THE ONE-CHINA POLICY: STATE, SOVEREIGNTY, AND TAIWAN'S INTERNATIONAL LEGAL STATUS

FRANK CHIANG
Fordham Law School, New York, NY, United States

ELSEVIER

Elsevier
Radarweg 29, PO Box 211, 1000 AE Amsterdam, Netherlands
The Boulevard, Langford Lane, Kidlington, Oxford OX5 1GB, United Kingdom
50 Hampshire Street, 5th Floor, Cambridge, MA 02139, United States

British Library Cataloguing-in-Publication Data
A catalogue record for this book is available from the British Library

Library of Congress Cataloging-in-Publication Data
A catalog record for this book is available from the Library of Congress

ISBN: 978-0-08-102314-3

Publisher: Glyn Jones
Acquisition Editor: Glyn Jones
Editorial Project Manager: Naomi Robertson
Production Project Manager: Debasish Ghosh
Cover Designer: Miles Hitchen

Typeset by MPS Limited, Chennai, India

CONTENTS

FOREWORD

This book is destined to be important. As I write these words, experts on China, Sino-American relations and international politics are again engaging in another of their recurrent debates over the prospect that the People's Republic of China (PRC) will in the foreseeable future use coercion to subdue Taiwan and reintegrate it into Mainland China. Despite immediate preoccupation with the threat of North Korean nuclear missiles and the possibilities of armed clashes in the South or East China Sea, many observers recognize that the gravest challenge to political stability in East Asia during the next decade may focus on the long-festering issue of the status of Taiwan.

This is why Professor Frank Chiang of Fordham University School of Law, an able and experienced American legal scholar, originally from Taiwan, has devoted himself to giving us a fresh review and analysis of the history and the complexities of the international legal aspects of this crucial problem.

Law may not turn out to be the decisive factor determining Taiwan's future, but, because of its intimate connection with public opinion as well as elite perceptions, it will surely be an influential factor. "Lawfare"—legal warfare—will be mobilized by the contending parties in an effort to justify, and summon domestic and international support for, its actions. Each of the contenders, of course, will claim that international law is on its side.

But what is the international law applicable to this potentially explosive situation? Is it the law of peace treaties that have traditionally transferred territorial sovereignty from wartime losers to victors? Should the rules of the world community instead emphasize not legal technicalities but broader aspects involving national intentions, policies, good faith, and diplomatic practice? Does it matter that the United States, one of the key players, has dramatically altered its position—perhaps twice—regarding Taiwan's legal status?

However sympathetic a government's claim, does contemporary international law permit resorting to the threat or use of force to vindicate it? Today, to what extent must the right to control territory reflect the wishes of its inhabitants? Is Taiwan's admirable transformation from dictatorship to democracy a relevant factor? Should the Taiwan of 2017 be regarded as the same polity as the Taiwan of more than seven decades ago when post-World War II arrangements that are still under scrutiny were first made?

If the island's legal status can no longer be legitimately determined by resort to coercion, how should it be decided if negotiations among the parties continue to fail? Since Beijing is adamant that the issue is a purely domestic one emanating from the Chinese civil war, international institutions are not likely to have a role. Moreover, because Beijing is a permanent member of the Security Council while Taipei has even been excluded from the General Assembly, the United Nations is not a promising venue. For similar reasons, the International Court of Justice is unlikely to be deemed appropriate. In principle it might be possible for Beijing to consider the possibility of submitting the legal arguments to a panel of arbitrators or conciliators entirely composed of Mainland and Taiwan nationals, but no participant would probably risk placing such an important issue in the hands of any such institution.

Persisting stalemate is therefore the most probable outcome for the foreseeable future unless Beijing succumbs to the temptation to use force. Yet, whatever develops, a new generation of diplomats, politicians, scholars, journalists, and other observers can only benefit from Professor Chiang's clear, careful, and stimulating study. His timely contribution deserves widespread appreciation.

Jerome A. Cohen
Professor of law, New York University School of Law, New York, NY, United States
Faculty Director, U.S.-Asia Law Institute, New York, NY, United States
Adjunct Senior Fellow for Asia Studies, the Council on Foreign Relations, New York, NY, United States

PREFACE

Taiwan is an island situated on the western edge of the Pacific Ocean. It lies 60 miles across the Taiwan Strait from the coast of China. To its northeast are the Ryukyu Islands of Japan, and to its south is Luzon Island of the Philippines.

The Taiwanese on the island have lived through 400 years of tumultuous history. The island has been successively ruled by the Dutch, Koxinga, the Qin Dynasty, Japan, and the Republic of China. Its legal status is still uncertain.

In 1894, Taiwan was part of China when the Sino-Japanese War started. In 1895 when China lost the war, the Qin government ceded the island, together with the nearby Pescadores Archipelago, to Japan in the Treaty of Shimonoseki. For the next 55 years, Taiwan was a part of Japan.

In 1945, when Japan surrendered at the end of the Pacific War, the United States (the U.S.) assigned Jiang (Chiang) Kai-shek, the leader of the Republic of China (the R.O.C.) government, to accept the surrender of the Japanese Army in Taiwan. It also assigned Jiang Kai-shek to administer the affairs of the islands until a peace settlement, which would determine the fate of the islands.

In 1951, the Allied powers and Japan signed the Peace Treaty of San Francisco. Although the treaty ended the Pacific War, it does not require Japan to cede Taiwan (Formosa) and the Pescadores to any country, it simply requires Japan to abandon the islands.

However, the R.O.C. government continued to administer the islands after the Peace Treaty was concluded. In 1949, having lost the control of China proper to Communist Revolutionaries in a civil war, the R.O.C. government fled to Taiwan and has been a government in exile since then. Meanwhile, the Chinese Communists established a new government called the People's Republic of China (the P.R.C.).

This leaves the legal status of Taiwan murky. While both the R.O.C. and the P.R.C. governments claim that Taiwan is a part of China, neither government ruled the island prior to 1945. Though Japan did not cede the island of Taiwan to China, it is still administered by the R.O.C. government. What does this mean for the legal status of Taiwan? Its status is far from clear.

From 1945 to 1986, Taiwan and the Pescadores were ruled by the Chinese leader Jiang Kai-shek, and, after his death, his son Jiang (Chiang) Ching-guo. At the death of Jiang Ching-guo in 1986, the presidency of the R.O.C. was succeeded by Vice-President Lee Teng-hui, a native Taiwanese, for Chiang's residual term. When Chiang's residual term expired in 1990, Lee was elected President of the R.O.C. by its National Assembly and again in 1996 in a general election in Taiwan.

In July 1999, during a Deutsche Welle TV interview, the then President, Lee Teng-hui made a controversial statement in international politics. He said, "The Republic of China is a sovereign independent State; the relationship between the Republic of China and the People's Republic of China is that of a special *state to state relationship*," implying that Taiwan was a state.

Yet, later in September of the same year, when a strong earthquake struck the central part of Taiwan leaving the area devastated, the then Secretary General of the U.N., Kofi Annan, refused to send a disaster assessment team to what he called the "Taiwan Province of China" because the P.R.C. government had not given the U.N. permission to do so.

Lee's statement and Annan's statement contradicted each other because if the R.O.C. in Taiwan was an independent State as Lee claimed, Taiwan could not be a Province of China as Annan stated; Taiwan could not be a State if it was a part of China. Whose statement carries greater weight? Is it that of the chief executive of the island or that of the Secretary General of the United Nations? Does either statement have any effect on the legal status of Taiwan?

Soon after Kofi Annan made the statement in September 1999, the Editor-In-Chief of Fordham International Law Journal (FILJ) asked me to write an article to be published in the Journal on the dispute between China and Taiwan over the legal status of Taiwan. He also asked the P.R. C.'s Permanent Mission to the U.N. to write on the same topic to be published in the same issue of the Journal. The P.R.C.'s Permanent Mission to the U.N. said that they had to ask for its government's approval to do so.

Early in February 2000, I submitted an article entitled "State, Sovereignty, and Taiwan" to the editor of FILJ. Toward the end of February, the Legal Advisor to the Chinese Permanent Mission to the U. N., Mr. Su Wei, informed the editor of FILJ that his government had approved the submission of a paper and he could submit a paper in one week. He then asked the editor for a copy of my article, but was refused. A week later, Mr. Su submitted an article entitled "Some Reflections on the One-China Principle" for publication.

At the time, I knew the term "one-China policy." It referred to the U.S.' new policy toward China over Taiwan announced in the 1972 Shanghai Communiqué. But I had never heard of the term "one-China principle." What happened was that not long after I submitted my article to the Journal, the P.R.C. government issued a position statement called "The White Paper on Taiwan," in which it announced a policy called "the one-China principle." Su Wei's position on the legal status of Taiwan based on China's one-China principle was opposite from the conclusion in my article.

After my article was published in New York, Professor Kazuomi Ouchi, a law professor of international law at Chuo University in Tokyo, read my article, and had it republished in Chuo Law Review of Chuo University and again in a book entitled "A Collection of Essays in Commemoration of the Retirement of Professor Kazuomi Ouchi" published by Chuo University Law Association.

In 2001, when the Japan Institute of Comparative Law was preparing to publish a special issue on "United Nations' Contributions to the Prevention and Settlement of Conflict," edited by Professor Ouchi and Professor Maki Nishiwumi of Chuo University, Professor Ouchi asked me to contribute an article for the issue. Thereupon, I wrote an article entitled "The Territorial State and Taiwan." It contains expanded analyses of some issues discussed in my earlier article.

Since the article "The Territorial State and Taiwan" was published in Japan, few people outside of Japan had the chance to read it. In 2003, the Editor-in-Chief of FILJ wanted to republish the article in the FILJ and suggested that the article be updated to include new developments during the two years since its publication in Japan. The result was an article entitled "One-China Policy and Taiwan." It compares the U.S.' one-China policy and China's one-China principle.

After the publication of "One-China Policy and Taiwan," three reasons prompted my idea of writing a monograph based on the three articles. One reason is, though the three articles deal with related subject matter, each of them has different areas of emphasis. The subjects in the three articles can be combined for discussions in a monograph.

The second reason is that in each of the three articles, the treatment of the concept of the State, the theory of sovereignty, and international law on territory, based on which the political and legal status of Taiwan was analyzed, is brief and superficial due to the nature of a law journal. A fundamental and thorough treatment of the subjects can be achieved only by a monograph.

The third reason is, a monograph will give the "one-China policy" an extensive treatment.

So, this book consists of two main parts. The first part is on State, sovereignty, and international law on territory. The book uses both inductive and deductive methods to draw some rules and principles on the concept of the State, the theory of sovereignty and the rules of international law on territory.

The second part initially applies the rules and principles drawn in the first part to analyze the political status of the R.O.C. and the legal status of Taiwan. It then analyzes the U.S.' position on the legal status of Taiwan under its one-China policy. Finally, it examines how the U.S.' one-China policy has impacted the life of the people of Taiwan.

Before I completed this book, Professor Ouchi and I coauthored an article entitled "The Legal Status of Taiwan in international law and the Japan–China Relations" published in two consecutive issues of the Comparative Law Journal of Japan. The article was based on my three articles mentioned above and is written in Japanese for Japanese readers.

This book is not geopolitical in nature. But Taiwan is situated among three economic and military powers, the United States, China, and Japan, in the West Pacific Ocean. Its strategic importance cannot be overstated. In the contest of influence in the region between the United States and China, the Taiwan Strait could be one of the flashpoints of international conflict. It is hoped that this book can serve as a guide to solve the conflicts by peaceful means through the application of international law.

F. C.
New York
October 26, 2017

AFTERWORD

Taiwan's "unsettled" status offers a rich and complex case study in the international law of sovereignty to scholars and diplomatists around the world. It is a particularly valuable case study because, after all, Taiwan is a fully-functioning and legally sovereign nation "State" of enormous prosperity, robust politico-cultural identity, vibrant democracy, modern defenses, broad global/regional geopolitical and trade power, widely-respected science and technology infrastructure, and a middling–large population of highly-educated and productive citizens about the size of Australia's. Its capital, Taipei, hosts hundreds of foreign diplomats (if one reads their business cards and happens to note the official email addresses linked to foreign ministries from all the earth's major nations—except China).

In the foregoing pages, Professor Chiang has shed legal and historical light on why Taiwan is now saddled with the dubious distinction of being the only State in the international community that all other States treat as fully sovereign, yet cannot bring themselves to call "sovereign." Major United Nations member States—except China—have formal foreign affairs missions in Taipei, but they are not called "diplomatic." To be sure, a dozen and a half States, all members of the United Nations, together with the Holy See, have formal diplomatic missions in Taipei. But even they do not recognize Taiwan diplomatically as a sovereign entity *separate* from "China." Taiwan even hosts thousands of uniformed foreign armed services personnel from Singapore who undergo basic ground-forces training at Taiwan military installations.[1]

As Professor Chiang explains, all this dates back four decades to the 1960s and 1970s when the Taipei government itself—anxious about the legitimacy of its authoritarian regime—could see no way to justify its existence in the Free World without a domestic political consensus that it was, legally, "China" and not, legally, "Taiwan." Hence, it eschewed the blandishments of the United States and Japan to consider a "Two China"

[1] The "Star Bright" program has been a joint Taiwan-Singapore training operation since the 1970s. see "Taiwan's Beleaguered Foreign Relations Find Stable Support in Singapore," Voice of America, October 6, 2017.

resolution.[2] Taipei's "Republic of China" regime would be the sole legal government of China or nothing. But it would not constitutionally be the democratic government of "Taiwan" without the democratic ratification of a plebiscite, because such a plebiscite overwhelmingly would reject the regime.

To abandon its pretentions as the rightful government of all "China" necessarily required that the Taipei government establish some basis for its legitimacy as the rightful government of the Taiwanese people, and this it could not do without the collapse of the existing power structure of émigrés and exiles.

Thus, in the international community, this could have been done without controversy in the 1960s and 1970s, but it was impossible within Taiwan's existing domestic politics. By 1991, however, the international community was unable to digest an independent Taiwan. Unable, even when Taiwan's political structure submitted to sweeping constitutional reforms that transformed Taiwan into a model of representational democracy, and the then-president of the Republic of China, Lee Teng-hui, proffered a formula that both his "Republic of China" and China's "People's Republic of China" both were "sovereign states, mutually non-subordinate, within a geographical, cultural, and historical 'one China.'"[3]

As Professor Chiang recounts, the peculiar diplomatic history of the United States policy that Taiwan's legal status remains "unsettled" dates to the end of the Second World War in the Pacific. While the United States fully intended that "Formosa" (Taiwan) would eventually revert to Chinese sovereignty even before the end of the war with Japan, planning documents prepared by both the Department of State and the Department of War anticipated that a legal transfer of sovereignty from Japan to China could be effected only through a formal peace treaty.

[2] See American Embassy Taipei telegram to the Secretary of State "Subj: Conversation of Vice Foreign Minister Yang Hsi-kun With Ambassador" dated November 30, 1971, at https://history.state.gov/historicaldocuments/frus1969-76v17/d174.

[3] The formula was unveiled at the November 1993 leaders' summit of the Asia Pacific Economic Cooperation forum in Seattle. See Wang Jinghong, "Taibei Burong Biansun, Beijing Peng Ying Dingzi, Shuangfang dou shi you junbei erlai, Zhonggong fan guixian che zhengzhi, Wo ti fanji weihu quanyi" (台北不容貶損 北京碰硬釘子 雙方都是有備而來 中共犯規先扯政治 我提反擊維護權益) [Taipei won't tolerate insults, Beijing hits hard nail, both sides came prepared, We launch counterstrike to protect interests], Taipei, *United Daily News*, November 24, 1993, p. 2.

By early 1947, mistreatment of Formosan citizens by occupying Nationalist Chinese armies and the gross maladministration of Taiwan by the military government firmed the US government's position that Taiwan's future status as a "part of China" remained to be determined. By 1949, with the Chinese Nationalists defeat in the Chinese Civil War by Soviet-supported Chinese Communists, the matter of Taiwan's international status was a central focus of post-War security concerns in Washington.

As early as December 1948, General Douglas MacArthur, Supreme Commander of the Allied Powers in the Far East, foresaw that Communist China aligned with the Soviet Union, was likely to be the only government of "China" in a position to take sovereignty over Taiwan if the Japan Peace Treaty went forward as written. "The subject is evidently close to his heart and mind," wrote a State Department officer of a December 7, 1948, conversation with General MacArthur: "From the strategic standpoint, he said, to permit the access of an unfriendly power to Formosa would be to invite rupture of our whole defense line in the Far East."[4]

In November 1949, the first drafts of a Japan Peace Treaty in which "Japan hereby cedes to China in full sovereignty the island of Taiwan (Formosa) and adjacent minor islands" were annotated in longhand that "McA[rthur] suggests considering trusteeship for Taiwan after a plebiscite."[5] The possibility of a UN trusteeship for Taiwan under the imprimatur of a popular plebiscite in Taiwan remained an American policy option even after the outbreak of the Korean War, but evaporated with Communist China's entry into the War in October 1950. Without other workable options, Washington simply acquiesced to the *status quo* of an "unsettled" status for Taiwan and continued recognition of Chiang Kai-shek's "Republic of China" government as the legitimate representative of the Chinese people but, paradoxically, without recognition that Chiang's regime had "sovereignty" in Taiwan.

The San Francisco Peace Treaty of 1951, at Washington's insistence, rebuffed attempts to address Taiwan's status, except to note that Japan

[4] Memorandum of Conversation, by the Counselor of Embassy in the Philippines (Flexer), December 7, 1948, *Foreign Relations of the United States, The Far East: China, Vol. IX, 1949*. pp. 265 – 265.

[5] "Japan Peace Treaty Working Draft and Commentary," Political Advisor, SCAP headquarters Tokyo, November 1949. National Archives NND 968099, accessed August 2011.

"renounced all right, title, and claim to Formosa." The "unsettled" rubric, always intended to be a stop-gap formula, has persisted for nearly seven decades. A Department of State memo to Secretary of State Dean Rusk of March 1966 explained, "As Taiwan is not covered by any existing international disposition, sovereignty over it is an unsettled question subject to future international solution. The United States recognizes the Government of the Republic of China as legitimately occupying and exercising jurisdiction over Taiwan, with a provisional capital at Taipei." The memo then got to the nub of the matter: "(CONFIDENTIAL) In our view the United States position is an important element of our legal case for declaring illegal under international law the use of force by Communist China to reassert its sovereignty over Taiwan."[6]

The problem of Taiwan's "unsettled" status was very much alive 10 years later in Secretary of State, Henry Kissinger's mind. On October 29, 1976, Secretary of State, Henry Kissinger asked his top China aides: "If Taiwan is recognized by us as part of China, then it may become irresistible to them. Our saying we want a peaceful solution has no force: it is Chinese territory. What are we going to do about it?" Arthur Hummel, then Assistant Secretary of State and later ambassador to Beijing, responded, "Down the road, perhaps the only solution would be an independent Taiwan." This, apparently, was not the response that Kissinger wanted to hear. Instead he mused, "Well, maybe the best solution would just be for Taiwan to be taken over by the mainland. Then that would solve everybody's problem." At which point Hummel's deputy, William Gleysteen, interjected, "I don't think that's ever going to happen."[7]

And 30 years after that, in August 2007, the Department of State remained militantly in favor of Taiwan's "unsettled" sovereign status. That month, Ban Ki Moon, the Secretary General of the United Nations, made a public pronouncement, *à propos* of Taiwan's attempt to adhere to a UN convention on women's rights, that the United Nations considers "Taiwan for all purposes to be an integral part of the PRC." To which the US representative to the United Nations delivered a *demarche* explicating, "while this assertion is consistent with the Chinese position, it is not universally held by UN member states, including the United States."

[6] Legal Status of Taiwan, prepared for Secretary's Appearance before House Foreign Affairs Far East Subcommittee, March 16, 1966, drafted by E.T. Herbert, Office of the Legal Advisor of the Department of State.

[7] William Burr, ed., *The Kissinger Transcripts: The Top Secret Talks with Beijing and Moscow* (New York: New Press, 1999), p. 464.

The *demarche* concluded with a promise that "If the UN Secretariat insists on describing Taiwan as a part of the PRC, or on using nomenclature for Taiwan that implies such status, the United States will be obliged to disassociate itself on a national basis from such a position."[8]

Professor Chiang astutely has pointed out that Taiwan indeed possess all four of the attributes of a nation-state in customary international law enumerated in the Montevideo Convention: a defined territory, a permanent population, an effective governmental administration and the capacity to conduct international relations. But Taiwan has yet to pull-the-trigger on the last, keystone attribute of a modern State: a declaration that it is, in fact, a State.

For the Taiwanese people, their country's "unsettled" international status has been a minor nuisance to their achievement of a highly prosperous and technologically developed democracy and to their position as a valuable and constructive member of the international community. But their "unsettled" state has undermined their ability to defend themselves against China's gathering military might. Unlike other States in the international system, Taiwan does not have a generally recognized right to arm itself. This has forced the United States, under the provisions of the Taiwan Relations Act, to assume full responsibility for Taiwan's defenses. Taipei is enjoined by US policy-makers from developing defense capabilities which Washington judges may be provocative to China. Yet, Washington is unwilling to make available to Taiwan the kinds of defense articles and services that effectively would deter Chinese military operations against the island and its people. To do so, Washington fears, would complicate American relations with China.

Perhaps the most potent insight that Professor Chiang proffers is that Taiwan does not yet face the necessity to declare itself a sovereign "State" separate from the cultural, geographic, and historical entity of "China" in the absence of an existential threat to its well-being. Given the pervasive

[8] The demarche was shared with the Taipei government, and a copy was made available to this author. It is reprinted in full in John J. Tkacik, Jr. "Taiwan's 'Unsettled' International Status: Preserving US Options in the Pacific", *Heritage Foundation Backgrounder* No. 2146, June 19, 2008. On August 16, 2007, the US Ambassador to the UN, Zalmay Khalilzad, reported "Ban said he realized he had gone too far in his recent public statements, and confirmed that the UN would no longer use the phrase 'Taiwan is a part of China,' as reported reftel." For a text of the cable see http://wikileaks.org/cable/2007/08/07USUNNEWYORK679.html

Chinese threat that "Taiwan independence means War,"[9] prudence may dictate that Taiwan need not take this last step. Certainly, as a final step, one may infer from Professor Chiang's thesis that Taiwan's most potent deterrent is the counterthreat that "war means Taiwan's independence."

By John J. Tkacik Jr.
Alexandria, Virginia
October 25, 2017

[9] "Peaceful reunification is a set policy of the Chinese Government. However, any sovereign state is entitled to use any means it deems necessary, including military ones, to uphold its sovereignty and territorial integrity. The Chinese Government is under no obligation to undertake any commitment to any foreign power or people intending to split China as to what means it might use to handle its own domestic affairs." *The Taiwan Question and the Reunification of China*, issued by the Taiwan Affairs Office and the Information Office under the State Council of the People's Republic of China on August 31, 1993. On January 28, 2000, Chinese Vice Premier, concurrently deputy chair of the Chinese Communist Party "Leading Group on Taiwan Work," Qian Qichen, said the decade of the 1990s has been filled with extremism and repeated struggles between China and "the splittist forces in Taiwan represented by Lee Teng-hui," and warned that "Taiwan Independence" only can mean war across the Taiwan Strait. Taipei, *United Daily News*, Saturday, January 30, 2000. Chinese military leaders first adopted this phrase when the election of pro-independence presidential candidate Chen Shui-bian seemed possible in March 2000. See "*Zhang Wannian: Taidu Yiweizhe Zhanheng; Fenlie meiyou heping; Baiwan Xiongshi Yanzhen Yidai*" (Zhang Wannian: Taiwan independence means war; no peace in separation; a million brave troops await the order), *Hong Kong Commercial Daily*, March 6, 2000, at www.pdf.sznews.com/hkcd/2000/0306/newsfile/n1-2.htm (accessed January 4, 2007). The PLA's then-most senior general, Zhang Wannian, suggested that China's nuclear weapons would be used to "deter moves to split the sovereign state" a clear reference to Taiwan. See Larry M. Wortzel, *China's Nuclear Forces: Operations, Training, Doctrine, Command, Control, and Campaign Planning* (Carlisle, PA: U.S. Army War College, Strategic Studies Institute, May 2007. Other top generals have envisioned nuclear weapons use at the outset of a Taiwan conflict. General Xiong Guangkai was quoted as saying in 1995 that China could act militarily against Taiwan without fear of intervention by the United States because US leaders "care more about Los Angeles than they do about Taiwan," See Patrick Tyler, "As China Threatens Taiwan, It Makes Sure US Listens," The *New York Times*, January 24, 1996, p. A-01; and Major General Zhu Zhenghu who in 2005 asserted to a gaggle of foreign journalists that "If the Americans interfere into [a Taiwan] conflict, if the Americans draw their missiles and position-guided ammunition into the target zone on China's territory, I think we will have to respond with nuclear weapons." See Danny Gittings, "General Zhu Goes Ballistic," *The Wall Street Journal*, July 18, 2005, p. A13 at http://online.wsj.com/article/0,SB112165176626988025,00.html.

ACKNOWLEDGMENT

I am grateful to many publishers and news media for providing materials and news items in paper, video, and electronic forms, either for the illustrations or analyses of the issues involved in the discussions. They include, but are not limited to (in alphabetical order) Arete Publishing, Aschendorff/Münster, Cambridge University Press, Central News Agency (Taiwan), China Post, Deutsche Welle Television, Encyclopaedia Britannica Publishing, Fordham International Law Journal, France Deux Television, the London Times, the L.A. Times, the New York Times, Oxford University Press, the Pacific Times, People's Daily, Taipei Times, Wall Street Journal, Washington Post, World Report, etc.

During more than 10 years in which I wrote this book, many have given me ideas and advice. Among them are my colleagues at the Fordham Law School 10-10 Workshop. My special gratitude goes to Professor Jerome A. Cohen and Professor Peter Dutton of New York University School of Law, and Mr. John J. Tkacik, Jr., a former US Diplomat and a book author, for their critiques and advice, and also for writing the Foreword, the blurb, and the Afterword of this book respectively. I am also grateful to Mr. Keng C. Wu, who is an Elsevier author, for his advice on the publication of the book. However, my opinions and the errors in the book are solely my own and should not be ascribed to anyone mentioned above.

I am indebted to Fordham University School of Law for providing facility and staff in the preparation of the manuscript. In particular, I thank Fordham Law Library Head of Reference/Adjunct Professor of Law Alison Shea, who not only searched cases and the Congressional records for me, but also advised my research assistant Tomisin Bolorunduro in the compilation of the bibliography.

Last but not least is my gratitude to my wife, Lisa, who has given me unreserved support while I was writing this book.

F. C.
New York
October 26, 2017

INTRODUCTION

On October 25, 1971, the members of the U.N. at the General Assembly, after a heated debate, expelled the Republic of China (the R. O.C.) and replaced it with the People's Republic of China (the P.R.C.) in the United Nations. The representatives of the R.O.C. immediately walked out of the U.N. Headquarters in New York City. The status of Taiwan, and the Republic of China, has been muddled ever since.

The event triggered a few intriguing questions. What is the political status of the R.O.C. in Taiwan after October 25, 1971? Has it become a State? Does the P.R.C. represent the people of Taiwan as well as the people of China in the U.N. after the Resolution? What is the present legal status of the island of Taiwan? Is it China's territory? If not, then whose territory is it? Does Taiwan belong to anyone besides the people that live there? This book will provide answers to these questions.

This book consists of two related parts. The first part explores the concept of the State, the theory of sovereignty, and their relations with international law. What makes a place or people a State? Does a state require territory? What is sovereignty? These are questions this part addresses. In doing so, it cites many historical treaties as precedents and treatises by well-known political philosophers and legal scholars as authorities.

The modern State has two characteristics. One is that the modern Sate is a territorial State: The State is predicated on territory. In the modern State, which replaced the feudal State, the ruler of the State governs the people within his territory directly. The second characteristic is that it is a sovereign State; the sovereignty of the modern State resides in its ruler (the king or the sovereign prince). For a republican State, which has no ruler, this work concludes that sovereignty resides in the State. This work employs the term "the neo-modern State" for a State where sovereignty resides in the State.

In the theory of the creation of State, a proposition commonly accepted is that a territorial political institution is a State once it has the four requirements prescribed in the Montevideo Convention: a permanent population; a defined territory; government; and the capability to enter into relations with the other States. However, by examining the

State practice on the creation of kingdoms and the modern States as well as the nature of the neo-modern States, this work concludes that a territorial political institution with all the requirements of a State prescribed in the Montevideo Convention does not become a State unless and until it declares the establishment of statehood or of similar import, such as a declaration of independence. Thus a territorial political institution does not evolve gradually into a State; it must openly and unambiguously declare itself into existence.

In the neo-modern State, like the modern State, territory is an essential element of the State. Sovereignty of a State over its territory and inhabitants is based on its title to the territory. In other words, unless a State has the title to a territory, it has no sovereignty over the territory and its inhabitants.

The second part of this work examines the political status of the Republic of China (the R.O.C.) in Taiwan[1] and the legal status of the island of Taiwan. It also attempts to shed light on the U.S.' one-China policy toward Taiwan. Is the R.O.C. in Taiwan a State? In Taiwan, after former President Lee Teng-hui announced that "the relationship between the Republic of China and the People's Republic of China is that of a special state-to-state relationship" in 1999, most people believe that Taiwan has become a State. The People's Republic of China (the P.R. C.), the U.N., and the U.S. have said "no." The R.O.C. government that controls Taiwan has at times said "yes" and at times said "no."

Taiwan cannot be a State if it is under the sovereignty of another State. The island of Taiwan was a territory that was ceded by China to Japan in 1895. After ruling the island for over 50 years, and Japan renounced it in the Peace Treaty of San Francisco after World War II while the island was under the administration of the R.O.C government. Both the P.R.C. government and the R.O.C. government claim that

[1] "Taiwan" as a geographical term in its strict sense refers to the island of Formosa, and in its broad sense, to a group of islands consisting of Formosa and a few adjacent islands, including the Pescadores (Penghu), Green Island, and Orchid Islet, but not Kinmen (Quemoy) and Matsu, two small islands off China's coast. The word "Taiwan" in the political term "Republic of China in Taiwan" is used in its broad sense. As used in this work, "Formosa" and "the island of Taiwan" are synonymous, both referring to Taiwan in its broad sense; the term "Taiwan" refers to the political institution existing on the island of Taiwan currently ruled by a government called the Republic of China. The term "Taiwan" used in this work accords with the definition of "Taiwan" defined in Taiwan Relations Act, *infra* note 503. Sec. 15(2). Hence, the term *Republic of China* (the "R.O.C.") refers to the governing authority of the political institution "Taiwan."

Taiwan is part of China. They claim that the island of Taiwan was returned to China after the Second World War.

The P.R.C. government's claim is based on four grounds: The first is based on the past ownership; the second is based on its own proclamations; the third is based on the Cairo Declaration and the Potsdam Proclamation; and the fourth ground is based on the administration of Taiwan by the R.O.C.'s government.

The second part of this work explores the historical facts relating to the issues raised above and provides answers to these questions from a legal perspective.

The people of Taiwan have lived through four centuries of unsettled history. They were ruled by the Dutch, General Koxinga, the *Qing* (Ching) Empire, Japan, and the R.O.C. government, successively. The entangling claims of sovereignty and statehood by various governments have put the people of the island in a schizophrenic environment, or a state of "political purgatory" as the U.S. Circuit Court Judge Brown called it, and even have the potential to lead to armed conflict between two superpowers, the United States and China.

This work is dedicated to determining the legal and the political status of Taiwan by applying international law, and sets forth a path forward to certainty for Taiwan's people and international powers that continue to struggle with the Taiwan problem. In the second part of this work, it applies the principles in the State theory and the rules of international law drawn in the first part of this work to the specific situation of Taiwan. It tries to answer the difficult questions about Taiwan raised above. It also examines the positions taken by various governments and why each matters.

Part I of this work consists of three Chapters: Chapter 1, The State, discusses the State in general; Chapter 2, The State and Sovereignty, analyzes the theory of sovereignty and the concept of State; and Chapter 3, The Territorial State, discusses the territorial State.

The second part of this work first reviews the State of China, its modern governments, and the sovereignty over Taiwan. It then examines U.S.' control over Taiwan. Part II (China and the Republic of China) consists of two Chapters: Chapter 4, The State and Governments of China, reviews the State and governments of China; Chapter 5, Political Status of the ROC in Taiwan, examines the political status of the R.O.C. in Taiwan.

Part III (Sovereignty over Taiwan) consists of four chapters (Chapters 6, 7, 8, and 9). Chapter 6, China's Sovereignty Over Taiwan Before the

U.S. One-China Policy, analyzes China's sovereignty over Taiwan, i.e., whether China reacquired title to the island of Taiwan after the Second World War under certain proclamations, declarations, treaties, or through administration of the island. Chapter 7, China's Sovereignty Over Taiwan Under the U.S.' One-China Policy, examines the U.S.' one-China policy and Taiwan Relations Act to see whether the U.S. concedes to China's claim over Taiwan under the policy or the Act. Chapter 8, The U.N.'s Position on the Sovereignty of Taiwan, examines the U.N.'s position on the legal status of Taiwan. Chapter 9, The Legal Status and the Political Status of Taiwan in International Law, analyzes the legal status of Taiwan—whether Taiwan is subject to any sovereignty—and the political status of Taiwan—whether Taiwan is a State—in international law.

Part IV (U.S.' control over Taiwan) analyzes the U.S.' control over Taiwan in three chapters (Chapters 10–12). Chapter 10, U.S. Policy on Taiwan, reviews the U.S.' policy on Taiwan; Chapter 11, Taiwan Under U.S. Protection and Control, examines the living conditions of the people in Taiwan under the control of the U.S; finally, Chapter 12, Solution, suggests a peaceful solution to the Taiwan problem.

This work expounds some of the author's ideas and theories which appeared in his earlier publications, in particular the following three law journal articles:

State, sovereignty, and Taiwan, Fordham International Law Journal, V. 23, No. 4 (Apr. 2000), New York; reprinted in Chuo Univ. Law Review, V. 104, Nos.5 & 6 (Apr. 2003), Tokyo, Japan.

The territorial state and Taiwan, The Comparative Law Journal of Japan, Special issue on "United Nations' Contribution to the Prevention and Settlement of Conflicts" (July 2003). Tokyo, Japan.

One-China Policy and Taiwan, Fordham International Law Journal, V. 28, No.1 (Dec. 2004), New York.

PART I

State, Sovereignty, and Territory

CHAPTER 1

The State

Contents

Part I examines the concept of the State and the theory of sovereignty, and then the territory of the modern State. This chapter examines the concept of the State and the various kinds of States.

The word "State" with a capital "S" as used in this work, except in cases of a quotation, applies broadly to a territorial political institution of any form commonly so described today. It includes kingdoms, the feudal States, and the modern States. As the State is a territorial political institution, when the term "political institution" is used for the State in this work, it means territorial political institution unless the context indicates otherwise.

1. THE STATE AND SOCIETY

State and society are two separate concepts, though the two are closely related. In discussing the evolution of humankind and the origin of the State, some writers equate the "State" with "civil society."[2]

But the State and civil society are different both in concept and in the process of their formation. Although the State exists only in a civil society,[3] not all civil societies are States.

[2] "In the early eighteenth century, the usual explanation of the origin of the state, or "civil society," as it was called, began by postulating an original state of nature, in which primitive man lived on his own." PETER STEIN, LEGAL EVOLUTION, THE STORY OF AN IDEA, Cambridge Univ. Press, 1980, at 1.

[3] Johnson, J. "I cannot but think that there are strong reasons for doubting the applicability of the epithet state, to a people so low in the grade of organized society as our Indian tribes most generally are." *Cherokee Nation v. The State of Georgia*, 5 Peters 1, at 20 (1831).

The One-China Policy: State, Sovereignty, and Taiwan's International Legal Status
DOI: http://dx.doi.org/10.1016/B978-0-08-102314-3.00001-X

It took a long time for human beings to form a society. The term "society" has been defined as "a community of people living in a particular country or region and having shared customs, laws and organizations."[4] The definition indicates that people formed a society in the place or region where they settled. This definition, however, describes a civil society, not a primitive one.

Human beings began with a savage society. Writers spoke of a "savage society,"[5] referring to a primitive society as "when mankind derived their whole subsistence from the fruits. . .hunting, fishing, and their flocks. . .they had no dwelling place nor settled habitations. . . . Such was the ancient manner of living [until] agriculture was introduced."[6] The primitive society began as a familial group, where parents cared for their young. This later expanded to extended family groups, called "clans," living in close proximity. This society eventually evolved to a civil society with a government and a functional political system. It took a long journey for a primitive society to develop into a civil society. The process was a gradual and slow one.

The process of establishing a State is different. From the beginning, the process for establishing a king and a kingdom, the earliest kind of the State, has been drastic. It is common that in a group of people, a strong person eventually emerges as the leader. The leader in an early society might initially have acquired his position by consent of the people or, sometimes, by brute force. At a certain point of time, the leader became their ruler—either by declaring himself their king (I am the king), or by accepting an acclamation of the people (Long live the king)—establishing a king, and a kingdom. Once a kingdom is established, a State is established. The State is an intangible political institution that has a life of its own. The State continues to exist, even though the king changes, until the State is extinguished, usually in a violent way.

2. VARIOUS KINDS OF STATES

A. The Medieval Feudal State

From ancient kingdoms, other kinds of States, mainly the feudal State and the modern State, developed. A brief review of the nature of the feudal State will help the reader understand the nature of the modern State.

[4] *See* Oxford Advanced Learner's Dictionary, 5th Ed., Oxford Univ. Press, 1995, at 1128 (providing the definition of "society").

[5] Stein, *supra* note 2, at 20.

[6] Antoine Yves Goguet, *De l'origine des lois, des arts, et des sciences, et de leurs progres, chez les anciens peuples,* in Stein, *supra* note 2, at 21.

In the 9th century, Europe began to fall into feudalism. Feudalism was a type of political order where a ruler only had the power to rule his vassals immediate below him, as opposed to all of the subjects within his territory. When the territorial magnates in the East Frankish Kingdom (what is known today as Germany) elected Arnulf, the Duke of Kaernten (Carinthia), as the King of Germany and Italy in 887,[7] feudalism began in the Kingdom. The Kingdom consisted of what is today Germany and northern Italy. Later, after Frederick I was crowned emperor of what would become the Holy Roman Empire, he created the rank of Prince for his chief vassals in 1155.[8] Similarly, in France, feudalism began when Hugh Capet was elected King of France in 987.[9] And in England, it began in 1066 when the (French) Duke William of Normandy conquered England and established the English Kingdom.[10] From then on, feudalism spread over Western Europe.

In the feudal system, the kingdom was built on the king's control of his vassals. The king no longer directly controlled all the people within his kingdom. Outside of his own domain, the king ruled his kingdom through his feudal vassals. In exchange for large parcels of land, called fiefdoms, the feudal vassals provided labor and military services to the king and made regular payments, as dues and taxes, to him. The common

[7] Charlemagne's territory included northern Italy. In the Treaty of Verdun (843) among the three sons of Louis I (the only surviving son of Charlemagne), northern Italy went to Lothair I, the eldest son of Louis I, as part of the Middle Kingdom. Lothair I divided (855) his territory between his two sons. Italy went to his elder son, Louis II, who became King of Italy until 875. After Louis II died, Italy went to Louis III. When Louis III died (882) without heir, Charles III (the Fat), a son of Louis the German, unified the East Kingdom and also became king of Italy. THE NEW ENCYCLOPEDIA BRITANNICA, 15th Ed., 2002, V. 7, at 483 (the entry of "Lorraine").

[8] Frederick I (Frederick Barbarosa) (r. 1152-90) created the rank of prince of the empire for his chief vassals, dukes. In Germany, the feudal vassals immediately under the emperor were the Electors, Princes, and States. Three bishops and four princes, known collectively as the Electors, voted on the succession of the Emperor. *See* HUGO GROTIUS, COMMENTARY on the LAW OF PRIZE AND BOOTY (*DE JURE PRAEDAE COMMENTARIUS*), eds. GWLADYS L. WILLIAMS AND W.H. ZEYDEL, Oxford L Clarendon Press, 1950, Vol. I: A Translation of the Original Manuscript of 1604 by GWLADYS L. WILLIAMS, with the collaboration of Walter Zeydel, at 504, footnote 3. *See also infra* note 53 on the Golden Bull. Frederick I also introduced the word "Holy" in the title of the Roman Empire, thus "Holy Roman Empire."

[9] From then on, Charlemagne's successors, as Roman Emperors, ruled only the Kingdom of Germany, which included the Kingdom of Italy.

[10] THE NEW ENCYCLOPEDIA BRITANNICA, *supra* note 7, V 12, at 141 (the entry of "United Kingdom.").

people, consisting mainly of peasants and workers, were subject to the rule of their feudal lords, not the rule of the king. The king ruled over and collected taxes from his feudal vassals, who in turn collected taxes from their subjects.[11]

To a feudal king and feudal lords, the lands (territories) in the king's domain and feudal lords' dominions were their personal properties—their estates—respectively. The rulers had ownership interests or title to the lands. Much like real property, territories could be transferred or acquired through the marriage of rulers. Developments in Western Europe provide an illustration. The Duke of Bavaria, Maximilian (later Holy Roman Emperor), married Mary of Burgundy (1477) and, through her, acquired Burgundy and the Low Countries, including the Austrian Netherlands (modern Belgium). In this way, Mary's territories went to the Duke of Bavaria as a dowry,[12] similar to the way common people would gain ownership interests in land by marriage. Likewise, the Hohenstaufen King Frederick I (Barbarossa) acquired the province of Burgundy by marriage.[13]

B. The Modern State

The modern State is a product of Western civilization.[14] "The modern State" is a generic term. It does not refer to any particular State.[15] There is no State that is *the modern State*. It is a collective name given to describe the States transformed from medieval feudalism that share some common characteristics.[16]

[11] This is a very general description of the European feudalism. In most feudal states, consent of the vassals was needed for the king to collect taxes from them. For instance, in 16th century France, Estates' consent was required for the king to collect tax from its members. *See infra* text accompanying note 64.

[12] ACADEMIC AMERICAN ENCYCLOPEDIA, Arete Publishing Co. (Princeton), 1980. V. 9, at 147, 150 (the entry of "History of Germany").

[13] *Id.* at 149.

[14] *See* H.C. Dowdall, *The word "state,"* 39 L.Q. Rev. 98 (1923). at 111. The development of the modern State may attribute to a few major factors. The foremost factor was the development of economy and a new monetary system. The second factor was the theological source of king's authority. The third factor was the introduction of the theory of sovereignty.

[15] *See* HEINTZ LUBASZ, ed. THE DEVELOPMENT OF THE MODERN STATE, The MacMillan Co. (New York), 1964, at 1.

[16] *See* Gerhard Ritter, *Origins of the Modern State,* 19–28 (*DIE NEUGESTALTUNG EUROPAS im 16. JAHRHUNDERT, BERLIN: VERLAG DES DRUCKHAUSES TEMPELHOF, 1950*) (Heinz Lubasz, trans., in LUBASZ, *supra* note 15, at 13–25).

The transformation of the feudal State into the modern State did not begin in every State at the same time.[17] It was a process that spread over time from one state to another. Although many historians regard France as the State where the modern State first developed in the 15th century, territorial political institutions with common characteristics of the modern State (e.g., the sovereign power) appeared in northern Italy as early as the 11th century. During this time, the Principalities of northern Italy, such as Florence, Genoa, Milan, Pisa, and Venice, asserted autonomy against their feudal lord, the Holy Roman Emperor.[18] In doing so, they turned their respective principalities or dominions into the modern States.[19]

Other parts of Europe did not begin the transformation to the modern State until the 15th century. After France defeated England in the Hundred Years War in 1453, starting with Charles VII the French kings began to strip away the power of their feudal vassals and centralize political power to themselves. Helped by the new economy based on money, the French kings also began to build their own army, thus, relying less and less on their vassals to defend the kingdom.[20] Eventually, France became a single unified monarchy State.

In Germany, when feudalism broke down at the end of the Thirty Years War,[21] hundreds of states appeared within the Holy Roman Empire. These German states were sometimes called the "secondary states" because structurally they were still constituent units of the Empire.

[17] For a discussion of the development of the modern state, *see* Ritter, *Id.*, at 19–28.

[18] *See* Dowdall, *supra* note 14. "[I]n the twelfth century, Alphonso VII of Castile is Emperor in Spain; and in the fourteen century, whether in France or in England, sovereignty [*imperior*] is claimed in the name of empire." *Id.* at 111. Thus, when Italian dominions exercised imperio (*Id.* at 111), the dominions defied Holy Roman Empire. "[A]n Italian Commune transformed, *through tyranny*, into a modern state." (Emphasis added). *See infra* text accompanying note 125.

[19] *Id.*

[20] Development of the modern State was attributed partly to the creation of the new monetary system. For major factors which led to the creation of the modern State, *see supra* note 14.

[21] The conflict between Protestants and Catholics and between Lutherans and Calvinists led to the Thirty Years War in 1618. *See* The Encyclopedia Britannica, V.19, 15th Ed., 1994, at 482–483 (the entry of "the Thirty Years War"). In 1648, the Catholic Emperor Ferdinand III, defeated by Protestant forces, signed Peace of Westphalia, *see infra* note 22.

Two provisions of the Peace of Westphalia (the "Treaties"),[22] which concluded the Thirty Years War, facilitated the creation of these states. One provision made all feudal vassals (e.g., the Electors, Princes, and States) who were immediately under the Emperor, large or small, powerful and weak, equal in position in the enjoyment of rights within the Empire, including voting rights in the Imperial Diet.[23] Another provision, in response to the demand of the German Princes, granted all "Estates of the Empire" the right to make alliance treaties between themselves and also with foreign rulers.[24] The grant, in effect, legally lifted whatever restriction that was placed on these Estates (Principalities) on making treaties between themselves and with foreign States. The removal of such restriction on the princes permitted them to claim sovereignty within the feudal structure of the Empire.[25]

[22] Peace of Westphalia, 1648. The Peace of Westphalia consists of two treaties signed by the Holy Roman Emperor Ferdinand III in 1648 ending the Thirty Years War. The two treaties are: One between the Emperor and his allies on one side and the Queen of Denmark and her allies on the other side, called *Instrumentum Pacis Osnarbrugensis* (IPO); and the other, between the Emperor and his allies on one side and the King of France and his allies on the other side, called *Instrumentum Pacis Monasteriensis* (IPM). Peace of Westphalia (*Die Westfaelischen Friedensvertaege vom 24. Oktober 1648. Texte under Uebersetzungen* (*Acta Pacis Westphalicae. Supplementa electronica,* 1). (http://www.pax-westphalica.de/6/1/07). The two Treaties contain many of the same provisions. Unless otherwise indicated, the English, the French, and the German translations of the Peace of Westphalia in this work are that of *Die Westfaelischen Friedensvertaege* in http://www.pax-westphalica.de/6/1/07. Last visited 6/1/10.

[23] "That there be an exact and reciprocal Equality amongst all the Electors, Princes and States of both Religions, conformably to the State of Commonweal, the Constitutions of the Empire, and the present Convention." Peace of Westphalia. *Id.* Art. V, 1 IPO; '47 IPM. 1.

[24] "[E]ach of the Estates of the Empire shall freely and forever enjoy the Right of making Alliances among themselves, or with Foreigners, for the Preservation and Security of every one of them: provided nevertheless that these Alliances be neither against the Emperor nor the Empire, nor the publick Peace, nor against this Transaction especially; and that they be made without prejudice in every respect to the Oath whereby every one of them is bound of the emperor and the Empire." *Id.* Art. VIII, 2 IPO; '63 IPM, 1.

[25] *See* John H. Herz, *The Rise and Demise of the Territorial State*, in 9 World Politics at 473–74 (1957), 479, reprinted in Lubasz, *supra* note 15, at 131–151. Michael P. Scharf observed that "[T]he power to conclude alliance formally recognized at Westphalia was not unqualified, and was actually a power that German princes had already possessed for almost half a century." *Seizing the "Grotian Moment: Accelerated Formation of Customary International Law in Times of fundamental Change*, Cornell International Law Journal, V. 43 Fall 2010. No. 3. at 442. Footnote 18. The princes who concluded alliance prior to Peace of Westphalia probably acted either with special sanction or without sanction of the Emperor. Otherwise, the princes would not have demanded the lifting of the restriction in the Peace. Since the restriction of the power of the princes was a legal restriction, in this writer's view, the restriction was legally lifted at Peace of Westphalia.

Thus, after the Peace of Westphalia went into force, these Estates (Principalities) asserted sovereignty by entering into relation with other States, even though they were nominally still parts of the Holy Roman Empire.[26] Other States began to recognize them as States and establish diplomatic relations with them. For instance, in 1665, the English King Charles II sent Walter Vane as the ambassador to the Elector of Brandenburg during the first Dutch War.[27] This act of sending an ambassador to Brandenburg served as a formal recognition of the status of Brandenburg as a State. These Princes and territorial magnates had turned their Principalities or dominions into the modern States.

Other feudal kings in Europe followed the trend and transformed their kingdoms into modern States. Eventually, a new political system emerged in Western Europe and the feudal system broke down. The transition from feudal States to the modern States signified the end of the Middle Ages.

In the modern State, the political system of the State changed. The fundamental change under the new system is that the ruler (the king or the sovereign prince) now governed his territory and the people within the territory directly, instead of through his feudal vassals. The king or the sovereign prince collects taxes directly from the people and also on the lands within his kingdom or principality, respectively. The king issued (sovereign) currency and maintained his own army. The transformation of the feudal State into the modern State was followed by the rise of modern intellectual movements leading to the Age of Reason.[28]

3. FUNDAMENTAL CHARACTERISTICS OF THE MODERN STATE

It is nearly impossible to sort out all common characteristics shared by the modern States. Various writers have described the modern State differently.[29] Some point out that the modern State is governed by a system of law. Some argue that it recognizes a distinction between the State and society. Others emphasize that the modern State is based on the principle

[26] After the Treaties were concluded, the German States continued to attend the Imperial Diet and Assembly.

[27] W.R. Sorley, A History of British Philosophy to 1900, Cambridge Univ. Press, 1965, at 106. John Locke served as secretary to Walter Vane. *Id.*

[28] *See* Ritter, *supra* note 16, at 19–28.

[29] *See* Lubasz, *supra* note 15, at 2–3. These points are not discussed here because they are not relevant to the analyses in this work.

of democracy. If the term "the modern State" is used generally to include all the States existing at the time, not all States will fit all these descriptions squarely. There are, however, two fundamental characteristics shared by the modern States. The first characteristic is that the modern State is a territorial State—a State predicated on territory. The second characteristic is that it is a State with sovereignty. A brief discussion of the two characteristics follows.

4. THE STATE PREDICATED ON TERRITORY

The territorial State means that the State is predicated on territory, or associated with a particular territory. In the feudal State, the ruler (the king or the emperor[30]) rules his kingdom or empire through the control of his feudal vassals. The territories ruled by his feudal vassals are their property (or estate). So, the exact outer limit of the territory is not crucial to the kingdom or the empire.[31]

The modern State is a territorial State. Its identity is tied to a particular area of land. The Italian princes who became autonomous from the Holy Roman Empire during the 11th century were territorial magnates and exercised a power similar to sovereign power in the lands in their dominions.[32] Under the new political system of the modern State, in order to rule his subjects directly, including collecting taxes from them and, in particular, on the lands, the ruler has to define the territory under his rule.[33] The definition of the State's territory now includes boundaries and a frontier. The frontier of the State creates a "hard shell" for the State,[34] not only for the protection of its peoples within its territory, but also for the ruler to exercise his power and authority over all the inhabitants and aliens within its boundaries. On the other hand, these

[30] In discussing the feudal system, the word "ruler" refers to a king and an emperor. "An emperor was an emperor only if he was a king first, and his role in the feudal system was an outgrowth of his kingship." William Y. Elliott and Neil A. McDonald, Western Political Heritage, Prentice Hall (New York), 1950, at 324.

[31] *See* Hurst Hannum, Autonomy, Sovereignty, and Self-Determination: The Accommodation of Conflicting Rights, U. of Pennsylvania Press, 1990, at 17.

[32] *See infra* text accompanying note 145 for the discussion of *dominio exercising imperio.*

[33] "Since the replacement of the Holy Roman Empire by a system of independent sovereign States having definite boundaries—what has been termed the 'birth of territoriality' during the sixteenth and seventeenth centuries." R.R. Churchill and A.V. Lowe, The Law of the Sea. Juris Publishing, Manchester University Press. 3rd Ed., at 71.

[34] *See* Herz, *supra* note 25.

boundaries also create a limitation of the State's authority. It has no power or authority beyond its territory.[35] The term "the territorial State" or "territoriality"[36] as used in this work refers to the notion of the modern territory-based State.

In the modern State, the sovereign ruler has title to his territory. Title to the territory still followed the sovereign ruler. For example, after the War of Polish Succession in 1738, the Holy Roman Emperor gave Lorraine to Stanishlaw, the Polish king. Later, Stanishlaw married his daughter to the French king, Louis XV. In 1766, when Stanishlaw died, Lorraine was incorporated into French territory because title to Lorraine passed to Louis XV through his wife, Stanislaw's daughter. In the modern State, the territory of the State was still treated as the private property of the ruler.

[35] The territory of a State also includes its territorial sea as recognized by international law.

[36] *See* U.N. Convention on the Law of the Sea, Dec. 10, 1982, Art. 2, 1833 U.N.T.S. 3, at 397; Rebecca M.M. Wallace, International Law, Sweet & Maxwell (London), 1986, at 120–123; R.R. Churchill and A.V. Lowe, *supra* note 33. For a discussion of the term *territoriality, see* Herz, *supra* note 25, at 473–485.

CHAPTER 2

The State and Sovereignty

Contents

The One-China Policy: State, Sovereignty, and Taiwan's International Legal Status
DOI: http://dx.doi.org/10.1016/B978-0-08-102314-3.00002-1

1. SOVEREIGNTY

A. The Power System of the Ruler

This chapter briefly examines the theory of sovereignty and its relationship with the State. The first characteristic shared by the modern states, as discussed briefly in Chapter 1, The State, is territoriality. The second characteristic shared by the modern States is sovereignty: The modern State is a State with sovereignty.

In discussing the theory of sovereignty in the modern State, in particular in describing rulers and their power, this work follows the words used by Jean Bodin and other writers: The word "ruler" includes "king" and "the sovereign prince"; the "sovereign prince" includes a feudal duke or noble of an autonomous dominion. The word "magnate" refers to a feudal vassal and the term "territorial magnate" is used to indicate a title with dominion over a territory, such as a duke or a prince, not just a high official.

The theory of sovereignty or similar concepts was advanced by jurists and political thinkers to explain or justify the political power of a ruler or rulers of a political institution of their time. While jurists used the Latin word *maiestas* (the medieval form of *majestas*) or *imperium* to describe the political power and authority of the emperor or the prince before the 16th century,[37] the modern theory of sovereignty was not formulated until the 16th century when Bodin first adopted the French word *souveraineté* (sovereignty)[38] to describe the political power of the ruler—whom

[37] "[I]n the fourteenth century, whether in France or in England, sovereignty is claimed in the name of empire." Dowdall, *supra* note 14, at 111. In the feudal Germany (Holy Roman Empire), the theories of sovereignty [*majestas*] flourished. But the word 'sovereignty [*majestas*]', usually not defined in the discussions, referred to public power of the people or the Emperor. *See* Otto von Gierke, The Development of Political Theories, as No. VII of the '*Untersuchungen zur Deutchen Staats- und Rechtsgeschiste*'. W.W. Norton & Company, Inc. 1880, trans. by Bernard Freyd. Howard Fertig, Inc. ed. 1966. In the English translation of the book, the word 'sovereignty' is used for Latin word *majestas*. *Id.* at 34.

[38] "We must now formulate a definition of sovereignty because no jurist or political philosopher has defined it." Jean Bodin On Sovereignty, ed. and trans. by Julian H. Franklin, Cambridge Univ. Press (Cambridge) 1992, 1. The book On Sovereignty is an English translation of four chapters (Chapters 8 and 10 of Book I, Chapters 1 and 5 of Book II) of Bodin's original work The Six Books of the Commonwealth (*Les Six Livres de la République*), 1576.

he called "the prince" or "the sovereign prince"—of the modern State.[39] Thus, discussions in this chapter will begin with the power system of the ruler in the modern State—the concept of the French word *état*.

The French word *état*, the modern form of *estat*, is from the Latin word *status*. (Hereafter the modern form "*état*" is used in this work unless the old form "*estat*" is in a quotation or is required by the context.) Initially, the word *état* had a meaning of the status of a person, particularly a person in a high position.[40] During the 15th century, the word *état* acquired the meaning of territorial magnate.[41]

B. Bodin's Theory of Sovereignty

After France transformed from a feudal State into a modern State, the word *état* also came to refer to the power system of the ruler.[42] Bodin describes the power system of the ruler of the modern State in his work *Les Six Livres de la République* (The Six Books of the Commonwealth)[43] written in French and published in 1576, about a century after the French King Charles VII began centralization of the political power in the king thus transforming France into the modern State.

[39] Bodin did not define the word "prince." He used the word for a person who had sovereignty as defined by him. Thus, he wrote that "[a] dictator (of Rome) was neither a prince nor a sovereign magistrate." *Id.* at 3. In using the word "prince," Bodin most likely followed its meaning in Machiavelli's work, THE PRINCE, published half a century earlier (1531). In 1152, when Holy Roman Emperor Frederick I created the title "Prince" for the magnates (mostly of the rank of duke) within the Empire, the Empire included northern Italy. For a short period (from 1499 to 1513) before Machiavelli published his work, northern Italy fell under the rule of French king Louis XII. But the magnates (mostly dukes) of northern Italy continued to use the title "prince." Thus, Dowdall wrote, "With Machiavelli, both the *Italicus* and the Duke would be described as a prince and the *civitas* as a republic." Dowdall, *supra* note 14, at 114. In Bodin's time, Philip II of Spain was Duke of Milan briefly from 1554 on.

[40] Dowdall, *supra* note 14, at 105, footnote 9.

[41] *Id.* 105, footnote 8. A territorial magnate is "one who exercised rights of government in his territory." *Id.* at 106.

[42] "The term *estat,* as distinguished from *république*, technically refers to the system of sovereign power and not to the organized political community over which the sovereign rules." BODIN, *supra* note 38, Translator's *Notes on translation*, at xli.

[43] *See Id. Also see* INGRID DELUPIS, INTERNATIONAL LAW AND THE INDEPENDENT STATE, Crane, Russak & Co., 1974, at 3; MICHAEL R. FOWLER & JULIE M. BUNCK, LAW, POWER, AND THE SOVEREIGN STATE: THE EVOLUTION AND APPLICATION OF THE CONCEPT OF SOVEREIGNTY, Penn. St. Univ. Press, 1995, at 36, footnote 15.

In his work, Bodin describes *état* of the ruler, either a single person or group, as the supreme and absolute power over his subjects.[44] The words *maiestas* and *imperium* were used for the power of a feudal king or a feudal emperor. But the power of the ruler which Bodin describes is more precise and different from the power of a feudal king or a feudal emperor, such as the Holy Roman Emperor. For the power of the king and the sovereign prince, Bodin adopts the French word *souveraineté* (sovereignty), which he defines as "the absolute and perpetual power of a commonwealth (*République*) that is the highest power of command."[45] In Bodin's theory, the power of the ruler is the supreme power in the commonwealth (*République*) because it "is the highest power of command."[46] Thus, it is the supreme power to rule the people. The power is absolute because he defines it as not "limited either in power or in function, or in length of time."[47] The power is unconditional "other than what is commanded by the law of God and of nature."[48] A sovereign prince is answerable only to God. The supreme and absolute power in Bodin's theory of sovereignty probably strengthened the power of the European feudal kings and princes during the 16th, 17th, and 18th centuries, culminating in the centralization of the political power in them, and precipitated the end of medieval feudalism.

The ruler acquires sovereignty by merely being in the position of a king or a prince, whether he acquires it by right of succession, acclamation of the people, or through brute force.[49] Bodin defined "sovereignty" so precisely that not every king or emperor had sovereignty by his definition. The territorial political institution with sovereignty described in Bodin's theory is now called "the modern State."

In Bodin's theory of sovereignty based on his definition, sovereignty has six characteristics. The first characteristic is that sovereignty resides in a ruler, a natural person: Sovereignty resides in a king or a prince. A king or a prince who has sovereignty is sovereign: A sovereign is the bearer of sovereignty. Although some power is exercised by other magistrates, sovereignty is held by the ruler. Bodin used historical events to illustrate that

[44] BODIN, *supra* note 38, at 1.
[45] *Id.* at 1.
[46] *Id.* at 1.
[47] *Id.* at 3.
[48] *Id.* at 8.
[49] *Id.* at 8. "[A] sovereign magistrate contrives to prolong the power entrusted to him (by the sovereign) by force is a tyrant [but] is a sovereign." *Id.* at 6.

the Spanish king and the English king, like the French king, had the sovereign power he defined.

The second characteristic of sovereignty is that the power is supreme and absolute. The concept of "sovereignty" developed by Bodin is a technical and narrow one, meaning the supreme and absolute power of the ruler to govern his subjects and manage the State. The power is supreme in the sense that the power is the highest in the State and not subject to the power of any other ruler or person. Not all emperors or kings have the supreme power described by Bodin. For instance, Holy Roman Emperors had *majestas*, but no sovereignty because "the emperor was subject to the Estates of the Empire, and did not claim sovereignty over the princes or the Estates."[50] Holy Roman Emperors had no sovereignty because, as Bodin said, "before he is consecrated, the (German) emperor, who has precedence over all other Christian kings, swears in the hands of the archbishop of Cologne to keep the laws of the Empire and the Golden Bull[51]; to obey the pope; to maintain the Catholic faith. That is the oath that Charles V took and which was sent to the pope by the papal ambassador in Germany."[52] The emperor who has no sovereignty is only "the chief person of the state."[53]

The sovereign power as formulated by Bodin means supreme power to command, including the exclusive executive power and the power to give law.[54] The supreme power of a sovereign includes the exclusive power to make law (the legislative power) in addition to the executive power. A sovereign is, in Bodin's theory, above his own law.[55] Bodin said,

[50] BODIN, *supra* note 38, at 15–16.

[51] The Golden Bull was the constitution for the Holy Roman Empire promulgated by Emperor Charles IV (of the House of Luxemburg) in 1356. It formally adopted the principle of elective monarchy with seven electors: the archbishops of Mainz, Trier, and Cologne, the Duke of Saxony, the margrave of Brandenburg, the Count Palatine of the Rheine, and the King of Bohemia. *See*, ACADEMIC AMERICAN ENCYCLOPEDIA, *supra* note 12, V.9, at 150 (the entry of 'History of Germany'); THE NEW ENCYCLOPEDIA BRITANNICA, *supra* note 7, V.5, at 339 (the entry of 'Golden Bull.').

[52] BODIN, *supra* note 38. at 15–16.

[53] *Id.* at 24.

[54] "[T]he very word 'law' in Latin implies the command of him who has the sovereign." *Id.* at 11.

[55] "This is why the law says that the prince is not subject to the law." *Id.* at 11. "[A] sovereign cannot tie his hands even if he wished to do so." *Id.* at 13. "[T]he laws of a sovereign prince, even if founded on good and strong reasons, depends solely on his own free will." *Id.* at 13.

"[P]ersons who are sovereign must not be subject in any way to the commands of someone else and must be able to give the law to subjects and suppress or repeal disadvantageous laws and replace them with others—which cannot be done by someone who is subject to the laws or to persons having power of command over him."[56] A monarch who has no exclusive power to make law has no sovereignty in Bodin's theory.

The sovereign power of the ruler is absolute in the sense that the power is not subject to any restriction imposed by other persons. If the power of an emperor or a king is not absolute, but is subject to another person other than god or is subject to a condition, he is not a sovereign, for Bodin said that "sovereignty given to a prince subject to obligations and conditions is properly not sovereignty or absolute power."[57] For instance, the 1791 First French Constitution made the king subject to another organ of the State when the French king was required to "take oath to the nation to be faithful to the nation ... [and] to maintain the Constitution decreed by the National Constituent Assembly."[58] In Bodin's theory, French King Louis XVI had no sovereignty under the First French Constitution[59] because the Constitution took away the power of French King Louis XVI to make law and placed the power to make law (legislative power) in the National Assembly.[60]

In Germany, the Holy Roman Emperors (of the First Reich), as pointed out earlier, had no sovereignty prior to the Peace of Westphalia

[56] *Id.* at 11.

[57] BODIN, *supra* note 38, at 8.

[58] The 1791 First French Constitution. Title III (Of Public Power), Chapter II, Section 1, Art. 4 provides, On his accession to the throne, or as soon as he has attained his majority, the King, in the presence of the legislative body, shall take oath to the nation to be faithful to the nation and to the law, to employ all the power delegated to him to maintain the Constitution decreed by the National Constituent Assembly in the years 1789, 1790, and 1791, and to have the laws executed. If the legislative body be not in session, the King shall have a proclamation published, in which said oath, and the promise to reiterate it as soon as the legislative body has assembled, shall be set forth. *available at* http://sourcebook.fsc.edu/history/constitutionof1791.html. Last visited 01/25/2010.

[59] BODIN, *supra* note 38, 56. "[T]he emperor, who swears to keep the laws of the Empire, to obey the Pope is subject to the Estates of the Empire and does not claim sovereignty." *Id.* at 15–16.

[60] The French Constitution of 1791. Title III. *See supra* note 56. Art. 3 provides, "The legislative power is delegated to a National Assembly composed of temporary representatives freshly elected by the people, to be exercised by it, with the sanction of the King in the manner hereinafter determined."

(the Treaties).[61] After the Treaties were concluded, while the territorial magnates (Princes, dukes) acquired sovereignty, the Emperors did not. Later, when William I became the Emperor (of the Second Reich), he did not have sovereignty either because under the 1871 Constitution the legislative power was in the Federal Council and the Imperial Diet.[62]

A restriction imposed by the ruler himself does not take away the sovereign power. A ruler often refrains from imposing harsh rules on his subjects out of his concern of their welfare. It is often also in the best interests of the ruler to keep his subjects happy in order to maintain the "consent" of the subjects. A ruler sometimes places certain rules above others in importance. These rules which he declares as more important are like a constitution. Bodin suggested that such a constitution could not be changed easily. He said, "I think it extremely dangerous to make any change in the law touching the constitution."[63]

The absolute power of the king and the sovereign prince defined by Bodin is subject only to god and the law of nature.[64] Thus, any restriction imposed by the natural law does not damage the power as the sovereign power. A principle of the natural law to which the sovereign power is subject to is the institution of contracts.[65] The sovereign cannot violate the natural rights arising out of the contract right. Thus, the sovereign was bound by a contract which he entered into.[66] Bodin distinguishes law issued by the sovereign (which he is above) and the contracts concluded by him (which he must keep). For example, in England, the king was bound by the Magna Carta, for it was considered the kings' contract with the Estates.[67]

[61] *See supra* text accompanying note 50.

[62] Constitution of the German Empire (1871) Art. 5 provides, "The legislative power of the Empire shall be exercised by the Federal Council (*Bundesrat*) and the Imperial Diet (*Reichstag*)," *available at* http://en.wikisource.org/wiki/Constitution_of_the_German_Empire#PREAMBLE. Last visited 01/25/2010.

[63] Bodin, The Six Books of the Commonwealth. Book IV, ch. III, 125 (M.J. Tooley trans. Basil Blackwell 1955), cited by Larry Cata Backer in *Reifying Law – Government, Law and the Rule of Law in Governance Systems*, Penn State Int. Law Review, Vol. 26, No.3, Winter 2008, The Pennsylvania State University, 521, at 523 footnote 2.

[64] Bodin, *Id.* at 8. *See also* Christian Purtschet, Histoire des institutions xe -xviiie siecle, Masson et C i.e., 1972, at 239.

[65] *See* discussions in von Gierke, *see supra* note 37, at 303.

[66] "[A] prince is bound by the just contract and promises that he has made." Bodin, *supra* note 38, at 13.

[67] Historically, in England "(Three) Estates" referred to the (three) groups constituting a political body subsequently called the Parliament. The New Shorter Oxford English Dictionary. 3d Ed., Oxford Univ. Press, 1993, V.1., at 853 (providing the definition of "estate").

Another principle of natural law, which the sovereign power is subject to, is the institution of private property.[68] The sovereign cannot violate the natural rights arising out of property rights. Thus, the sovereign in the modern State cannot impose tax on his subjects without the consent of the people, for, as Bodin said, "there is no prince in all the world who has the power to levy taxes on the people at his pleasure any more than he has the power to take another's goods."[69] Thus, by agreeing not to levy taxes without consent of common counsel in the Magna Carta,[70] the English king's sovereign power was not subjugated.

The ruler with such supreme and absolute power will be called the "absolute ruler," or the "absolute monarch" in the case of a king or a prince, in this work in order to be distinguished from the monarch of a constitutional monarchy.

The third characteristic of sovereignty in Bodin's theory is that sovereignty belongs undivided to the ruler. This is the notion that sovereignty is indivisible. As mentioned earlier, sovereignty, as formulated by Bodin, includes the power to give law. Bodin said that "the first prerogative of sovereignty is to give law to all in general and to each in particular, the latter part refers to privileges without the consent of any other, whether greater, equal, or below him."[71] Bodin said that "a (sovereign's) attributes are [his] properties not shared by [his] subjects,"[72] which included the senate and the people, and were not subject to or shared by the

[68] *See* von Gierke, *supra* note 37, at 303.

[69] Bodin, *supra* note 38, *at* 21. "[T]he inviolability of a subjective right was to be strictly maintained only if, and in so far as, this right could be based on some ground of Natural Law independent of positive law. [T]wo principles became the ground work of the whole doctrine. First, that the institution of private property is rooted in '*ius gentium*,' a Law which flowed from the pure Law of Nature without the aid of the State. Secondly, that the binding force of contracts comes from the Law of Nature, so that the sovereign, though he cannot bind himself or his successors by statute, can bind himself and his successors to his subjects by contract." von Gierke, *supra* note 37, at 303.

[70] Article 12 of Magna Carta (1215) provides, "No scutage or aid shall be imposed in our kingdom unless by common counsel of our kingdom." The New Encyclopedia Britannica, *supra* note 7. V.7, at 673–674 (the entry of 'Magna Carta').

[71] Bodin, *supra* note 38, at 56.

[72] *Id.* at 46.

Parliament or the Assembly of the Estates of the people.[73] Speaking of the relationship between the English king and the Estates of the people, Bodin said that "[t]he main point of sovereign majesty and absolute power consists of giving the laws to subjects in general without their (the Estates') consent."[74] In France, the resolutions of the French Parliament were mere recommendations.[75] Thus, in Bodin's theory, not only was the king's sovereignty indivisible, his power to exercise sovereignty (the sovereign power) was also not shared by the legislature or the people.

The fourth characteristic of sovereignty in Bodin's theory is that sovereignty is personal and perpetual: the power rests in the ruler. Sovereignty is personal in the sense that it follows the person—the sovereign. The power is perpetual in the sense that it resides in the sovereign until his death. Bodin said that "[w]e must understand the word *perpetual* to mean 'for the life of him who has the power.'"[76] When a sovereign dies, his power to rule ceases. Bodin said that "[f]or it is well known that the laws, ordinances, letters patents, privileges, and concessions of (sovereign) princes, have force only during their lifetimes unless they are ratified by the express consent, or at least the sufferance of a (sovereign) prince who is cognizant of them."[77]

The fifth characteristic of sovereignty is that the sovereign power of the ruler extends to his entire territory. As discussed before, the modern State is predicated on territory. Thus, the king's power extends to all of his territory. Bodin says that "the prerogative of sovereignty is to give law to all . . . which are in the *jurisdiction* of sovereign princes to the exclusion of all others."[78] Under the new political system of the modern State, the lands previously owned and controlled by the king's vassals now become the king's territory under his direct control.[79] In the modern State, sovereignty over its territory and the people is based on title to the territory.

[73] *Id.* at 23.

[74] *Id.* at 23.

[75] Subsequently, Louis XV stripped the power of the parliaments and left them to function only as appellate courts.

[76] BODIN, *supra* note 38, at 6.

[77] *Id.* at 12. In Bodin's work, the word "prince" refers to the sovereign princes of northern Italy. *See infra* text accompanying note 125.

[78] *Id.* at 56 (emphasis added).

[79] "[T]he first prerogative (marque) of a sovereign prince is to give law to all in general." *Id.* at 56. *See also supra* text accompanying note 33.

The concept that sovereignty of the modern State is based on title to the territory is sometimes known as "territorial sovereignty."

The sixth characteristic of sovereignty in Bodin's theory is independence or autonomy. Because a sovereign is not subject to the rule or interference of other rulers, the sovereign is independent of the other States or autonomous within an empire. Although Bodin did not elaborate, the sovereign power which he described was the power of the king of the modern State in which the king ruled the people directly without need for the cooperation of feudal vassals. The sovereign king or the sovereign prince need not follow the commands of the pope or an emperor. The king also built his own army and centralized the power, including military power, in him, thus eliminating his reliance on others for protection or aid. A sovereign employed his power to protect both the independence of the commonwealth (or autonomy of the principality) and his own.

In adopting the word "sovereignty" to describe the power system of the ruler, Bodin defines the word with specific terms. At the time, when Bodin adopted the word to describe this political power system, the prevailing form of State in Europe was the monarchy or principality. Thus, his theory of sovereignty is based on the power of the king or "the prince," whom he calls "the sovereign prince."

Writers after Bodin have criticized his theory of sovereignty. The most significant criticisms of Bodin's theory attack two premises: first, the sovereign power of the ruler is absolute; and second, sovereignty is indivisible.

On the first point—that sovereign power is absolute—the most prominent critic was John Locke. Locke argues that a sovereign's power is never absolute. On the second point—that sovereignty is not divisible—a prominent critic was Otto von Gierke. Von Gierke argues that sovereignty is not indivisible as Bodin claims, but is shared with the parliament.

Both criticisms may be disposed in a simple way. Much of the criticism was mainly on the nature and extent of the power of the ruler. But the word "sovereignty" was first adopted and *defined* by Bodin as the absolute and exclusive power of the ruler. For instance, in Bodin's theory, the sovereign power includes power to make law without consent of others.[80] When a ruler shares the power with others, he is *not* sovereign.

[80] *See supra* text accompanying note 74.

Thus, sovereignty defined by Bodin does not apply to monarchs in constitutional monarchies where the legislative power is not in the monarch. Though others may claim that such absolute political power never existed, they cannot disagree with *his* definition. These critics have used the word "sovereignty" for different meanings. But this is not a place for lengthy discussions on this issue.

C. Theories of King's Authority

From early on, political thinkers have attempted to support or limit the authority, or the legitimate power, of rulers by theorizing the source of their authority. For many centuries, the theory accepted by most, if not all, writers, was set forth by Thomas Aquinas.[81] It is that the rulers receive their authority to govern their subjects from the god. As late as the middle of the 16th century, Bodin writes that "sovereign princes are established by Him (God). Contempt for one's sovereign prince is contempt toward God, of whom he is (the) earthly image."[82] In other words, a sovereign ruler receives the absolute power to rule from god. Such theory was acccpted without much question until the 17th century. Even in feudal Germany, where the theory of popular sovereignty was introduced early on among the scholars, the parties to the 1648 Peace of Westphalia (the "Treaties"), in signing the Treaties, invoked the power of god. The Preamble to the Treaties states, "In consequence (of the Assembly or Congress of Plenipotentiaries), the Ambassadors and Plenipotentiaries lawfully established on both sides, ... After having invoked *the Assistance of God*, ... they transacted and agreed among themselves, to the Glory of God, and Safety of the Christian world (the Electors, Princes, and States of the Sacred (Holy) Roman Empire being present, approving, and consenting) the Articles of Peace and Amity, whereof the Tenour follows...."[83]

In the middle of the 17th century, a new theory emerged. Thomas Hobbes,[84] in his work, Leviathan, describing his version of the modern

[81] For Thomas Aquinas (1224–1274)'s political theory, *see* THE POLITICAL IDEAS OF ST. THOMAS AQUINAS, DINO BIGONGIARI ed., Free Press (New York), 1953, at 188, 191.

[82] BODIN, *supra* note 38, at 46.

[83] English translation of Preamble of Peace of Westphalia, *supra* note 22. *Supplementa electronica*, at 1 (emphasis added).

[84] For a brief statement of Thomas Hobbes (1588-1679)'s theory, *see* STEIN, *supra* note 2 in Chapter 1, at 2–3.

State, advocated the theory of social contract.[85] Hobbes expounds the theory that the king obtains his authority from his subjects by a conjectured social contract, where each of the parties, both the ruled and the ruler, agree to abide by an unwritten agreement to live in an ordered society for mutual benefit. Such a condition implies that the king's authority is not from God, but from the people. Hobbes regards the king as the sovereign, who acquires unlimited political power to rule by the consent of the people. The people consent because the "state of [human] nature must have been so dangerous and unpleasant for man that he would gladly agree to surrender all the freedom and power over himself, which he had hitherto enjoyed, to a *sovereign person* or body who was strong enough to protect him from its perils."[86] Hobbes argued, however, that once the people had given up their public power to a king, the king's power became absolute and could not be retracted by the people. Therefore, according to Hobbes, it was wrong to overthrow a king because it would be breaking the social contract.

Toward the end of the late 17th century, John Locke,[87] in his work The Second Treatise of Government,[88] expounds another theory of social contract based on his ideas that men are rational and that human beings are equal in nature.[89] Locke says that "[C]ivil society was consciously created by rational men ... who first agreed to combine in a community by one contract, and then, by another ... agreed to entrust its government to a *ruler* chosen by themselves."[90] Locke differs from Hobbes in the extent of a king's authority. In Locke's theory, the political power to rule,

[85] Thomas Hobbes, Leviathan, first published in 1651, ed. by C.B. Macpherson. Penguin Books, Ltd. Republished by Pelican Books, Ltd. (1968).

[86] A quotation from Stein, *supra* note 2, at 2 (emphasis added). It is the best summary of the central theme of Hobbes' theory. For a discussion of theory of social contract, *see* Hobbes, *supra* note 85, at 189–221. This writer adds the word "human" because Hobbes refers to the state of human being, not of the nature in general. *Id.*

[87] Locke lived from 1632 to 1704.

[88] John Locke, The Second Treatise of Government, (1690) ed. by Thomas P. Pearson. The Liberal Arts Press, Inc., 1952. The work expounding the theory of social contract was published in 1690. John Locke, Treatise of Civil Government in Charles L. Sherman, ed. Treatise of Civil Government and A Letter concerning Toleration. Appleton-Century-Crofts, Inc. (New York), 1937.

[89] Locke, The Second Treatise of Government, *id*, at 5 and 54.

[90] This description is taken from Stein, *supra* note 2, at 2.

which the king receives from the people under a social contract, is limited and revocable.[91] Locke theorizes that the people entrust the government to their ruler, who governs with the consent of the people.[92] The ruler who betrays their trust can be deposed. Thus, the Glorious Revolution that replaced a king with another was justified.[93]

In Hobbes's theory of social contract, sovereignty resides in the ruler (the king) even though the ruler receives the political power to rule from the people by contract. In his theory, as described in Leviathan published 75 years after Bodin's work, the sovereign power to rule is absolute and unrestricted by the social contract. On the other hand, in Locke's theory, as described in his The Second Treatises of Government, published 114 years after Bodin's work, the king's power is restrained by the contract with the people.

The theory of social contract expounded by Locke eventually replaced the theory of the theological source of a king's authority during the late 18th century. His democratic idea of equality among men influenced Charles Montesquieu, who in his work, The Spirit of the Laws (*Les Esprit des Droit*),[94] published half a century later, favored a republican over a monarchical and aristocratic form of government.[95] The liberal political ideas of Locke and Montesquieu became the core of political thought of 18th century Europe, known as the Age of Enlightenment. But liberal political thought remained just an ideal and was not realized until the American Revolution in the second half of the 18th century when it was incorporated into the American Declaration of Independence (1776) and

[91] John Locke, who supported the Glorious Revolution of 1688 that replaced the English king with another argued that "[T]he ruler was limited in what he could command his subjects to do, and these limitations were prescribed by nature." STEIN, *supra* note 2, 2-3.

[92] Charles L. Sherman, the editor of TREATISE OF CIVIL GOVERNMENT, *supra* note 88, said that by "consent of the people," Locke had in mind the people who had property. Sherman in Introduction to the book said, "It is safe to say that Locke had little interest in the great mass of town and country laborers who had not succeeded in scraping together more than the immediate needs of the day.... Consent to him included the merchant, the business man, the intellectual, who now disputed the exclusive claims of the landed aristocracy to control government and through government the sources of free opinion and individual improvement." *Id.* at xiv–xv.'

[93] King James II was overthrown in the Glorious Revolution of 1688.

[94] The work was published in 1748.

[95] ACADEMIC AMERICAN ENCYCLOPEDIA, *see supra* note 12, Vol. 13, at 553.

enshrined into the Constitution of the United States of America (The "U.S.") upon the establishment of the U.S. in 1789.

By the time of the American Revolution, the theory of the theological source of a king's authority was discarded. The U.S. is a republic. Its Presidents are elected by the people to serve for a limited period of time. So, their authority, given by the constitution enacted by the people, is limited and is retracted at the end of their term. In Europe, the French Revolution of 1789 was justified on the ground that the king's authority was not derived from God.[96] The resulting government established a similar system where the ruler was clearly chosen and empowered by the people. This began a worldwide shift away from the modern state.

2. THE MEANING OF THE WORD "STATE"

A. The Origin of the Word "State"

While the English word "State," with a capital S, applies to all kinds of territorial political institutions described as such in this work, the word "state" has not always carried the same meaning in the past.

The English word "state" is derived from the French word *état.*[97] Etymologically, it has had the same meaning as *état*. Thus, the meaning of *état* will be first examined. Although the French word *état* has a meaning of "territorial political institution with the sovereign power" today, the word was not commonly used for that meaning probably until the 18th century. The word *état* has had many meanings in the past. As mentioned earlier, it started with the meaning of position or status of a person. After the word acquired the meaning of "territorial magnate" in the 15th century,[98] the word was used for such meaning throughout the 16th, 17th and the first half of the 18th century.[99] For instance, in translating the Peace of Westphalia (the "Treaties") of 1648, the Latin word *status*

[96] "The revolutionaries justified their actions by the principle of national sovereignty. It meant that political legitimacy no longer rested on the divine right to rule of a monarch." THE FRENCH LEGAL SYSTEM, AN INTRODUCTION, by ANDREW WEST, YVON DESDEVICES, ALAIN FENET, DOMINIQUE GAURRIER, and MARIE-CLET HEUSSAFF, Fourmat Publishing (London), 1992, at 156.

[97] The English word "state" is from Old French *estat.* MERRIAM WEBSTERS COLLEGIATE DICTIONARY, 10th Ed. 1993, at 1148.

[98] *See supra* text accompanying note 41.

[99] The word *état* was occasionally also used for government from the 17th century on. *See* Dowdall, *supra* note 14, at 115–19.

meaning territorial magnate was rendered as *estat* in the 1684 as well as the 1754 French translation.[100]

Bodin used the word *état* for the power system of the ruler[101] and also used it to refer to a sovereign ruler in his work, The Six Books of the Commonwealth (1576). Thus, when Louis XIV claimed "*L'état c'est moi*" (The state, it's me) in the 17th century, his claim probably alluded to two things: one was his sovereignty—his absolute power to rule; the other was that he was the sovereign.[102]

The English word "state," like the French word *état*, acquired the meaning of "territorial magnate" during the 15th century.[103] This can be seen from the English translation of the word "state" for the Latin word *status* in the Peace of Westphalia.[104] That the Latin word *status* in the Peace of Westphalia referred to a person, rather than a political institution, can be seen from its context. The phrase "*Sacri Romani Imperii electores, principes, status*"[105] in the original Latin text of the Treaties was translated into English as "the Electors, Princes, and States of Holy Roman Empire."[106] It is clear that the Treaties regard the s*tate*, along with the Elector and Prince, as a person in the top position immediately below the Emperor. So, the word "state," which included the "Nobility,"[107] undoubtedly referred to a person. Thus, until the late 18th century, the

[100] The phrase "*Sacri Romani Imperii electoribus, principibus ac stantibus*" in the Peace of Westphalia (Preamble) were rendered "*les Electeurs, Princes & Etats du saint Empire Romain*" in the French translation. The words *les Electeurs, Princes,* and *Etats* all refer to natural persons. Peace of Westphalia, *supra* note 22.

[101] According to the translator of Bond's book, the word "estate" refers to the system of sovereign power. *See supra* note 42. The word "ruler" in this work refers to a natural person: a king or a sovereign prince.

[102] William Y. Elliott and Neil A. McDonald, Western Political Heritage, Prentice Hall (New York), 1950, at 422. Louis XIV or Louis The Great lived from 1638 to 1715. *Also at* http://hisotry-world.org/louis_xiv.htm. Last visited 01/11/2007.

[103] Dowdall, *supra* note 14, at 105–106.

[104] *See* Peace of Westphalia, *supra* note 22.

[105] *Id.* Preamble.

[106] *Id.* Art. I IPO; '1 IPM, Art. III, 1 IPO; ' 5 IPM. The English translation of Peace of Westphalia, *supra* note 22.

[107] *Id. See also* Art. III, 1 IPO; ' 5 IPM III. The English translation of Peace of Westphalia; October 24, 1648. The Avalon Project at the Yale Law School, *at* http://www.yale.edu/lawweb/avalon/westphal.htm. Last visited 03/14/2000. "therein comprehending the Nobility, [that] depend immediately on the Empire." *Id.*

English word "state" referred to either territorial magnate or king, but not to a political institution.[108]

B. The Word for a Territorial Political Institution

a. The Word for a Territorial Political Institution Prior to the use of "state"

From the 16th century through the 18th century, the French called the territorial political institution or "the collective existence of a territory"[109] under the rule of a king *république*. Bodin in his work said that "a *république* is a just government, with sovereign power, of several households and of that which they have in common."[110] Likewise, the 1648 Peace of Westphalia used the Latin word *reipublicae*[111] for the territorial political institution under the rule of the German (Holy Roman) Emperor. The 1649 German translation of the Treaties also interpreted it as *Republic.*[112]

For such territorial political institutions, English writers employed the word "commonwealth." Richard Knolles, in his 1606 English translation of Bodin's work, used "Commonwealth" for the French word *république.*[113] Hobbes in Leviathan (1651)[114] and Locke in The Second Treatise of Government (1690)[115] also used the word "commonwealth" to refer to the English kingdom. Locke explained the use of the word "commonwealth" as follows: "By commonwealth, I must be understood all along to mean, not a democracy or any form of government, but any independent community which the Latins signified by the word *civitas*, to which the word which best answers in our language is commonwealth, and most properly expresses such society of men, which 'community' or 'city' in English does not for there may be subordinate communities in a

108 Dowdall, *supra* note 14, at 106.

109 The words of Jacob Burckhardht in his *Die Kulter Der Renaissance in Italien*, *id.*, at 105.

110 Bodin, *supra* note 38, at 1. Translator's "Notes and translation 3" at xli. "*république* means organized political community." *Id.*

111 Peace of Westphalia, *supra* note 22. Art. V, 1 IPO; '47 IPM. The original text was in Latin.

112 *Id.* The 1649 German translation of the Treaties. Peace of Westphalia also calls the territory under the rule of the Electors, Princes and States the "country." *Id.* Art. V 37 IPO 30; '47 IPM 30. Also Art. V 43 IPO; '47 IPM 33.

113 *Id.* Art. III. King James the First (1566–1625) also used the word 'commonwealth' for the country under his rule. *See* Locke, *supra* note 88, at 74.

114 The full title of the book is "LEVIATHAN, or The Matter, Forme, & Power of a Common-wealth Ecclesiasticall and Civill" Hobbes, *supra* note 85.

115 Locke, *supra* note 88, at 87.

government; and city amongst us has quite a different notion from commonwealth; and therefore, to avoid ambiguity, I crave leave to use the word commonwealth in that sense I find it used by King James the First; and I take it to be its genuine signification; which if anybody dislike, I consent with him to change it for a better."[116] In Locke's time, the word "state" could not be appropriately used for an "independent community" because the word "state" had a different meaning- it referred to the king or a territorial magnate. Thus, until the middle of the 18th century, the English word "state" did not apply to territorial political institution. The 1713 English translation of the Peace of Westphalia also used "commonweal[th]" for the Latin word *reipublicae.*[117]

The meaning of the English word "state" has not been static. In the 18th century, the word "state" acquired a different meaning: territorial political institution. There is some controversy over the etymology of the word. Dowdall argued that the English word "State"(or *Staat* in German) meaning political institution was not derived from the Latin word *status* as some German writers suggested.[118] He demonstrated in his article *The Word "State"* that the Latin word *status* meant position of a person, usually a territorial magnate and never meant political institution.[119] His view is supported by the use of the word *status* in the Latin text of the 1648 Peace of Westphalia discussed above.[120]

[116] *Id. at* 87.

[117] The phrase "*Sacri Romani Imperii electoribus, principibus ac stantibus*" in Peace of Westphalia was rendered "the Electors, Princes, and States of the Sacred Roman Empire" in English translation. Peace of Westphalia, *supra* note 22, Preamble. The words "*the Electors,*" "*Princes,*" and "*States*" all refer to persons. Art. V. 1 IPO; '47 IPM. *Id.*

[118] Dowdall discussed extensively the source and the meaning of the word "State" in his article *The Word "State."* *See* Dowdall, *supra* note 14, at 115. The 1649 German translation of Peace of Westphalia renders the word *Stand,* not *Stat,* for the Latin word *statibus.* Thus, the German word *Staat* (State) was not a derivative of Latin *statibus.* According to Professor Georg Jellinek, the use of the German word *Stat* meaning *stato* preceded the use of the English word "state" [and French *état*] meaning territorial political institution. In Germany, the word *Stat* meaning a territorial political institution was used for Italian *stato* in the early 16th century. "(German) Professor Georg Jellinek (in his work *ALLGEMEINE STAATSLEHRE*, ed. 1875) says that 'from the beginning of the sixteenth century *stato* is the current expression [of German *Staat*] for a State.'" *Id.* at 99.

[119] *Id.* at 105.

[120] Peace of Westphalia, *supra* note 22. The Latin word *status* was translated as *estat* in French and *state* in English, both meaning a magnate.

b. The Italian Word stato

According to Dowdall, the English word "state" acquired its meaning of territorial political institution from the Italian word *stato* as defined by Machiavelli.[121] Because the word *stato* had a defined technical meaning, which influenced the adoption of corresponding words in other languages, a closer look at the word is in order.

The meaning of the Italian word *stato* changed several times. Initially, the word meant property in general.[122] Later, but before the time of Machiavelli, the word *stato* applied to feudal estates.[123] Machiavelli, in his work, The Prince, written in Italian and completed in 1513,[124] defines the Italian word *stato* and applies it to describe one type of territorial political institution.

Machiavelli used the word *stato* to describe some northern Italian principalities that by the 11th century had, in reality, become autonomous—no longer under the effective control of the Holy Roman Empire.[125] These principalities bore the essential characteristics of the modern State at a time when they were nominally still constituent units of the Empire. "(German) Professor Villari," referring to Duchy of Duke Gian Galeazzo in northern Italy, "said that [a]t Milan, for the first time, we find an Italian Commune transformed, through tyranny, into a modern state."[126] Machiavelli defines the word *stato*, in essence, according to Dowdall, as *dominio* which exercises *imperio* or "the *status* or estate of an effectively sovereign prince, together with the rights and powers belonging thereto."[127] Machiavelli, in short, defines the word *stato* as "an effectively sovereign government."

c. The Word "state" for the Territorial Political Institution

At some point in time the English word "state" acquired the meaning of territorial political institution. However, the exact time when the English word "state" acquired such meaning is not clear. It is impossible to

[121] Dowdall, *supra* note 14, at 125.
[122] But the word "ha[s] no special reference to land." *Id.* at 107.
[123] *Id.* at 108.
[124] The draft of The Prince was completed in 1513 and was widely available before the Italian edition was published in 1532. *Id.* at 115.
[125] The present day northern Italy came under the rule of the Holy Roman Empire in 882 when Emperor Charles III also became King of Italy. *See supra* note 7.
[126] Dowdall, *supra* note 14, at 108.
[127] *Id.* at 102. "[*I*]*mperium* meant sovereignty or independent." *Id.* at 111.

pinpoint a time because, in general, the usage of words develops slowly from a random use to general acceptance, except when a word, like *stato* or "sovereignty," is defined by initial users. The following analysis is an attempt to trace the use of the word "state" for territorial political institution in the past.

The Italian word *stato,* as defined by Machiavelli, for political institution had such a specific meaning that it did not have a corresponding concept and word in other contemporaneous languages in the 16th century.[128] The Latin translations of The Prince, rendered Machiavelli's *stato* as "*imperium, principatus, ditio,* or the like" depending on the context, but not by *status.*[129] The 1571 French translation of The Prince by Gohory rendered "stato" as "*estat, seigneurie, pais, province,* or *maniement d'affaires,*" also depending on the context.[130] Machiavelli once said to Cardinal Rohan of France that "the French did not understand *stato,*" implying that French scholars had not properly interpreted the word *stato* used by him.[131]

The German word corresponding to the Italian word *stato* is *Staat.* The adoption of the German word *Staat* for territorial political institution with sovereign power took place most likely after the 1648 Peace of Westphalia. In 1603, when German jurist Johannes Althusius published his work, The Politics, in Latin, he referred to territorial political institutions as *politia, imperium, regnum, populus,* or *respublica.*[132] But Althusius' concept of the state was different from the concept of "the State" today. In his concept, the constituents of the state are not individuals, but "cities or provinces which have agreed to unite and incorporate themselves into one body."[133] Thus, it is doubtful that Althusius employed any German word for a political institution corresponding to the State of modern time. In 1513, when Machiavelli completed his work, The Prince, German principalities were still constituent units of the Holy Roman Empire. While by that time, the Italian princes had acquired sovereign power, German princes had not. The meaning of *stato* as defined by Machiavelli describing the Italian principalities with the sovereign power

[128] *Id.* at 109–116.

[129] *Id.* at 101.

[130] *Id.* at 116.

[131] "When Cardinal Rohan said to [Machiavelli] that the Italians did not understand war, he replied that the French did not understand *stato.*" *Id.* at 109.

[132] VON GIERKE, *supra* note 37, at 39.

[133] *Id.*

would not apply to the German principalities. It is only after the 1648 Peace of Westphalia in which German princes acquired sovereign power, that the Italian word *stato* became equally applicable to German principalities.

Although the 1649 German translation of the Peace of Westphalia used the German word *Stande* for the Latin word *statibus*[134] or *status*[135] meaning magnate, the corresponding German word adopted for the Italian word *stato* was *Staat* when the definition of *stato* was applicable to German principalities. It indicates that the Germans, instead of giving a new meaning to the word *Stande,* adopted a different word *Staat* for the Italian word *stato.* Thus, the word *Staat* is not a derivative of the Latin word *status,* but more likely a derivative of the Italian word *stato.*

The French word *état* with the meaning of territorial political institution exercising the sovereign power is also derived from the Italian word *stato.*[136] In the 16th century, Gohory, in writing the 1571 French translation of The Prince, probably could not find an exact French word for the Italian word *stato* and rendered *estat* for the word, even though at the time *estat* commonly referred to a territorial magnate.[137] Thus, neither Bodin in his work of 1576 nor the translator of the 1684 French translation of Peace of Westphalia followed the new use of the word *estat* by Gohory, most likely because they adhered to the traditional meaning of the word *état,* referring to a territorial magnate or a king. But Gohory already implanted a seed for a new meaning to the word *état* in the second half of the 16th century. Thus, in the 18th century, when a word in French corresponding to the Italian word *stato* was needed, the word chosen was *état.* In other words, the French word *état* acquired a new meaning. Likewise, in the 18th century, the English word "state" which meant

[134] *See supra* note 117.

[135] "*Bewilligung des eil. Roem. Reiches' Fuersten und Stande.*" Peace of Westphalia, *supra* note 22, Preamble (the German translation).

[136] M. Ernest Nys said "*Dans la nomenclature politique et juridique, le mot francais 'Etat' derive du mot italien stato.*" *See* Dowdall, *supra* note 14, at 105, footnote 8. "He(Nys) also says that *estat* is used for the State in (French) *Code Civil,* and that the corresponding word in the late eighteenth century was *nation,* and, before that, *république* ('*Revue de droit International,*' 1901, at 420–21), Dowdall, *Id.*

[137] Dowdall talked about the difficulty in translating the Italian word *stato* defined by Machiavelli. Dowdall, *Id.* Gohory rendered the French word *estat* for Italian word *stato* whether it "refers to a government as such, to its form, authority, or proprietary character" or to "feudal superiority" or to "the extent of territory." *Id. supra* note 14, at 116.

territorial magnate acquired a new meaning, the territorial political institution.

d. The Word "State" for a Constituent Unit of an Empire or a Commonwealth

When the English word "state" was initially used to refer to a territorial political institution—the word applied to what was later called "the modern State"—the state, at the time, had three characteristics. The first was that the state initially referred to a political institution that was a constituent unit of a kingdom or an empire. In 1765, Governor Stephen Hopkins of Rhode Island, which was a British colony at the time, referred to German principalities as "(German) states,"[138] while he referred to the Holy Roman (German) Empire as the "empire of Germany," not as a State, in his article *The Rights of Colonies Examined.*[139]

Hopkins also referred to Great Britain as "the emigrant *state*"[140] and "the mother *state*."[141] The term "mother state" applied only to Great Britain, which consisted of England, Wales, and Scotland, but not to the entire British Empire.[142] He referred to the "whole British Empire" as the "whole commonwealth."[143]

A conclusion may be drawn that when the English word "state" was initially applied to a territorial political institution, the institution it referred to was a constituent unit of an empire, not an independent entity. Such a conclusion is consistent with Machiavelli's definition of *stato*, which meant *dominio* exercising *imperio*. At the time when Machiavelli used the word *stato* to describe Italian principalities or duchies, they were

138 Stephen Hopkins, The Rights of Colonies Examined, 1764. Introduction and ed. by Paul Campbell, (Reprinted by) The Rhode Island Bicentennial Foundation, (Providence, Rhode Island), 1974, at 46. By Hopkins' time, the German word *Staat* (meaning *State*) was in use for the German States under Holy Roman Empire. *See infra* text accompanying note 157.

139 *Id.* at 45. "[T]he empire of Germany, which consists of many states." *Id.* at 45–46.

140 *Id.* at 29 (emphasis added).

141 *Id.* at 30–33 (emphasis added).

142 *See* Oxford Advanced Learner's Dictionary, *supra* note 4, at 521 (providing the definition of "Great Britain").

143 "[T]he commerce of the whole British empire, taken collectively, and that of each kingdom and colony in it, as it makes a part of that whole: Indeed, everything that concerns the property interest and fit government of the whole common-wealth, of keeping the peace, and subordination of all the parts towards the whole must be considered in this light." Hopkins, *supra* note 138, at 5–36.

constituent territorial units of the Holy Roman Empire.[144] Also consistent with such a conclusion, Dowdall explains that "*dominium* is the regular word for feudal lordship, whether subordinate or not"[145] and "*status* and *stato* were applied to the position of a prince or bishop, but not to that of the (Holy Roman) Emperor or the Pope."[146] In supporting his view, Dowdall points out that when Professor Villari declared that [Duke Gian Galeazzo's] Milan transformed into a modern State, "Gian Galeazzo (the ruler of Milan) got his ducal title from the Emperor and, in that rather shadowy way, held the duchy as a fief."[147] Thus, despite Milan being a "modern state," it was still a unit within the Holy Roman Empire, rather than an independent entity.

The second characteristic of the state referred to by Hopkins is that until the middle of the 18th century, it applied to a territorial political institution headed by a sovereign person. In the case of Great Britain, as a part of the British Empire, it was headed by the English king; in the case of German principalities in the Holy Roman Empire, they were headed by German princes.

The third characteristic of the state is that it was autonomous. Machiavelli defined the word *stato* when the principalities (the *dominio*) in northern Italy were autonomous in reality, yet nominally still part of the Holy Roman Empire. In 1648, when the German princes acquired equal status between themselves and the power to enter alliances (treaties) with other princes and rulers in the Peace of Westphalia, the principalities became autonomous, and the word *stato* then also applied to these German principalities. Equal status between the states and the power to engage in relations with other states are two attributes of the states and also the foundation based on which international law developed. Thus, until the middle of the 18th century when Hopkins compared the British Colonies in North America with "German states" in the Holy Roman (German) Empire after the Peace of Westphalia, the English word "state" still referred to a territorial political institution that was a constituent unit of an empire. He said, "[I]n an emperial[sic] state, which consists of many separate governments, each of which hath peculiar privileges, and of which kind it is evident the empire of Great Britain is; no single part,

[144] Although from 1499 to 1513 northern Italy was temporarily seized by a French king.
[145] Dowdall, *supra* note 14, at 111.
[146] *Id.* at 108.
[147] *Id.*

though greater than another part, is by that superiority intitled[sic] to make laws for, or to tax such lesser part; but all laws, and all taxations, which bind the whole, must be made by the whole: This may be fully verified by the empire of Germany, which consists of many states, some powerful and other weak, yet the powerful never make laws to govern or to tax the little and weak ones, neither is it done by the emperor, but only by the diet, consisting of the representatives of the whole body."[148]

The American Colonies were similar, but not parallel, to German states during the period from the conclusion of the Peace of Westphalia (1648) to the dissolution of the German Empire (1806). The two were similar in that both were constituent units of an empire (for the former, the British Empire, and for the latter, the German empire). But the two differed in that, while American Colonies were under the sovereignty of the English king, the German states were already sovereign "states" within the Holy Roman Empire.[149]

Hopkins' article indicates that by the middle of the 18th century, the English word "state" already referred to a territorial political institution (the mother state; the German states), rather than a ruler (the sovereign prince or the territorial magnate), albeit the state was still a constituent unit of a commonwealth or an empire.

By referring to the German political structure and the relations among German States, Hopkins implied that Rhode Island, a small Colony which he represented, should have the equal status as other larger Colonies, such as New York and Pennsylvania. Eventually, the German system served as a model for the political structure of the American States after the American Revolution: First, each American State was independent; second, the American States, large or small, were equal in rights and power among themselves; third, the American States stayed together and formed a confederation; fourth, each State acquired, as the German States had, sovereign power, a point which will be explored later.

In summary, during the 17th century the English word "state" still referred to a ruler, not a political institution. By the middle of the 18th century, the word had already acquired the meaning of a territorial political institution that was a constituent unit of a commonwealth or an

[148] HOPKINS, *supra* note 138, at 45–46. *See also supra* text accompanying note 23 in Chapter 1 on the structure of Holy Roman Empire after Peace of Westphalia.

[149] KURT RABLE, CHRISTOPH STOLL, MANFRED VASOLD, FROM THE U.S. CONSTITUTION TO THE BASIC LAW OF THE FEDERAL REPUBLIC of GERMANY. Verlag Moos & Partner, 1988, at 17.

empire. It is also notable that such a commonwealth or empire was headed by a ruler—a monarch or an emperor.

In the 17th century, the Latin word *status*, meaning territorial ruler, was rendered *state* in English and *état* in French. Thus, when subsequently the words "state" and "*état*" acquired the meaning of territorial political institution, the words "state" and "*état*" were given a new meaning.

C. The Word "State" for an Independent Territorial Political Institution

a. The American Revolution

As just mentioned, until the American Revolution, the English word "state" applied to a political institution that was a constituent unit of an empire. The American Colonies, while calling themselves "Colonies" or "provinces,"[150] called Great Britain, which was a part of British Empire, the "parent state."[151]

By the time of the American Revolution, the word "state" acquired an additional meaning: an independent territorial political institution. Richard Lee used the English word "State" for an independent territorial political institution. Before a committee to prepare the Declaration of Independence was appointed, Richard Lee of Virginia introduced three resolutions, one of which stated that the "colonies are, and of right ought to be, free and independent States."[152]

In drafting the Declaration of Independence, Thomas Jefferson incorporated Lee's statement in the document. The Declaration of Independence of 1776 uses the word "States" for the English Colonies in North America when it states "*We, the representatives of the united States of America ... solemnly publish and declare, That these United Colonies are, and of Right ought to be Free and Independent States*; that they are Absolved from all Allegiance to the British Crown, and that all political connection

[150] As in "The Province of Pennsylvania and Territories." *Pennsylvania Charter of Privileges, Oct. 28, 1701.* DOCUMENTS OF AMERICAN HISTORY, 3rd Ed., ed. by Henry Steele Commanger, F.S. Croft & Co. (New York), 1943, at 40.

[151] American Colonies referred to Great Britain as "parent state." "These were our sentiments toward Great Britain while she continued to act the part of a *parent state*" (emphasis added). *The Movement For Independence – Instructions from the town of Malch, Massachusetts, for a Declaration of Independence, May 27, 1776.* AMERICAN HISTORY, *id.* at 96.

[152] On June 7, 1776. *See* Editor's note to *The Declaration of Independence*, AMERICAN HISTORY, *id.* at 100. The letter "S" in the word "state" was capitalized.

between them and the State of Great Britain, is and ought to be totally dissolved."[153] While the word "State" in "the State of Great Britain" refers to a constituent unit of the British Empire, the word "States" in "Free and independent States" refer to the *independent* territorial political institutions established upon the declaration. Unless further research proves otherwise, Richard Lee was the first prominent politician who used the word "State" for independent territorial political institution, and the Declaration of Independence is the first formal document that used the word for the new meaning.

Upon the collective declaration of independence by the 13 American Colonies, each Colony became an independent territorial political institution. Each one claimed to be a "State."[154] Each State had the same and equal status as "the State of Great Britain." So, the 13 States had competence to collectively sign a treaty of alliance with France in 1778.[155]

The States in North America formed, first, a confederation and, then, a federation. In 1777, the 13 States in North America formed a Confederation of the United States.[156] In 1789, these States united to form a federation and established a single State, the United States of America (thc "U.S."). Though each State retained its name "State," it became a constituent unit of the federation, much like part of a commonwealth or an empire.

The "German States" referred to by Hopkins in his 1764 article also subsequently became separate independent territorial political institutions ruled by territorial magnates. In June 1806, secondary German states (Principalities) along the Rheine formed the Confederation of the Rheine, but remained constituent units of the German Empire.[157] Later, in August of the same year, a few days before the dissolution of the Empire, the Confederated states proclaimed their secession from the Holy

[153] *The Declaration of Independence*, AMERICAN HISTORY, *id.* at 100, 102 (emphasis added).

[154] "That this state (Massachusetts) being at Present destitute of a Properly established form of government, it is absolutely necessary that one should be immediately formed and established." *The Concord Town Meeting Demands A constitutional Convention.* AMERICAN HISTORY, *id.* at 105.

[155] *The Treaty of Alliance With France. Feb. 6, 1778.* AMERICAN HISTORY, *id.* at 69. The treaty was signed by representatives of each of the thirteen States.

[156] The Article of Confederation was agreed by Congress on November 15, 1777, and was ratified and in force on March 1, 1781. *Id.* at 111.

[157] THE NEW ENCYCLOPEDIA BRITANNICA, *supra* note 7, V 20, at 101 (the entry of "Germany").

Roman Empire, and became independent States. At the dissolution of the Empire,[158] the other German states which did not join the Confederation also became independent States.

As a result, Germany was divided into more than 200 independent States, which were later consolidated into about three dozen States by Napoleon Bonaparte. These independent political institutions, no longer under an empire, continued to call themselves "State (*Staat*)." When the German Confederation (*Deutscher Bund*) was formed in 1815, the term "German States" (*deutschen Staaten*) was used[159] for the member institutions, which varied in size and power and included the Great Powers (Austria and Prussia), kingdoms, electorates, grand duchies, dukedoms, principalities, earldoms, and self-governing cities.[160] The Confederation of Germany lasted until 1866. In 1870, the Prussian King William I unified them into a single federal State (*Bundesstaaten*).[161] In the unified federal German State, although each individual state retained its name "State (*Staat*)," it became a constituent unit of the federation.

b. The Republican State: The Neo-Modern State

The American Revolution ushered in a new kind of "modern State"—the republican State. When the leaders of the American Revolution chose a republic, instead of a monarchy, as a new form of State for their Colonies, the ideas of liberalism and democracy conceived in Europe by Locke and Montesquieu during the Age of Enlightenment were for the first time realized, not in its birthplace, but in North America. After the American Revolution, most newly established States are republican States. Some monarchies also turned into republics. For instance, in the State of France, the Revolution of 1789 eventually resulted in the abolishment of monarchy, and the establishment of a republic; the State of Germany also transformed into a republic in 1918.

In a republican State, the nature of the State changed. In a monarchy, the king and the commonwealth which he rules are two related but separate entities. While the commonwealth is an intangible abstract entity, the

[158] Holy Roman Empire was formally dissolved on August 6, 1806 when Francis II resigned from the title of Holy Roman Emperor.

[159] Act of the German Confederation, Art. 2.

[160] For Confederation of Germany, *see* THE NEW ENCYCLOPEDIA BRITANNICA, *supra* note 7, V. 20, at 104 (the entry of "Germany").

[161] The German Empire (*Deutsches Reich*, 1871–1918). *See* http://www.deutsche-kaiser-reich.de/. Last visited 02/10/2011.

ruler is a tangible natural person. When American Colonies established new States, the States were republican States. In a republican State, the State takes the place of both the king and the commonwealth, and becomes a purely abstract entity[162]; the form of the State is now analogous to a juristic person, such as a corporation or an association, in municipal law.[163]

c. The Terms "Nation," "Nation-state," and "Country"

The word "State" meaning territorial political institution has a technical meaning. The meanings of other synonymous words, such as "nation" or "country," are less precise. The term "nation" has many meanings. After the French Revolution of 1789, France eventually adopted a republican form of State. The French began to call their republican State "the *nation*."[164] Thus, in France while the political institution under the king before the French Revolution was called *république*, the republican State is called "nation." To the French at least, the word "nation" implies that the form of the State is a republic.[165]

The word "nation" also has other meanings. It may refer to an ethnic group of people or a large group of people sharing a common history, culture, and language.[166] In this sense, a nation is a group of people, not an independent political institution. For instance, American Indians in

[162] THE FRENCH LEGAL SYSTEM, *supra* note 96, at 155. "The state becomes a 'legal person.'" MICHAEL STOLLEIS, A HISTORY OF PUBLIC LAW IN GERMANY 1914–1945, trans. by Thomas Dunlap, Oxford University Press (New York), 2004, at 48.

[163] BARRY E. CARTER & PHILLIP R. TRIMBAL, INTERNATIONAL LAW, Little Brown & Co., 2d Ed., 1995, 456. "The idea of 'nation' plays an important role in the French political system. It is rooted in the French Revolution, and paradoxically is particularly strong because of its *abstraction*." THE FRENCH LEGAL SYSTEM, *supra* note 96, at 155 (emphasis added). In a monarchy, though the "commonwealth" is an abstract concept, its ruler is not.

[164] THE FRENCH LEGAL SYSTEM, *supra* note 96, at 155.

[165] "The idea of 'nation' ... rooted in the French Revolution. The national sovereignty implies state sovereignty and vice versa." THE FRENCH LEGAL SYSTEM, *Id.* at 155. "[S]ince the American Independence and the French Revolution [the word *state*] has acquired a democratic character." Dowdall, *supra* note 14, at 125. Subsequently, the word *état* came into use. *See supra* note 136.

[166] OXFORD ADVANCED LEARNER'S DICTIONARY, *supra* note 4, at 773 (providing the definition of "nation-state."). "The term 'nation', strictly speaking, as evidenced by its etymology indicates relation of birth or origin and implies a common race, usually characterized by community of languages and customs." HACKWORTH, DIGEST OF INTERNATIONAL LAW, U.S. Government Printing Office, (Washington D.C.), 1940, Vol. 1 Chap. 2, at 47.

the United States have called their tribes "nations" since the 18th century.[167] These "nations" are not States meaning independent political institutions. The U.S. Supreme Court in *Cherokee Nation* v. *The State of Georgia* held that American Indians were not "independent nations," but "domestic dependent nations," which were subject to the U.S. federal government's regulations.[168]

Similarly, in 2006, Stephen Harper, the prime minister of Canada, proposed that the seven million "Quebecoi form a *nation* within a United Canada," and Parliament recognize it as such.[169]

In the 19th century, the word "nation" began to be used for another meaning: the "nation-state." The term "nation-state" initially refers to a State established by a large ethnic group of people, or a "politically organized nation."[170] Thus, a nation-state simply means a State formed by a people or a nation. For example, Germany was formed by the Teutonic people; France was formed by the Franks. But now the term "nation-state" is used by some writers to emphasize that a political institution is a State.

From the turn of the 20th century, the term "State" and the term "nation" have been used interchangeably. Both the League of Nations and the United Nations are formed by States. Both organizations use the word "Nations" in their names, even though not all members are republics and not all member States are nation-states.

Another word used synonymously with State is "country." Unfortunately, the word "country" is ambiguous. It may mean territory or a government.[171] It may refer to a political institution with or without sovereignty.[172] While Great Britain is a State, England, a part of Great

[167] *See Cherokee Nation* v. *The State of Georgia*, *supra* note 3.

[168] *Id.* at 17.

[169] Christopher Mason, *Canadian Prime Minister Is Ready to Loosen Federal Ties to Quebec.* N.Y. Times, 11/23/2006, Sec. A, C. 1, p. 11 (emphasis added).

[170] A term used in Dowdall, *supra* note 14, at 125.

[171] The U.S. Supreme Court in *Burnet v. Chicago Portrait Co.*, 285 U.S. 1 (1932) in interpreting the term "foreign country" stated, "It may be taken to mean foreign territory or a foreign government." *Id.* at 5.

[172] The U.S. Court of Appeals in *Rogers v. Cheng Fu Sheng* said that "the word 'country' is not limited to national sovereignties in the traditional diplomatic sense." 280F.2d 663 (U.S. App. D.C. 1960) at 665. *See infra* note 510 for citation of the lower court.

Britain, is also called a "country."[173] This work uses the word "State," instead of "nation" or "country" for independent territorial political institution because the words "nation" and "country" both lack precise meaning.

3. SOVEREIGNTY AND THE NEO-MODERN STATE

A. Sovereignty in the Republican State

a. The Sovereignty in the Modern State

As discussed here before, in Bodin's definition and theory of sovereignty, sovereignty is the power of a ruler; it resides in the ruler of the modern State. In the theories of social contract, sovereignty is also in the king. In Hobbes' theory, sovereignty resides in the ruler. Hobbes, who was the first in England to advocate the theory of social contract, stated that in a monarchy "one man (the king) has it (sovereignty)."[174] Locke, who advanced a different version of the theory of social contract, never denied that sovereignty could be in the king, even though in his theory, the people in a commonwealth retain the public power under the social contract. While Locke advocated that the supreme public power of the people was the legislative power,[175] he did not call such a power of the people "sovereignty" or "sovereign power." Locke did not advocate abolishment of the English monarchy because he supported the Glorious Revolution of 1688 that replaced an English king with another. In fact, he said that the majority of the people might choose to put the legislative power—the power to make law—in a monarch.[176]

For two centuries after Bodin formulated his theory, sovereignty was claimed in the name of a king or a sovereign prince—who was a natural person—because until the American Revolution, with a few exceptions,[177]

[173] "England, prominent *country* of the United Kingdom and Northern Ireland." (emphasis added). The New Encyclopedia Britannica, *supra* note 7, V.4, at 496 (the entry of "England").

[174] Hobbes, *supra* note 85, at 245.

[175] "This legislative is not only the supreme power of the commonwealth, but sacred and unalterable in the hands where the community have once place it." The Second Treatise of Government, *supra* note 88, at 75.

[176] Locke said, "The majority ... may (put) all that power in making laws for the community into the hands of one man: and then it is monarchy." *Id.* at 73.

[177] Such as Republic of Venice and ancient Athens of Greece. The City of Augsburg was a republic ruled by two Presidents. *See* Peace of Westphalia, *supra* note 22. Art. V, 4 IPO; '47 IPM. These republics were all short-lived.

all States[178] were headed by a monarch or a prince. Thus, the nature of sovereignty is that it is the power of an absolute monarch or a sovereign prince. He is the bearer of sovereignty.

That sovereignty resides in the absolute ruler of a political institution is also true when the English word "state" refers to a political institution that was a constituent unit of an empire or a commonwealth, such as "the German states" or "Great Britain." As discussed earlier, when the German principalities became German States after the Peace of Westphalia, sovereignty was in the princes. Likewise, the sovereignty of Great Britain, as part of the British Empire, was in the English monarch.

b. Claim of Sovereignty by the Republican States

The power asserted by the 13 American States was the power which, until the American Revolution, only a sovereign ruler (a king or a sovereign prince) had. When the American Colonies declared the establishment of States by the Declaration of Independence, the form of State adopted by the American States was a republic. These republican States also claimed to have all the political power of a king. In their Declaration of Independence these States stated that "as Free and Independent States, [the American States] have the full Power to levy War, conclude Peace, contract Alliances, establish Commerce, and to do all other Acts and Things which Independent States may of right do."[179] While the first phrase "(Free and) Independent States" in the quoted passage above refers to the American States, the second phrase "Independent States" referred to other States, such as Great Britain and France. At the time these other "independent States" were all monarchies ruled by kings. The "full power" claimed in the name of the American States is the sovereign power of an absolute ruler (a king or a sovereign prince), though the American States did not call the power *sovereignty* in the Declaration of Independence.

In the following year (1777), when the 13 American States formed a confederation, they formally claimed to have *sovereignty.* Article II of the Articles of Confederation provides that "Each state *retains its sovereignty,* freedom and independence, and every Power, Jurisdiction and right, which is not by this confederation expressly delegated to the United

[178] The word "states" is used here for various kinds of political institutions.
[179] *The Declaration of Independence.* AMERICAN HISTORY, *supra* note 150, at 100, 102.

States, in Congress assembled."[180] The phrase "retains its sovereignty" in the provision indicates that the States already had sovereignty at the time of signing the Articles of Confederation. The only occasion at which the American States claimed a power similar to the sovereign power of the king and the sovereign prince was a year earlier when they established the States by the Declaration of Independence.

Not only did the original 13 American States claim to have sovereignty at the time of their establishment, but also allowed the Western Territories which subsequently joined the Confederation as States to have sovereignty. The Report of Government For the Western Territory, which was approved by the Congress assembled in 1784, provided that "Such (new) State shall be admitted by its delegates into the Congress of the United States on equal footing with the original States."[181] The phrase "on equal footing with the original States" indicates that the new States would acquire sovereignty upon joining the Confederation and became equal with the original 13 States. The Northwest Ordinance drafted in 1787 confirmed the equal treatment of the new States.[182]

In 1778, France not only recognized but also guaranteed each American State's sovereignty in the Treaty of Alliance between her and the united States collectively. Article XI of the Treaty provides that "His Most Christen Majesty (referring to Louis XVI) guarantees on his part to the United States their liberty, *sovereignty* and independence, absolute and unlimited."[183] When the American Revolutionary War with Great Britain ended with a peace treaty in 1783,[184] Great Britain also acknowledged each State's sovereignty in the treaty. Article I of the Treaty of Paris between Great Britain and the United States provides that "His Britannic Majesty (referring to King George III) acknowledges the said United States, viz. New Hampshire, Massachusetts Bay, Rhode Island, and

[180] *The Article of Confederation. Id.* at 111 (emphasis added).

[181] *Report of Government For the Western Territory, April 23, 1784. Id.* at 121, 122.

[182] On July 13, 1787. Art. 5 of The Northwest Ordinance provides, "There shall be formed in the said territory, not less than three no more than five States .... And whenever any of the said States shall have sixty thousand free inhabitants therein, such State shall be admitted, by its delegates, into the Congress of the United States, on an equal footing with the original States in all respects whatever." *Northwest Ordinance of 1787. Id.* at 128, 131.

[183] *The Treaty of Alliance between the United States and France* (1778). *Id.* at 105, 106 (emphasis added).

[184] *The Treaty of Peace between Great Britain and the United States (The Treaty of Paris,* 1783*). Id.* at 17.

Providence Plantations, Connecticut, New York, New Jersey, Pennsylvania, Delaware, Maryland, Virginia, North Carolina, South Carolina, and Georgia, to be free, *sovereign* and independent States."[185]

c. The Nature of Sovereignty Claimed by the Republican States

The American States claimed a different kind of sovereignty. The sovereignty claimed in the name of these republican States was not the same as the sovereignty of the king or the sovereign prince. When the French king recognized and the British king acknowledged the sovereignty claimed by the American States, they did not question the nature of sovereignty or define the sovereignty which they had recognized or acknowledged, except that the French king recognized it as absolute and unlimited.

The sovereignty claimed by these republican States and the sovereignty described by Bodin are different in their nature. These republican States had no rulers. They could not have the same kind of sovereignty as defined by Bodin because in his theory the sovereignty resides in an absolute ruler, who is a natural person. Thus, the sovereignty claimed by the republican States is a new kind of sovereignty.

The American States claimed a new kind of sovereignty without defining the word. At the time when Bodin wrote his work setting forth his theory of sovereignty, Bodin needed a word other than *majestas* or *imperium* to describe precisely the power of the rulers whom he observed at the time. He adopted the word *souveraineté* (*sovereignty*) for the power of the absolute ruler and gave it a precise definition from which he expounded his theory. Although Thomas Jefferson, in drafting the Declaration of Independence, spelled out the kinds of power which only an absolute ruler (a king or a sovereign prince) had at the time, he did not use the word "sovereignty" in the document for the power of the American States. Was it because Jefferson knew that the kinds of power which he listed in the Declaration of Independence were the kinds of power only an absolute ruler could have? No one can tell.

B. Characteristics of Sovereignty in the Republican State

Although the new sovereignty claimed by the republican States is not the sovereignty of the absolute ruler of the modern States, the two kinds of sovereignty have many common characteristics. Several characteristics of

[185] *Id.* at 117 (emphasis added).

the new sovereignty may be deduced from analyzing the nature of the sovereignty claimed by the united States of America, and was recognized by the French king and the British king.

The first characteristic is that the new sovereignty is the power of the State. The American States, as newly established States, had power to do all acts and things which an absolute ruler had right to do. When the united Colonies declared the establishment of republican States, they claimed that "the States *have* full Power to do all Acts and Things which Independent States may of right do."[186] Thus, the new States had the power similar to that of the French king and the British king.

The sovereign power which the American States claimed included the power to make law, which was an attribute of the sovereign power of a king or a sovereign prince. The Constitution of the United States of America adopted by the American States in 1789 at the formation of a federal State demonstrates that it also has power to make law when it provides that "The Constitution of the United States, together with the laws and treaties made pursuant to it, is the supreme law of the land."[187] For instance, the State now known as the united States of America imposes a rule on the form of each constituent State and its government. The U.S. Constitution provides that "The U.S. shall guarantee to every state in this union a republican form of government."[188] The power to impose such rule is an attribute of sovereignty in Bodin's theory.

The States which claimed sovereignty were republican States. Although the attribute of the new sovereignty is similar to that of sovereignty in the modern State, the nature of new sovereignty is different. While sovereignty in the modern State is the power of the absolute ruler, the new sovereignty is the power of a republican State.

In the republican State, sovereignty resides in the State. The new sovereignty is claimed in the name of the American States. These republican States, being pure abstract political entities, had no kings. If the core concept of sovereignty was to survive as a new kind of sovereignty, as it survived, the new sovereignty had to reside in some entity. The new entity was the State.

Thus, a republican State is a new kind of the modern State. The State is a kind of the modern State because the State has sovereignty and is

[186] *The Declaration of Independence. Id.* at 100, 102 (emphasis added).
[187] Art. V of the U.S. Constitution. *Id.*
[188] Sec. 4 of Art. IV of the U.S. Constitution. *Id.*

predicated on territory; it is a new kind of the modern State because its sovereignty resides in the State instead of the ruler. That sovereignty resides in the State is the core characteristic of the new kind of the modern State. For lack of a more suitable term, the State where sovereignty resides in the State is called "the neo-modern State" hereinafter in this work for reference. That sovereignty resides in the State is the core characteristic of the neo-modern State.

The second characteristic of the new sovereignty is that the sovereignty is the supreme and absolute power to govern the people and territory within the State. A characteristic of the new sovereignty claimed by the American States is the power itself. The United States had the same power which an absolute ruler had. The Declaration of Independence states that "(American States) have full Power to levy War, conclude Peace, contract Alliances, establish Commerce, and to do all other Acts and Things which Independent States may of right do."[189] The power which these American States asserted and that was recognized by the French king is a power no less than the sovereign power of an absolute ruler described in Bodin's theory.

But the power of the neo-modern State must be defined in light of the nature of the new sovereignty—that sovereignty is claimed in the name of the State: the new sovereign power is the State power. There are two aspects of the State power: the internal power and the external power. The second characteristic of the new sovereignty refers to the internal power of the State. American Colonies in their Declaration of Independence claimed to have the power "to do all other Acts and Things which Independent States may of right do."[190] Such power is the internal power of the State to govern the people and its territory.

The neo-modern State's internal power to govern the people and its territory is supreme in the sense that no other power within the State is higher. The most important internal power is the power to make law. The power of the neo-modern State to make law is supreme in the sense that within the State, no one else has higher authority to make law.

The internal power of the neo-modern States is absolute in the sense that the power is not subject to any condition or limitation. The French king in the Treaty of Alliance recognized the sovereignty of American

[189] *The Declaration of Independence. Id.* at 100, 102 (emphasis added).
[190] *Id.* at 100, 102 (emphasis added).

States to be "absolute and unlimited." Such power is equal to that of the absolute ruler.

In the 19th century, the concept of absolutism of the sovereign power to govern the people was challenged. But the absolute sovereign power of the neo-modern State can be explained as follows. The concept of bearing the sovereignty is different from the concept of exercising the sovereign power. The distinction between the two is not apparent in the modern State because in the modern State the absolute ruler not only bears the sovereignty but also exercises the sovereign power. However, in the republican State while the sovereignty resides in the State, the power to exercise the sovereign power is in the government chosen by the people. Due to the influence of the modern democratic thoughts, the people restrict the power of the government to exercise the sovereignty—the governing power—over them, often by a constitution. Thus, while the government's power to exercise the sovereign power is not absolute, the internal State power of the neo-modern State is absolute in the sense that the law enacted by the State according to the prescribed procedure is absolute.[191] No person is above it.

The third characteristic of the new sovereignty is that sovereignty means independence. This characteristic refers to the external power of the neo-modern State. In the modern State, a sovereign is independent of other States or autonomous within an empire. The republican State is independent, as opposed to being a part of an empire or kingdom. In its Declaration of Independence, the American Colonies declared that "these United Colonies are . . . independent States."

The external power of the neo-modern State is the power to engage with the other States, including power to wage war and competence to conclude treaties with other States. As an independent State, each State has "full power to levy war." Thus, it builds its own army to protect itself, and if necessary engages other States in war.

Each independent State has unrestricted capacity "to conclude Peace, contract Alliances, establish Commerce"[192] with other States. The external power of the neo-modern State is supreme because the power of an independent State is not subject to the sovereign power of another State. Its capacity to engage in relations with other States is not subject to the limitation or restriction imposed by others. When the American Colonies

[191] Art. V of *the U.S. Constitution. Id.*

[192] *The Declaration of Independence. Id.* at 100, 102 (emphasis added).

in 1776 "solemnly publish[ed] and declare[d], That as Free and Independent States, they [had] full power to levy war, conclude Peace, contract Alliances, establish commerce,"[193] they claimed a power that was an attribute of an absolute ruler. The British king acknowledged that the States of the united States were "independent States" in the 1783 Treaty of Paris.

The fourth characteristic of the new sovereignty is that the new sovereignty is a concept inseparable from the neo-modern State. Just as the ruler of the modern State acquires sovereignty when he assumes the position, a republican State acquires sovereignty at the establishment of the State and becomes the neo-modern State.[194] Thus, while the ruler of the modern State and his sovereignty are inseparable, a republican State and its sovereignty are also inseparable. That means, only the neo-modern State has this new kind of sovereignty. After the American declaration of independence in 1776, each State of the Confederation of the United States was a *sovereign State.*[195] When the United States of America was formed in 1789, the newly unified federal State acquired sovereignty and each individual member State gave up sovereignty, although they retained some residual sovereign power, such as the power to enact state laws. As sovereignty is the *supreme* power of the State, there cannot be sovereign States within a sovereign State.

The fifth characteristic of the new sovereignty is that the sovereign power is indivisible. As mentioned before, sovereignty of the modern State belongs undivided to the ruler in Bodin's theory. When Hobbes stated that in a monarchy "one man (the king) has it (sovereignty),"[196] the statement indicated that the king did not share his sovereign power with others.

In the neo-modern State, sovereignty is also indivisible. Both sovereignty and the State are abstract concepts, and the new sovereignty is inseparable from the neo-modern State as mentioned above. The State cannot and does not share sovereignty with any other entity or person. French writers agree. Referring to the sovereignty claimed by the French Republic, five French writers (West, Desdevices, Fenet, Gaurrier, and

[193] *Id.* (emphasis added).

[194] *See supra* text accompanying note 179. "The nation is necessarily regarded as being sovereign." The French Legal System, *supra* note 96, at 155.

[195] Martin Weinstein, Summary of American Law, The Lawyers Co-operative Publishing Company (Rochester, New York), 1988, at 105.

[196] *See supra* text accompanying note 174.

Heussaff) say that "National sovereignty is unitary and cannot be divided."[197]

However, in the neo-modern State the power to exercise sovereignty (the sovereign power) can be and is divided. As mentioned earlier, the power to exercise sovereignty (the sovereign power) is different from sovereignty itself. While the sovereignty is indivisible, the function of exercising the sovereign power and the power to perform the function of the government may be divided. Thus, the U.S. Constitution and the French Constitution, largely due to the influence of Locke and Montesquieu, who advocated separation of power, divide the sovereign power into three kinds: the executive, the legislative, and the judiciary, and distribute the function of exercising the sovereign power among three branches of the government.

The sixth characteristic of the new sovereignty is that the sovereign power is perpetual. In the modern State, sovereignty of a ruler ceases when the ruler dies. Each of the succeeding kings of the same State acquires his own sovereignty. The neo-modern State is an abstract entity. It, unlike a natural person, is immortal in the sense that its life does not terminate in its normal course. The sovereignty of the State, once coming into existence, continues to reside in the State without interruption unless the State becomes extinct. In this sense, the sovereignty of the neo-modern State is perpetual. Therefore, the sovereignty of the neo-modern State continues notwithstanding constant changes of its governments or administrations.

The seventh characteristic of the new sovereignty is that the sovereign power extends to the entire territory of the State. Like the modern State, the neo-modern State is predicated on territory. Thus, its power extends to the outer limit of its territory. Aliens within the territory, as well as its people, are subject to the law of the State. In the neo-modern State, like the modern State, sovereignty over its territory and the people is based on title to the territory.

Based on the analyses above, the new sovereignty may be defined as "the supreme and absolute power of the State to govern its people and territory and to enter relations with other States." The power is supreme because the State is not subject to the power of another State; it is absolute because within the State the power is not subject to any condition or limitation.

[197] THE FRENCH LEGAL SYSTEM, *supra* note 96, at 157.

C. The Neo-Modern State and Its Territory

a. Nature of Territory in the Neo-Modern State

In the feudal State, territory was proprietary in nature. The feudal king ruled his own domain; a feudal vassal, as a territorial magnate, ruled his dominion. Each one "exercised rights of government in his territory."[198] The territory under the rule of a king or a feudal vassal was considered his private property.

In the modern State, the sovereign ruler also treated the territory under his rule as his private property. When the feudal State turned into the modern State, the king, who had stripped the power of his feudal vassals and ruled the territory directly, had no reason to change the nature of the territory. For instance, France acquired Lorraine by a marriage of its King in 1766.[199]

In the neo-modern State, sovereignty is now in the State. Thus, the State owns the territory: Territory is the public property of the State. Since the State is an abstract entity, and does not marry or die, the territory of the State can no longer be modified through marriage or inheritance.

b. Territory as an Element of the Neo-Modern State

The modern State is a territorial State: the State is predicated on the territory. Thus, territory becomes an essential element of the State. The neo-modern State, like the modern State, is also predicated on the territory, and thus, territory is still an essential element of the State. The neo-modern States are associated with a defined territory.

D. The Neo-Modern State and Its Government

a. Nature of Government in the Neo-Modern State

In the feudal State, government is proprietary in nature. The feudal kings and their vassals all set up their governments in their domains or dominions, respectively, to manage their estates. The government established by the ruler was regarded as his property.[200]

[198] Dowdall, *supra* note 14, at 106.

[199] The New Encyclopedia Britannica, *supra* note 7, V 7, at 483 (the entry of "Lorraine").

[200] Dowdall describes that, in 15th century, a magnate "was necessarily a territorial magnate, who exercised rights of government in his territory." Dowdall, *supra* note 14, at 106.

In the modern State, the government is also proprietary in nature. When a ruler centralized the political power within the territory in him and created the modern State, he became an absolute ruler and directly governed the people, including collecting taxes from them, within the territory.

The absolute ruler, as the bearer of sovereignty, also exercises the sovereign power. To manage the affairs of the State, the ruler sets up a government, of which he is the head. For efficient operation, the ruler appoints an officer as a deputy, usually called the prime minister (premier) or chancellor, who serves at his pleasure, and delegates the governing power to the officer.

The nature of the government of the modern State is that it is the management of the State. Dowdall said that "[g]overnment being at (Machiavelli's) time regarded as property, rather than a trust, it follows that government, from the point of view of a (sovereign) prince, closely resembled estate management."[201] In the terminology of the modern political science, the absolute ruler of the modern State is the head of the State and also the head of the government.[202]

A State may have successive rulers. Once a king established a kingdom—a State—each succeeding king set up his own government to manage the State. Although the government changed when a new king was installed, the State remained the same. For instance, the State of France was established by Charles I in A.D. 843.[203] During more than 11 centuries in existence France changed its government numerous times, going through Dynasties, Houses, Empires, and republic governments.[204] Great Britain also changed its governments many times, going through many Houses since its establishment in 1066 by William the Conqueror, but the State, as a political institution, had not changed.[205] This point is

[201] *Id.* at 109.

[202] Even in the 20th century, British prime ministers referred to the British government as "His Majesty's Government." *See infra* text accompanying notes 772, 773; 3, 1049, 1050.

[203] A.D. 843 was the year the Treaty of Verdun, which divided the Charlemagne's Empire, was concluded. Some French historians argued that the state of France was established much earlier, in 481 by Clovis I.

[204] French Dynasties were, in chronological order, Carolingian, Capacian, Carolingian, Capacian, and Valois. The two Houses were Bourbon and Orleans.

[205] English Houses were Normandy, Blois, Anjou, Tudor, Stuart, Orange, Hanover, and Windsor. The Royal Line of Succession, Patrick W. Montague-Smith, Late Editor, Debrett's Peerage, Pitkin Guides LTD., Andover, 1986.

reflected in a rule in international law: the debt incurred by a government owing foreigners is a State (sovereign) debt, and its succeeding governments are obliged to repay it.

In the neo-modern State, the nature of the government is different. Almost all new States established after the American Revolution are republics. They are the neo-modern States—sovereignty resides in the State—referred to in this work. In the neo-modern State, the nature of government changed. The government is not formed by the ruler to manage the affairs of the State because there is no ruler.

The government of the neo-modern State is in the nature of a trust. The neo-modern State is a purely abstract entity. It, unlike a ruler, has no will and ability to manage the affairs of the State. Thus, the people set up a government formed by natural persons and entrusted the management of the affairs of the State to the government.

The government of the neo-modern State exercises the sovereign power. While in the modern State, the concept of bearing sovereignty and the concept of exercising the sovereign power need not be clearly distinguished because the absolute ruler, who is the bearer of sovereignty, also exercises the sovereign power,[206] the neo-modern State is different. In the neo-modern State, while the sovereignty is in the State, the power to exercise sovereignty (the sovereign power) is in the government. The government represents the people, who elect its officials, either directly or indirectly. Thus, the power to exercise the sovereignty is subject to the ultimate public power of the people.[207]

Almost all republican States have a constitution (or a basic law). The people enact a Constitution for their State for two major purposes. One is setting up a political structure for the complex organization of the State and its government. The other is delineating the fundamental rights of the individual which the government cannot deprive or encroach upon. To achieve these two purposes, the constitution (the basic law) provides how the State (sovereign) power is exercised.

The power of the State, by its nature, may be divided into three kinds: the executive, the legislative, and the judicial. Many constitutions, following the U.S. model, distribute the three kinds of State power to three

[206] In a constitutional monarchy, the people also put the power to exercise the sovereign power in the government.

[207] France enacted in 1791 Declaration of the Rights of Man and Citizen to restrict the power of the government over the individuals. For the Declaration, *see infra* note 218.

different branches of the government—the executive power to the Executive; the legislative power to the Congress or Parliament; and the judicial power to the court—either for checks and balances (e.g., the United States), or for distribution of power (e.g., France).

Thus, in the neo-modern State, the power of government is different from that of the modern State. In the modern State, the word "government" refers to the executive chief who has and exercises the executive and the law-making powers.[208] In the neo-modern State, the government is formed by the people to manage the State and, adopting the idea of Locke,[209] includes the legislature. Thus, in the neo-modern State, though sovereignty held by the State is indivisible, the power to exercise the sovereign power is shared by two or three branches of the government usually pursuant to the constitution (the basic law). In the neo-modern State, the government also changes from time to time, yet the State remains the same.

b. Head of the Government in the Neo-Modern State

In the modern State, the absolute ruler, as the head of the State, is also the head of the government. In the neo-modern State, the head of the State and the head of the government may not be the same person.

In a republican State, the head of the State is the President. The head of the government may be the President of the republic or the Prime Minister (or Chancellor), depending on the power system of the government adopted by the Constitution (the Basic law). If the government is a presidential system, such as the United States, the executive power is in the President. Thus, the president is the head of the State and also the head of the government. If the government is a parliamentary system, such as the Federal Republic of Germany, the executive power is in the Prime Minster or Chancellor, who is elected by the Parliament or Diet. Thus, though the head of the State is the President, the head of the government is the Prime Minster or the Chancellor.

France has a unique system. It has a dual heads system. While the President, the head of the State, who is elected by popular votes, and the

[208] "[T]he main point of sovereign *majesty* and absolute power consists of giving the law to subjects in general without their consent." BODIN, *supra* note 38, at 23. *See* text accompanying note 52.

[209] "[H]e who takes away the freedom or hinders the acting of the legislative in its due seasons in effect takes the legislative and puts an end to the government." LOCKE, *supra* note 88, at 121.

Premier, the head of the government, who is appointed by the President, share the executive power, the President has the exclusive power to conduct the foreign affairs.[210]

c. Government as an Element of the Neo-Modern State

The modern States share some common features. They have four common features: (1) the people; (2) a territory in which the people inhabit; (3) a ruler—a king or a sovereign prince—who bears sovereignty; and (4) the capability to engage in relations with other States. The ruler is an essential feature of the modern State because a kingdom or a principality without a ruler (the king or the sovereign prince) is unthinkable. Modern writers list "government" as a requirement of the modern State. The practice may be justified since the ruler always sets up a government to manage the affairs of the State or the principality.

The last feature—the capability to engage in relations with other States—is implied in the theory of sovereignty. In the case of the modern State that is a constituent unit of an empire or of a commonwealth, capability means an unrestricted capability. As discussed earlier, until the conclusion of the 1648 Peace of Westphalia, German principalities under the Holy Roman Empire were legally restricted from forming an alliance between themselves and with foreign States.[211] By gaining a legally unrestricted power to engage in relations with other States in the Peace Treaties, they became States.

In the neo-modern State, its government is a feature of the State. In contrast with the modern State, the government of the neo-modern State is more than the management of the State. It now exercises the sovereign

[210] In France, there is an ambiguity as to who, between the President and the Premier, has power to conduct the foreign affairs. The French Constitution does not specify whether the President or the Premier has such power. General De Gaulle, at the time of establishing the Fifth Republic, said that the foreign policy was a "reserved domain" of the President. During the 1986 cohabitation between the socialist President and the RPR conservative Premier, President Francois Mitterrand introduced the concept of "shared domain" in conducting the foreign policy. In 2000, during the cohabitation between the RPR conservative President Jacques Chirac and the Socialist Premier Lionel Jospin, Jospin speaking in *Bir Zeit* on or about February 28, 2000, referred to the Islamic group Hezbollah army in Lebanon as "terrorists." President Chirac immediately reminded him that the President "conducts" the foreign policy. (Part of the information is from France 2 News television broadcast, Feb. 29, 2000).

[211] *See infra* text accompanying note 293 for the elements of the State.

power. As a consequence, the government replaces the ruler as a feature of the neo-modern States.

Consequently, the neo-modern States share four common features. They are (1) people; (2) territory in which the people inhabit; (3) a government formed by or for the people; and (4) an unrestricted capability to engage in relations with other states. These features eventually turned into elements of the State in the State theory and international law.

To be an element for the formation of a State, the government must be formed by its own people, and formed under the constitution when the people have enacted a constitution. The U.S. Restatement (Third) of the Foreign Relations Law (the "Restatement"), in prescribing elements of the States, provides that, "a State is an entity that has a defined territory and a permanent population, under the control of *its own government*."[212] Thus, a government formed by a foreign State to control the territory or a government formed under the constitution of another State is not a government of the territory effective for establishing a State.

In discussing the internal sovereign power of the neo-modern State, the term "government" is used in a broad sense to include all of its branches. However, in discussing the external power of the State, the term "government" is usually used in its narrow sense, referring to the Executive branch.[213] From this point on, unless otherwise indicated, the word "government" refers to the Executive branch in this work.

4. SOVEREIGNTY AND THE CONSTITUTIONAL MONARCHY

Thus far, in discussing sovereignty two kinds of independent States have been examined. The first kind is the absolute monarchy. The second kind is the republican State seceded from a monarchy. There are two other kinds of independent States: One is a constitutional monarchy transformed from absolute monarchy; the other is a republican State

[212] The Restatement of the Foreign Relations Law of the United States, (3d Ed. 1987).' 202, Comments a, b.' 201(emphasis added).

[213] The word "government" is defined as "the group of people who are responsible for controlling a country or a state: to form a government." Oxford Advanced Learner's Dictionary, 6th Ed., Oxford Univ. Press, 2000, at 557 (providing the definition of "government"). Apparently, the word is defined in the narrow sense, referring to the executive branch only. The word "government" may be used in a broad sense. E.g., The same Dictionary defines "the executive" as "the part of a government responsible for putting laws into effect" *Id.* at 435.

transformed from a constitutional monarchy. This section discusses the sovereignty in a constitutional monarchy transformed from an absolute monarchy.

A. Constitutional Monarchy

From the 11th century to the middle of the 18th century, the modern State was an absolute monarchy. Some monarchs promulgated a constitution which set forth the organization of the government but did not limit their power. The power of the absolute monarch and the sovereign prince was the sovereign power described by Bodin, even though his power was subject to some limitations described before. For instance, Bodin considered that the 1215 Magna Carter signed by the English king was the king's contract with the Estates,[214] and thus did not deprive the English king of his sovereignty because the king retained the exclusive power to make law.

The democratic thoughts of Locke and Montesquieu produced two new forms of State: one is the republic; the other is the constitutional monarchy. Constitutional monarchies appeared during the 18th century, and replaced most absolute monarchies in the 20th century.

An English dictionary defines "constitutional monarchy" as "A country with a king or queen, whose power is controlled by a set of laws and basic principles."[215] The definition describes the British political system because Great Britain has no single piece of document called "the constitution."[216] For monarchies which have a single piece of document called "the constitution," "constitutional monarchy" means a country with a king (queen) or a prince, whose power is controlled by the constitution. The constitution is a central set of laws, which govern the organization of government, and set limits on the power of the government. The monarch (the king or the prince) in a constitutional monarchy is not an absolute ruler for two reasons. Firstly, the power of the monarch is always limited by "a set of laws and basic principles" or the constitution. Secondly, the constitution of a constitutional monarchy places the law-making power in the legislature, whether or not the legislature has the exclusive legislative power.

[214] For English Estates, *see* The New Shorter Oxford English Dictionary, *supra* note 65.

[215] Oxford Advanced Learner's Dictionary, *see* note 4, at 243 (providing the definition of "constitutional monarchy").

[216] Legal scholars say that Great Britain has an "unwritten constitution."

Many absolute monarchies turned into republics later. Historically, while all new States established by secession from an existing State adopted a republican form, the transformation of a State from an absolute monarchy to a republic was often not direct. During the 19th century many absolute monarchies became constitutional monarchies first, then further transformed into republics.

B. Sovereignty in a Constitutional Monarchy

When an absolute monarchy turned into a constitutional monarchy, the monarch was still the head of the State, but lost sovereignty because the constitution deprived him of the exclusive law-making power. In France, after the 1789 Revolution, the French people turned their State from an absolute monarchy into a constitutional monarchy. The French First Constitution enacted by the National Assembly in September of 1791 established a constitutional monarchy. It expressly took away the sovereignty from the king when it required that "[o]n his accession to the throne, or as soon as he has attained his majority, the King, in the presence of the legislative body, shall take oath to the nation to be faithful to the nation and to the law, to employ all the power delegated to him to maintain the Constitution decreed by the National Constituent Assembly in the years 1789, 1790, and 1791, and to have the laws executed."[217] As stated before, a king who had to "take oath to the nation to be faithful to the nation and to the law" had no sovereignty under Bodin's definition.

But the constitutional monarchy still claimed a power similar to sovereignty. Before the French National Assembly adopted the First Constitution, it in August of 1789 adopted the Declaration of the Rights of Man and Citizen (hereinafter the "Declaration of the Rights"), in which Article 3 provides that "[t]he principle of all sovereignty resides essentially in the nation. No body nor individual may exercise any authority which does not proceed directly from the nation."[218] The drafters of the Declaration of the Rights, like the drafters of the American Declaration of Independence, probably were aware that a power not in the monarch was not *sovereignty*, and used the words "the principle of all

[217] French Constitution (1791), Title III, Ch. II, Sec. 1, Art. 4. *See supra* note 56.

[218] *See* the 1789 Declaration of the Rights of Man and Citizen. Yale Law School, The Avalon Project, *available at* http://avalon.law.yale.edu/18th_century/rightsof.asp. Last visited 01/22/2010.

sovereignty" to describe the power instead.[219] The French National Assembly proclaimed in the Declaration of the Rights that "the principle of all sovereignty resides essentially in the nation" without much explanation.[220] Even if the Declaration had no immediate legal effect at the time, it laid down a principle for the foundation of the future French State.

Germany also turned from a monarchy into a constitutional monarchy before it transformed into a republic. As mentioned earlier, Holy Roman Emperors (of the 16th century) had *majestas*, but no sovereignty as defined by Bodin because they had to obey the Pope.[221] On the other hand, the principalities within the Empire became sovereign States after 1648.

When the German Empire (the Second Reich) of 1871 was established, it was a constitutional monarchy. The 1871 Constitution of the German Empire did not claim "sovereignty" or a power of similar import. It placed the legislative power of the Empire in the Federal Council and the Imperial Diet.[222] Thus, the German Emperor William I did not have sovereignty under Bodin's definition because he had no exclusive law-making power under the 1871 Constitution.

C. The Sovereignty Claimed by a Constitutional Monarchy

Nevertheless, sovereignty was claimed by some constitutional monarchies. When the French people turned the absolute monarchy into a constitutional monarchy in 1791, the constitutional monarchy claimed sovereignty. Title III Art. 1 of the 1791 First French Constitution provides that "Sovereignty is one, indivisible, inalienable, and imprescriptible."[223]

The constitutional monarchy claimed sovereignty in the name of the State. The concept of sovereignty in the State created by the American Revolution probably influenced the French revolutionaries. The French Constitution claimed sovereignty in the name of the State (nation), even though there was a king.[224] Title III, Art. 1 provides that "Sovereignty

[219] *Id.*

[220] The Declaration of the Rights of Man and Citizen. *Supra* note 218. Art. 3, *Id.*

[221] *See supra* text accompanying note 54.

[222] Art. 5 of the Constitution of the German Empire (1871) provides, "The legislative power of the Empire shall be exercised by the Federal Council (*Bundesrat*) and the Imperial Diet (*Reichstag*). A majority of the votes of both bodies shall be necessary and sufficient for the passage of a law." CONSTITUTION OF THE GERMAN EMPIRE (1871). *See supra* note 60.

[223] French Constitution (1791), *Id.* Title III, Art. 1, *supra* note 56.

[224] *Id.* Title III, Art. 2.

appertains to the nation."[225] Art. 2 provides, "The nation, from which alone all power emanates, may exercise such power only by delegates."[226] Under the Constitution, all public power belonged to the nation.[227] Thus, the Constitution explicitly placed the sovereignty in the State.

Some constitutional monarchies by a proclamation, either announced or implied, claimed sovereignty in the name of the State. An example is Liechtenstein. In February 2008, when the German government in a tax evasion case pressed the principality of Liechtenstein to provide information of secret accounts held by wealthy Germans in a bank owned by Liechtenstein's crown prince Alois, he retorted that "We are also a *sovereign state* and, we hope, do not live in an era when might makes right rather than international law and international agreement."[228]

Liechtenstein is a constitutional monarchy. Prince Alois was the head of the State. When he proclaimed that "We are also a *sovereign state*," he was a "sovereign." But the statement "the sovereign State" had a subtle implication: the Prince claimed sovereignty in the name of the State.

In constitutional monarchies, sovereignty is not in the parliament. Although the constitution of a constitutional monarchy places the legislative power in parliament, the parliament does not claim sovereignty because it exercises only part of the sovereign power. In addition, parliament's power to make law is subject to the restriction of the constitution. Perhaps, British Parliament is the only parliament that claims parliamentary sovereignty due to the nature of the British constitution. In the British constitutional system, Parliament has the supreme power to make law. There is no single document called "the constitution" in Great Britain. A law enacted by the British Parliament supersedes any conflicting prior law. The British Parliament claims parliamentary sovereignty because "[t]here are no restrictions on the law that Parliament cannot pass."[229] In December 2008, after Scotland Yard police raided an office of

[225] *Id.* Art. 1.
[226] *Id.* Art. 2.
[227] *Id.* Art. 2.
[228] *See* Eric Pfanner and Mark Landler, *Tax Inquiry? Principality Is Offended,* N.Y. Times, 02/20/2008, C1, Column 6 (emphasis added). In December 2008, Liechtenstein entered into an agreement with the U.S. in which Liechtenstein agrees to provide the U.S. limited information of its bank customers involving tax fraud cases, but not tax evasion cases. Lynnley Browing, "*Liechtenstein To Share Some Secrets Of Its Bank*" N.Y. Times, 12/5/2008, B7, C6.
[229] Oxford Advanced Learner's Dictionary, *supra* note 4, D2, at 1110–1111.

a Conservative M.P. in the Parliament, many members "described [the police raid] as the most threatening assault on Britain's parliamentary sovereignty in memory."[230] Even though in Locke's theory the legislative power was the supreme power in England, he never asserted that British Parliament had sovereignty. Although British Parliament has supreme power to make law, it exercises only part of the sovereign power. The executive power is in the Prime Minster. Thus, the word "sovereignty" in "parliamentary sovereignty" simply means the supreme power to make law.

D. The Monarch of a Constitutional Monarchy

In constitutional monarchies, the monarch is the head of the State, but does not have sovereignty as defined by Bodin because the monarch has no exclusive power to make law. Some monarchs, such as the Emperor of the German Empire of 1871, or princes, however, retained some executive power (the power to make political decisions), including power to conduct foreign affairs, under their constitutions.

But some monarchs, such as the English King (and Queen) and Japan's Emperor, have no executive power. The executive power is in the head of the government, usually the Prime Minster or the Premier. These monarchs are ceremonial figures, though they also serve to stabilize the country during a period of political turmoil.

5. SOVEREIGNTY AND THE REPUBLICAN STATE TRANSFORMED FROM CONSTITUTIONAL MONARCHY

This section discusses sovereignty in the republican State transformed from constitutional monarchy. After the American Revolution, some constitutional monarchies transformed into republics. For instance, from 1791 on, France changed among three forms of State—constitutional monarchy, republic, and absolute monarchy, not necessarily in that order,—until 1870 when it settled at the Third Republic.[231] So far, the

[230] "It was the Commons' first opportunity to respond, in formal session, to what many members have described as the most threatening assault on Britain's parliamentary sovereignty in memory." John F. Burns, *Britain's Parliament Opens With Uproar Over Police Raid*, N.Y. Times, 12/4/2008, A12, C3.

[231] France was proclaimed republic by National Convention in 1792. The Third Republic of France was established in 1870.

French people have established five republics including the present Fifth Republic.

When a constitutional monarchy transformed into a republic, the State also claimed sovereignty. The First French Republic claimed sovereignty when there was no longer a king. Its 1793 Constitution provided that "Sovereign power rests in the entirety of French citizens. It is inalienable and eternal. No individual, no fraction of the people has the rights to exercise."[232]

The present Fifth Republic of France continues to claim sovereignty. Article 3 of the 1958 Constitution provides that "National sovereignty shall vest in the people, who shall exercise it through their representatives and by means of referendum. No section of the people nor any individual may arrogate to itself, or himself, the exercise thereof."[233]

However, the language of the 1958 French Constitution raises a question—where does sovereignty reside? The provision in Article 3 of the Constitution seems to indicate that sovereignty is in the people when it provides that "National sovereignty shall vest in the people."[234] But it, like the Constitution of the First French Republic,[235] incorporates the Declaration of the Rights. The constitution's Preamble provides that "The French people solemnly proclaim their attachment to the Rights of Man and *the principles of national sovereignty as defined by the Declaration of 1789*, confirmed and complemented by the Preamble to the Constitution of 1946."[236] As it was pointed out before, the French Declaration of the

[232] The Constitution of the First French Republic (drafted in 1793), Ch. 1, Sec. 1. At http://sourcebook.fsc.edu/history/constitutionof1791.html. Last visited 01/01/2010. The Constitution of the First French Republic also incorporated the Declaration of Rights of Man and Citizen in its preamble. It used the term "popular sovereignty" to indicate that sovereignty was to be exercised by "all French citizens." Art. 7.

[233] The Constitution of the Fifth French Republic (1958) Art. 3.

[234] *Id.*

[235] *See supra* note 232.

[236] *Id.* (emphasis added). The Preamble of the 1946 Constitution also incorporated the Declaration of Rights of 1789. It provides that "In the morrow of the victory achieved by the free peoples over the regimes that had sought to enslave and degrade humanity, the people of France proclaim anew that each human being, without distinction of race, religion or creed, possesses sacred and inalienable rights. They solemnly reaffirm the rights and freedoms of man and the citizen enshrined in the Declaration of Rights of 1789 and the fundamental principles acknowledged in the laws of the Republic." Constitution of the Republic of France, 1946, adopted 27th of October, 1946. http://www.elysee.fr/elysee/anglais/the_institutions/founding_texts/preambule_to_the_27th_of_october_1946_constitution/preambule_to_the_27th_of_october_1946_constitution.20243.html. Last visited 01/01/2010.

Rights places the "national sovereignty" in the "nation": Sovereignty resides in the "nation."[237] Thus, the Preamble and Art. 3 of the Constitution seem not to be consistent with each other on where the sovereignty resides.

The Constitution should be read in its entirety and construed in favor of its consistency. A preamble in a document is where the fundamental principles of the document are laid down. It is presumed that the drafters of the Constitution were familiar with the principle laid in the 1789 Declaration of the Rights that the sovereignty resides in the "nation" when they incorporated it into the Preamble of the 1958 Constitution. It is also presumed that the drafters were careful not to make conflicting statements in the same document, especially a document which lays down the foundation of the Nation. Thus, the two provisions can be explained as consistent with each other as follows.

As it was discussed in Section 3 of Chapter 2, sovereignty and the power to exercise sovereignty (the sovereign power) may be placed in different bodies. Thus, a consistent construction of the 1958 French Constitution on sovereignty is: in the French Republic, while the sovereignty resides in the nation as the Preamble prescribes, the *power to exercise* the sovereignty "vests" in the people who "shall exercise [the sovereignty] through their representatives and by means of referendum."[238]

The construction of the Constitution that sovereignty of the French Republics lies in the State can also be found in the term "national sovereignty" itself. Semantically, the word "national" in "national sovereignty" of Art. 3 is a possessive adjective, signifying that sovereignty is "national," meaning belonging to the "nation." Such construction also finds a support from French writers. Referring to France after it became a republic, the five French writers (West, Desdevices, Fenet, Gaurrier, and Heussaff) in their coauthored work stated that "[S]overeignty resided not in the people as a collection of individuals but in the nation as a whole."[239] This means that the Nation or State is sovereign and that the State has the power to rule, though the people have the power to exercise the sovereign power through their representatives.

In contrast, Germany's State structure clearly indicates that sovereignty resides in the State. After World War I, Germany transformed into a

[237] *See supra* text accompanying note 218.
[238] *Id*. Art. 3.
[239] The French Legal System, *supra* note 96, at 156, footnote 14.

republic in 1919. It became a federation of the States, similar to the United States of America. The Constitution of the German Federation (The Weimar Constitution)[240] adopted a republican form of State.[241]

The Weimar Constitution claimed a power called *Staatsgewalt*. Article 1 provided that "The State-authority (*Die Staatsgewalt*) derives from the people."[242] The power is properly called "the governing power" because it referred to the power of the government organizations to exercise the "State affairs." Art. 5 provided that "The State-authority (*Die Staatsgewalt*) is exercised in Reich (the State) affairs by the government organizations of the Reich, based on the Reich constitution."[243] The power of the Reich (the State) included the power to make law, which applied to the entire territory of the Federation.[244]

Under the Weimar Constitution, Germany's governing power was in the State. In the republican State, the governing power could not be in a ruler because there was no ruler. The governing power was claimed in the name of the State. The German Constitution called the governing power "the state-authority (*Die Staatsgewalt*),"[245] signifying that the governing power is of the State. A German Dictionary defines *Staatsgewalt* as

[240] Weimar Constitution (in English). http://www.zum.de/psm/weimar/weimar_vve.php *Die Verfassung des Deutchen Reichs* (in German). http://www.documentarchiv.de/wr/wrv.html.

[241] *Id.* Art. 1. provides, "The German Reich is a republic."

[242] Art. 1 of Weimar Constitution: (2) "*Die Staatsgewalt geht vom Volke aus.*" DIE VERFASSUNG DES DEUTSCHEN REICHS, ["*Weimarer Reichsverfassung*"] *vom 11. August 1919*.http://www.documentarchiv.de/wr/wrv.html. Last visited 02/04/2010.

Weimar Constitution (in English), *available at* http://www.zum.de/psm/weimar/weimar_vve.php

INTRODUCTION, CONSTITUTIONAL CRISIS, THE GERMAN AND THE AMERICAN EXPERIENCE, WEIMAR, A JURISPRUDENCE OF CRISIS, ed. by ARTHUR JACKSON and BERNHARD SCHLINK, translated by Belinda Cooper, University of California Press, (Berkeley), 2000, at 9. In The Constitution of the German Federation, GERMAN CONSTITUTIONAL DOCUMENTS SINCE 1871, SELECTED TEXTS AND COMMENTARY, ed. by Louis W. Holborn, Gwendolen M. Carter, John H. Herz. Praeger Publishers (New York), 1780, at 19, the word "sovereignty" is used instead of "the state-power." *Id.* Art. 1. The word "sovereignty" is not a German word. The German word corresponding to sovereignty is *Staatsgewalt* (the state-authority). *See* NEW WILDHAGEN GERMAN DICTIONARY, Follett Publishing Company, Chicago, 1965, at 1013 (defining "*Staatsgewalt*" as "supreme authority.")

[243] WEIMAR CONSTITUTION (in English), *id.* The Reich Constitution of August 11th 1919 (WEIMAR CONSTITUTION) with Modifications, *at* http://www.zum.de/psm/weimar/weimar_vve.php. Last visited 02/04/2010.

[244] *Id.* Art. 6 through Art. 11.

[245] *Id.* Art. 1(2).

"supreme authority."[246] Since the German word *Staat* means State, *Staatsgewalt* refers to the supreme authority of the State.

The Weimar Constitution did not claim that the governing power was in the people, or "sovereignty in the people." The phrase "derives from the people" in Art. 1 meant that the state power *came from* the people; not that the power was in the people. Michael Strolleis, commenting on the principles of the Weimar Constitution of 1919, wrote: "[T]he solution to the competition between princely sovereignty and popular sovereignty had been 'state sovereignty,'"[247] meaning that the state, not the people or any ruler, was sovereign. German-English dictionaries define the English word "sovereignty" as "the highest *state* authority."[248] Strolleis's "state sovereignty" simply emphasizes that the highest authority is the authority of the State. Thus, the Constitution of 1919 claimed a state power, which was neither the prince's sovereignty nor popular sovereignty (sovereignty in the people).

The 1949 Basic Law (*Grundgesetz*) of the Federal Republic of Germany established after World War II also claims a power called *Staatsgewalt*.[249] Art. 20(2) of the Basic Law provides that "All state-authority (*Staatsgewalt*) emanates (derives) from the people. It shall be exercised by the people by means of election and voting and by specific legislative, executive, and judicial organs."[250] The power called *Staatsgewalt* is the governing power. The provision claiming the governing power in the 1949 Basic Law (*Alle Staatsgewalt geht vom Volke aus*) and the provision claiming the governing power in the 1919 Weimar Constitution (*Die Staatsgewalt geht vom Volke aus*) are, in essence, the same. Consequently, in the 1949 Basic Law, the governing power is also claimed in the name of the State though it is emanated from the people.

[246] New Wildhagen German Dictionary, *supra* note 242, at 1013 (providing the definition of *Staatsgewalt*.)

[247] Michael Stolleis, *supra* note 162, at 48.

[248] *Die hoechste Staatsgewalt*. New Wildhagen German Dictionary, *supra note* 242, at 808 (providing the definition of "sovereignty"). Cassel's New German Dictionary (1959), at 475 (providing definition of "sovereignty") (emphasis added).

[249] Basic Law for the Federal Republic of Germany (*Grundgesetz für die Bundesrepublik Deutschland*), 1949, *available at* http://www.documentarchiv.de/brd/1949/grundgesetz.html. Last visited 04/01/2011.

[250] *Artikel 20, (2) Alle Staatsgewalt geht vom Volke aus. Sie wird vom Volke in Wahlen und Abstimmungen und durch besondere Organe der Gesetzgebung, der vollziehenden Gewalt und der Rechtsprechung ausgeübt. Id.* Thus, the word "emanate" in the translation has the same meaning with "derive" in Art. 1 of Weimar Constitution. *See supra* note 242.

The sovereignty claimed by the French Republics and the State-authority (*Staatsgewalt*) claimed by the German Republics is also a new kind of State power. Such state powers are not the same with the sovereignty as defined by Bodin. Although the French and the German Constitutions did not spell out the power of the State in detail as the American States did in their Declaration of Independence, both powers are claimed in the name of the republican State, analogous to the nature of sovereignty claimed by the American States. Consequently, both France and Germany under the present constitutions are properly called the neo-modern States in this work. The sovereignty or the state-authority claimed by the neo-modern States may be called the new sovereignty.

As it was pointed out before, in an absolute monarchy (the modern State), the monarch and the commonwealth which he ruled are two related but separate entities. While the commonwealth is an abstract entity, the monarch, who bears sovereignty, is a tangible natural person. When an absolute monarchy transforms into a republic, a purely abstract entity,[251] the State replaces both the monarch and the commonwealth. The State assumes the position of the monarch and his power—the power to govern the people and its territory. Thus, when the neo-modern State claims sovereignty, the entity in which the sovereignty resides is the State.

As observed thus far, there are two types of neo-modern States. One, exemplified by the States of North America, is a newly established State which adopts the republican form. The other, exemplified by France, is a republican State transformed from a monarchy.

The neo-modern States have one common feature: the new sovereignty of the neo-modern States resides in the State itself. The characteristics of the new sovereignty derived from the American States discussed before also apply to the sovereignty claimed by these neo-modern States established after the American Revolution.

6. SOVEREIGNTY CLAIMED IN OTHER NAMES IN THE 20TH CENTURY

Thus far, this work has examined the sovereignty claimed in the name of two kinds of independent State: republican State and constitutional monarchy. During the 20th century, sovereignty was also claimed in the name

[251] *See supra* text accompanying note 162.

of an entity other than an independent State. In particular, it was claimed in the name of (A) a State that was a constituent unit of a commonwealth and (B) the people as a whole. A brief discussion of such claims follows.

A. State That Is a Constituent Unit of a Commonwealth

As it is pointed out before, after the Peace of Westphalia, the principalities of the Holy Roman Empire, like northern Italian principalities, became States. Historically, when the word "State" acquired the meaning of a territorial political institution, the political institution was a constituent unit of an empire. After the word "state" acquired the meaning of an independent political institution in the second half of the 18th century, it has continued to apply to a territorial political institution that is a constituent unit of an empire or a commonwealth. Canada, Australia, and New Zealand are such States.[252]

Canada, Australia, and New Zealand acquired the status of States when the First World War ended. Formerly they were British colonies under the administration of the Governors-General appointed by the British monarch. In the 19th century, ministerial governments responsible to the elected assembly replaced the Governors-General, who became ceremonial figures.[253] The three British colonies participated in the First World War and when the War ended, they were permitted by their mother State—Great Britain—to sign the Treaty of Versailles (1919) in their own names. By such permission, the three colonies acquired an unrestricted capability to conclude treaties with other States—a feature of the State. With the unrestricted capability to conclude treaties, the colonies acquired statehood when they asserted the State power by signing the Treaty, at the time when they were still constituent units of the British Empire. The Statute of Westminster of 1931, which recognized the self-governing units as dominions with status equal to that of Great

[252] So was India before her independence.

[253] In the case of Canada, the change took place between 1848 and 1855. *See* ACADEMIC AMERICAN ENCYCLOPEDIA, *supra* note 12. V. at 4 (the entry of "History of Canada") at 83. In the case of Australia 1850 (*Id.* V. 2, at 340) and New Zealand, 1856 (*Id.* V. 14. at 162). The Governors-General still play a ceremonial role. At the opening ceremony of the 2010 Winter Olympic Games in Whistler, Canada, the Governor-General representing Queen Elizabeth II "opened" the Games.

Britain,[254] merely confirmed the political status which they had attained in 1919.

Canada, Australia, and New Zealand are sovereign States, even though they are still constituent units of the British Commonwealth. Historically, sovereignty is also claimed in the name of a constituent unit of an Empire. Bodin called the princes of the principalities of the Holy Roman Empire "the sovereign princes." However, even though the head of these States is Queen Elizabeth II of Great Britain, their sovereignty is not in Queen Elizabeth II, the Governors-General appointed by the English Queen, or the Prime Minister elected by Parliament. Since these States claim sovereignty, the sovereignty, like that of a republican State, can only reside in the State. Thus, though these States are not independent States, they have the same State power of a republican State. Since their sovereignty resides in the State, similar to the neo-modern States described in this work, they may be classified as "neo-modern States."

B. The People as a Whole

a. The Doctrine of Popular Sovereignty

During the 20th century, sovereignty was also claimed in the name of the people. After the Second World War, "popular sovereignty" became a political slogan. The doctrine of "popular sovereignty," also called "sovereignty in the people," had been used to advance the power of the people or to advocate democracy. The doctrine holds that sovereignty lies or resides in the people as a whole; the people as a group are the bearers of sovereignty.

The notion of "popular sovereignty" has been widely accepted.[255] Although the people as a whole hold the ultimate public power, the notion of popular sovereignty conflicts with the nature of sovereignty examined thus far. A brief review of the doctrine follows.

[254] ACADEMIC AMERICAN ENCYCLOPEDIA, *id.* V. 2 History of Australia, at 341; V. 4. History of Canada, at 86; V.14 (the entry of "History of New Zealand"), at 162.

[255] For an example, Judge Ammoun of the International Court of Justice stated, "Sovereignty, which is inherent in every people did not cease to belong to the people subject to mandate." Separate Opinion in the Advisory Opinion of 21 June 1971 regarding Legal Consequences for States of the Continued Presence of South Africa in Namibia (South West Africa) notwithstanding Security Council Resolution 276 (1970), I.C.J. Rep. 1971, at 68.

b. The Origin of the Doctrine

The doctrine of popular sovereignty has a long history. In Medieval Germany, before Bodin defined the French word "sovereignty" in his work, the power of the German Emperor, who was elected by electors, was not absolute as shown by the Golden Bull of 1356.[256] The Emperor had *majestas*, but not sovereignty as later defined by Bodin. Some German jurists expounded the theory that the German Emperor's power came from the people either by "transference" or "concession."[257] In the doctrine of "popular sovereignty" as it was called later, the word used for describing the power of the people was *majestas.*[258] The theory that *majestas* came from the people later faded out. After the Protestant Reformation some German writers "sought to wrest the power of the State itself from the hands of the monarch and revived the doctrine of the sovereignty of the people."[259] After Bodin published his work, the German scholar Althusius published his work The Politics in 1603. In his work he consolidated the theories of previous writers and advocated that sovereignty (*majestas*) was *in* the people.[260] However, his theory was widely criticized at the time.

c. The Proponents and Critics

In discussing the German theory of "popular sovereignty," this writer relies on the English translation of von Gierke's work The Development of Political Theory (originally written in German). Since the English translation of the work uses the term "sovereignty" without qualification on the meaning of the German term, the following discussion will likewise treat the German term to mean *sovereignty* defined by Bodin.[261]

According to von Gierke, the doctrine of popular sovereignty never built roots in the European Continent. Von Gierke in his work observed

256 *See supra* note 54.

257 For the development of the doctrine of popular sovereignty in Germany, *see* VON GIERKE, *supra* note 37, at 143–240.

258 *Id.* at 155.

259 A quotation from VON GIERKE *supra* note 37, at 154.

260 *Id.* German writer Johannes Althusius wrote about "popular sovereignty" in POLITICS (1603) when Germany was part of Holy Roman Empire. "He laid the groundwork of his theory in a broader in a more rigorous fashion than any one before him; he above all expounded the absolute inalienability of the sovereign rights of the people." *Id.* at 16.

261 To treat it otherwise will lead to a lengthy discussion outside of the scope of this work.

that during the 17th and the 18th centuries, the doctrine of sovereignty in the people was not employed in the European Continent but in England. He said that "from Althusius to Rousseau there arose on the Continent no system of politics in which the doctrine of popular sovereignty was fully and completely worked out; during this period its proper home was in England."[262] In supporting his view that the proper home for the doctrine of popular sovereignty was in England, von Gierke stated that "Locke derived his scheme of the three powers from the original sovereignty of the people."[263]

Von Gierke's reasoning for his point was not well founded. In supporting his conclusion that Locke "derived his scheme of the three powers from the original sovereignty of the people," von Gierke cited in the footnotes two sections in Locke's work The Second Treatises of Government.[264] He paraphrased one section stating "[F]rom the nature of society there arise the legislative, executive and 'federative' power,"[265] and another section stating "[T]he forms of government are established according as the majority either retains the legislative power, or transfers it to one man or a few men, or else institutes mixed forms as it may see fit."[266]

Neither of the two sections in Locke's work cited by von Gierke supports a conclusion that Locke considered sovereignty in the people. Although Locke spoke of the public power of the people or of the supreme power of the legislative,[267] he did not use the word "sovereignty" to describe people's public power, or the legislative power.

In Bodin's theory, sovereignty in the modern State does not reside in the people. In describing the power of the king or the sovereign prince in the modern State, Bodin does not say that sovereignty is in the people or that sovereignty of the ruler comes from the people. The notion of "sovereignty in the people" is not consistent with Bodin's theory of sovereignty in five aspects. First, according to Bodin, the ruler acquires

262 VON GIERKE, *supra* note 37, at 163.

263 *Id.* at 164.

264 *Id*, at 209, footnote 121.

265 *Id.* Citing "Locke, II. c. 12."

266 *Id.* Citing "Locke, II. c. 10. '132."

267 "[T]he legislative ... [is] the supreme power in every commonwealth." LOCKE, *supra* note 88, at 76.

sovereignty by merely being in the position of a king or a prince.[268] This position or power did not come from the people. Second, under Bodin's definition and theory of sovereignty, the sovereign power is "for the life of him who has the power."[269] Thus, a sovereign, being a natural person, dies at some point in his life. In the notion of "sovereignty in the people," the word "people" necessarily means the people as a body. Such a body does not die, even though its individual constituents do. Third, as the sovereign power includes giving law to the subjects, there can be only one who has such sovereign power in the State. Bodin said that "Law depends on (a prince) who has the sovereignty and he can oblige all his subjects (by a law) but cannot oblige himself."[270] Such theory is inconsistent with the notion of sovereignty in the people. Fourth, according to Bodin, the king or the prince who had sovereignty was not subject to the Estates.[271] He said that "if a sovereign prince is subject to the Estates, he is neither prince nor sovereign, and the state is neither a kingdom nor a monarchy, but a pure aristocracy of many lords with equal power, where the greater part commands the smaller part collectively, and each individual particularly . . . all of which is absurd and inconsistent (in a monarchy)."[272] If the sovereign is not subject to the Estates, he is much less subject to the people. If the king or the prince is not subject to the people, it means that the people have no sovereignty (meaning that they do not hold the absolute power to rule). Fifth, the doctrine of sovereignty in the people has no satisfactory explanation on the power to govern. Sovereignty as defined by Bodin is the absolute power to rule the people. In other words, the people are the objects of the sovereign power.[273] However, sovereignty in the people means that the people collectively are the bearers (the subject or possessor) of the sovereignty. Even though people have the ultimate public power, they cannot be the bearers of the sovereign power that governs them. The notion of "sovereignty in the people" means that the people are the rulers and the ruled at the same time. No one can be the subject of a power and also the object of the same power.

[268] *See supra* text accompanying note 49.
[269] *See supra* text accompanying note 76.
[270] Bodin, *supra* note 38, at 15.
[271] *Id.*
[272] *Id.* at 19.
[273] "[P]eople is object of [sovereign's] care." Dowdall, *supra* note 14, at 114.

Thus, in the theory of Bodin, sovereignty of the modern State is in the ruler, not in the people. Any power with different connotations is not sovereignty defined by Bodin.[274]

In the republican States, sovereignty is not in the people either. This is so when a republican State is established by secession from an existing State. When American Colonies declared establishment of States—republican (the neo-modern) States, they claimed that the new American States *had* the power which the kings had. The American States in Declaration of Independence declared that "as Free and Independent States, they have the full Power which Independent States may of right do."[275] Thus, the American States in the Declaration said that the States, not the people, had the sovereign powers of English and French kings.

That sovereignty is not in the people is also true in a republican State which was transformed from a monarchy. These republican States also claimed sovereignty in the name of the State. As it was observed earlier, the French Republic claimed sovereignty in the name of the "Nation." In Germany, when the Federal Republic of Germany was established, it claimed a state-power, which, as Strolleis pointed out, was not popular sovereignty. In fact, in Germany, where the doctrine of popular sovereignty was once a popular political thought among the German theorists, the doctrine was never adopted by the German States in practice.

If sovereignty is not in the people as just explained, "sovereignty in the people" is just a political slogan and must be given a different meaning: The concept of holding the sovereignty and the concept of exercising the sovereign power must be distinguished. In the neo-modern State, while the sovereignty is in the State, the power to exercise the sovereign power is in the government formed by the people. Thus, "sovereignty in the people" properly means that the ultimate public power is in the people.

[274] Bodin calls a ruler who has no sovereign power described in his theory "the chief person of the state." *See* BODIN, *supra* note 38, 71. *See supra* text accompanying note 55. Bodin said that "the (German) emperor is subject to the Estates of the Empire, and does not claim sovereignty over the princes or the Estates." BODIN, *supra* note 38, at 16.

[275] *The Declaration of Independence*. AMERICAN HISTORY, *supra* note 150, at 100, 102.

7. SOVEREIGNTY AS A DEFENSE OF THE STATE ACT

During the 20th century, the concept of sovereignty was denounced. Sovereignty was attacked as "obsolete,"[276] "a dead duck,"[277] "extinct,"[278] or "not helpful."[279] However, it was not abandoned. From 1943 to December of 2008, 126 new States jointed the U.N.,[280] more than double the number of States that existed in history before World War II. All these new States are republics. As neo-modern States, they are properly called "sovereign States." The sovereignty is properly called "State sovereignty" or "national sovereignty."

The term "the sovereign State" has also been used to justify or as a defense of a State act. It was often used to emphasize or defend the independence or autonomy of a State. In the incident of Liechtenstein discussed earlier, when the German government sought to pressure Liechtenstein to, breaking its own law, disclose the names of German depositors in Prince Alois's bank, the prince used the term "the sovereign State" to defend his refusal.[281]

During the 2008 Summer Olympic Games hosted by China, the Chinese government blocked some Websites, including that of Amnesty International. Jacques Rogge, the president of the International Olympic Committee (IOC), was under pressure to criticize the Chinese government. Rogge replied that "the IOC was not in the business of criticizing *sovereign states*."[282] By using the term "sovereign states" in a plural form, Rogge not only defended the act of the State of China, a republic, but also of other States.

The concept of sovereignty may have changed, but it is too late to abandon it or to dissociate it from the State. It is almost inconceivable

[276] Hans J. Morgenthau, *The Intellectual and Political Functions of a Theory of International Relations*, *in* THE ROLE OF THEORY IN INTERNATIONAL RELATIONS 116 (Horace V. Harrison ed., 1964).

[277] J.P. Nettl, *The State as a Conceptual Variable*, 20 WORLD POLITICS, at 560 (1968).

[278] ALI KHAN, THE EXTINCTION OF NATION-STATES, at 193 (1996).

[279] For a general discussion, *see* JAMES CRAWFORD, THE CREATION OF STATES IN INTERNATIONAL LAW. 2nd Ed. Oxford University Clarendon Press, 1979.

[280] *See* THE ENCYCLOPEDIA BRITANNICA, *supra* note 21, V.3, at 464 (15th Ed. 1994) and the U. N. membership, *available at* http://www.un.org/en/members/index.shtml, Last visited, 12/10/2008.

[281] *See supra* text accompanying note 228.

[282] George Vecsey, *Turn Out the Lights, The Party's Over*, 08/25/2008 Sports Monday, D1 (emphasis added).

to say that an independent political institution is a State, but not a sovereign State.

8. STATE, SOVEREIGNTY, AND INTERNATIONAL LAW

A. Creation of International Law

This is not a work on general international law. It does not intend to cover all the rules of international law on the topics mentioned here. In principle, discussions of international law in this work focus only on its relationship with concept of the State and the theory of sovereignty, or when it is to be applied to the issues raised in the Introduction. In discussing international law hereinafter, the term "State" applies to all forms of territorial political institutions, including the modern States, the neo-modern States, constitutional monarchies, and states that are constituent units of a commonwealth, unless otherwise specified.[283]

International law was created after the modern States appeared. After the Peace of Westphalia, hundreds of German principalities became modern states with the unrestricted capability to enter into relation with other states. These modern States with sovereignty defined by Bodin were not subject to the rule of other States. Each State, in theory, had unlimited sovereign power.

A consequence of State autonomy and State independence is the creation of international law. The sovereign power of the modern State, if not restrained, may encroach on the rights or interests of other States. Therefore, the States by consent created international law to restrain or limit their own power[284] by regulating the conduct of the States. Thus, international law was created for self-limitation and self-regulation.[285]

B. Sources of International Law

International law was created by consensus of the States. There are three major sources of international law: (1) treaties, including international conventions; (2) international custom; and (3) the general principles of

[283] *See* The Restatement, *supra* note 212. Sec. 201.

[284] *Id.*; *see also* Arthur M. Weisburd, *The Executive Branch and International Law*, 41 Vand. L. Rev. 1205, 1206 (1988).

[285] *See* Hannum, *supra* note 31, at 19.

law recognized by civilized nations.[286] These sources are all based on the consensus of the States, albeit in different ways. Treaties and international conventions are the most explicit demonstration of a consensus. They are signed by the contracting States.

International custom arose out of the consensus of the States through State practice, or based on the writings of ancient influential writers. This point was discussed in detail by Hugo Grotius, who proved by the method of *a posteriori* in his work, The Law of War and Peace, that a body of international law was created by the common consent of the States.[287]

Many international customary laws are based on the theory of sovereignty. Grotius published his influential work in international law almost 50 years after Bodin published his work, The Six Books of the Commonwealth.[288] In developing a body of international customary law based on State practice of the Western European States, Grotius was influenced by Bodin's theory of sovereignty.

The general principles of law recognized by civilized nations also formed a basis for the creation of international law where there was no international convention or custom. When a rule of international law was based on the general legal principles recognized by civilized nations, the rule was also based on the consensus of civilized nations. Samuel Pufendorf in The Law of Nature and Nations used the method of *a priori* deduced logically from the rational and social nature of man "certain universal legal principles" which were accepted by different societies and "binding . . . on all men."[289] Such principles "could then be regarded as the basis of an international law."[290]

[286] *See* Statute of the International Court of Justice, June 26, 1945, Art. 38, 59 Stat. 1055, T.S. No. 993, 3 Bevans 1179; WALLACE, *supra* note 36, at 7–33. Decisions of International Court of Justice, in theory, only bind the parties before the Court, though they may provide future guides for the Court and for other States.

[287] *De jure belli ac pacis* (1625). *See* STEIN, *supra* note 2, at 3 (holding that Hugo Grotius (1583–1654) was one of "most influential writers" in first half of 18th century).

[288] *See supra* note 38.

[289] Quotations from STEIN, *supra* note 2, at 4. (discussing *de iure naturae et gentium*).

[290] *Id*. at 3, 51.

C. Nature of the State in International Law

The States are legal persons in international law: They have a legal status similar to that of a natural person in a civil society. International law was developed by the States to provide norms of conduct among them. Thus, the States, as legal persons in international law, are subject to international law, albeit the law is not a positive law in the strict sense, meaning that there is no higher authority to enforce the law.[291]

D. Common Elements of the States in International Law

The neo-modern States share some common elements. Although the States may differ in size, economic development, and political system, they share some common features. These features have turned into elements of the States in State theory and international law. The Convention on Rights and Duties of States, commonly known as the Montevideo Convention,[292] prescribes four qualifications of the States. Article 1 of the Convention provides that "The State as a person of international law should possess the following qualifications: (a) a permanent population; (b) a defined territory; (c) government; and (d) capacity to enter into relations with the other States."[293] Likewise, the Restatement[294] also prescribes four requirements of the States. Section 201 of the Restatement provides that "[u]nder international law, a State is an entity that has a

[291] Positive law, in the view of John Austin, is "law set by political superiors to political inferiors" in his Lecture I, quoted in STEIN, *supra* note 2, at 72. H.L.A. Hart sees "[positive] law as coercive orders separate from morals." H.L.A. Hart, *Positivism and the Separation of Law and Morals*, 71 HARV. L. REV. 593, 594 (1958). For a discussion of positive law, *see* H.L.A. HART, THE CONCEPT OF LAW (2d Ed. 1994). For the positions of international law scholars, *see* Brian H. Bix A Dictionary of Legal Theory, Oxford University Press Inc. (New York), 2004, at 103 (the entry of 'international law').

[292] *See* Convention on Rights and Duties of States, Dec. 26, 1933, Art. 1, 49 Stat. 3097, 3100; 165 L.N.T.S. 21, 25, entered into force Dec. 26, 1934 [hereinafter "the Montevideo Convention"]. It was adopted by the Seventh International Conference of American States.

[293] The Montevideo Convention, *id.* Art. 1. "For all purposes of International law, state (*onnos, civitas, volk*) may be defined to be a people permanently occupying a fixed territory, bound together by common laws, habits, and customs into one body politic, exercising, through the medium of an organized government, independent sovereignty and control over all persons and things within its boundaries, capable of making war and peace, and of entering into all international relations with the other communities of the globe." MOORE, INTERNATIONAL LAW DIGEST (1906), V. 1. Sec. 3, at 14.

[294] THE RESTATEMENT, *see supra* note 212.' 202, Comments a, b (3d Ed. 1987).

defined territory and a permanent population, under the control of its own government, and that engages in, or has the capacity to engage in, formal relations with other such entities."[295] These qualifications or requirements are common elements of the neo-modern States.

These four elements are all objective factual matters and can be observed. Population and territory are undoubtedly factual matters. Population is the people who form the State. Territory is the land in which the people establish the State. Often the name of the people becomes the name of the land where they reside. Most States adopt the name of its people or the name of its territory as the name of the State. The government of a territorial political institution is formed by natural persons. Such government is manifested in documents, associations of the people, and other observable features.

"Capacity to enter into relations with the other States" is also a factual matter. The "capacity" as a qualification of a State in the Montevideo Convention or a requirement in the Restatement must be distinguished from "legal capacity" of the State.

Legal capacity is an attribute of a person. It is a general rule recognized by civilized nations that a natural person acquires legal capacity to enjoy rights at birth. Art. 1 of the German Civil Code[296] provides that "The legal capacity of a human being (*Rechtsfähigkeit*) begins with the completion of birth."[297] Legal capacity is also an attribute of a person which enables the person to perform.[298] Thus, the legal capacity is the attribute of a natural person to hold or enjoy rights or to engage in legal relationships.

Likewise, as discussed before, all States have power to engage in relations with other States. The public power of the State in political theory may be translated as competence[299] in legal theory and in international law. Thus, the legal term of the State power to engage in foreign affairs is competence to enter into relations with other States. Such competence is an attribute, rather than a qualification or requirement, of the State.

[295] *Id.* '202, Comments a, b (3d Ed. 1987);' 201.

[296] GERMAN CIVIL CODE, *BUERGELICHESGESETZBUCH.*

[297] GERMAN CIVIL CODE, Art. 1. Trans. by Chung Hui Wang. Stevens and Sons, Ltd., London, 1907. Reprinted 2000, Gaunt, Inc. Holmes Beach, Florida.

[298] *See* BLACK'S LAW DICTIONARY, 6th Ed. 1990, at 207 (providing the definition of "capacity").

[299] *See* THE NEW SHORTER OXFORD ENGLISH DICTIONARY, 5th Ed., Oxford Univ. Press, 2002. at 467 (providing the definition of "competence").

Interpreting the word "capacity" in the Montevideo Convention and the Restatement to mean "legal capacity" or "competence" to enter into relations with the other States as a qualification or a requirement of a State creates a circuitous problem. If the term "capacity" in the Montevideo Convention and the Restatement is interpreted to mean "competence" in law (legal capacity), then only an established State has such competence to meet the requirement. As a consequence, a political institution without statehood can never have the "capacity" to meet the qualification or the requirement and become a State.

The term "capacity" in the Montevideo Convention and the Restatement means ability in fact or capability to conduct foreign affairs and "enter into relations with other States,"[300] rather than legal capacity or competence.[301] For the purpose of analysis in this work, the word "capability" will be used to mean the ability in fact.

The qualification of "capacity to enter into relations" in the Montevideo Convention and the requirement of "the capacity to engage in formal relations" in the Restatement mean the unrestricted capability (ability-in-fact) to enter into relations with the other States. When the capability of a territorial political institution is restricted, it has no "capacity" to enter into relations with other States. In most cases, such a political institution with restricted capability is a constituent unit of an empire or a federation. In an empire or a federated State which consists of many constituent units (territorial political institutions), it is the empire or the federal State that has the capability to engage in relations with other States. Its constituent units do not because their capability to engage in relations with other States is restricted by the empire or the federation. Several examples in history support such an interpretation. As mentioned earlier, before the 1648 Peace of Westphalia, within the feudal structure of the Holy Roman Empire, the Emperor had the capability to engage in relations with other States, but the German princes of the Empire did not. The princes' capability to enter into alliances with other princes was restricted by the Empire. The structure of the British Empire before the First World War was also similar to the Holy Roman Empire before 1648. Canada, Australia, and New Zealand were former British colonies

300 *See* Oxford English Dictionary, 2d Ed. 1989, at 2 (providing the definition of "ability" as "holding power").

301 *See* The New Shorter Oxford English Dictionary, 5th Ed., *supra* note 299.

and members of the British Empire. These British colonies' capability to conduct foreign affairs was restricted by Great Britain.[302]

After the 13 States in North America formed a single, federated State—the United States of America—in 1789, only the united States of America has the capability to engage in relations with foreign States. The member States do not. Their capability to engage in relations with other States is restricted by the federation. Likewise, in Germany, within the federal structure of Federal State of Germany, the Federal State (*Bundesstaat*) has such capability, but its constituent "States (*Staaten*)" do not because their capability to do so is restricted by the federation.

A restriction on the capability to engage in relations with other States means a restriction imposed by a higher authority. The restriction on a territorial political institution is imposed by either an empire or a federation of which the political institution is a constituent unit. Alternatively, when a State, by an agreement, delegates the power to engage in foreign affairs to another State, the State does not lose its political status as a State. Monaco, for instance, delegates its power to conduct foreign affairs to France, but is still an independent State.

The restriction is a legal restriction. In the case of an empire, the restriction is imposed by an order or a law of the empire. In the case of a federation, the restriction is imposed by the Constitution (e.g., of the United States) or the Basic Law (e.g., Federal Republic of Germany) of the federation. A territorial political institution whose capability to engage in relations with other States is restricted by law cannot be a State. On the other hand, after the empire grants its constituent units the right to enter into treaties between them or with other States, the restriction on their capability is lifted and they acquire unrestricted capability to enter into relations with other States. They then have "capacity" prescribed in the Montevideo Convention and the Restatement and become States.

E. Creation of a State in International Law

a. The Nature of the Creation of a State in International Law

International law jurists have different views on the nature of the creation of a new State. Some writers, such as Oppenheim, regard the formation of a new State "a matter of fact, and not of law."[303] Some writers hold

[302] *The Declaration of Independence*. AMERICAN HISTORY, *supra* note 150, at 100, 102 (emphasis added).

[303] LASSA OPPENHEIM, INTERNATIONAL LAW: Vol. I. at 544 (H. Lauterpacht ed., 8th Ed. 1955).

that the creation of States in international law is a "mixed question of law and fact."[304]

Oppenheimer's view is preferred. The law referred to is international law. Since States existed before the creation of international law, law cannot be the base for the creation of a State.

b. Effect of Recognition in the Creation of a State

Two theories have dominated the discourse as to how a State is created: the constitutive theory and the declaratory theory. The two theories differ on the effect of diplomatic recognition by other existing States in the creation of a new State.

The Constitutive Theory

The constitutive theory holds that the statehood of a political institution in international law derives only from diplomatic recognition by the other States.[305] According to this theory, diplomatic recognition of other States has constitutive effect and a political institution which exists with all common elements of the States is not a State in international law unless and until it is recognized by other States.

The constitutive theory has difficulty not only in theory, but also in its application.[306] Its difficulty in theory is that it cannot explain the status of kingdoms before the doctrine of recognition was conceived in international law. For instance, the kingdom of China was established by First Chin Emperor in 221 B.C.[307] According to the constitutive theory, China would not be a State until the middle of the 19th century when Western States began to establish diplomatic relations with her, thus, recognizing her as a State. Prior to the modern time, there could not be recognition of China by other States because the recognition of a State in international law is based on concept of the equality of the States. Recognition signifies that the recognizing State considers and treats the recognized State as an equal. But premodern China never considered the

[304] *See* James Crawford, *supra* note 279. (stating that some courts held that problem of state is "mixed question of law and fact.").

[305] "A State is, and becomes, an International Person through recognition only and exclusively." Justice Johnson, *Cherokee Nation v. The State of Georgia*, *supra* note 3. OPPENHEIM, *supra* note 303, at 125. For a discussion of this view, *see* CRAWFORD, *supra* note 279, at 4.

[306] CRAWFORD, *supra* note 279, at 17-20.

[307] For First Chin Emperor (*Shih-huang Ti*), *see infra* text accompanying note 433.

other States its equal until the Opium War, in which it was defeated by Great Britain.[308] Furthermore, the constitutive theory cannot explain the character of the agreements signed by a new political institution with existing States before the former is widely recognized. More troubling is the question of how the first State ever came into existence. If recognition by other States is a requisite of the establishment of a State, then who recognized the first State?

The difficulty in the application of the constitutive theory is that its proponents never indicate, much less prove, the number of the existing States required to recognize a new political institution as a State in order that the political institution turns into a State. State practice in the past does not shed any light on the matter.

The Declaratory Theory

The declaratory theory holds that the State exists independent of diplomatic recognition by other States. According to this theory, a political institution with the common elements of the States is, by virtue of its mere effective existence, a State and has legal personality in international law.[309] The State exists by itself.[310] Thus, recognition of a State is *declaratory* in nature only,[311] and not a requirement for establishing the State. Other States which have not recognized it as a State must treat it as one.[312] For example, the three Swiss Cantons (Uri, Schwyz, and Unterwalden) became independent from their ruler, the Holy Roman Emperor, by declaring the formation of an alliance among themselves in 1291.[313] The alliance later developed into the Swiss Confederation. The Swiss consider that the declaration and the entry of the mutual alliance pact established statehood, though the Emperor did not recognize the

[308] China's emperors before the Opium War of 1840 considered other kingdoms as tributaries.

[309] CRAWFORD, *supra* note 279, at 4.

[310] *Id.* at 21.

[311] *Id.* at 4.

[312] THE RESTATEMENT, *see supra* note 212.

[313] In 1291, Uri, Schwyz, and Unterwalden signed a mutual defense pact against their common enemies, which included their ruler, Holy Roman Empire. The pact later developed into Swiss Confederation. The Swiss consider the announcement in the 1291 mutual alliance pact as a declaration of independence from the Empire. "In 1991 the Swiss celebrated 700 years of the country's history." THE NEW ENCYCLOPEDIA BRITANNICA *supra* note 7, V. 28, at 352 (the entry of 'Switzerland').

independence of the Swiss Confederation until over 300 years later, in 1499.[314]

Under the declaratory theory, diplomatic recognition of the State means that the recognizing State recognizes another State, which effectively exists in fact, as an equal with her, and signifies to the recognized State and international community that she is willing to enter into diplomatic relations with the recognized State on an equal footing.[315]

The declaratory theory has become the predominant view in the 20th century. The Montevideo Convention[316] adopts this theory. In the Convention, recognition of a political institution as a State by other States is not a qualification of a State. Article 1 of the Convention prescribes four "qualifications" of a State. Recognition by other States is not one of them.[317] In fact, the Convention is more explicit on the point. Article 3 provides that "The political existence of the State is independent of recognition by the other States."[318]

The Restatement also adopts the declaratory theory.[319] It does not consider recognition by other States an essential element of a State. Section 201 prescribes the four common elements of the State more as the features of a State than as requirements of a State,[320] though the comments refer to them as requirements.[321] Recognition by other States is not a requirement. On the contrary, a comment to Section 202 states,

314 The Empire did not recognize the independence of Swiss Confederation until 1499 when Emperor Maximilian, not being able to defeat the Swiss, abandoned a plan to retake Switzerland, and "unofficially [recognized] Swiss independence." *Id.* The official recognition occurred in the 1648 Peace of Westphalia.

315 For instance, Israel was recognized as a new state by other states in 1948 after Israel established statehood by Declaration of the Establishment of the State of Israel. *See* Declaration of the Establishment of the State of Israel, May 14, 1948, 1 L.S.I. 3 (1948).

316 *See* The Montevideo Convention, *supra* note 292.

317 *Id.* Art. 3. A recent example is Macedonia. It declared independence from Yugoslavia in 1991, but was not recognized by any state until two years later. By June 2012, only a few States had recognized it. Many states refuse to recognize it because of Greece's objection to its name "Macedonia," not because of the legality as to its existence. By 2017, many more States have recognized Macedonia.

318 *Id.*

319 THE RESTATEMENT, *see supra* note 212. '202, Comments a, b.

320 *See id.* '202, Comments a, b (stating that requirements are (a) population; (b) territory; (c) government; and (d) capacity to engage with other States).

321 *Id.* '201, Comment b; Reporter's Notes 1 to '202.

"An entity that satisfies the requirements of Section 202 is a state whether or not its statehood is formally recognized by other states."[322]

The Nature of the Convention and the Restatement

It is important to recognize that the Montevideo Convention does not *create* a binding law on the requirements of a State. Although it is sometimes said that Article 1 of the Convention prescribes the *requirements* of a State in international law, it does not. The Convention is not municipal legislation. It cannot create the requirements of a State as a positive law can. Where it is relevant is that, as stated earlier, treaties are a source of international law. But the Montevideo Convention is a treaty among 13 American States, and the subsequent Seventh International Conference of American States which adopted it, was signed by 16 States.[323] A convention signed by a small number of States does not have the force of international law binding the other nonsignatory States.

The Montevideo Convention simply codifies a customary rule in international law. As stated earlier, the neo-modern States have four common elements. From these common elements of the neo-modern States a customary rule of international law developed: a political institution requires these four elements for it to be a State. The Montevideo Convention codifies the customary rule and prescribes the four elements as four qualifications of the State. Similarly, the Restatement *restates* the customary rule, rather than creates the rule.

c. The Declaratory Theory and Creation of the State

The declaratory theory does not address the question of *how* the State is created. While the constitutive theory, by the theory itself, provides how a new State is created—recognition by the other States—the declaratory theory does not. Although the proponents of the declaratory theory hold that "the State exists by itself," few of them have fully explained how a State comes to exist. The Montevideo Convention and the Restatement merely describe the common qualifications or requirements of existing States after they have come to exist. Neither one provides *how* a new State is established. While the four elements[324] prescribed in the Montevideo Convention and the Restatement are necessary qualifications

[322] *Id.*
[323] *See* The Montevideo Convention, *supra* note 292.
[324] *See supra* text accompanying note 292.

to be a State, they alone do not establish the State. For instance, Palestine is a political institution with all four qualifications prescribed in the Montevideo Convention, but it is not considered a State.[325]

[325] Whether Palestine became a State on December 4, 2012 is an intriguing question. In the Peace Treaty of Sevres concluded with the Allied Powers after World War I, Turkey renounced all her rights and title over Palestine. The territory of Palestine then came under the U.K.'s trusteeship in "A Proclamation, by the President of the U.S.A., in Convention between the U.S. and Great Britain in respect to rights in Palestine," signed at London, Dec. 3, 1924, proclaimed Dec. 5, 1925. After the Second World War, the territory came under the administration of the Palestine Authority. After the 1967 war between Israel and the surrounding States, part of Palestine was occupied by Israel. On November 15, 1988, Palestine National Council meeting in Algeria issued a declaration of independence for a State of Palestine in the West Bank and Gaza Strip. Although about 25 countries accorded recognition to "the State of Palestine," their recognition seemed to be politically motivated. The declaration of 1988 was generally considered not to have effectively established the State of Palestine because the "Arafat's government," being not established within the territory it claimed by the inhabitants of the territory at the time, did not effectively control the territory it claimed and is not a government-in-exile. *See* INTERNATIONAL LAW, CASES AND MATERIALS, LESTER B. ORFIELD and EDWARD D. RE. The Bobbs-Mererrill Co. Inc. New York (1965), at 268. "Edwin Martin, Assistant Secretary of State for Inter-American Affairs states, 'Our consistent policy has been to recognize governments-in-exile only when they have a direct constitutional connection with the last legally constituted government of the country, usually when they have actually exercised power in the country just prior to being forced out.'" *Id*, at 262.

On December 4, 2012, the U.N., upon the application of the Palestinian Authority, adopted a resolution to change the status of Palestine in the U.N. from *the Permanent Observer Mission of Palestine* to *No-member Observer State. See* Sharon Otterman, *Cheering U.N. Palestine Vote, Synagogue Tests Its Members*, N.Y. TIMES, 12/5/2012. Whether Palestine became a State by the Resolution is questionable. If Palestine was a State at the time, it should have applied to be a member of the U.N. to the Security Council as prescribed by the U.N. Charter. If the voting in the General Assembly on December 4, 2012 constituted a collective recognition of the State of Palestine, a question is: When did the State of Palestine come to exist? Under the declaratory theory, a State exists before other States recognize it. Can one consider the application of the Palestine Authority to the U.N. to change its status in the U.N. as a declaration of establishing statehood? If so, it would be an unusual way of declaration to establish statehood. As of March 20, 2013 when the U.S. President Obama visited West Bank, he did not treat Palestine as a State. For the statehood of Palestine, *see* James Crawford, *The Creation of the State of Palestine: Too Much Too Soon?*, 1 EUR. J. OF INT'L LAW 307 (1990). *Butsee* Francis A. Boyle, *The Creation of the State of Palestine*, 1 EUR. J. OF INT'L LAW 301 (1990). On October 30, 2014, Sweden officially recognized Palestine as a State. But it may be politically motivated. New Swedish Prime Minster Lofven, in his inauguration, told the Parliament "that a two-state solution was the only way to resolve the conflict between Israel and the Palestinians. Sweden will therefore recognize the state of Palestine." Other Western European countries which have recognized Palestine as State are Malta and Cyprus. Source: http://www.nytimes.com/2014/10/31/world/europe/sweden-recognizes-palestinian-state.html?ref'world&_r'1. Last visited 11/1/2014. In contrast, in case of Israel, the United Nations General Assembly passed a resolution on November 27, 1947 calling for the establishment of a Jewish State in Eretz-Israel. The government of Israel on May 14, 1948 formally declared establishment of the State of Israel by The Declaration of the Establishment of the State of Israel, *supra* note 315.

A political institution with the required elements of the State becomes a State by an act of declaration. This proposition is drawn from State practice. As it was pointed out at the beginning of this work, historically the process for establishing a kingdom was by a drastic act. The leader of a group of people at a certain point of time became their ruler either by declaring himself their king, or by accepting their acclamation to be their king. The declaration or the acceptance of the acclamation was an instant act which established a kingdom. This state practice turned into an international customary rule forming part of international law. This customary rule applied to the establishment of early kingdoms as well as the modern States.[326]

Historically, the act of declaration to establish a State took two forms: formal and informal. A formal form of declaration was an explicit declaration. It was used to establish a king and, thus, a kingdom. Bodin, writing about the establishment of a kingdom, described a drastic process of establishing a king: "[The duke] is lifted on high (by the people), and acclaimed king of the Tarars."[327]

Initially, the formal form to establish a kingdom or the modern State was by an oral declaration. Hobbes and Locke, notwithstanding their differences in the theory for forming a commonwealth(the State), in advocating a social contract as the method of forming a state, proposed that the commonwealth was created at the formation of an agreement between the people and the ruler—the second agreement—after they had made the first agreement among the people themselves. In this second agreement, the people "agreed to entrust its government to the ruler"[328] and the ruler orally declared his acceptance to be the king, and established a commonwealth.[329]

Subsequently, a formal announcement or document called "declaration of independence" was used by a constituent part of a State to secede from its ruling State. In practice, a declaration of independence by a constituent political community of a ruling State not only declared that the political community severed its political ties from its ruling State, but also simultaneously established a new State.

[326] THE RESTATEMENT, *supra* note 212. The Restatement provides a similar rule. *Id.* '202, Comments a, b (3d Ed. 1987).

[327] BODIN, *supra* note 38, at 8.

[328] *See supra* text accompanying note 90.

[329] The acceptance may be inferred from a gesture of gratitude or a promise to protect them.

Most political institutions became States by a formal declaration. The early examples are Switzerland from Holy Roman Empire in 1291[330]; the Netherlands from Spain in 1648[331]; and Belgium from the Netherlands in 1831.[332] The State practice of establishing a State by a declaration became a customary rule by the time international law began to develop.

The rule that a State is established by an act of declaration also applies to republican States. The 13 British Colonies of North America became States by declaring independence from Great Britain in 1776. After the American Revolution, democratic thought spread to other parts of the world. Almost all newly established States since then were republics. During the 20th century, more than 120 new States were established.[333] All of them were republican States.[334] Many colonies were granted independence by their ruling States either at will or under pressure of a revolt. These former colonies became new States by a declaration of independence.

On the other hand, where a territorial political institution was not under the sovereignty of an existing State, it became a State by a declaration of the establishment of a State. For instance, Israel became a State by a declaration in 1948 while it was not under the sovereignty of another State.[335]

In addition to State practice as a source of the rule that a republican State is established by an act of declaration, the rule can also be deduced *a priori* from the general principles of law recognized by civilized nations. The nature of the neo-modern State is different from that of the modern State. Although the modern State is called "a moral person,"[336] it is not a

330 *See supra* text accompanying note 314.

331 The New Encyclopedia Britannica, *supra* note 7, V. 24, at 888.

332 *Id.* V. 14, at 867. Recent examples are: Slovenia and Croatia declared independence from the Socialist Federal Republic of Yugoslavia in 1991; Bosnia and Herzegovina declared independence from Serbia on March 22, 1992 by the parliament. Wikipedia, http://en.wikipedia.org/wiki/Bosnian_War. Last visited 11/2/06.

333 *Id.* V. 3, at 464. About new 118 states became members of the U.N. from 1943 to 2006. The exact number of the States existing today depends on the definition of State.

334 This form was used where the declaring entity was a colony or part of an existing state.

335 The document establishing the State is titled, "The Declaration of the Establishment of the State of Israel." *See supra* note 315.

336 Samuel Pufendorf called "state" "a moral person." Crawford, *supra* note 279, at 6. From the beginning the word "state" "refers to positions of a general or abstract type." Dowdall, *supra* note 14, at 103.

purely abstract entity because while the commonwealth is an abstract entity, its ruler, an essential element of the modern State, is a natural person. A natural person is tangible. Once a person is born, the person's existence may be observed and is never questioned. The person who becomes a king has been in existence as a human being for many years since birth. When the person becomes a king by an act of declaration, the declaration does not change the nature of the person—a natural person. A republican State is different. It has no ruler. It, as a purely abstract political institution,[337] is akin to a corporation in municipal law.

A corporation is different from a natural person, though both have legal personality. A corporation, as a purely abstract legal entity, is intangible and cannot be seen or touched. The creation of a corporation in all civilized societies that recognize such a legal institution is accomplished by registration with the municipal authority in a public record after the requirements prescribed by a municipal law are fulfilled. Until the registration, the corporation does not and cannot exist in the eyes of law. Registration of a corporation, therefore, is equivalent to a formal declaration of the formation of the corporation by the incorporators to the society that the corporation comes to exist.

The nature of a republican State is akin to that of a corporation. A republican State is a legal entity in international law. Like a corporation, it is a purely abstract entity and cannot be seen or touched. But, unlike a corporation in the municipal law, the State is not and cannot be established by registration. There is not, and has never been, an office for such registration; neither the League of Nations nor the United Nations serves such function. Consequently, a declaration of establishment is essential for a political institution to become a republican State. In State practice, a formal act of declaration establishing a republican State was made by a political leader or representatives of the people.

An informal act of declaration is an act signifying the existence of sovereign power and the State. Such a declamation is implied in an act. In ancient times, when a group of people acclaimed their leader to be their king, raising both hands high signifying acceptance of the position by the leader was an informal act of declaration establishing a king and a kingdom. A constituent unit of an empire or a commonwealth also established statehood while remaining in the empire or the commonwealth by this method. The earliest example is the Principalities of the Holy Roman

[337] Lubasz, *supra* note 15, at 1.

Empire. Prior to the end of the Thirty Years' War in the 17th century, the Principalities in the Holy Roman Empire were not States (*statos*) because their Princes' capability (capacity in fact) to enter into relations with other Princes or States—an element of the State—was legally restricted by the Empire. At the end of the Thirty Years' War, Holy Roman Emperor Ferdinand III was forced to lift the legal restriction and granted the Princes right to make alliance treaties with other Princes and rulers in the Peace of Westphalia.[338] Upon the conclusion of the Treaties, the Princes acquired an unrestricted capability to enter into treaties with other Princes or rulers. With such capability, the Principalities became States when they asserted or claimed the sovereign power, including the power (competence) to enter into treaties with the other Principalities or States. The assertion or claim of the sovereign power signifying the existence of the State was an implicit declaration to establish statehood and the principalities became the modern States (*statos*).[339] Thus, the fourth elements of a State—capability to engage in relations with other States—prescribed in the Montevideo Convention refers to the "unrestricted capability" of the territorial political institution to enter into relations with other States. As discussed before, in the 20th century the British colonies of Canada, Australia, and New Zealand also took this form of declaration to establish States while officially remaining in the British Commonwealth.[340]

This State practice subsequently turned into a customary rule in international law that a territorial political institution with the required elements becomes a State by an act of declaration. In summary, a political institution with all the qualifications prescribed in the Montevideo Convention does not transform itself into a State unless and until an act of declaration signifying that it is a State. As an act of declaration is a drastic act, every State was established at a definite time. Thus, every State has a birthday.[341] A political institution does not evolve gradually into a State.

[338] *See supra* text accompanying notes 24–26; *see also* THE ENCYCLOPEDIA BRITANNICA, *supra* note 21, v. 19, at 482.

[339] *See supra* text accompanying note 25. *Also see* Herz, *supra* note 25, at 473–93.

[340] *See supra* text accompanying note 254.

[341] *See* the CIA World's Facebook, *at* https://www.cia.gov/library/publications/the-world-factbook/fields/2088.html. Last visited 04/20/2011.

An act of declaration to establish a State has two implications. The first implication is that the political institution claims statehood. A political institution with all the required elements of the State must itself claim that it is a State in order to establish a State. A declaration to establish a State implies such a claim. This requirement is also pointed out by the drafters of the Restatement. The Comment to Section 201 of the Restatement states that "[w]hile the traditional definition does not formally require it (claiming statehood), an entity is not a state if it does not claim to be a state."[342] A political institution that does not assert itself a State cannot be a State.

A claim of statehood is based on the common will of the people inhabiting the territory. For a political institution to establish statehood, it is not enough that it has the four objective elements of the States listed in the Montevideo Convention and the Restatement. To establish a State, there must be a subjective element—the common will of the people to establish a State.

Common will of the people as an essential element to establish a State is implied in the declaration. Where a king was installed by an acclamation of the people, the common will to establish a kingdom was explicit. Again, as Bodin describes it, "[the duke] is lifted on high, and acclaimed"[343] by the people their king. The requirement of common will is also implied in the theory of social contract expounded by Hobbes and Locke. When the people desired to establish a State, they first entered into an agreement among themselves (the first agreement), then, by their common will, chose a ruler by entering into "the second agreement" with him.[344] Even if a ruler acquired his position by a brutal force, he could not retain his position for long without the consent (common will) of the people ratifying his act. Von Gierke observes that when "the State was the product of violent conquest or revolution or successful usurpation . . . a retroactive legitimation express or tacit consent of the people was indispensable if the ruler was to have a good title to rulership."[345]

When the common will of the people was not clear, a referendum was the most common method to ascertain the wish of the people. Many States were established in the 20th and the 21st centuries after a

[342] THE RESTATEMENT, *supra* note 212. '201, Comment f (3d Ed., 1987).

[343] *See supra* text accompanying note 327.

[344] *See supra* text accompanying note 328.

[345] *See* VON GIERKE, *supra* note 37, at 93.

referendum. East Timor, Montenegro, and South Sudan provide good examples.

On the other hand, if the people did not have the common will to establish a State, then no other States can force them to do so. The Commonwealth of Puerto Rico, a U.S. Territory, is not a State because there is no common will among the people to establish a State as shown by repeated referenda. Madeira, an island located in the middle of Atlantic Ocean, is a territory of Portugal. It has a defined territory, population, and a government.[346] But the people had no common will to become a State and only asked for autonomy within the State of Portugal in the 1970s.

A State set up without the support of the common will of the people is void. The Japanese government seized Manchuria in northeastern China and set up Manchukuo State in 1932.[347] Manchukuo State was not considered a valid State because the establishment (State) was not created or supported by the people.

The second implication of a declaration is that the declaring political institution becomes a State instantly. The declaration is an announcement to the international society that the declaring institution is a State from the moment of the declaration onwards. A declaration to establish a State takes effect instantly.[348] As the act of declaration to establish a State is, by definition, the beginning of the State's existence, it does not have retroactive effect. Accordingly, for a political institution to become an effective State, its conduct in the international arena after the declaration must be consistent with the fact that it is a State, i.e., asserting its statehood and acting like a State in international affairs. This point is self-explanatory.

This work will not discuss the length of time in which the new State must be effective and stable after the declaration so that the new State is considered to be validly established because the issue is not relevant to the issues involved in this work.

[346] The head of the government is the President. In May 2006, the President was Jardim Alberto.

[347] For Manchukuo State *see* Academic American Encyclopedia, *supra* note 12, at 109.

[348] In theory, such a declaration may at the same time announce that it will take effect at a later time, but there has been no such instance in the past.

F. State Power and International Law

The sovereign (State) power of the neo-modern State in the context of modern international law will be explored next. The power may be analyzed from two aspects: internal and external.

a. Internal Power

As described before, internally the power of the neo-modern State is the highest authority in the State to govern its territory and people. The power of the State to govern its territory, including making and enforcing the law within its territory, is not subject to the intervention of other States. Justice Holmes in *Mateo Carino* v. *Insular Government of Philippine*[349] stated that "in legal theory, sovereignty is absolute, and that, as against foreign nations, the United States may assert absolute power (over its territory)."[350] Oppenheim states that "The importance of State territory lies in the fact that it is the space within which the State exercises its supreme authority."[351]

In Bodin's theory of sovereignty, the State also has the exclusive power to make law for the people within its territory without the intervention of other States. In Western Europe, during the migration period, the law was personal law. Personal law was the law, mostly customary law, of the people. When the peoples, such as Angles, Saxons, Thuringians, Salian Franks, Burgundians, Visigoths, Lombards, Alemanni, migrated westward since the 3rd century A.D., the law of the peoples followed the peoples wherever they moved.

After the peoples settled down, the law became territorial law. Sometime around the 5th century A.D., these peoples settled down. The peoples identified themselves with the territory where they settled and established political communities. The new communities developed the territorial law to replace the personal law. Under the territorial law, all peoples, regardless of their race or national origin, in a territory were subject to the law of the territory. In the feudal State, the people were subject to the law promulgated by the feudal lord; in the modern State, the law of the king or the sovereign prince. After the neo-modern State

[349] *Mateo Carino v. Insular Government of Philippine*, 212 U.S. 449 (1909).

[350] *Id.* While the 20th century doctrine of international human right imposes restrictions on a sovereign power over its subject, the doctrine does not apply to a state's right to its own territory.

[351] *See* OPPENHEIM, *supra* note 303.

appeared, the people were subject to law of the State. Thus, in general, a foreigner within the territory of a State is subject to the laws of the State.

For centuries, a State had exclusive power, free of the intervention of other States, over the people, including foreigners, within its territory. However, after the Second World War, the exercise of the State power over the people within its territory, as well as the people in the foreign territory under its occupation, may be restricted by newly developed international human rights law. There are two sources of international human rights law that may restrict or limit the power of the State. One is international conventions. The international conventions entered into by States may impose some restrictions or limitations on their State power. The Convention on the Prevention and Punishment of the Crime of Genocide[352] and almost all human rights conventions concluded after the Second World War do so.[353]

The other source of international law which may restrict the State power over its people is international customary law developed from State practice in the international society. As observed before, the exercise of the State power is subject to international law, which developed along with the formation of the modern States.[354] After the Second World War,

[352] Adopted on December 9, 1948.

[353] The U.N. adopted the following conventions on human rights: Universal Declaration of Human Rights, Dec. 10, 1948, U.N. G.A. Res. 217 (1948); International Covenant on Civil and Political Rights. Dec. 16, 1966, 999 U.N.T.S. 171; International Covenant on Economic, Social and Cultural Rights, Dec. 16, 1966, 993 U.N.T.S. 3; International Convention on the Elimination of All Forms of Racial Discrimination, 5 I.L.M. 352 (1966); Optional Protocol to the International Covenant on Civil and Political Rights, 999 U.N.T.S. 171, 6 ILM. 383 (1967); Convention on the Rights of the Child, Nov. 20, 1980, 28 I.L.M. 1448 (1980); Convention on the Elimination of All Forms of Discrimination Against Women, Dec. 18, 1979, 19 I.L. M. 33 (1980); Convention Against Torture and Other Cruel, Inhuman, or Punishment, Dec. 10, 1984, 23 I.L.M. 1027 (1984), as modified, 24 I.L.M. 535 (1985).

European Unions adopted the following conventions on human rights: European Convention for the Protection of Human Rights and Fundamental Freedoms, Nov. 4, 1950, 312 U.N.T.S. 221, E.T.S. 5, as amended by Protocol No.3, E.T.S. 45, Protocol No. 5, E.T.S. 55, and Protocol No. 8 S.E.T.S. 118 and Protocol No. 11 E.T. S. 155.; Protocols to the European Convention for the Protection of Human Rights and Fundamental Freedoms, Mar. 20, 1952, 213 U.N.T.S. 262, E.T.S. 9.

Other conventions are: American Convention on Human Rights, Nov. 22, 1969, 9 I.L.M. 673 (1970); American Charter on Human and Peoples' Rights (Banjul Charter), Jun. 27, 1981, 21 I.L.M. 59 (1981).

[354] *See supra* text accompanying note 290.

a new concept of human rights developed. The concept was adopted in many international human rights conventions, which have been so widely accepted by the international society that they are in the process of developing into international norms of conduct, binding members as well as nonmembers of the conventions, as international customary law.[355]

Under a new doctrine based on the concept of international human rights, if a government, in exercising its State power over the people within its territory particularly over an ethnic minority group, or the people in the foreign territory under its occupation, disregards the generally accepted new norms of conduct, other States or international organizations, such as the U.N., the North Atlantic Treaty Organization (NATO), or European Union, may intervene. For instance, NATO intervened in Serbia in 1999 on the grounds that the Serbian government was committing atrocities against its Muslim minority population within its own borders.[356] The U.N. Security Council in March 2011 authorized the creation of a no-flight zone inside Libya to prevent the Libyan government from bombing its own people. The government officials who authorized the atrocious acts committed war crimes and were personally responsible for their acts.

However, this new doctrine of international human rights has not been universally accepted by the end of the 20th century. Some States denounced the doctrine on the grounds that it encroached upon their sovereignty. When world opinions criticized China for its mistreatment of the ethnic people in Tibet during the early 21st century, China accused the critics of interfering with its internal affairs concerning its own people and territory.[357] Some States simply ignored the criticism of other States on its conduct. The government of Myanmar (formerly Burma) formed by a military Junta put Aung San Suu Kyi, an opposition leader, under house arrest for nearly fifteen years between July 1989 and May 2009 without charging her of any crime. The government ignored

[355] "The State Department issued a statement on Friday calling on China to release Mr. Liu [Xiaobo], saying that the 'persecution of individuals for the peaceful expression of political views is inconsistent with international recognized norms of human rights.'" Andrew Jacobs, *In Sentence of Activist, China Gives West a Chill*, N.Y. TIMES, 12/26/2009. A4 C1.

[356] *See infra* text accompanying note 432.

[357] "Hu says Tibet issue an 'internal affair.'" CHINA POST, 04/13/2008, *available at* http://www.chinapost.com.tw/china/national%20news/2008/04/13/151644/. Last visited 07/04/2009.

the criticism of the international society and the U.N.[358] Like the manners of natural persons, such international norms may be encouraged by other States, but they are not always enforceable.

b. External Power

Power to Engage in War

As discussed earlier, externally the State power includes the power to engage in war and the power to engage in diplomatic relations with other States.

The State is an independent or autonomous political institution. As stated earlier, a characteristic of the state sovereignty is independence or autonomy. As such, the State is not subject to the rule of other States.[359] The State, being independent or autonomous in international society, has the power to exclude foreign elements—e.g., foreign civilians and armies—from its territory. Thus, a foreigner enters the State only with its consent or invitation. The border of the State forms an invisible shell protecting the territory and the people within. Since ancient times, one of the main purposes for establishing a kingdom or a duchy was the protection of its people from outsiders. A society that has not formed a State cannot enjoy peace and order within the society[360] and has no protection from outside invaders.[361] The State may build its army to defend its independence or autonomy, and, if necessary, wage war with another State. The American Declaration of Independence states that "[American States] have full Power to levy War."[362] But in conducting a war, States are subject to the international law of warfare.

358 *Myanmar Junta, Wary of Outsiders, Is Accused of Delaying Storm Aid*, NY TIMES, 05/8/2008. A1. It was reported in March 2010 that the U.N. planned to send a team to investigate the human rights violation by the ruling government to Myanmar.

359 *See* LUBASZ, *supra* note 15, at 2.

360 Dowdall states, "[W]arfare was chronic in each land until there had been established therein a power of recognized and effective supremacy, under whose protection the life of the community might, if circumstances were favourable, be integrated. This process began in the West, and the States thus established were kingdoms and duchies." Dowdall, *supra* note 14, at 112. The U.S. Constitution Preamble states "the People of the United States, in Order to form a more perfect Union, establish Justice, insure domestic Tranquility, provide for the common defense, promote the general Welfare, ordained and established the Government of the United States..." AMERICAN HISTORY, *supra* note 150.

361 "[W]hoever has the ... supreme power of any commonwealth is bound to ... employ the force of the community ... to prevent or redress foreign injuries, and secure the community from inroads and invasion." LOCKE, *supra* note 88, at 73.

362 *The Declaration of Independence,* AMERICAN HISTORY, *supra* note 150.

Power to Engage in Diplomatic Relations

The external State power includes power (competence) to engage in diplomatic relations with other States on equal footing. Diplomatic relations, though conducted by the kings or the representatives of governments, are between States. The concept of State independence or State autonomy gives rise to the concept of equality among the States. The level of equality inherent in the concept of sovereignty is meaningful only when the State deals with the other States. Equal status with the other States means that the State can engage in formal relations with the other States—e.g., diplomatic exchanges or concluding treaties—on equal footing. The concept of equality between States existed long before the formulation of the modern theory of sovereignty. In the early days, leaders of two or more groups of people who had common interests entered into military alliance agreements against others. These leaders also divided territories by agreements.[363] After these leaders established kingdoms—the States, the agreements made by two kings were between two kingdoms and called "treaties." When two kingdoms entered into a treaty, the two were equal in their legal status. Equal legal status between two kingdoms, however, did not mean that the two kingdoms had equal bargaining power.[364] After the neo-modern States appeared, international treaties are concluded

[363] *See* THE ENCYCLOPEDIA BRITANNICA, *supra* note 21, V.12, at 316. When Emperor Charlemagne's son, Louis I, died in 840, Louis I's three sons, Charles, Emperor Lothair I, and Louis, fought over the vast territory. *See Id.* The war among the three brothers ended with the Treaty of Verdun(843). *See Id.* The treaty divided the empire into four parts (The western part, the middle part, the eastern part, and the far eastern part). *See Id.* The western part consisting the land mostly of what is today France went to Charles (later Charles I), who declared establishment of the West Frankish Kingdom (*Francia Occidentalis*) and was considered the first true king of France. The middle part consisting of the Low Countries, Alsace, Lorraine, Luxembourg, Provence, Burgundy, and northern Italy was retained by Emperor Lothair I and was called the Middle Kingdom. The eastern part consisting of the land east of Rhein River and mostly of what is today Germany went to Louis (later Louis the German), who declared establishment of the East Frankish Kingdom (*Francia Orientalis*). The far eastern part consisting of the eastern tributary provinces did not come under the direct rule of any brother. *See Id.*

[364] For instance, the losing party to a war always has weaker bargaining power than the winning party. The losing party that surrenders unconditionally has no bargaining power at all.

between two political institutions with statehood. Only a State may conclude a treaty with another State.[365]

Diplomatic Recognition

Diplomatic relations begin with diplomatic recognition.[366] The competence of a State to engage in relations with the other States includes the competence of granting diplomatic recognition. There are two kinds of diplomatic recognition in international relations: recognition of a State and recognition of a government. Diplomatic recognition of a State, or State recognition, is an act by which the recognizing State declares that it will deal with the recognized State on an equal footing. When a State desires to engage in a formal relationship with another State for the first time, the former first communicates to the latter that it recognizes the latter being its equal and that the latter has competence to engage in such relations. In discussing the two theories in the creation of the State earlier in this work, recognition refers to the recognition of the State.[367]

Recognition of the State takes many forms. The most formal one is a direct communication by the recognizing State to the recognized State. A less formal form of recognition is that the Executive head of a State sends an envoy to meet with the Executive head of another State with credentials prescribing the envoy's authority, usually a plenipotentiary.

In contrast, recognition of a government, or government recognition, is recognition by a State of a particular government as the representative of another State. As a State may have only one government representing the State, other States may recognize only one government as the representative government of the State at a time. Recognition of a new government also takes many forms. A less formal form of government recognition is sending an envoy to attend the inaugural ceremony of a new government head. When a new State is established, the State recognition and the government recognition by other States may occur

[365] *See* Vienna Convention on the Law of Treaties, May 23, 1969, Art. 2.1(a), 1155 U.N. T.S. 331, 340 [hereinafter Vienna Convention].

[366] *See* Hackworth, *supra* note 166, at 167, 168; M.J. Peterson, Recognition of Governments: Legal Doctrine and State Practice, 1815–1995. St. Martin's Press, Inc. (New York), 1997, at 87.

[367] *See supra* text accompanying note 315.

simultaneously, and the recognition of the government also implies the recognition of the State, which the government represents.[368]

The nature of recognition of a government is different from the nature of recognition of a State. Recognition of a State is permanent and cannot be withdrawn unless either State becomes extinct.[369] A State continues to exist once it is established. There has been no incident in history where a State withdrew its recognition of another State. On the other hand, recognition of a government of another State may be withdrawn. For instance, the United States recognized the ROC (the Republic of China) government as the new government of China in 1913 after the Qing ("Ching" in the Wade-Giles system) government was overthrown.[370] When the United States subsequently recognized the PRC (the People's Republic of China), as the new representative government of China in 1979, it simultaneously withdrew its recognition of the ROC government.[371]

Power to Grant Diplomatic Recognition

Decisions to grant recognition are political questions.[372] Consequently, the power of the State to grant diplomatic recognition is exclusively in the ruler or the executive head. In the modern State, the king or the prince as the head of the State is also the head of the government, who exercises the sovereignty power, including the power to conduct foreign affairs.[373] Such power, including power to grant diplomatic recognition, is a prerogative of the ruler.

In the neo-modern State, the executive head has the executive power, which includes the power to conduct foreign affairs, though in some States the executive shares the power to conduct foreign affairs with the legislative. However, the power to grant diplomatic recognition is always in the executive head because decisions to grant recognition are political questions. The United States has the presidential system: the President, as

[368] When a new State is established, sending an envoy with credentials by another State to congratulate the government of the new State constitutes recognition of the new government as well as the new state.

[369] *See* The Restatement, *supra* note 212. Comment g to Section 202.

[370] The U.S. recognized the R.O.C. government on May 2, 1913, *available at* http:/usinfo.org/sino/chronology(1)_e.htm. Last visited 12/13/2006.

[371] *See infra* text accompanying note 502.

[372] *See infra* text accompanying note 965.

[373] *See supra* text accompanying note 52.

the head of the State and also the head of the government, is the Executive head. The President has exclusive power to grant diplomatic recognition, even though the President shares some power to conduct foreign affairs with the Congress.[374] The Federal Republic of Germany has a parliamentary system: the Chancellor elected by the Diet, as the head of the government, is the Executive head.[375] The Chancellor has exclusive power to grant diplomatic recognition, even though the Chancellor also shares the power to conduct foreign affairs with the Diet. France has a dual heads system: while the Premier is the head of the government, the President, the head of the State, has the power to conduct foreign affairs, including granting diplomatic recognition.[376]

In most constitutional monarchies, the monarchs reign but do not rule. The executive power, including the power to grant recognition, is in the head of the government—the prime minster elected by the parliament or the Diet.[377]

Recognition and De Facto Government

As the granting of recognition is a political question, whether or not to extend recognition is a prerogative of the Executive, on which the judicial branch cannot encroach.[378] For instance, after the 1917 Revolution in Russia, the U.S. Government refused to recognize the new Soviet

[374] The President of the U.S. has exclusive executive power. *U.S. v. Pink*, 315 U.S. 203, 62S.Ct. 552 (1942); *Cherokee Nation v. The State of Georgia*, *supra* note 3, at 21. The President has exclusive power to recognize a state, its government and territory. Zivotofsky v. Kerry, 725F.3d 197, 406 U.S. App. D.C. 324 (2013), 135S. Ct. 2076 (2014). However, the legislative often tries to influence the Executive by controlling the financing.

[375] If the head of the State, under its constitution, is a ceremonial figure, such as Queen of the United Kingdom or the President of Germany, then the head of the government, e.g., the Prime Minster in the United Kingdom and the Chancellor in Germany, possesses the executive power.

[376] France presents a unique situation. *See supra* note 210.

[377] E.g., the United Kingdom and Japan. One exception is the German Emperor under the Constitution of 1871. Although the legislative power is in the Federal Council (*Bundesrat*) and the Imperial Diet (*Reichstag*) (Art. 5), the Emperor has some executive power, including the power to conduct foreign affairs (e.g., concluding treaties with other States. "The Emperor shall represent the Empire among nations, declare war, and conclude peace in the name of the same, enter into alliance and other conventions with foreign countries, accredit ambassadors and receives them." Art. 11, CONSTITUTION OF THE GERMAN EMPIRE (1871). *See supra* note 60.

[378] *See Baker v. Carr*, *infra* note 965.

government established by the revolutionaries until 1936. Thus, until 1936, to the United States, there was no legitimate or *de jure* government of the USSR. The U.S. Government and the courts treated the Soviet government as a *de facto* government.[379] While the term "*de facto* government" is a recognized term in international law, the term "*de facto state*" is not a generally accepted term. Under the State theory, a political institution is either a State or not. Likewise, under the theory of sovereignty, a political institution either has sovereignty or has not. The term "*de facto* sovereignty" is an abnormal term,[380] and simply means the supreme power to control.

G. Basic Principles of International Law Based on Sovereignty

Many basic principles of international law are based on the theory of sovereignty,[381] which is accepted by all Western States. The following are some of them:

a. In the neo-modern State, sovereignty is a concept inseparable from the State; only a State has sovereignty. A political institution without statehood has no sovereignty. For instance, Palestine is not a State (before it declares statehood), thus, it has no sovereignty. As will be discussed later, the Republic of China has no sovereignty because it is not a State.

b. In the neo-modern State, the State, not its government, has title to its territory. Both government and territory are elements of the neo-modern State. The government in exercising sovereign power only controls and manages the territory. The government does not "own" the territory. A transfer of a territory is between two States, not between two governments.

c. Diplomatic relations are between States, although they are conducted by their governments. Likewise, international treaties are between States, though they are negotiated and signed by their respective representative governments. The State, not its government, has the competence to engage in formal relations, e.g., conducting diplomatic exchanges or concluding treaties, with other States. Each neo-modern

379 *See Wulfsohn v. Russian Socialist Federated Soviet Republic*, 234 N.Y. 372(1923).

380 *Cf.* The U.S. Supreme Court Justice Gray stated, "Who is the sovereign, de jure or de facto, of a territory, is not a judicial, but a political, question." *Jones v. United States*, *infra* note 973.

381 The term "sovereignty" refers to the theory developed by Bodin.

State, being sovereign, can and may enter into relations with the other States on an equal footing. On the other hand, a political institution without statehood cannot enter into formal relations with a State. It may sign an agreement or an accord, but not a treaty. For instance, the Oslo Accords between Israel and the Palestine Liberation Organization (PLO) were only a set of agreements, not a treaty, because the PLO did not represent a State.[382]

d. Only a State may be a full member of an international organization. Thus, a political institution without statehood cannot be a full member of an international organization, such as the U.N.[383] Palestine (before declaration of statehood) was not a State and, thus, could not be a member of the U.N. but only an observer. The Republic of China also cannot be a member of the U.N. because it is not a State, only a government.

e. Wars are between States, even though they are conducted by their governments. Thus, a peace treaty concluding a war is between the warring States, not the governments, even though the governments negotiate and sign on behalf of their respective States.

f. The sovereign power of a State is limited by international law. While sovereignty is not subject to any other State's rule,[384] in order to avoid conflicts arising out of unrestrained sovereign power of the States, the States have, by consensus, subjected themselves to a body of law—international law—created to limit the exercise of their sovereign power.

g. A State may have only one government. Sovereignty is the highest State power and is indivisible. Thus, there can be only one which is the highest authority within a State. Accordingly, each State has only one government which represents the State in international affairs.

[382] Oslo Accords (1993). *See* http://en.wikipedia.org/wiki/Oslo_Accords. Last visited 04/15/2011.

[383] CHARTER OF THE UNITED NATIONS, June 26, 1945; 59 Stat. 1031, 1038, T.S. No. 993, 3 BEVANS 1153. Art. 4. 1.

[384] *See Mateo Carino v. Insular Government of Philippine*, 212 U.S. 449(1909). Justice Holmes stated, "[I]n legal theory, sovereignty is absolute, and that, as against foreign nations, the United States may assert absolute power (over its territory)." *Id.* at 458.

CHAPTER 3
The Territorial State

Contents

1. THE TERRITORIAL STATE AND INTERNATIONAL LAW

This chapter examines the rules of international law on territories. As mentioned in the previous chapters, one characteristic of the State (both the modern State and the neo-modern State) is that it is a territorial State. The term "territorial State" means that the State is predicated on territory. Thus, a defined territory is an essential element of the State in international law[385]: the sovereignty of a State over a territory is based on its title to the territory. The word "territoriality" will be used as a short term for the notion that the State is a territorial State.

The principle of territoriality is accepted by all States and is the basis for many principles and rules of international law relating to territory. Some basic principles of territoriality are listed below:

1. A State has the sovereign power over its territory and the people within its territory.[386] A State's territory includes its airspace. A coastal State's territory includes the territorial sea. Aliens within the State are subject to the laws of the State.

[385] *See* the Montevideo Convention, *supra* note 292, Art. 1; The Restatement, *supra* note 212. '201 (3d Ed. 1987).
[386] *See* Oppenheim, *supra* note 303.

The One-China Policy: State, Sovereignty, and Taiwan's International Legal Status
DOI: http://dx.doi.org/10.1016/B978-0-08-102314-3.00003-3

2. The power of a State ceases at its border. The States have, by consensus, limited the exercise of their sovereignty to the territory within their borders.[387] A State that exercises the police power in another State without the other State's consent encroaches upon the other's sovereignty.[388] However, an exception based on the relatively new concept of human rights has developed in the second half of the 20th century.[389] Under the new concept, if a State oppresses the people within its territory in violation of the concepts of human rights, another State and/or international organizations may intervene in order to protect them.[390]
3. In a war between two States, when the defeated State surrenders unconditionally, the victorious State may occupy the territory of the defeated State and may dispose of its territory at will. The victorious State has such power because the defeated State has limited or no bargaining power.[391] Thus, some States have annexed a weaker State without its consent. In 1801, Russia annexed its protective State, Georgia[392]; in 1910, Japan annexed Korea[393]; and in 1951, China annexed Tibet.[394]

   When a State annexes another State without its consent, no treaty is needed or is possible for taking the territory because the defeated State is extinct and the victorious State has no party with which to conclude a treaty.

[387] "The operation of the Federal (the U.S.) Constitution is coextensive with the political jurisdiction of the United States." WEINSTEIN, *supra* note 195, at 108.

[388] *See* Barbara Crossette, *The Summit in New York: The Overview; Leaders Debate Broad New Role For U.N. Council*, N.Y. TIMES, 09/8/2000, at A1.

[389] *See Id.*

[390] *See Id.*; *see also* Richard Reeves, *United Nations: A Tale of Two Speeches*, TULSA WORLD, 09/24/1999. For instance, NATO attacked Serbia's army in Kosovo in 1999. *See* WALLACE, *supra* note 36, at 263; *See also* David Whippman, *Kosovo and the Limits of International Law*, Fordham Law Review, V. 25, November 2001, at 129–150.

[391] *See*, e.g., John Foster Dulles, *The San Francisco Conference on Proposed Japanese Peace Treaty*, Statement to the Press (Aug. 15, 1951), *in* DEP'T ST. BULL., Aug. 1951, at 347. At the Conference, John Foster Dulles, representing the United States, stated that "[t]he United States, which for [six] years has been and is *the occupying power* [in Japan], could practically do much as it wanted." (emphasis added). *Id.*

[392] James Traub, *Taunting the Bear*, N.Y. TIMES, 08/10/2008, Week in Review, p. 1. The Bolshevik government of Soviet Union signed a treaty with Georgia recognizing Georgia's independence. *Id.* Georgia declared independence from Russia in 1991.

[393] AN ENCYCLOPEDIA OF WORLD HISTORY, compiled and ed. by WILLIAM L. LANGER, Houghton Mifflin Co. (Boston), 1948, at 887.

[394] For China's annexation of Tibet, *see* ACADEMIC AMERICAN ENCYCLOPEDIA, *supra* note 12, V. 19, at 189 (the entry of "Tibet").

4. The victorious State in a war may take a piece (part) of territory from the defeated State by a treaty. From the defeated State's point of view, ceding part of its territory to the victorious State is a price to pay in order to preserve its entity.

By State practice,[395] taking a piece of another State's territory by a State is accomplished by a treaty.[396] This is true even if the victorious State wants to acquire an enemy's territory under its occupation during the war. In 1828, Chief Justice Marshall in *American Insurance Co.* v. *Cantor*[397] said that "[t]he usage of the world is, if a nation be not entirely subdued, to consider the holding of conquered territory as a mere military occupation, until its fate shall be determined at the treaty of peace."[398]

The usage has turned into an international customary law: if title to a piece of territory of the defeated State is to be changed after a war, then it must be achieved by a treaty.[399] The corollary of the rule is that no part of a State's territory can be taken away or transferred by other States without a treaty. The Hague Convention Respecting the Laws and Customs of War on Land confirmed this international customary law rule and codified it. Art. 55 of the said Convention provides,

[395] For example, King Louis II of the East Frankish Kingdom (later the Holy Roman Empire) acquired Alsace by the Treaty of Mersen in 870. France acquired Alsace in the Treaty of Ryswick in 1697 and Lorraine by marriage in 1766 (Acquisition of a territory by marriage is analogous to acquisition by a merger agreement). After the Franco-German War, Germany reacquired Alsace and Lorraine by the Treaty of Versailles in 1871. After the First World War, France again acquired Alsace and Lorraine under the Treaty of Versailles of 1919. Other examples include: the Treaty of Paris (1898), concluded at the end of the Spanish-American War, in which Spain ceded Puerto Rico to the United States; the Treaty of Nanjing (Nanking) (1842), concluded at the end of the Opium War, in which China ceded Hong Kong to the United Kingdom; and the Congress of Vienna (1815), concluded at the end of the Napoleonic War, which settled the territories among the European States. *See* COLUMBIA ENCYCLOPEDIA, 6th Ed. (2001), *available at* www.bartleby.com/65. Last visited 10/04/2004. In 1987, the United Kingdom transferred Hong Kong to China by an agreement.

[396] *See,* e.g., Herz, *supra* note 25.

[397] *American Insurance Co. v. Cantor,* 26 U.S. 511 (1828). 1 Pet. 511 (1828).

[398] *See Id.* at 541.

[399] *See* OPPENHEIM, *supra* note 303, '216; GEORGE H. KERR, FORMOSA BETRAYED, Houghton Mifflin Co., Boston (1965), "[S]overeignty could not be transferred until a peace treaty could be worked out, agreed upon, and signed." at 39; *see also* Hague Convention Respecting The Laws and Customs of War on Land, with Annexed Regulations, Oct. 18, 1907, 36 Stat. 2277, at 'III, Art. 55.

The occupying State [of a territory of the hostile State] shall be regarded only as administrator and usufructuary of public buildings, real estate, forests, and agricultural estates belonging to the hostile State, and situated in the occupied country. It must safeguard the capital of these properties, and administer them in accordance with the rules of usufruct.[400]

A good example is the relationship between Japan and the United States on Ryukyu Islands. After Japan surrendered, the United States occupied and administered the Ryukyu Islands, which are Japan's territory. The Peace Treaty of San Francisco of 1951[401] did not require Japan to cede its Ryukyu Islands to the United States, but acknowledged the United States' right to exercise all and any powers of administration, legislation, and jurisdiction over the territory and inhabitants of the islands. Thus, the United States did not acquire title to the Islands. It, as the occupying power (State), occupied the Islands until 1972 when it returned the Islands to Japan.[402]

5. A treaty which transfers a territory, called "the territorial treaty" in this work, has special characteristics which other kinds of treaties do not have. A separate treatment of territorial treaties follows.

2. TERRITORIAL TREATIES

Treaties between States have different functions. A treaty may be political, economic, military (i.e., defense alliances), cultural, or scientific in nature.

[400] Hague Convention Respecting The Laws and Customs of War on Land, 1907. *Id.* Annex to the Convention, Regulations Respecting the Laws and Customs of War on Land, Section III Military Authority Over the Territory of the Hostile State, Art. 55. The U.S. Department of the Army also incorporates the rule in the DEPARTMENT OF THE ARMY FIELD MANUAL (FOR) THE LAW OF LAND WARFARE. FM 27-10, Department of the Army, July 1956, amended July 15, 1976. Ch. 6 (Occupation) Sec.1 (General), Par. 353 (Subjugation or Conquest Distinguished) provides, "Belligerent occupation in a foreign war, being based upon the possession of enemy territory, necessarily implies that the sovereignty of the occupied territory is not vested in the occupying power. Occupation is essentially provisional." *Id.* par. 353. It further provides that "Being an incident of war, military occupation confers upon the invading force the means of exercising control for the period of occupation. It does not transfer the sovereignty to the occupant, but simply the authority or power to exercise some of the rights of sovereignty. It is unlawful for a belligerent occupant to annex occupied territory or to create a new State therein while hostilities are still in progress." *Id.* par. 358.

[401] *See infra* note 403.

[402] *See infra* text accompanying note 1044. The Treaty of San Francisco, Art. 3, *infra* note 403.

There is another type of treaty which is referred to as "territorial treaties" in this work. A territorial treaty affects the territories of the parties, e.g., delineating the territorial boundary, transferring the title to a piece of territory, dividing, or abandoning a territory. Historically, major wars between States ended through concluding peace treaties between the warring States.[403] Most peace treaties are also territorial treaties that reallocate territories of the defeated States.[404]

By their nature, territorial treaties are different from other types of treaties in many ways. They have the following characteristics. First, territorial treaties are proprietary as well as contractual in nature, while other types of treaties are purely contractual. Such territorial treaties, like deeds in municipal property law, involve a transfer of interest in a piece of land and affect the sovereign power of the parties to the treaties. Second, territorial treaties provide a final settlement of the territories between the parties. It has the characteristic of finality. Other types of treaties are executory and forward looking. For instance, these treaties may provide for cooperation in the future, or establish new rules of conduct between the contracting parties. Third, territorial treaties are self-executing: unless otherwise agreed, they take effect immediately when they enter into force. Other types of treaties usually require implementation and execution afterward by the parties. These characteristics of territorial treaties create the following principles and rules relating to territorial treaties.

1. The victorious State in a war may validly force the defeated State to dispose of its territories by a treaty. Title to the territories transferred or ceded by the defeated State is valid. A territorial treaty binds its parties even though the treaty benefits only one side. In concluding a treaty, both parties are on equal footing. Equal footing does not mean equal bargaining power, but both parties are bound by the treaty. This

[403] *See,* e.g., The Treaty of Verdun (845); Peace of Westphalia (1648); Treaty of Paris (1898); Treaty of Versailles (1915); Treaty of Peace With Japan, Sept. 8, 1951, 136 U.N.T.S. 46 (entered into force Apr. 28, 1952) [hereinafter the "Peace Treaty of San Francisco"]; *see also* Herz, *supra* note 25. Both sides in the Korean War signed an armistice when cease-fire took place in 1953. North Korea has demanded the United States and the other parties to the war signing a peace treaty to end the hostility between two sides. Since the signing of the armistice, both sides have maintained hundreds of thousands of troops at both sides of the border between North Korea and South Korea. N.Y. TIMES, 07/22/2005, A6, C3.

[404] For example, The Treaty of Versailles, 1919 (after WW I).

is particularly true in a peace treaty between the warring States concluding a war.

2. A territorial treaty's disposition is final. A territorial treaty in which a State cedes a territory to another State or renounces its title to a territory provides a final settlement of the territory. Once the territorial treaty enters into force, the treaty's disposition of the territory becomes effective.
3. A territorial treaty cannot be revoked, abrogated, or terminated. A treaty of executory nature may be revoked, abrogated, or terminated by one side subsequent to the conclusion,[405] but a territorial treaty cannot be revoked, abrogated, or terminated no matter how unfair it seems.[406]

   The only way for the transferor of a piece of territory by a treaty to regain the transferred territory is through a transfer by the transferee to the transferor by another treaty. Thus, a ceding State may regain title to the ceded territory from the acquiring State only through another treaty. This rule is drawn from State practice and the characteristics of a territorial treaty discussed earlier.[407] For example, Alsace and Loraine changed hands between Germany and France several times. Each time, the transfer was achieved by a treaty or an agreement.[408]
4. In a territorial treaty, only a party to the treaty can receive title to the territory. No State which is not a party to the treaty can receive title to the territory disposed of by the treaty. This rule is derived from the general principles of law recognized by civilized nations *a priori*. Under the general principles of law recognized by civilized nations, when title to a piece of land is conveyed by the grantor in a deed, only the other party to the deed can be the grantee to receive it.

[405] For instance, in 1939, after Japan blockaded British and French concessions in Tientsin City, China, the United States denounced its treaty of commerce with Japan. *See* Brad DeLong, *Review of Akira Iriye's The Origins of the Second World War in Asia and in the Pacific, available at* http://www.j-bradford-delong.net (Last visited 10/4/2004); *see also* Ibiblio, *A Chronological Collection of Documents Relating to the U.S. Entry Into WWII, available at* http://www.ibi8blio.org/pha/timeline/144chap4.html. Last visited 10/04/2004.

[406] Except, probably, on the ground of fraud in the execution or direct duress on the representatives who signed the treaty. Both are rare instances. *See,* e.g., David Wippman, *Treaty-Based Intervention: Who Can Say No?*, 62 U. Chi. L. Rev. 607, 634 (1995) (providing an example of possible grounds for condemnation of a treaty because of coercion).

[407] *See supra* text accompanying note 399.

[408] *See supra* note 395.

5. A territorial treaty binds the parties to the treaty. Under customary international law, it is a general rule that the parties to a treaty are bound by the treaty under the principle of *Pacta Sunt Servanda*.[409] The ceding State is bound by the treaty in which it ceded territory to another State; a treaty to cede a territory concluded at the end of a war is binding on both parties however unfair it may seem. This is because the defeated State is in a weaker bargaining position. No such treaty has ever been effectively revoked or terminated on the grounds of unfairness or unjust.

   A territorial treaty also binds other States which are not parties to the treaty. The general rule that a third party to a treaty is not bound by the treaty is subject to exceptions created by international customary law.[410] The Vienna Convention of 1969 also recognizes exceptions to the general rule. Article 38 of the Vienna Convention provides that "[n]othing in Articles 34 to 37 precludes a rule set forth in a treaty from becoming binding upon a third [S]tate as a customary rule of international law, recognized as such."[411] One exception created by the international customary law applies to territorial treaties.[412] The exception is that territorial treaties produce obligations which third parties must observe.[413] This exception is one of customary international law that has developed from long-held State practice that territorial treaties are rarely challenged by a third party. For the same reason, such treaties also bind international organizations, such as the United Nations.
6. Words and language used in territorial treaties are precise and unambiguous. Since territorial treaties stipulate the final settlement between the parties, or provide the final disposition of territories, they cannot leave room for doubt or dispute on its meaning. The treaties use definite and precise terms, such as "cede," "divide," "relinquish," or "renounce" to dispose of a territory. In rare cases where there is a dispute on the meaning of a term or terms, the ordinary meaning of the

[409] *See* Mark W. Janis, An Introduction to International Law, 2d Ed. 1993, at 9–11 (discussing the principle of *pacta sunt servanda*). *See also* Vienna Convention, *supra* note 365, Art. 26. *See Id.*

[410] *See* Wallace, *supra* notes 36, at 241–42 (discussing the principle of *pacta tertiis nec nocent nec prosunt*).

[411] Vienna Convention, *supra* note 365, Art. 38. *See Id.* (discussing the binding authority of customary international law on third parties).

[412] *See* Wallace, *supra* note 36, at 242.

[413] *Id.*

words of the treaty and the intention of the parties control. This approach is the general rule of interpreting treaties,[414] which was recognized and adopted by the 1969 Vienna Convention.[415] In addition, when a provision in a territorial treaty enumerates specific items or places, the enumeration is also a word of limitation. Items or places not enumerated are excluded.

3. SECESSION AND THE TERRITORIAL STATE

A. Meaning of Secession

The PRC (the People's Republic of China) government promulgated an "Anti-secession Law" in 2005 to intimidate the Taiwan independence movement.[416] Whether China has such a right in international law and whether or not such a law would apply to the people in Taiwan are issues to be discussed later. This section addresses the concept of secession in the context of the territorial State.

Secession is defined as "the fact of an area or group becoming independent from the country or larger group that it belongs to."[417] Thus, secession and independence are closely related concepts. Secession by a region in a State often leads to independence of the region from the State. The most common justification for a group of people to seek secession is the desire for independence.

As discussed earlier, both the modern State and the neo-modern State are territorial States: the State is predicated on territory; territory is an element of the State. Thus, a secession of a region from a ruling State to establish a new State invariably means that the secessionists establish a new State based upon territory inside its ruling State. The ruling State loses a portion of its territory and sovereignty over that portion of its territory and its inhabitants.

[414] *Id.*, at 240. In the Peace Treaty of Sevres, Turkey "renounces" all her rights and title over Palestine. *See supra* note 325.

[415] Vienna Convention, *supra* note 365. Art. 2.1(a). The Convention essentially codified customary international law. *See* WALLACE, *supra* note 36, at 230. Article 31 of the Convention provides interpretive methodologies for all treaties. *See Id.* at 240.

[416] The Anti-secession Law, *infra* note 889.

[417] *See* OXFORD ADVANCED LEARNER'S DICTIONARY, *supra* note 213, at 1152 (providing the definition of "secession").

Historically, beginning in the 5th century A.D., after the peoples settled down in Europe and established their kingdoms, most new States were established by secession from existing States. One such case was the secession of three Swiss Cantons from the Holy Roman Empire in the 13th century. A more recent case is the secession of Kosovo from Serbia in 2008.[418] The reason why secession is the most common way of State creation is that nearly every inhabitable land on the earth is already a territory claimed by some State, so that usually a new State has to be established within the territory of an existing State. For instance, most States created after World War II were former colonies of the West European powers.

B. Justification for Secession—Self-Determination

In many European States, a minority group of people within the State declared independence and seceded from it after the Second World War. They established the new States in the name of self-determination.

The doctrine of self-determination was a heated issue in the 20th century, especially after World War II. In its historical context, during the 18th and 19th centuries, self-determination was a concept in the ideology of nationalism,[419] meaning a minority group of people inhabiting in an area within a State deciding their own future.[420] Such a group of people usually have the same social, ethnic, or cultural backgrounds, or a combination thereof, and are different from the majority of the people of the State. During the 20th century, the concept of self-determination was strengthened by the doctrine of human rights that it is the human right of a group of people to secede from its ruling State and establish a new State.[421]

[418] Kosovo declared independence on February 17, 2008. N.Y. TIMES, 02/18/2008, A. p. 1., C6.

[419] *See* HANNUM, *supra* note 31, at 27; *see also* Otto Hintze, *The Emergence of the Democratic Nation-State,* [*DAS DURCHBRUCH DES DEMOKRATISCHEN NATIONALSTAATES IN DER AMERIKANISCHEN UND FRANZOESISCHEN REVOLUTION*] *STAAT UND VERFASSUNG* at 503-10 (2d Ed. Guettingen, Vandenhoeck & Ruprecht) (*trans. By* LUBASZ,) *in THE DEVELOPMENT OF THE MODERN STATE*, *supra* note 15, at 69.

[420] *See* HANNUM, *supra* note 31, at 36.

[421] Although some States are not as ready to recognize such right for minority groups of people who reside in their territories, e.g., Russia for Chechens, Turkey for Kurds. Anatol Lieven, Letters-Review, NAT'L INTEREST, Winter 2000 (reviewing Zbigniew Brzezinski, *Living with Russia* (Fall 2000)), *available at* http://www.findarticles.com/p/articles/mi_m2751/is_2000_Winter/ai_68547483/print. Last visited 11/18/2004.

At issue in international law is whether a minority group of people inhabiting in a region or a constituent unit of the State has the right to secede from its ruling State in the name of self-determination without the consent of its ruling State. If self-determination is recognized as a *right* in international law, then it sets a limitation on the sovereign power of the ruling State.[422]

C. Attitude of the Ruling States

In some cases, the secession by a region or a constituent unit of a State which led to the establishment of a new State was achieved with the consent or the grant of its ruling State. In such cases, the ruling State then recognized the new State almost immediately.

In many cases, however, a ruling State would not permit a region or a constituent unit to secede.[423] The attempt of 11 southern States of the United States to secede from the Union led to the American Civil War in 1861. Many colonies or constituent units succeeded in seceding from their ruling State after bloodshed. In such a case, the ruling State usually refused to recognize the new State, at least initially. The three Swiss Cantons that declared independence from the Holy Roman Empire in 1291 were not formally recognized by the Empire until 1648 in the Peace of Westphalia, more than 350 years later.[424] In the case of the 13 English Colonies in North America, it took 7 years (including 5 years of bloody battles) from July of 1776 when they declared independence until September of 1783 when the Treaty of Paris was signed for Great Britain to recognize their independence.[425]

[422] The conflict is described to be one between natural law and positive law. *See* ANTONIO CASSESE, SELF-DETERMINATION OF PEOPLES: A LEGAL REAPPRAISAL 44–46 (Cambridge Univ. Press, 1995). Antonio Cassese states:

> *[S]elf-determination is a powerful expression of the underlying tensions and contradictions of international legal theory: it perfectly reflects the cyclical oscillation between positivism and natural law, between an emphasis on consent, that is, voluntarism, and an emphasis on binding "objective" legal principles, between a "statist" and a communitarian vision of world order.*

Id. at 1.

[423] Examples are Turkey to Kurds; Russia to Chechens.

[424] *See supra* note 314.

[425] British General Lord Cornwallis surrendered on Oct. 19, 1781.

D. Attitude of the Other States

Internationally, a secession of a region or a constituent unit from its ruling State without the latter's consent has been objected to by some other States. South Ossetia in 1991 and Abkhazia in 1992 declared independence from the State of Georgia against its will. Georgia refused to recognize their independence on the grounds that their declarations were instigated by Russia. In 2008, Russia sent its army into South Ossetia to fight Georgia's army on the grounds of protecting the right of the people of South Ossetia to secede. Other States refused to recognize South Ossetia and Abkhazia as States. By March 1, 2017, only six States have recognized South Ossetia and six States have recognized Abkazia as States.

On the other hand, some States recognized a new State immediately after it had seceded from its ruling State without its consent. In the case of Kosovo's independence from Serbia, Western States were quick to recognize it. One day after Kosovo declared independence from Serbia and established statehood, the United States, the United Kingdom, France, and Germany were quick to recognize the new State. But Russia and China condemned Kosovo's independence. Spain also refused to recognize it. Russia and China claimed that "Kosovo's independence was a reckless breach of international law that would spur other secessionist movements across the world."[426] They condemned Kosovo's independence as a "breach of international law" without specifying the rule of international law that was breached. The motive of Russia and China in condemning Kosovo's independence and Spain's refusal to recognize the

[426] *Id.* Dan Bilefsky *World Court Rules Kosovo Declaration Was Legal*, NY TIMES. 07/22/2010. *Also available at* http://www.nytimes.com/2010/07/23/world/europe/23kosovo.html?_r = 1. Last visited 04/11/2011. During the hearing in International Court of Justice for giving an advisory opinion on the Declaration of Independence by Kosovo, the PRC government submitted the following opinion: "There is no doubt that after the breakup of the Socialist Federal Republic of Yugoslavia, Kosovo was a part of the Federal Republic of Yugoslavia, that is, Serbia. Integral parts of sovereign states, under international law, do not have a right to unilateral secession ... while the principle of protection of territorial integrity is a cornerstone of international legal order. Sovereign states have a right to prevent unilateral secessions and protect their integrity. The unilateral proclamation is a violation of mandatory UNSC Resolution 1244 and this resolution is binding. In 1999 China insisted that the provision on the territorial integrity and sovereignty be included in the resolution, which came after NATO's illegal military attack and for this reason China did not block Resolution 1244," *available at* https://en.wikipedia.org/wiki/International_Court_of_Justice_advisory_opinion_on_Kosovo's_declaration_of_independence. Last visited 04/11/2011.

State of Kosovo was clear. They all had secessionist activities within their own borders. The International Court of Justice in July 2010 ruled in an advisory opinion requested by the UN General Assembly that Kosovo's declaration of independence was legal.[427] By July 2010, more than 69 States recognized Kosovo.[428]

In the 20th century, a great majority of the international community supported the right of self-determination.[429] International conventions concluded after World War II also embraced this principle.[430] Article I of the UN Charter describes one of its purposes as "[t]o develop friendly relations among nations based on the principle of equal rights and *self-determination* of peoples."[431] One argument of the West supporting Kosovo's independence from Serbia was that "Serbia's brutal subjugation of Kosovo's ethnic Albanian majority cost it any right to rule the territory."[432] This argument indicates that a condition for Kosovo's independence was the suppression of the ruling State against the Muslim minority group. However, no convention that embraces the right of self-determination imposes suppression of the ruling State as a condition for the right of self-determination.

The concept of the State, the theory of sovereignty, and international law on territory discussed above will be the bases of analyses that follow on the issues raised in the Introduction on the political status of the Republic of China and Taiwan, as well as on the legal status of the island of Taiwan.

[427] Mike Corder, *World court says Kosovo's independence is legal*. Associated Press, 07/22/2010. *available at* http://news.yahoo.com/s/ap/eu_world_court_kosovo. Last visited 07/22/2010.

[428] *Id.*

[429] William R. Cumming, *Self-Determination and National Security Concerns*, *available at* http://faculty.lls.edu/~manheimk/ns/cumming.htm. Last visited 11/08/2004.

[430] *See* The U.N. Charter, *supra* note 383, Art. 1; *see also Int'l Covenant on Civil and Political Rights*, *supra* note 353; *Int'l Covenant on Economic, Social and Cultural Rights*, *supra* note 352. Article 1 of the two Covenants provides that "All peoples have the right of self-determination. By virtue of that right they freely determine their political status and freely pursue their economic, social and cultural development." *Int'l Covenant on Civil and Political Rights*, *supra*; *Int'l Covenant on Economic, Social and Cultural Rights*, *supra*.

[431] The U.N. Charter, *Id.*, Art. 1, Sec. 2 (emphasis added).

[432] Dan Bilefsky, *In a showdown, Kosovo declares its independence*, N.Y. Times, 02/18/2008, Sec. A p. 1.

PART II

China and The Republic of China

CHAPTER 4

The State and Governments of China

Contents

A question raised in the Introduction concerns the political status of the Republic of China (the ROC): whether the ROC in Taiwan is a State. Both former President Lee Teng-hui and his successor former President Chen Shui-bian of the ROC made some controversial remarks while in office implying that the ROC was a State. This chapter discusses the political status of the ROC in State theory and international law. It begins with a brief overview of the State known as China in the West followed by an examination of the relationship between the ROC and China. It then discusses whether the Republic of China in Taiwan has become a State under the traditional concept of State and international law discussed in Chapter 2, The State and Sovereignty. Whether or not Taiwan has become a State is a different issue to be dealt with in Chapter 9, The Legal Status and The Political Status of Taiwan in International Law.

The One-China Policy: State, Sovereignty, and Taiwan's International Legal Status
DOI: http://dx.doi.org/10.1016/B978-0-08-102314-3.00004-5

1. THE STATE OF CHINA

The largest State in the world by population is in East Asia. The English call the State "China." The French call it *La Chine,* and the German, *Das China*. The Chinese call their country *Zhong* (*Chung*) *Guo* or "Middle Country."

The state of China was established in 221 BC. During the Warring States Period of the feudal *Zhou* (Chou) Dynasty,[433] the king of Chin, who succeeded his father as a king of a secondary state within feudal *Zhou* (Chou) Dynasty, began to conquer other secondary states within the Dynasty. By 221 BC, he unified the country by annexing the feudal king's domain and the territories of other secondary states. The king of Chin established an empire called "Chin" and named himself "Chin *Shih Huang*" or the First Emperor of Chin. The name "Chin" became the name of the unified country.[434] Historians consider 221 BC the year in which the State of China was established. The English name "China" was derived from the Latin word "Chin," which was the Latin name for the country later known

[433] Traditional historians divide the *Zhou* (Chou) Dynasty (1122-221 BC) into Western *Zhou* (Chou) (1122-770 BC) and Eastern *Zhou* (Chou) (770-221 BC). The Warring States Period was named for a period (403-221 BC) toward the end of feudal Eastern *Zhou* (Chou) Dynasty, during which seven major secondary autonomous states under *Zhou* (Chou) Dynasty fought among them. The secondary states were Chin, Han, *Zhao* (Chao), Wei, Chu, Yen, and *Qi* (Chi). The Warring States Period ended in 221 BC when the king of Chin established Chin Empire. For romanization of the Chinese characters, this work uses the *pingyin* system adopted by the PRC government but uses the Wade-Giles system when it is used in a quotation, and for the surname of the First Emperor of Chin and the name of the Empire he created. The spellings (in roman) in parentheses which follow *pingyin* (in *italic*) are the phonetic equivalent in the Wade-Giles system.

[434] In the Wade-Giles system, the Chinese word 秦 [pronounced "chin" in Chinese], which was the surname of the king who established the Empire, was romanized as "Chin." *See* A Chinese-English Dictionary by Herbert A. Giles, Shanghai, China (1892), 2nd Ed.(1912), Shanghai and London; reprinted in 1967 by Che'eng-Wen Publishing Co. Taipei, Taiwan.

as "China."[435] Since then, China was a monarchy for 2000 years until 1912 when it became a republic.

Many Chinese political philosophers prior to the establishment of Chin Empire advanced their political theories regarding ways and means by which a king should rule his kingdom. There were three major schools of political philosophers who proposed to the kings the statecraft of ruling their subjects: the Taoist School, which theorized a direct connection between the king and Heaven, maintained that nonactivity or passivity was the best way for a king to govern his kingdom; the Confucianist (*Ru*) School stressed that a king should govern his subjects with the principles of benevolence and virtues; the Legalist (*Fa*) School emphasized the use of penal laws to rule the king's subjects. The First Emperor of Chin appointed a Legalist as his chancellor and adopted the Legalist theory to rule the country.

Adhering to the Legalist philosophy, the First Emperor of Chin established two major institutions to govern the country. One was the administrative system: a political system of a centralized administration to

[435] *See* SHIN EIWA CHU JI TEN (NEW COLLEGE ENGLISH-JAPANESE DICTIONARY), Kenkyusha Co. 7th Ed., Tokyo, 2003. The Japanese adopted many Chinese characters into their written language and called them Kan Ji (Kan character) or Kan Go (Kan language). They pronounced Kan characters different from the Chinese pronunciations. Its entry of English word "China" defines the word as "[in Kan characters] 中国 [pronounced 'chukoku' in Japanese: middle country]; [Latin] Chin 秦 [pronounced 'shin' in Japanese], name of a dynasty in the 3rd cen. BC," *Id.* at 304. The definition indicates that the origin of the English word "China" is the Latin word "Chin."

In *ZHENG ZHONG XING YING YI ZONG HE DA ZI DIAN* or *CHENG CHONG'S* CHARACTER, PHONETICS, AND SEMANTICS COMPREHENSIVE DICTIONARY [正中形音義綜合大字典 in Chinese], Cheng Chong Book Co., Taipei (1971), the entry of the Chinese word 秦 [romanized as "chin"] defines it as "The name which in ancient time Western Regions called what is today China (BOOK on HAN DYNASTY: Western Regions)." *Id.* at 1232. This definition cites BOOK on HAN DYNASTY as its source. Han Dynasty succeeded Chin Dynasty in 206 BC and lasted until AD 189 in the 2nd century. Thus, according to BOOK on HAN DYNASTY, after Han Dynasty succeeded Chin Dynasty, peoples in the western regions continued to call the country "Chin." This definition of the Chinese word 秦 (ch'in) is in accord with the definition of the word 秦 (chin) in A CHINESE-ENGLISH DICTIONARY, *supra* note 434, which defines the Chinese word 秦 [romanized as "ch'in"] as "Used down to the 2nd cent. AD as a name for China." *Id.* at 261 (Entry of the Chinese word 秦). These definitions agree that subsequent to Chin Dynasty the western regions continued to call the country "Chin." Thus, during the early Roman Empire, the Roman called the empire in the East "Chin" in Latin. Consequently, when subsequently the French, German, and English languages developed, the French word *la Chine*, the German word *das China*, and the English word "China" were derived from the Latin word "Chin."

replace the feudal system of the earlier *Zhou* (Chou) Dynasty. The system divided the Empire into provinces; provinces into prefectures. The Emperor ruled his subjects directly through governors of the provinces and prefects of the prefectures appointed by him. The new political system was similar to the modern State in Europe discussed in this work in that the Emperor ruled his subjects directly, but the nature of the power of the Emperor was different from sovereignty as defined by Bodin.[436] The other institution that the Chin Empire established was a judicial system with a penal code to govern his subjects.

The administrative and the judicial systems were adopted by successive Chinese Dynasties. After the Chin Dynasty, for 2000 years imperial China was ruled by successive dynasties: chronologically the *Han*, *Sui*, *Tang*, *Song* (later divided into Northern *Song* and Southern *Song*), *Yuan* (The Mongolian), *Ming*, and the last, *Qing* (Ching) (The Manchu).[437] The Chinese Dynasties, like British Houses and French Dynasties, were governments in terms of modern political science. While the governments changed, the Empire (State) remained the same. Many systems of Chin government including the administrative and the judicial systems were adopted by the successive Dynasties. By the time of *Qing* (Ching) Dynasty, the last dynasty before the republic, the penal code, the Great *Qing* (Ching) Code, had expanded to consist of more than two thousand articles.[438]

The traditional Chinese political philosophers did not make a clear distinction between the concept of State and the concept of government.[439]

436 For instance, Chinese Emperors did not treat other kings their equal. *See infra* note 450.

437 The names in the parentheses following the name of Dynasty are the peoples who ruled the dynasties.

438 The first edition of the *Qing* (Ching) Code (*Ta Qing L Li* or *Ta* Ching Lü *Li*) or The Laws and Statutes of Great *Qing* (Ching) promulgated in 1644 contained about 450 sections of Laws (*L*) and about 2000 sections of Statutes (*Li*).

439 A Chinese-English Dictionary, *supra* note 434, defines the Chinese word 国 [romanized as *guo* or "kuo"] in English as "A nation; a kingdom; a State; a country; the capital of a country; a dynasty; a house or line." *Id.* at 836. Thus, the Chinese word *guo* may mean "country" or "dynasty." It also defines the Chinese term 清国 [romanized as *qingguo* or "ching kuo"] as "The Manchu Dynasty; China." *Id.* at 837. Again, the Chinese word 国 [romanized as *guo*] may mean "dynasty."

Dynasty means government or house. The Manchu Dynasty is called 清朝 [romanized as *qing* (ch'ing) *chao*] in Chinese. A Chinese-English Dictionary, *Id.*, defines the Chinese term 清朝 (romanized as *qing chao* or ch'ing chao) as "The Pure Dynasty-of the Manchu Tartars or the present [The year 1892 when the Dictionary was first published] rulers of China." *Id.* at 277. Likewise, it defines the Chinese term 明朝 [romanized as "ming ch'ao"] as "The Ming dynasty, AD 1366–1644." *Id.* at 985. In sum, the Chinese word 朝 (*chao*) means dynasty (house) or government of China. Thus, the Chinese word "guo" may mean government.

In the prerepublic China, the two concepts were not clearly delineated and the traditional Chinese political theories rarely touched upon the distinction between the two concepts; consequently, discourse on the relation between State and government was conspicuously lacking.

Until the 20th century, the Chinese did not use an official country name for the country established by the First Emperor of Chin known to the West as "China." From the Chin Dynasty on, while the West called the country "Chin" or its derivatives such as French *la Chine,* English "China," and German *das China,* Chinese called their country by the name of the Dynasty of their time. Thus, Tang Dynasty (618–907) was also called Tang Empire; *Qing* (Ching) Dynasty (1644–1911) was also called "*Da Qing* (Ching) *Di Guo*" (Great *Qing* (Ching) Empire) or simply "*Qing* (Ching) *Guo*" or "*Qing* (Ching) country."

During the Tokugawa and the Meiji Japan, the Japanese called China *Shin or Shin koku*[440] which are the Japanese pronunciation of the Chinese characters *Qing* (Ching) or *Qing* (Ching) *guo* (*Qing* country) respectively. Thus, while the English version of the Treaty of Shimonoseki (1895) between Japan and China begins with "His Majesty the Emperor of Japan and His Majesty the Emperor of China, desiring to restore the blessings of peace to their countries and subjects . . .," the literal English translation of the official Japanese version of the Treaty is, "The Peace Treaty between His Majesty the Emperor of Great Japan Empire and His Majesty the Emperor of Great *Shin* Empire"[441] because Japan also called the State of China by its dynasty's name, *Shin* (*Qing* in Chinese). The Japanese began to call China *Shi na* toward the end of the 19th century

[440] Tokugawa Shogunate, a military government established by Tokugawa Iyeyasu and ruled Japan from 1603 to 1867, was with some variation contemporary to *Qing* (Ching) Dynasty of China (1644–1911). The Chinese words 清国 (romanized as *qing-guo* in Chinese) are pronounced *Shin koku* in Japanese. Shin Sen Koku Go Ji Ten (Shin Sen Dictionary of National [Japanese] Language), Rev. Ed., ed. by Ichi Kyotsuke Kinda, Shou Gaku Kan Co. Tokyo, 1965. Its entry of the Japanese word シン(Kan character 清) [pronounced "shin" in Japanese] defines the term as "China's Dynasty from 17th cen. to the beginning of the 20th century," *Id.* at 421.

[441] The Treaty of Shimonoseki, *see infra* note 454. The Treaty concluded the Sino-Japan War in 1895 during Meiji Emperor's reign. In Mei Kai Dictionary of National [Japanese] Language, Rev. Ed., ed. by Ichi Kyotsuke Kinda, Sansei Do Co. Tokyo, 1966, the entry of the Japanese words ニッシン(Kan characters 日清) [pronounced "nii shin" in Japanese] defines the term as "(between) Japan and Shin koku (Kan character 清国 or China)" *Id.* at 645.

during the Meiji era.[442] The term *Shi na* is considered by the Chinese as a derogatory expression, and ceases in use after World War II.

After the 1911 Revolution overthrowing the *Qing* (Ching) government, the name that the Chinese call their country is *Zhong* (Chung) *guo* or "Middle Country." Although *zhong* (chung) *guo* or "middle country" was a term used by the Chinese since ancient times to refer to "the kingdom situated in the center of the earth,"[443] the Chinese term was not used as a formal name of the country until the 20th century, after China became a republic.

In contrast, the States in the West have had a name for the State since their establishment. By practice, peoples adopted the name of their people or the land they inhabited as the name of their country. For instance, what is France today was part of Charlemagne's Empire of Salian Franks and was called *Francia Occidentalis* where Salian Franks established a kingdom.[444] The French have called their country "France" since then.

The English have used the name "Britain" or "England" for their country since its establishment. In 927, when Athelstan became the first king to rule all England, he called himself "King of all Britain."[445] King John in the 1215 Magna Carta signed his name as "John, King of England."[446]

In the Western political theories, the State and the government are distinguished, as witnessed by the writings of Bodin, Locke, and

[442] For the country name of China, the Japanese adopted Japanese words "シナ" [in katakana form of Japanese characters, pronounced "shi na"] after Japanese students sent by Meiji government to study in Germany returned to Japan. The words pronounced as "shi na" are the Japanese phonetic equivalent of the German word "China." For the Kan characters of the Japanese term シナ (*shi na*), the Japanese adopted the characters 支那 (pronounced "shi na"). MEIKAI DICTIONARY of NATIONAL [JAPANESE] LANGUAGE, *Id.* Its entry of Japanese words シナ (Kan characters 支那 or China) defines the term as "The old name of the country called 中国 [pronunced "chukoku" in Japanese]," *Id.* at 357. *See also* SHIN SEN DICTIONARY of NATIONAL [JAPANESE] LANGUAGE, *supra* note 440. Its entry of the Japanese words シナ (支那 or China) defines the term, using Kan characters, as "中国," *Id.* at 305.

[443] A CHINESE ENGLISH DICTIONARY, *supra* note 434, defines the Chinese term 中国 [romanized as *zhong* (chung)-*kuo* (guo)] as "middle kingdom, from a belief that it was situated at the center of a vast square earth, surrounded by Four Seas, beyond which lay islands inhabited by barbarians." *Id.*, at 358. In Tang Code (AD 618–907) and the Code of Great Qing (Ching), referred to in note 438, the term *zhong* (chung)-*kuo* (guo) (middle kingdom) was never used, let alone as the official name of the country.

[444] The Treaty of Verdun, 843.

[445] THE NEW ENCYCLOPEDIA BRITANNICA, 15th Ed. *supra* note 7 in Chapter 1, V 29, at 29 (the entry of "United Kingdom.")

[446] *Id.* V.7. at 674 (the entry of "Magna Carta.")

Montesquieu. Thus, during the 19th century, even though the Chinese regarded *Qing* (Ching) as their country's name,[447] to the West, China was the name of the State and *Qing* (Ching) Dynasty was the name of the government of China.

That *Qing* (Ching) Dynasty was a government of the State of China can be seen from the following several instances of State practice in international relations. The first instance was in diplomatic recognition. As mentioned in Chapter 2, The State and Sovereignty, diplomatic relations are between States. During the era when the European States were expanding trade to the East, the Empire of China was ruled by *Qing* (Ching) Dynasty, which lasted from 1644 to 1911. Great Britain was the first among the Western States in modern times to establish formal diplomatic relations with China. In 1793, King George III sent George Macartney as an envoy to China to open trade in northern China.[448] When the English envoy presented his credentials to Emperor Qian (Ch'ien) Lung[449] of *Qing* (Ching) Dynasty, Great Britain established diplomatic relations with the Empire of China. The act of Great Britain was recognition of the State of China as it was the first time Great Britain made formal diplomatic contact with the State of China.[450] And it also

[447] *See supra* text accompanying note 441. The Chinese Americans living in New York City call China Town "*Tang-ren* Street" today. *Tang-ren* means the people of Tang, referring to Tang Dynasty of the 6th century. CONTINENTAL'S CONCISE ENGLISH-CHINESE DICTIONARY, Ta Lu Book Co. Rev. Ed., Taipei, Taiwan, 1978. Its entry of "China town" defines the term in Chinese as "唐人街 (*Tang-ren* Street)." *Id.* at 225.

[448] *See* JOHN K. FAIRBANK & EDWIN O. REISCHAUER, CHINA, TRADITION AND TRANSFORMATION 256-57 (Rev. Ed, 1989); DWARF TREES FROM LORD MACARTNEY, *available at* http://www.pjoenixbonsai.com/pre1800Refs/Macartney.html. Last visited 03/23/09.

[449] Qian (Ch'ien) Lung Emperor reigned from 1736 to 1796. A CHINESE ENGLISH DICTIONARY, *supra* note 434, at 23.

[450] George Macartney was the first British envoy to China. "Macartney, along with visiting Mongols and Burmese, was then given a single imperial audience and presents for his mission and the King. He received no state dinner. Macartney was received only as a tribute bearer. The prepared verdict (of Emperor Ch'ien Lung) acknowledged King George III's 'sincere humility and obedience' in sending a tribute mission to the Emperor. It also absolutely rejected the proposals for changing the existing trade arrangements since they did not conform to the Celestial Empire's ceremonial system.' The edict also admonished the British monarch to 'act in conformity with our wishes by strengthening your loyalty and swearing perpetual obedience.'" *Available at* http://www.pjoenixbonsai.com/pre1800Refs/Macartney.html. Last visited 03/23/09.

signified recognition of the *Qing* (Ching) authority as China's legitimate government.[451]

The second instance of State practice indicating that *Qing* (Ching) Dynasty was the government of the State of China was in the treatment of wars and peace treaties. As stated in Chapter 2, The State and Sovereignty, wars are between States in international law, though they are conducted by their governments. A treaty signed by the governments to end a war is also an agreement between the warring States. Thus, the Opium War of 1841 was a war between the British Empire and the Empire of China, though the fighting was between the British Navy and *Qing* (Ching)'s armed forces. When *Qing* (Ching)'s Army was defeated, the *Qing* (Ching) Emperor and the English King signed the Treaty of Nanjing (Nanking) (1842).[452] The treaty was between the British Empire and the Empire of China.

Likewise, the Sino-Japanese War of 1894 was a war between the Empire of China and the Empire of Japan.[453] When *Qing* (Ching)'s armed forces were defeated in that war, the treaty of peace mentioned earlier known as the Treaty of Shimonoseki signed by the *Qing* (Ching) government and the Japanese government was an agreement between the Empire of China and the Empire of Japan.[454] Thus, although the English version of the treaty begins with "His Majesty the Emperor of Japan and

[451] *See* HACKWORTH, *supra* note 166, at 167,168; *see also* The Montevideo Convention, *supra* note 292, Art. 7. According to Fairbank and Reischauer, the Chinese Emperor regarded other countries tributes, and Emperor Chien Lung praised King George III's "respectful spirit of submission." FAIRBANK & REISCHAUER, *supra* note 448, at 257. The *Qing* (Ching) Emperor lacked the concept of state equality and asked the English envoy, Macartney, to kowtow like emissaries from tribute countries, which he refused. The Emperor would probably have executed Macartney, if Macartney had said to the Emperor that the King of England would recognize him as equal. Nevertheless, the visit should be considered recognition from the viewpoint of the English king. But in 1816 British ambassador, Lord Amhurst, was sent away from Peking without being received. ENCYCLOPEDIA OF WORLD HISTORY, *supra* note 393, at 877.

[452] This is the Treaty of Nanjing (Nanking), signed August 29, 1842 in which China ceded Hong Kong to the United Kingdom.

[453] The Japanese call the war of 1894 between Japan and China "the Nii-Shin War." "Nii" is romanized Japanese Kan character 日, meaning Japan; "Shin" is romanized Japanese Kan character 清, meaning Qing (Ching) Dynasty: China. *See supra* text accompanying note 440.

[454] This is the Treaty of Peace, signed on Apr. 17, 1895, China–Japan, 181 Consol. T.S. 217 [hereinafter the "Treaty of Shimonoseki"]. In the Treaty, China ceded Formosa and the Pescadores to Japan.

His Majesty the Emperor of China,"[455] the English title of the Treaty is "Treaty between China and Japan, signed at Shimonoseki, April 17, 1895."[456] Other States, such as the United States, France, Germany, and Russia, which signed treaties with *Qing* (Ching) Dynasty during the 19th century also regarded the treaties as between them and the State of China.[457] Consequently, a treaty signed by the government of a State binds the State and its succeeding governments.

The third instance of State practice indicating that *Qing* (Ching) Dynasty was the government of the State of China was in the treatment of the sovereign debt. A debt which a government incurs is the debt of the State. Thus, bonds issued by the *Qing* (Ching) government were sovereign bonds, for which succeeding governments were also liable.[458]

2. THE GOVERNMENTS IN MODERN CHINA

China saw two drastic transformations of its political system during the 20th century. Both took place when a new government was established. The first transformation of China's political system was from a monarchy to a republic when *Qing* (Ching) Dynasty was replaced by the ROC. The ruling class in China during *Qing* (Ching) Dynasty was the Manchu people from Manchuria in the northeast of China, who established *Qing* (Ching) Dynasty in 1644. It ruled China for 266 years when the Han Chinese, led by the Nationalists, overthrew it and established a republic in 1912, replacing the monarchy.

The Nationalist Chinese who established the ROC believed that they had established a State. That the prerepublic Chinese did not make a clear distinction between the concept of State and the concept of government most likely had contributed to the modern Chinese characterization of "the Republic of China." They called their country "the Republic of China (ROC)," and their government "the ROC

455 *Id.*

456 *Id.*

457 For instance, the French version of the original text of the Second International Conference (Convention) of Peace, singed in 1907 at the Hague, lists "La Chine" as a party to the Conference. MARTENS, NOUVEAU RECUEIL GENERAL DE TRAITES. T. III Ser. 3, 1910, 323 at 329. The German translation of the same Convention also lists "China" as a party.

458 *See infra* text accompanying note 472.

Provisional Government," "the ROC Beiyang Government," or "the ROC Nationalist Government."[459]

Their perception that the ROC was a "State" at the time was also reflected in the ROC Constitution of 1946.[460] Article 2 of the Constitution provides that "The sovereignty *of* the ROC or *Zhong* (*Chung*) *Hua Min Guo* belongs to the entire body of nationals."[461] If the ROC had sovereignty, then the ROC was a State because as explained in Chapter 2, The State and Sovereignty, in a neo-modern State sovereignty resides in the State. The Nationalist Chinese also regarded the title to the Chinese territory to be in the ROC. Article 3 provides that "The territory *of* the ROC, consisting of the originally owned areas, cannot be changed without a resolution of the National Assembly."[462] If the title to the Chinese territory is in the ROC, then the ROC is a State because, as discussed in Chapter 2, The State and Sovereignty, territory is an element of the neo-modern State and belongs to the State.

Other instances also reflected their perception. For instance, Jiang (Chiang) Kai-shek, the leader of the Chinese Nationalists, idolized the revolutionary leader, Sun Yat-sen, by installing him as "Father of the Country," mimicking the characterization of George Washington as "Father" of the United States of America.

The Nationalist Chinese called the ROC a "country." The English name "the Republic of China" is a translation of the Chinese name *Zhong* (Chung) *Hua Min Guo*, a name adopted by the Nationalists who had overthrown the *Qing (*Ching) government. The last character *Guo* in *Zhong* (Chung) *Hua Min Guo* means "country."[463] They adopted the

[459] The ROC Provisional Government, 1912–13, seated in Nanjing (Nanking). It effectively governed southern China only. In the north, Beiyang Government, 1912–28, seated in Beijing (Peking) was controlled by warlords, *available at* http://en.wikipedia.org/wiki/Beiyang_Government. Last visited 10/8/2013. In the south, the R.O.C. Nationalist Government, 1925–1948, seated in Nanjing(Nanking).

[460] *Zong* (Chung) Hua Minkuo Hsienfa (Constitution of the Republic Of China) (adopted by the National Assembly on Dec. 25, 1946, promulgated by the National Government in Nanjing (Nanking) on Jan. 1, 1947, effective Dec. 25, 1947, *available at* http://www.oop.gov.tw/roc/charter/echarter.htm. The 1991 Amendment to the Constitution of the Republic of China, Articles 1–10, was promulgated on May 1, 1991; The 1992 Amendment, Articles 11–18, was promulgated in May of 1992.

[461] Constitution of the ROC in Article 2 (emphasis added).

[462] *Id.* (emphasis added).

[463] While the Chinese word 国 (*guo*) generally means "country," it may also mean "dynasty" or "government." *See supra* text accompanying note 439.

name *Zhong* (Chung) *Hua Min Guo* (the ROC) because they believed they established a country in 1912.

In joining the United Nations, Jiang (Chiang) Kai-shek also used the name "the Republic of China" as the name of his country.[464] When the United Nations was formed in 1945, China was a founding member and was also a permanent member of its Security Council. But the name that China used to join the United Nations was "The Republic of China," not "China."

Whatever the Chinese people characterized "the Republic of China," to other States, "the Republic of China" was only a government of the State of China. The Nationalist Chinese established a new government, not a new State. Although the form of the State changed from a monarchy to a republic, the territorial political institution as a State remained the same because the essential components of the political institution—the people and the territory—remained the same.

That the ROC was a government of the State of China before it moved to Taiwan can be seen from a few instances of State practice in its relations with other States. The first instance was in the diplomatic recognition by other States. The US Government recognized the ROC in 1913. In 1979 when the US Government recognized the People's Republic of China (PRC) as the new legitimate government of China, it simultaneously withdrew its recognition of the ROC. As discussed in Chapter 2, The State and Sovereignty, that the recognition of the ROC could be withdrawn demonstrated that the recognition of the ROC in 1913 was recognition of a new government, not a new State.

The second instance was in the Pacific war with Japan. The Pacific War was a war between States even though the war was conducted by the governments. The day after Japan attacked Pearl Harbor in 1941, the US Government declared war against Japan. The war was between the

[464] *See* THE U.N. C.HARTER *supra* note 383 Art. 7, Sec. 1. Article 23, Sec. 1 provides, "The Security Council shall consist of fifteen Members of the United Nations. The Republic of China, France, the Union of Soviet Socialist Republics, the United Kingdom of Great Britain and Northern Ireland, and the United States of America shall be permanent members of the Security Council. The General Assembly shall elect ten other Members of the United Nations to be nonpermanent members of the Security Council, due regard being specially paid, in the first instance to the contribution of Members of the United Nations to the maintenance of international peace and security and to the other purposes of the Organization, and also to equitable geographical distribution." *Id.*

United States and the Empire of Japan. A few days later, the ROC also declared war against Japan. The war was between the State of China and the Empire of Japan, not between the ROC government and Japan. The 1952 Treaty of Peace signed by the ROC government and the government of Japan which ended the war was the treaty concluded between the State of China and the State of Japan even though the treaty was executed by the two governments, which had conducted the war.

The third instance was in the ROC's previous participation in the United Nations. The United Nations was an organization formed by territorial political institutions with statehood.[465] It regarded the State of China as its original member, notwithstanding that China used the name "the Republic of China."[466] To the United Nations, "China" was its member's name. Thus, in listing the permanent members of the Security Council alphabetically in the UN Charter, the Charter placed the name "the Republic of China," despite the words "the Republic of," before the name "France."[467] The words "the Republic of" were considered words of description indicating the form of the State and were disregarded in arranging the member States in their alphabetic order. Therefore, until 1971, when the General Assembly of the United Nations and its Security Council were in session, the nameplate on the desk where the Chinese representatives sent by the ROC government sat stated "China," not "the Republic of China."

The State of France provides an illustration of State practice to support the above analysis. The State of France was established by Charles I in the 9th century.[468] After the 1789 revolution, France changed from a

[465] *See* JOHN N. PETRIE, *AMERICAN NEUTRALITY IN THE 20TH CENTURY: THE IMPOSSIBLE DREAM* (Inst. for Nat'l Strategic Stud., McNair Paper 33, Jan. 1995). The U.S. Government wanted to invite all States, except the Axis States, to join the United Nations. It also invited some States, such as Australia, New Zealand, and India, which were constituent units of a commonwealth or empire. *See supra* text accompanying note 252.

[466] *See* THE U.N. CHARTER *supra* note 383, Art. 7, Sec. 1.

[467] One possible explanation is more political. In 1945, when the United Nations was being organized, Jiang (Chiang) Kai-shek, the leader of the ROC government, foresaw the imminent rise of Chinese Communists, and insisted that the name of "the Republic of China" be put in the Charter, so that his government could represent China in the United Nations in case the Communists overran part of China's territory.

[468] *See supra* text accompanying note 203.

monarchy to a republic.[469] It changed the form of State, as well as the form of government, but the territorial political institution remained the same. In international law, the State was still France. France was also an original member of the United Nations and one of the five permanent members of the Security Council. To the United Nations, "France," not the "Republic of France," was its member's name. Thus, the United Nations in listing its members by alphabetic order places "Republic of France" before "Federal Republic of Germany" because both "the Republic of" and "Federal Republic of" are descriptive words. When the General Assembly and the Security Council are in session, the name-plate on the desk where the French representatives to the United Nations sit states "France," not "the Republic of France."[470]

In the United Nations, after the PRC replaced the ROC as the representative government of the State of China in October 1971, the United Nations, in listing the permanent members of the Security Council, lists the State of China as "China," not "the People's Republic of China."[471]

The fourth instance of State practice which demonstrates that the ROC was a government of the State of China before the ROC moved to Taiwan was in the treatment of sovereign debts. In characterizing *Qing* (Ching) as the government of China earlier, it is observed that the debt incurred by the *Qing* (Ching) government is the sovereign debt for which the succeeding governments are liable. The ROC agreed to be liable for the bonds

[469] The Encyclopedia Britannica, *supra* note 21, V19, at 524 (15th Ed. 1994). The First Republic of France was established in 1789.

[470] Where a state was split into two independent States, and both States wanted to use the original State's name as part of their new State's name in order to retain their identity, the two States might use the government's name as the State's name to avoid the confusion. For instance, in 1945, Germany was split into two: The Federal Republic of Germany (West Germany) and the German Democratic Republic (East Germany) until 1990, during which period the State's name and the government's names were the same.

[471] "The Security Council has 15 members. The U.N. Charter designates five States as permanent members and the General Assembly elects ten other members for two-year terms. The term of office for each nonpermanent member of the Council ends on 31 December of the year indicated in parentheses next to its name. The five permanent members of the Security Council are China, France, Russian Federation, United Kingdom and the United States." Department of Public Information • News and Media Division • New York Membership Of Principal United Nations Organs in 2009. 5 Feb. 2009. Press Release ORG/1507.

issued by the *Qing* (Ching) government.[472] In summary, the instances of State practice discussed above show that when the ROC was established, it was a new government of the State of China, and not a new state.

The second drastic transformation of China's political system in the 20th century occurred when the Chinese Communists established the PRC in 1949. The new political system was influenced by the Soviet Union. Since the 1930s, the Chinese Communists with the support of the Soviet Union (the Union of Soviet Socialist Republics or "USSR") engaged in a revolution against the Nationalist's ROC government. After Japan surrendered in World War II, the Chinese Communists shoved the ROC government out of China proper and established the PRC government in 1949.[473] The PRC government was modeled on the Soviet system based on Marxist Socialism.[474]

The Chinese name of the PRC also indicates that it is a country. The English name "the People's Republic of China" is a translation of the Chinese name *Zhong* (Chung) *Hua Jen Min Kung Ho Guo*. The last word *Guo* in the name also means "country." The Chinese Communists called their country "the People's Republic of China" and called their government the "Central People's Government."

[472] *See Jackson v. The People's Republic of China*, 794 F.2d 1490, at 1492 (11th Cir. 1986). "In 1911 the Imperial Government of China issued bearer bonds (called 'Hukuang bonds') to assist in financing the building of a section of the Hukuang Railway. The Republic of China made interest payments on the Hukuang bonds until mid-1930's." *Id.* at 1491. By paying interest on the bonds issued by the previous government, the ROC government acknowledged the debt created by the *Qing* (Ching) government as the sovereign debt of the state of China, and it, as the succeeding government, was obliged to pay. In 1947, the ROC government, through its Prime Minister, announced that "China pledges her honorable intention to repay those external loans the service of which was suspended in the course of the Sino-Japanese War." *See* DEBRA TARNAPOL, *The Role of the Judiciary in Settling Claims Against the PRC*, 25 HARV. INT'L L.J. 355, 360, n.21 (1984).

[473] The term "China proper" refers to the territory legally owned by China, including two offshore islands, Kinmen (Quemoy) and Matsu. It does not include the island of Taiwan used in the broad sense. *See supra* note 1. *See* KERR, *supra* note 399.

[474] *See* the Constitution of the People's Republic of China, adopted on December 4, 1982, by the 5th National People's Congress, with further revisions in 1988, 1993, 1999, and 2004. "Under the leadership of the Communist Party of China and the guidance of Marxism-Leninism and 'Mao Zedong Thought,' the Chinese people of all nationalities will continue to adhere to the people's democratic dictatorship and follow the socialist road, steadily improve socialist institutions, develop socialist democracy, improve the socialist legal system . . . step by step to turn China into a socialist country." Preamble of the Constitution of the People's Republic of China, *Id.*

However, to other States, the Chinese Communists also established a new government, not a new State. That "the People's Republic of China" is a government of the State of China can also be seen from several instances of State practice in its relations with other States. The first instance is in diplomatic recognition by other States. When the Chinese Communists established the PRC in October of 1949, they established a new government, not a new State. While the States belonging to the Soviet bloc immediately recognized the new government, Western States for more than a decade refused to recognize the PRC because they regarded the new Chinese government as a satellite regime of the Soviet Union, which plotted to create a political hegemony in the world. In 1950, the UN members engaged in a military conflict with the Chinese army in the Korean Peninsula when the Chinese army intervened in the Korean War.

Western States began to change their attitude in 1964. After a long period of withholding their diplomatic recognition of the PRC by the Western States, France was the first among them to recognize the PRC. Other Western States followed. Whenever a State recognized the PRC, it also simultaneously withdrew its recognition of the ROC. This demonstrated that both the ROC and PRC are governments of the State of China and that other States can recognize only one as the representative government of the State of China.

The second instance indicating that the PRC is a government, not a State, is in its participation in the United Nations. After the PRC was established in 1949, it did not apply to join the United Nations as a new member. Under the UN Charter, an application of a State to join as a new member requires the affirmative resolution of the Security Council before the application is forwarded to the General Assembly for determination.[475] Instead, the PRC claimed that it was entitled to represent an existing member State, China, in the United Nations on the ground that it was China's sole legitimate government. After the UN General Assembly adopted Resolution No. 2758[476] in 1971, the PRC government replaced the ROC government to represent the State of China in the United Nations. Thus, when the General Assembly and the Security Council are in session, the nameplate on the desk behind which sit the Chinese representatives sent by the PRC government still states "China," not "the People's Republic of China."

In summary, the ROC was a government, not a State, before it moved its seat to Taiwan.

[475] THE U.N. CHARTER, *supra* note 383, Art. 4, para. 2; Art. 27, para. 3.
[476] *See infra* text accompanying note 548.

CHAPTER 5

Political Status of the ROC in Taiwan

Contents

1. THE ROC IN TAIWAN

It was observed in Chapter 4, The State and Governments of China, that the Republic of China (ROC) was not a State before it moved its seat to the island of Taiwan, but was a government of the State of China. This chapter reviews the position of the government officials in Taiwan as well as that of foreign governments on the political status of the ROC, or more specifically whether the ROC has become a State, after it moved to Taiwan.

The One-China Policy: State, Sovereignty, and Taiwan's International Legal Status
DOI: http://dx.doi.org/10.1016/B978-0-08-102314-3.00005-7

In 1945, immediately after Japan surrendered to the United States and its allies, the United States entrusted the ROC government with the administration of Taiwan.[477] Thereupon, Jiang (Chiang) Kai-shek sent his army in the US ships to the island in October of 1945. On October 25, 1945, the Chinese Military Commander accepted the surrender of the Japanese Military Authority in an official ceremony in Taipei.

Jiang (Chiang) Kai-shek immediately established a military authority to rule Taiwan. In less than 2 years, a conflict between the Chinese Military Security Guards and the Taiwanese civilians led to bloodshed in the whole island. On February 28, 1947, the brutal treatment of a female sidewalk vendor in Taipei by a Chinese tobacco inspector angered the Taiwanese bystanders, who began to defend the woman. The ensuing conflict between the Taiwanese civilians and the Chinese military police turned into a revolt by the Taiwanese people against the ROC authority throughout the island. To suppress the revolt, Jiang (Chiang) Kai-shek in Nanjing (Nanking) quickly sent enforcement troops to Taiwan. Upon arrival in Taiwan, the troops shot thousands of unarmed Taiwanese indiscriminately on sight. After the revolt was put down, the ROC authority arrested and executed without trial thousands more of the Taiwanese, including many elites such as medical doctors and lawyers. The atrocity committed by the Chinese army was later called "the 228 Incident" or "the 228 Massacre."[478] Subsequent to the 228 Incident, further oppression of the Nationalist Chinese incited an anti-Chinese sentiment among the Taiwanese people, especially the intellectuals.

In 1949, the ROC government moved its seat to Taiwan. In the winter of 1949, the ROC government, having lost China proper to the

[477] *See infra* text accompanying note 654.

[478] On February 28, 1947, a Chinese official of the Taiwan Tobacco and Liquor Monopoly Bureau, while inspecting street vendors in Taipei, used a pistol to hit a Taiwanese female sidewalk vendor for selling smuggled cigarettes, who subsequently died. The official's brutal treatment of the woman angered the bystanders, who began to defend the woman. The ensuing scuttle between the police and the civilians led to a large-scale protest by the Taiwanese against the repression of Jiang (Chiang) Kai-shek's Chinese Nationalists. During the following days, Chiang's government sent a re-enforcement troop from China to the island and began an indiscriminate killing. It is estimated that at least 18,000 Taiwanese lost their lives during the atrocity. Tillman Durdia, *Formosa killings are put at 10,000; foreigners say the Chinese slaughtered demonstrators without provocation* (Nanking, March 28), N.Y. TIMES, 3/29/1947. For a vivid description of the incident, *see* Li-Thian-Hok, AMERICA'S SECURITY AND TAIWAN'S FREEDOM, Xlibris, www.Xlibris.Com, at 46–48.

Communists in a civil war, was forced to take exile in Taiwan on December 8, 1949. Jiang (Chiang) Kai-shek moved the political structure of the ROC to Taiwan, even though Taiwan was under a military occupation.

Before Jiang (Chiang) Kai-shek moved the seat of his government to Taiwan, he had ruled China under the authority of the ROC Constitution. After the 1911 revolution, the State of China became a republic. Several constitutions were promulgated by different governments until 1946 when the present ROC Constitution was promulgated by the ROC government seated in Nanjing (Nanking). The ROC Constitution was based on the political doctrine, "the Three people's principles," formulated by Sun Yat-Sen, the nominal leader of the 1911 revolution.[479]

The Constitution provides a presidential system with a National Assembly and five Institutes (*Yuan*). The President of the republic is the head of the State and also the head of the government exercising the executive power. The National Assembly "exercises political powers on behalf of the whole body of citizens," in particular the function of electing and recalling the President and the Vice-president.[480] Jiang (Chiang) Kai-shek, who was Chairman of the Chinese Nationalist Party (the Kuomintang or the KMT) at the time, was elected the first President in 1948 by the National Assembly convened in Nanjing (Nanking) pursuant to the ROC Constitution.[481]

The five Institutes (*Yuan*) are five organs of the government (in the broad sense) collectively exercising the various powers of the State. They are the Executive Institute (The Executive *Yuan*), the Institute of Legislation (The Legislature *Yuan*), the Institute of Judiciary (The Judiciary *Yuan*), the Examination Institute (The Examination *Yuan*), and the Institute of Control (The Control *Yuan*). The Executive Institute, headed by the Premier, is the administrative organ under the President to implement the law enacted by the Institute of Legislation

[479] "The three people's principles" referred to Sun Yat-sen's three principles of nationalism, democracy, and social well-being. The Constitution of the Republic of China, A COMPILATION OF THE LAWS OF THE REPUBLIC OF CHINA, V. 1. 1967. Publisher: Kang Chi-Chao. Taipei, Taiwan, at 3.

[480] Arts. 25 and 27 of the Constitution of the Republic of China, A COMPILATION OF THE LAWS OF THE REPUBLIC OF CHINA. *Id.*

[481] In 1949, when Jiang (Chiang) Kai-shek's army was overrun by the Chinese Communists, he stepped down from the Presidency for a few months until 1950 when he resumed the presidency.

and the ordinances of the President.[482] The Institute of Legislation (The Legislature *Yuan*) is the highest legislature of the country.[483] The Institute of Judiciary (The Judiciary *Yuan*) is the highest judiciary.[484] The Examination Institute is the highest organ in charge of matters relating to the selection and promotion of civil servants.[485] The Institute of Control (The Control *Yuan*) exercises the power of impeachment and the power of reprimanding government officials, as well as auditing the governmental expenditures.[486]

The National Assembly, the Institute of Legislation, and the Institute of Control together are subsequently referred to as the three houses of the "congress." Each house of the "congress" is composed of deputies elected from all Provinces and Autonomous Regions. The number of deputies to be elected from each Province is proportional to the size of its population and the number of deputies from each Autonomous Region is fixed. The Autonomous Regions included Mongolia and Tibet. Where it is relevant is that in 1946 when the ROC Constitution was promulgated Taiwan was not part of China: it was Japan's territory.

In 1948 when the ROC government was losing the civil war to the Chinese Communists, the National Assembly, meeting in Nanjing (Nanking) in May of 1948, promulgated "Temporary Provisions Effective During the Period of Communists Rebellion Act" ("Temporary Provisions Act"), which allowed the President to enlarge his power without following certain procedural requirements prescribed by the Constitution.[487] After the ROC government took exile in Taiwan in December of 1949, the ROC government also applied the Act to the island.

The 1948 Temporary Provisions Act allowed Jiang (Chiang) Kai-shek to rule Taiwan until his death. It suspended an article of the Constitution which limits the term of the President and the Vice-President to two

[482] *Id.* Art. 53.
[483] *Id.* Art. 62.
[484] *Id.* Art. 77.
[485] *Id.* Art. 83.
[486] *Id.* Art. 90.
[487] Temporary Provisions Effective During the Period of Communists Rebellion Act (Temporary Provisions Act) was adopted by the ROC National Assembly on April 18, 1948, and promulgated on May 10, 1948. A COMPILATION OF THE LAWS OF THE REPUBLIC OF CHINA, V. 1., *supra* note 479. The Act was repealed on May 1, 1991 when the 1991 Amendment to the Constitution was adopted. *See infra* text accompanying note 554.

terms, thereby allowing Jiang (Chiang) Kai-shek to be reelected many times by the National Assembly until his death.[488]

In Taiwan, Jiang (Chiang) Kai-shek controlled the government apparatus including the "congress" during his life time. After the ROC government moved its seat to Taiwan, the Constitution continued to apply to the entirety of China in theory. When the ROC government and the "congress" went into exile in the island of Taiwan, most deputies of the "congress," who were elected by the people in China, also followed the government to Taiwan. They continued to represent the people in China under the rule of the Chinese Communists. The National Assembly amended Temporary Provisions Act by adding a provision which authorized the President to issue ordinances for electing new congressional delegates in addition to the original delegates.[489] The original delegates continued to represent their old congressional districts even after their original terms expired. Thus, for 40 years the congressional deputies were in fact permanent members of the "congress" until the 1991 amendment of the Constitution. Jiang (Chiang) Kai-shek could control the congressional deputies as his puppets because their livelihood depended on the KMT Party's support.

Ever since Jiang (Chiang) Kai-shek arrived in Taiwan, he imposed a totalitarian rule on the Taiwanese. In 1954, Jiang (Chiang) Kai-shek had Martial Law amended to authorize trials of civilians by court martial for offenses against national security, and then declared implementation of the Martial Law in Taiwan. Special penal laws were enacted to suppress opposition. National security was placed under the control of the Military Security Guards. Many dissidents were tried and sentenced to death by court martial, or simply disappeared without trace.[490]

[488] Temporary Provisions Act, *Id.* Art. 3, referring to Art. 47 of the ROC Constitution. Jiang (Chiang) Kai-shek resigned in 1949 to negotiate with the Chinese Communist Party. He resumed the Presidency in 1950 and continued in the position until his death in 1975.

[489] *Id.* Art. 6 was amended to authorize President to issue ordinances for electing new congressional delegates in addition to the existing delegates.

[490] The Martial Law was enacted in 1940, amended in 1954. The amendment permitted the President, with a resolution of the Conference of the Executive Institute (The Executive *Yuan*) and the consent of the Institute of Legislature (The Legislative *Yuan*), to declare the implementation of martial law. In the following three decades, the Chinese Nationalists continued to rule Taiwan under the Martial Law until 1987. As early as 1949, the US Department of State Policy Planning Staff at one time suggested that the US issue a "White Paper on China dealing with Formosa with particular emphasis being laid upon Chinese misrule of the islands since VJ-Day." US Department of State/Foreign relations of the United States 1949. The Far East: China. Vol. IX (1949). "Chinese administration on the islands has been rapacious and oppressive and the chaos." *Id.*

Jiang (Chiang) Kai-shek took three steps to legitimize his rule of the island of Taiwan and its inhabitants. The first step was that while in China he claimed that the island of Taiwan was returned to the ROC by the surrender of the Japanese military authority to the Chinese authority in Taipei in 1945, notwithstanding that the island was still Japan's territory. The second step was that the ROC government in China issued a decree in January of 1946 announcing that all the Taiwanese people residing in Taiwan "are restored" the citizenship of the ROC retroactively to October 25, 1945 when Japan surrendered,[491] even though the Taiwanese people still resided in Japanese territory and had neither renounced nor been deprived of their Japanese citizenship.

After the ROC government moved its seat to Taiwan, Jiang (Chiang) Kai-shek took a third step to legitimize his authority to rule Taiwan. He created some political slogans collectively characterized here as the "one China dogma." The one China dogma is, "There is only one China; China means the Republic of China; the Republic of China's territory consists of China proper and the island of Taiwan; and the People's Republic of China (PRC) illegally occupies the Republic of China's territory."[492]

From the beginning, Jiang (Chiang) Kai-shek's one-China dogma was a myth. When the ROC took exile in Taiwan in 1949, it had lost China forever. The Nationalists lost the trust of the people in China due to the mismanagement of the ROC officials. By 1950, the PRC government was firmly established, controlling China proper except for two small offshore islands (Kinmen and Matsu). In contrast, the ROC government only controlled the two Chinese small offshore islands and the island of Taiwan which was not China's territory. Thus, while there is only one China, China could not mean the ROC; the PRC did not "illegally occupy the ROC's territory" as the one-China dogma claimed. Although Jiang (Chiang) created the myth to legitimize his authority and power in Taiwan, since he was the paramount leader of the KMT Party, the Party and the government were able to permeate the dogma throughout the Taiwan society.

[491] *See* Chen Yi-nan, *ROC forced citizenship on unwary Taiwanese*, The Taipei Times, Jan 20, 2011, p. 8., *available at* http://www.taipeitimes.com/News/editorials/archives/2011/01/20/2003493942. Last visited, 07/16/2015.

[492] "One China dogma (*i zhong jiao tiao* in Chinese)" is not an official name of a teaching or political philosophy. Rather, it is a general term referring to the collective political slogans of Jiang (Chiang) Kai-shek described in the quotation.

2. POSITION OF TWO JIANG (CHIANG)S ON THE POLITICAL STATUS OF THE ROC IN TAIWAN

Jiang (Chiang) Kai-shek, like most of the Chinese people, did not distinguish the concept of State and the concept of government and treated the ROC as a State. In addressing his countrymen Jiang (Chiang) Kai-shek often used an expression "our country the ROC." After Jiang (Chiang) Kai-shek moved to the island of Taiwan, he still considered himself the legitimate leader of his country "the ROC." He regarded the PRC as a traitor regime established by the Chinese Communists, who "had stolen the territory of his country the ROC."

In Taiwan, Jiang (Chiang) Kai-shek never intended to establish a new State limiting its territory to the island of Taiwan. After the 1951 Peace Treaty of San Francisco was concluded, he still intended to retake the China mainland. In an attempt to motivate his army, he created a slogan: "Counter attack the mainland (Chinese Communists); retake the lost territory." In 1964, on the eve of France switching its recognition from the ROC to the PRC, French President De Gaulle called Jiang (Chiang) Kai-shek and advised him of the imminent French action and that if Jiang (Chiang) would declare the ROC a new State limiting its territory to the island of Taiwan, France would recognize the new State and the ROC as its legitimate government. Jiang (Chiang) refused.[493] He refused because such a move would lose the legitimacy of his ambition to recover his homeland.

After Jiang (Chiang) Kai-shek died in 1978 during his term of the presidency, his son Jiang (Chiang) Jing-guo succeeded to his power. Upon the death of Jiang (Chiang) Kai-shek, the Vice President Yen Chia-kan succeeded to the Presidency pursuant to the ROC constitution, but soon resigned to allow Jiang (Chiang) Jing-guo to become the President.[494] During the lifetime of Jiang (Chiang) Kai-shek, Jiang (Chiang) Jing-guo had already built up a strong position in the ROC government. Jiang (Chiang) Kai-shek appointed him the Premier

[493] This is an account of Dean Rusk, the former Secretary of State during the presidency of John Kennedy and Linden Johnson. When he began to teach international law at the University of Georgia, School of Law after Johnson's term expired, he and this writer taught international law together for one year. This writer learned of this historical episode during a private conversation at this writer's residence.

[494] Jiang (Chiang) Jing-guo, President of the ROC (1978–88).

(officially "The President of the Executive Institute") of the ROC,[495] who also controlled the KMT Party.

Jiang (Chiang) Jing-guo never established a new State in Taiwan either. As the President of the ROC, Jiang (Chiang) Jing-guo never intended to establish a State limiting its territory to the island of Taiwan. He also relied on the one-China dogma to legitimize his rule of Taiwan. But he had no intention to retake the China mainland, and simply adopted a new slogan, "Unification of China by the Three People's Principles."

To other States, the ROC in Taiwan was a government of China in exile. Until the conclusion of the Peace Treaty of San Francisco, the island of Taiwan, while under the administration of the ROC government at the assignment of the US Government, was Japan's territory. In 1951, when the United States and other Allied powers signed the Peace Treaty of San Francisco with Japan, the ROC was not a party to the Peace Treaty, though it also had conducted the war with Japan. When the United States and the United Kingdom were drafting the peace treaty, they could not include "the Republic of China" as a party because the War was between States, and the ROC was not a State, just a government. They did not include China as a party because they did not want either government to represent China in the Treaty: the PRC government which fought the United Nations (UN) forces in the Korean War[496] was not recognized by most Western States as the legitimate government of China; the ROC government, which had lost most of China's territory, had no legitimacy to represent the State of China.

As stated earlier, in 1964 when France recognized the PRC and simultaneously withdrew its recognition of the ROC, the ROC did not become a State.[497] Other Western States which followed France to accord

[495] Jiang (Chiang) Jing-guo, Premier of the ROC (1972–78).

[496] On June 27, 1950, the Security Council resolved to "[recommend] that the Members of the United Nations furnish such assistance to the Republic of Korea (South Korea) as may be necessary to repel the armed attack and to restore international peace and security in the area." S.C. Res. 83, UN SCOR, 474th mtg. at 85, UN Doc. S/1511 (1950). On July 7, 1950, the Security Council then resolved to "[recommend] that all Members providing military forces and other assistance pursuant to Security Council resolutions [82 (1950) and 83 (1950)] make such forces and other assistance available to a unified command under the United States of America." S.C. Res. 84, UN SCOR, 476th mtg. at 85–86, UN Doc. S/1588 (1950).

[497] Jean-Luc Domenach, *Sino-French Relations: A French View* in CHINA'S FOREIGN RELATIONS, NEW PERSPECTIVES 87 (Chun-tu Hsüeh, ed. 1982).

recognition to the PRC also recognized it as the government of China. The ROC continued to be a government of China in exile after the Peace Treaty of San Francisco entered into force.

In 1970 when the UN General Assembly debated which government, the ROC or the PRC, should take China's seat, the PRC accused the US Government and Japanese government of plotting to create two "Chinas." The Japanese Ambassador to the UN Min Aichi replied that "Japan will continue to espouse the '1-China' policy,"[498] implying that the ROC was not a new State.

When the United States withdrew recognition of the ROC in 1979, the ROC did not become a State. Then President Jiang (Chiang) Jing-guo did not intend to establish a new State limiting its territory to the island of Taiwan. Other States followed the United States, leaving only a number of small States which continued to recognize the ROC as China's representative government. The ROC government became isolated in the international community.

In Taiwan, since 1945 when the ROC government took over the administration of the island, the political power was in the Chinese people. For 43 years, the political power was in Jiang (Chiang)'s family: first Jiang (Chiang) Kai-shek and then his son Jiang (Chiang) Jing-guo. Most government officials and deputies of the "congress" were Chinese, whom the Taiwanese referred to as "the mainlanders" or "people from the other Provinces."

The Chinese totalitarian rule finally aroused anti-Chinese sentiment among the Taiwanese people. When the Chinese soldiers arrived in Taiwan on US Navy ships in 1945, they called themselves "the liberators" and were welcomed by the Taiwanese. But since 1947, for decades, the people lived in fear of persecution under the shadow of the 1947 "228 Incident." In the 1960s, after a long period of the totalitarian rule under the martial law, a Taiwan independence movement began to sprout. In 1979, the year after the United States withdrew its recognition of the ROC government, an incident, subsequently called "The Incident of

[498] On November 22, 1970, the then Japanese Ambassador Min Aichi said "that Japan will continue to espouse the '1-China' policy despite closeness of the vote [in the UN]." *See* N.Y. TIMES ABSTRACTS, 11/ 22/1970, at 9. *See infra* note 536 and the accompanying text for the voting in the United Nations.

Formosa magazine,"[499] illustrated the KMT's totalitarianism. In December of that year, Taiwanese political leaders gathered in Kaohsiung City to celebrate the 31st anniversary of the signing of the UN Convention of Human Rights. After the meeting, as the Taiwanese politicians and the audience were preparing to march on the street they were blocked and beaten by the ROC's Military Security Guards and police. The conflict between them resulted in the arrest of many Taiwanese politicians. Many were sentenced to a long-term imprisonment.

Another incident occurred in 1981. A Professor Wen-chen Chen of Carnegie-Mellon University, while visiting Taiwan in July 1981, was found dead from falling from a second floor in the campus of his alma mater, The National Taiwan University, after being questioned by the Military Security Guards on the day before. Although the authority announced suicide as the cause of death, many people would not rule out a political assassination.

While Jiang (Chiang) Kai-shek called Taiwan "Free China," the Taiwanese people subsequently called the period under the two Jiang (Chiang)s "the White Terror era."[500] Although the ensuing unrest in the Taiwanese society eventually forced Jiang (Chiang) Jing-guo to lift the martial law in 1987, a year before his death, the Taiwanese people were still mistreated by the Nationalist Chinese.

The next section will closely examine the position of the United States on the political status of the ROC during the era of the two Jiang (Chiang)s.

[499] A brief narration of the incident follows: "In November of 1979, the publisher of 'Formosa' magazine requested the government for a permit for an outdoor rally to celebrate the 31st anniversary of the UN Convention of Human Rights. The permit was issued but was restricted to a rally, no parade. On December 10, 1979, after the rally, the participants began to walk on the street. The Military Security Guards and police attempted to stop them from walking on the street and a conflict began. The police used tear gas to disperse the civilians. Both sides had light casualties. Next day, the Military Security Guards and the police began to arrest Taiwanese political leaders who participated at the rally as well as those who did not. Many of them were sentenced to long imprisonment terms. Senator Edward Kennedy made a statement criticizing the method of handing by the ROC government." The US Congress Record, 126, No. 35. (March 5, 1980).

[500] *See* A MEMORIAL FOR PROFESSOR CHEN WEN-CHEN—A TAIWANESE, published by Chen Wen-chen Memorial Foundation, Inc. Ann Arbor, Michigan, 1982.

3. US POSITION ON THE POLITICAL STATUS OF THE ROC BEFORE LEE TENG-HUI

Whatever the two Jiang (Chiang)s' characterization of the ROC in the one-China dogma, there was no doubt to other States that the ROC was a government of the State of China from the very beginning when it was established in 1912 and was a government after it moved its seat to the island of Taiwan in 1949.

The United States' treatment of the ROC is particularly relevant, since it became the occupying state of Taiwan and the dominant power in the region after World War II. Its Executive, Legislative, and Judicial branches all held the same position—that the ROC was only a government of the State of China. A closer analysis of the view of each branch follows.

A. The Executive Branch

As discussed in Chapter 2, The State and Sovereignty, it is the power of the Executive head, the President in the United States, to grant diplomatic recognition. It was pointed out before that the Executive branch of the United States considered the ROC a government of the State of China from the time when it was established in 1912. Its recognition of the ROC in 1913 was recognition of the government, since the United States had long recognized the State of China before 1913.

The ROC did not become a State independent of China after it moved its seat to the island of Taiwan. From October 25, 1971 on, the PRC government has replaced the ROC government to represent China in the United Nations. The US Government, however, continued to recognize the ROC in Taiwan as the representative government of China until 1979.[501] On December 30, 1978, the Carter Administration finally accorded recognition to the PRC and simultaneously withdrew its recognition of the ROC[502]. When the US recognized the PRC, it did not recognize the PRC as a new State, but recognized it as the representative government of China. Since the State which the PRC represented was still China, the United States had to withdraw simultaneously its

[501] *See* Ruan Ming, *Time to Put an End to Fallacy of "One China,"* TAIPEI TIMES, 11/14/2003, *available at* http://taiwansecurity.org/TT/2003/TT-141103-1.htm. Last visited 11/08/2004.

[502] The United States established diplomatic tie with the PRC and terminated the tie with the ROC on January 1, 1979. *See President's Memorandum for All Departments and Agencies: Relations with the People of Taiwan*, reprinted in 1979 U.S.C.A.N. 36, at 75.

recognition of the ROC Upon withdrawal of its recognition of the ROC, the United States also terminated the US–China (the ROC) Mutual Defense Treaty because the treaty had lost its purpose—defending against the invasion of the PRC government, which was now recognized as the representative government of the other party to the treaty.

The withdrawal of the recognition of the ROC by the US demonstrated that the US regarded the ROC as a government. As it was discussed in Chapter 2, The State and Sovereignty, in State practice, while recognition of a State cannot be withdrawn, recognition of a government may be withdrawn. The withdrawal of recognition of the ROC by the United States and other States did not make the ROC a new State as some people in Taiwan have claimed. Withdrawal of recognition is an act of destruction of a relationship, not an act of creation of a new entity.

B. The Legislative Branch

Nor did the US Congress consider the ROC a State. When the United States terminated the US–China (the ROC) Mutual Defense Treaty, the US Congress enacted the Taiwan Relations Act (the "Act")[503] to protect the people of Taiwan against the invasion of the Chinese Communists as well as the security and interest of the United States in the Western Pacific. If the ROC was a State, then the US Government could enter into a mutual defense treaty with it, instead of employing such a roundabout maneuver. The United States does not have South Korea Relations Act or Japan Relations Act. It does not need such domestic law because both South Korea and Japan are States. The two States and the United States have signed mutual defense treaties.[504] Thus, the United States has obligations and power under the treaties to protect them. Some may say that Taiwan Relations Act treats the ROC like a State.[505] It is true that in

[503] Taiwan Relations Act, Pub. L. No. 96-8, '2, 93 Stat. 14 (1979) (codified as amended at 22 U.S.C.'3301–3316 (2004)). Approved by the 96th Congress on April 10, 1979, effective January 1, 1979 (Sec. 18).

[504] Agreement between the United States and the Republic of Korea relating to military assistance was signed on June 27, 1974. Mutual Assistance Agreement between the United States and Japan was signed on March 8, 1954.

[505] Taiwan Relations Act, *supra* note 503. "Whenever the laws of the United States refer or relate to foreign countries, nations, states, governments, or similar entities, such terms shall include and such law shall apply with such respect to Taiwan." *Id.* Sec. (4)(b).

the Act, the ROC is treated *like* a State by the United States and enjoys some of the same prerogatives and courtesy accorded by the US Government to other States. But if the United States treats the ROC like a State, the implication is that the ROC is not a State, only similar to one. In fact, after the United States withdrew recognition of the ROC, it no longer regarded the ROC as a "government." Taiwan Relations Act calls it "the governing authorities."[506]

Taiwan Relations Act is a US domestic legislation, not a treaty. If the PRC government uses force against Taiwan,[507] the US Government has no treaty obligation toward the ROC government to protect Taiwan, though the US Government may, as the occupying power, defend Taiwan pursuant to the Taiwan Relations Act or other considerations.

C. The Judicial Branch

Furthermore, the judicial branch of the United States has not considered the ROC a State either.[508] In the United States, a constitutional principle is that on matters of recognition of a foreign State and a foreign government, the judicial branch follows the decisions and opinions of the Executive branch because they are political questions.[509] The Court in *Cheng Fu Sheng v. Rogers*[510] stated,

> *"It is fundamental that such questions as whether a foreign country or a foreign government should be formally recognized are problems that are not to be solved by the courts, but are political matters that are to be decided by the executive and legislative departments of the Government. On such topics the President and the Secretary of State speak for the United States, and the courts are obligated to follow their pronouncements."*[511]

[506] The Act calls it "[t]he governing authorities on Taiwan recognized as the Republic of China prior to January 1, 1971." *Id.* Sec. 15(2).

[507] It would be considered exercise of sovereignty beyond its border.

[508] One exception is *New York Chinese TV Programs, Inc. v. U.E. Enterprises, Inc. et al.*, 954 F. 2d 847, 853 (2d. Cir. 1992). *See infra* discussions at note 526.

[509] *U.S.* v. *Pink*, *supra* note 372.

[510] *Cheng Fu Sheng* v. *Rogers*, 177 F. Supp. 281 (D.D.C. 1959), remanded; 280 F.2d 663 (US App. D.C. 1960), remanded; 294 F 2d 26 (US App. D.C. 1961). 177 F. Supp. 281 (D.D.C. 1959).

[511] *Id.* The court cites *Jones* v. *US*, *infra* note 973, as authority.

Nevertheless, the US courts, in deciding the application of an international treaty or a municipal law, had occasions to give their reasons that the ROC was not a State. Two cases involving the application of the Warsaw Convention[512] confirmed that the ROC was not a State. In the first case, *John Lee and Margaret Lee* v. *China Airlines Ltd.*,[513] two passengers on a flight from Hong Kong[514] to San Francisco sued China Airlines in a US federal court sitting in California for injuries caused by a sudden drop of the airplane of 31,000 ft in the air, off the coast of California. The defendant argued that the US federal court had no jurisdiction to try the case. The plaintiffs argued that the federal court had jurisdiction, and, if their action were dismissed for lack of jurisdiction, they would be compelled to bring the action abroad, either in Taiwan[515] or in Hong Kong,[516] where they would not receive an adequate hearing of their claims because, they argued, the Warsaw Convention would not apply to either Hong Kong or Taiwan. The court, in holding that the Warsaw Convention applied and it had no subject matter jurisdiction according to the Convention, dismissed the action.[517] The court added that if the plaintiffs sued in either Hong Kong or Taiwan, "[t]he Warsaw Convention will figure prominently in the decision making process over there because both Hong Kong and *Taiwan* adhere to it."[518]

The court statement that "Taiwan adhere[s] to [the Warsaw Convention]" implied that Taiwan was a contracting party of the Warsaw Convention. It should be noted, however, that at the time when the accident occurred, while the PRC government of China ratified and adhered to the Warsaw Convention in July 1958, the ROC government in

[512] Convention for the Unification of Certain Rules Relating to International Carriage by Air, Oct. 12, 1929, 49 Stat. 3000, T.S. No. 876, 137 L.N.T.S. 11 [hereinafter "Warsaw Convention"].

[513] 669 F. Supp.979 (C.D. Cal. 1987).

[514] Hong Kong was still a territory of the United Kingdom at the time. *Id.* at 980.

[515] Taipei was the carrier's principal place of business. *Id.* at 979.

[516] Hong Kong was the passenger's place of destination, because the plaintiffs purchased round trip tickets in Hong Kong. *Id.*

[517] The court said, "Under Article 28 of the Convention, an action can be brought under the terms of the Convention only in the following places: (1) the carrier's domicile; (2) the carrier's principal place of business; (3) the place where the ticket was purchased; or (4) the passenger's place of destination." *John Lee and Margaret Lee*, 669 F. Supp. at 980. California was none of the locations mentioned above. For applicability of Warsaw Convention, *see infra* note 522.

[518] *Id.* at 984 (emphasis added).

Taiwan had neither ratified nor adhered to the Warsaw Convention. Thus, the reason that the court ruled that Taiwan was a contracting party was because it regarded Taiwan a part of China and covered by the Warsaw Convention; the ROC was not a State.

The second case in which an American court held that the ROC was not a State was *Atlantic Mutual Insurance Co.* v. *Northwest Airlines.*[519] In this case, Tacoma Boat Building Co. (Tacoma) delivered some machinery to Northwest Airlines ("Northwest") for shipment from Milwaukee, Wisconsin, to Taipei, Taiwan. Tacoma claimed that certain parts of their machinery components were damaged due to Northwest's negligence during the air transport of the components. Atlantic Mutual Insurance Co.[520] and Tacoma jointly sued Northwest in Milwaukee for damages. In the federal district court sitting in Milwaukee,[521] the issue was whether the state court or the federal court had the subject matter jurisdiction to try the case. The plaintiffs, which argued that the state court had the jurisdiction, claimed that the Warsaw Convention did not apply on the grounds that Taiwan was not a party to the Convention and, thus, the federal court lacked subject matter jurisdiction. The defendant, Northwest, argued that the Warsaw Convention applied to the case and, thus, the federal court had jurisdiction. In reaching the conclusion that the Warsaw Convention applied, the federal court said that it had "federal subject matter jurisdiction ... only if Taipei, Taiwan—the flight destination—also was a party to the convention."[522]

[519] 796 F. Supp. 1188, 1191 (E.D. Wis. 1992).

[520] It had paid Tacoma for the loss under an insurance policy and was subrogated Tacoma's right against Northwest.

[521] The plaintiffs originally brought the case to the circuit court for Milwaukee County, Wisconsin, a state court, which at the defendant's motion, remanded the case to the federal court sitting in Milwaukee. *Id.* at 1189.

[522] The court stated:

> *"[T]he convention is applicable where ... the contract of transportation (e.g., a plane ticket) involves travel from one 'High Contracting' party to another ... [A] High Contracting party is a state which is an original signatory to the convention or one which ratified the convention or filed declarations of adherence to the convention after it went into force. Further, a declaration of adherence to the convention by a state may include colonies or territories of that state."*

Id. 1190–91 (citations omitted).

Holding that Taiwan was a party to the convention, the federal court explained as follows:

> *Since 1949 to the present [1992], two governments—the Republic of China and the People's Republic of China [PRC]—claim to be the sole legitimate government of "China," which both governments agree is comprised of mainland China and Taiwan. In reality, the Republic of China retains control only over the island of Taiwan while the PRC retains control over the mainland; neither government has asserted that they are two separate countries.*[523]

The court further stated:

> *The world community was compelled to determine whether the ROC or the PRC would receive formal recognition as the legitimate government of China. On December 30, 1978, the US formally recognized the PRC as the sole government of China, in its entirety, and withdrew recognition from the ROC. Over 100 other nations and the UN have done the same.*[524]

Although the ROC in Taiwan had never adhered to the Warsaw Convention in its own name, the court accepted the defendant's argument that Taiwan was a party to this convention because of the declaration made by the PRC when it ratified the Warsaw Convention. The PRC's declaration stated that the convention "shall of course apply to the entire Chinese territory including Taiwan," and that "the recognition of the PRC as the sole government of China by the United States, the United Nations and over 100 other nations legitimizes this declaration despite the continued existence of the ROC."[525]

[523] *Id.* at 1190 (citations omitted).

[524] *Id.* (citation omitted).

[525] *Id.* at 1191. The court then stated that it "is not vested with the power [to review]" the executive branch's recognition of the PRC as the sole government of China. *Id.* Subsequent to the decision, the parties attempted to settle before a magistrate judge of the US District Court for the Eastern District of Wisconsin. Coordination Council For North American Affairs (The ROC's office in New York City having the functions of a general consulate) intervened contesting the district court's finding that Taiwan was a province of the People's Republic of China. The US District Court dismissed its petition and the Council appealed to the US Court of Appeals For the Seventh Circuit. The Seventh Circuit affirmed the judgment below on the ground that the Council was not a proper party to intervene. *Atlantic Mutual Insurance Company and Tacoma Boatbuilding Company, Inc. (Plaintiffs-Appellees)* v. *Northwest Airlines, Inc. (Defendant Appellee), and Coordination Council For North American Affairs, (Intervenor-Appellant)*. 24 F. 3d 958.

The two cases discussed above demonstrated that the US courts did not consider the ROC a State after the ROC moved its seat to Taiwan, but regarded it only as a government of China.[526] Whether the courts were correct in stating that "Taiwan was a part of China" is a different issue to be dealt with later in this work. However, regardless of the characterization of the ROC by Jiang (Chiang) Kai-shek and Jiang (Chiang) Jing-guo while they were in Taiwan, the United States at the time did not regard the ROC as a State.

4. UN POSITION ON THE STATUS OF THE ROC IN TAIWAN BEFORE LEE TENG-HUI

In 1949, the Chinese Communists did not establish a new State. As stated earlier, the PRC is a new government of China. Thus, the PRC did not apply to join the United Nations as a new member. Instead, it claimed that it was entitled to represent an existing member, China, in the United Nations on the ground that it was China's sole legitimate government.

Until 1972, the State of China was represented by the ROC government in the United Nations. When the United Nations was formed in 1945, the ROC was the government that represented China. To the United Nations, the ROC was still the representative government of China after Jiang (Chiang) Kai-shek took exile in the island of Taiwan.

The PRC attempted to replace the ROC in the United Nations for 22 years. In its attempt to replace the ROC, the PRC solicited the assistance of its allies in the Soviet block. In September 1950, a year after the PRC was established, Cuba proposed in the United Nations to include in

[526] One exception that an US court held that Taiwan was a "nation" was *New York Chinese TV Programs, Inc.* v. *U.E. Enterprises, Inc. et al.*, 954 F.2d 847 (2d Cir. 1992), in which the court stated that Taiwan was a nation, and thus the Treaty of Friendship, Commerce, and Navigation between the Republic of China and the United States was still in force. However, the court could have reached the same conclusion without determining the political status of Taiwan. When the United States shifted the recognition from the ROC to the PRC government in 1979, the US President issued a Memorandum stating that "Existing international agreements and arrangements in force between the United States and Taiwan shall continue in force." US Code Cong. & Admin. News 75. In *Mingtai Fire & Marine Insurance Co., Ltd.* v. *United Parcel Service*, 177 F.3d 1142, at 1144–46 (9th Cir. 1999), the Ninth Circuit Court of Appeals decided the applicability of the Warsaw Convention to the territory of Taiwan based on "the political departments' position that Taiwan is not bound by China's adherence to the Warsaw Convention" without "independently determin[ing] the status of Taiwan." *Mingtai*, F.3d at 1142.

the annual meeting agenda of the General Assembly a discussion of the question of China's representation. The General Assembly established a Special Committee consisting of seven members to consider the question.[527] In December 1950, the General Assembly adopted a resolution recommending that the representation question "should be considered in the light of the Purposes and Principles of the Charter and the circumstances of each case,"[528] but did not address directly the question of China's representation.

During the 1951 and 1952 General Assembly sessions, no proposal to decide China's representation was made. The UN's armed forces were fighting the PRC's "volunteer army" in the Korean Peninsula. Perhaps, no State thought it appropriate to raise the question.

After the armistice of the Korean War, the proposal to include the question of China's representation in the General Assembly annual meeting agenda was resurrected. Each year from 1953 to 1960, a member of the Soviet bloc made the proposal. Each time the proposal was rejected by a majority vote.[529]

In the 1960s, the US Government insulated the ROC's position in the United Nations by a procedural maneuver. When a similar proposal was made again in 1961, the US Government (the Kennedy Administration) invoked an article in the UN Charter to create a procedural barrier for any proposal to change the representation with respect to China in the United Nations. The General Assembly adopted a resolution proposed by the US Government to designate the representation question

[527] *See* G.A. Res. 490, UN GAOR, 5th Sess., 277th plen. mtg., Supp. No. 20, at 153, UN Doc. A/1775 (Sep. 19, 1950), *available at* http://www.un.org/depts/dhl/resguide/r5.htm. Last visited 02/15/2011.

[528] G.A. Res. 396, UN GAOR, 5th Sess., 325th plen. mtg., Supp. No. 20, at 98, UN Doc. A/1775 (Dec. 14,1950). *Id.*

[529] *See* G.A. Res. 800, UN GAOR, 8th Sess., 432d plen. mtg., Supp. No. 17, at 225, UN Doc. A/2630 (1953); G.A. Res. 903, UN GAOR, 9th Sess., 473d plen. mtg., Supp. No. 21, at 171, UN Doc. A/2890 (1954); G.A. Res. 990, UN GAOR, 10th Sess., 516th plen. mtg., Supp. No. 19, at 231, UN Doc. A/3116 (1955); G.A. Res. 1108, UN GAOR, 11th Sess., 580th plen. mtg., Supp. No. 17, at 159, UN Doc. A/3572 (1956); G.A. Res. 1135, UN GAOR, 12th Sess., 686th plen. mtg., Supp. No. 18, at 245, UN Doc. A/3805 (1957); G.A. Res. 1239, UN GAOR, 13th Sess., 755th plen. mtg., Supp. No. 18, at 151, UN Doc. A/4090 (1958); G.A. Res. 1351, UN GAOR, 14th Sess., 803d plen. mtg., Supp. No. 16, at 235, UN Doc. A/4354 (1959); G.A. Res. 1493, UN GAOR, 15th Sess., 895th plen. mtg., Supp. No. 16, at 184, UN Doc. A/4684 (1960).

as an "important question" under the UN Charter.[530] "Important questions" require a two-thirds majority vote of the members present.[531] From 1962 to 1964, every year when a proposal was made in the General Assembly to replace the ROC with the PRC in the United Nations, the General Assembly adopted a resolution making the question of China's representation an "important question."[532] Each time the proposal to replace the ROC government with the PRC government did not receive the required two-thirds majority vote.

A crucial event in the international politic occurred in 1965: France broke her diplomatic ties with the ROC and accorded her recognition to the PRC. Soon after that, other Western States began to follow. However, attempts to replace representatives of the ROC with representatives of the PRC failed again in the UN General Assembly in 1967,[533] 1968,[534] and 1969[535] because the proposals did not receive the required two-thirds majority vote for the "important question."

In September 1970, the US Government began to change its policy toward the PRC. By 1970, more than one half of the UN members recognized the PRC as the representative government of China.[536] At the same time, the number of the States which recognized the ROC

[530] The General Assembly "[d]ecides, in accordance with Article 18 of the Charter of the United Nations, that any proposal to change the representation of China is an *important question*." G.A. Res. 1668, UN GAOR, 16th Sess., 1080th plen. mtg., Supp. No. 17, at 296, UN Doc. A/5100 (1961) (second emphasis in italic added).

[531] *See* UN CHARTER *supra* note 383 ART. 18. Sec. 2 (Decisions of the General Assembly on important questions shall be made by a two-thirds majority of the members present and voting.).

[532] For the Soviet Draft Proposal, *see* Adlai E. Stevenson, *United Nations Rules Out Change in Representation of China, Plen. Statement Before the General Assembly* (Dec. 1 and Dec. 14, 1961), in DEP'T ST. BULL., Jan. 1962, at 117.

[533] *See* G.A. Res. 2271, UN GAOR, 22d Sess., 1610th plen. mtg., Supp. No. 16, at 241, UN Doc. A/6716 (1967).

[534] *See* G.A. Res. 2389, UN GAOR, 23d Sess., 1724th plen. mtg., Supp. No. 18, at 116, UN Doc. A/7218 (1968).

[535] *See* G.A. Res. 2500, UN GAOR, 24th Sess., 1808th plen. mtg., Supp. No. 30, at 213, UN Doc. A/7630 (1969).

[536] There were 125 members at the 1970 UN General Assembly plenary session. The ROC government "is recognized diplomatically by more than 60 of the members of this organization." Christopher H. Phillips, *Twenty-fifth General Assembly Rejects Move to Change Representation of China in the United Nations*, Plen. Statement Before the General Assembly (Nov. 12, 1970), *in* DEP'T ST. BULL., Dec. 1970, at 734.

decreased correspondingly. In 1970, the Nixon Administration was willing to allow representatives of the PRC to take China's seat in the General Assembly and in the Security Council on a condition that the representatives of the ROC remained in the General Assembly.[537] The PRC, on the other hand, insisted that it would take over China's seat only if the representatives of the ROC were expelled from the United Nations.[538] The US Government refused to accept the PRC's condition, and again proposed that the representation question was an "important question."[539] The proposal was adopted by a narrower margin this time.[540] A proposal by Albania, which followed, to expel the representatives of the ROC was again defeated.[541]

In 1971, the United States sustained defeat in the United Nations. In September 1971 when the General Assembly convened, the US Government (the Nixon Administration) again proposed a dual representation: both the PRC and the ROC were represented in the UN General Assembly, and the PRC also occupied China's seat in the Security

[537] *See Id.*

[538] *See Id.* at 733–34.

[539] Resolution 2642 of the General Assembly, entitled *Representation of China in the United Nations*, was adopted by the 1913th plenary session of the General Assembly on November 20, 1970. *See* G.A. Res. 2642, UN GAOR, 25th Sess., Supp. No. 28, at 6, UN Doc. A/8028 (1970).

Recalling the recommendation contained in its resolution 396 (V) of 14 December 1950 that, whenever more than one authority claims to be the Government entitled to represent a Member State in the United Nations and this question becomes the subject of controversy in the United Nations, the question should be considered in the light of the purposes and principles of the Charter of the United Nations and the circumstances of each case.

Recalling further its decision in resolution 1668 (XVI) of 13 December 1961, in accordance with Article 18 of the Charter, that any proposal to change the representation of China is an important question, which, in General Assembly resolutions 2025 (XX) of 17 November 1965, 2159 (XXI) of 29 November 1966, 2271 (XXII) of 28 November 1967, 2389 (XXIII) of 19 November 1968 and 2500 (XXIV) of 11 November 1969, was affirmed as remaining valid,

Affirms again that this decision remains valid. 1913th plenary meeting 20 November 1970.

[540] The votes were 66 in favor and 52 against, with 7 abstentions. *See* Taiwan Documents Project, Resolution on the Representation of China in the United Nations (Nov. 20, 1970), *available at* http://www.taiwandocuments.org/un2642-XXV.htm. Last visited 09/09/2004.

[541] The votes were 51 in favor and 49 (including US vote) against, with 25 abstentions. *See* Phillips, *supra* note 536, at 735 footnote 2.

Council.[542] The General Committee[543] prepared a General Assembly agenda which included both the United States proposal calling for "the continued right of representation of the ROC [in the General Assembly]"[544] and Albania's proposal calling for the representatives of the PRC to take China's seat as well as for the expulsion of the representatives of the ROC from the United Nations.[545] In the General Assembly, the United States proposal to make the question of expelling the representatives of the ROC from the United Nations an "important question" was, for the first time, defeated.[546] Thus, China's "representation question" was to be decided by a majority vote.

[542] On August 2, 1971, Secretary of State William Rogers said at a press conference, "The United States accordingly will support action at the General Assembly this fall calling for seating the People's Republic of China. At the same time the United States will oppose any action to expel the Republic of China." William Rogers, *Sec'y Rogers Announces US Policy on Chinese Representation in the UN*, Statement to News Correspondents (Aug. 2, 1971), *in* DEP'T ST. BULL., Aug. 1971, at 193.

[543] One of the General Committee's functions is to recommend the General Assembly agenda.

[544] The US proposed Resolution is entitled, "The Representation of China in the United Nations." The draft resolution, in part, reads, "The General Assembly ... 1. Hereby affirms the right of representation of the People's Republic of China and recommends that it be seated as one of the five permanent members of the Security Council; 2. Affirms the continued right of representation of the Republic of China." George H. W. Bush, *UN Votes to Seat People's Republic of China and Expel Representatives of Republic of China*, Plen. Statement Before the General Assembly (Oct. 18, 1971), *in* DEP'T ST. BULL., Nov. 1971, at 549.

[545] G.A. Res. 2758, UN GAOR, 26th Sess., Supp. No. 29, at 2, UN Doc. A/8439 (1971). The Proposal stated:

> *Restoration of the lawful rights of the People's Republic of China in the United Nations.*
> *The General Assembly, Recalling the principles of the Charter of the United Nations,*
> *Considering that the restoration of the lawful rights of the People's Republic of China is essential both for the protection of the Charter of the United Nations and for the cause that United Nations must serve under the Charter,*
> *Recognizing that the representatives of the Government of the People's Republic of China are the only lawful representatives of China to the United Nations and that the People's Republic of China is one of the five permanent members of the Security Council,*

Decides to restore all its rights to the People's Republic of China and to recognize the representatives of its Government as the only legitimate representatives of China to the United Nations, and to expel forthwith the representatives of Chiang Kai-shek from the place which they unlawfully occupy at United Nations and in all the organizations related to it.

Id. See also Phillips, *supra* note 536, at 735 footnote 2.

[546] *See Id.* at 556 footnote 3.

The proposed resolution of Albania put to the vote at the end of the debates on October 25, 1971 was adopted.[547] In the General Assembly, the United States again attempted to create dual representations, but failed. When Albania's proposed resolution to replace the ROC with the PRC was presented for voting, the Nixon Administration voted against Albania's proposal. But Albania's proposed resolution was carried by a large margin.

Resolution No. 2758 of the General Assembly stated,

> *The General Assembly ...* decides *to restore all its rights to the People's Republic of China and to recognize the representatives of its Government as the only legitimate representatives of China to the United Nations, and to expel forthwith the representatives of Chiang Kai-shek from the place which they unlawfully occupy at the United Nations and in all the organizations related to it.*[548]

The Resolution became effective immediately and the representatives of the ROC left the UN Headquarters.

Resolution 2758 of the United Nations did not involve an expulsion of a member State. When the General Assembly expelled the ROC, it did not remove a member even though "the Republic of China" was the name of a member and also a permanent member of the Security Council. As mentioned earlier, in 1945 when China joined the United Nations under the name "The Republic of China," international society

[547] The votes were 76 in favor 35 against. *See Id.*

[548] The full Resolution is entitled, "Restoration of the Lawful Rights of the People's Republic of China in the United Nations." G.A. Res. 2758, GAOR, 26th Sess., Supp No. 29, at 2, UN Doc. A/8439 (1971) [hereinafter 'Resolution 2758'].

The full Resolution 2758 follows:

The General Assembly,

Recalling the principles of the Charter of the United Nations,

Considering that the restoration of the lawful rights of the People's Republic of China is essential both for the protection of the Charter of the United Nations and for the cause that United Nations must serve under the Charter,

Recognizing that the representatives of the Government of the People's Republic of China are the only lawful representatives of China to the United Nations and that the People's Republic of China is one of the five permanent members of the Security Council,

Decides to restore all its rights to the People's Republic of China and to recognize the representatives of its Government as the only legitimate representatives of China to the United Nations, and to expel forthwith the representatives of Chiang Kai-shek from the place which they unlawfully occupy at United Nations and in all the organizations related to it.

Id. See Phillips, *supra* note 536, at 735 footnote 2.

regarded that the State that joined the organization was the State of China and that the ROC was the government representing China at the time. During the 1971 debate in the General Assembly resulting in the passage of Resolution 2758, the State involved was the State of China. The proposal was to expel the ROC government, not to expel one of its members, China.

The Resolution of the United Nations involved a question of representation in the United Nations. Since in principle only one government was allowed to represent a member in the United Nations, the question at the time was: Which government, the ROC or the PRC was to represent the member China. The Resolution made this point clear in the language adopted. It "[*d*]*ecides* to restore all its rights to the People's Republic of China and to recognize the representatives of its Government as the only legitimate representatives of China to the United Nations."[549] Thus, when the United Nations expelled the ROC, what it expelled was a government, not a State. After the representatives of the PRC replaced the representatives of the ROC in the United Nations, the UN documents listing its members state "China" as its member and also indicates that China was admitted on October 24, 1945, a date prior to the establishment of the PRC. The name plate on the desk where the representatives of the PRC to the UN sit states "China," not "the People's Republic of China" or "the PRC."

Resolution 2758 created the UN's China policy. The Resolution has three propositions: there is only one China; its government is the PRC; in the United Nations, the people in China will be represented by the PRC government thereafter. If the propositions have become the UN's policy over China, it is quite different from "the UN's one China policy" that subsequently developed.

5. POSITION OF LEE TENG-HUI ON THE POLITICAL STATUS OF THE ROC

A. Lee's Initial Position—The KMT's One-China Dogma

In 1988, the political power of the ROC fell on a Taiwanese. When Jiang (Chiang) Jing-guo died in January 1988 before his second term expired, Vice-President Lee Teng-hui assumed the presidency for the rest of Jiang (Chiang)'s term. Lee was the first Taiwanese to become the

[549] *Id.*

ROC President.[550] He, at the same time, became the Chairman of the Chinese Nationalist Party (The KMT). In 1990 when Jiang (Chiang) Jing-guo's residual term expired, the National Assembly elected Lee to be the President for a term of six years.[551]

When Lee first assumed the presidency in 1988, the ROC was already isolated in the international society. An overwhelming number of the States recognized the PRC as the representative government of China. Fewer than 40 States still recognized the ROC as the representative government of China. All of those States were small and, except the Holy See (the Vatican), had received significant financial aid from the ROC government.

From the beginning, Lee Teng-hui, like his predecessors, considered the ROC a "country" that had sovereignty over the entire China as well as the island of Taiwan. As the Chairman of the KMT, Lee adhered to the KMT's one-China dogma. He had no intention to establish a new State limiting its territory to the island of Taiwan.

The people of Taiwan were confused as to the political status of the ROC. Throughout the rule of Jiang (Chiang) Kai-shek and Jiang (Chiang) Jing-guo, the people of Taiwan lived under the shadow of the one-China dogma. But to them, China, *Zhong* (*Chung*) *Guo* or the "Middle Country," referred to the country called the PRC or *Zhong* (*Chung*) *Hua Jen Min Kung He Guo* across the Taiwan Strait. They, however, had different perceptions on the political status of the ROC. Although some people understood that the ROC was a government of the State of China exiled on the island of Taiwan, most people regarded the ROC as a country, largely due to the influence of the Chinese name of the ROC, *Zhong* (*Chung*) *Hua Min Guo*, and the one-China dogma.

After Lee took the office of the presidency of his own term in 1990, he embarked on some political reforms. In 1991, he terminated the Temporary Provisions Effective During the Period of Communists Rebellion Act[552] pursuant to its provision.[553] The most important reform was restructuring of the "congress" to reflect the reality that the ROC no longer governed the territory and the people under the control of the

[550] Lee Teng-hui, President of the ROC (1988–2000).

[551] Lee was elected on March 21, 1990 by the National Assembly, and inaugurated on May 20, 1990.

[552] For Temporary Provisions Effective During the Period of Communists Rebellion, *see supra* note 487.

[553] *Id.* Art. 9 of the Temporary Provisions provides, "The termination of the Period of Communist Rebellion shall be declared by the President." *Id.*

PRC. Up until that time, the "congress" included "representatives" of regions in mainland China that were under the control of the PRC. In order to reform composition of the deputies in the three houses of the "congress" to reflect the reality, Lee initiated an amendment to the ROC Constitution by the National Assembly in 1991. The Amendment of the Nanjing (Nanking) Constitution of 1946[554] changed the structure of the "congress." The "permanent" deputies who represented the people who never elected them were persuaded to retire with favorable entitlements to quell their opposition. The amendments were welcomed by the people of Taiwan.

However, the amended ROC Constitution does not forsake the one-China dogma, in particular the ROC's claim of sovereignty over "Mainland China." The 1991 Amendment consists of 10 Articles. The most important provisions concern the formation of the members of the three houses of the "congress." The first three Articles provide the number of deputies in the National Assembly,[555] the Institute of Legislation (the Legislature *Yuan*),[556] and the Institute of Control (the Control *Yuan*).[557] The Amendment creates two geographic regions for the purpose of selecting the deputies: "the Free Region" and "the Entire Country."[558] The term "the Free Region," by implication, refers to the territory under the actual control of the ROC: the "Province of Taiwan" and China's two offshore islands, Kinmen and Matsu. The term "the Entire Country," by implication, refers to both the territory under the control of the ROC and the territory under the control of the PRC. Thus, the amended ROC Constitution still applies, in theory, to entire China as well as Taiwan.

[554] The Amendment of the Constitution, adopted by the second extraordinary session of the First National Assembly on April 22, 1991 and promulgated by the President on May 1, 1991 (The 1991 Amendment), *available at* http://www.ey.gov.tw/en/Upload/WebArchive/4697/Constitution.pdf. Last visited 10/9/2013.

[555] Art. 1 of the (1991) Amendment, *Id.*, replaces Articles 26 and 135 of the Constitution providing the number of deputies in the National Assembly.

[556] Art. 2 of the (1991) Amendment, *Id.*, replaces Art. 64 of the Constitution providing the number of deputies in the Institute of Legislation (The Legislature *Yuan*).

[557] Art. 3 of the (1991) Amendment, *Id.*, replaces Art. 91 of the Constitution providing the number of deputies in the Institute of Censorship (or the Institute of Control—The Control *Yuan*).

[558] Another geographical term created by the (1991) Amendment is "the Mainland Region." The term is not used for the election of deputies. Art. 10 of the Amendment, *Id.*, provides that "The rights and obligations between the people in the Free Region and the Mainland Region, and the disposition of other affairs may be regulated by other law."

Under the amended Constitution, the people in "Mainland China" still have representation in the ROC's new "congress." For each house of the "congress," the number of deputies elected by the residents of cities or prefectures in the Free Region (Taiwan) is determined by the size of the population of the cities or the prefectures. In addition, a fixed number of deputies collectively represent the entire population of "the Entire Country."[559] The latter are appointed by political parties according to a system of proportional representation: each political party gains additional seats proportionate to the votes it receives in the congressional election. Thus, the people in "Mainland China" are represented by the deputies selected to represent "the Entire Country."

In 1992, Lee persuaded the National Assembly to make another amendment to the ROC Constitution.[560] The major change of the 1992 Amendment to the Constitution was on the method of electing the President and the Vice-President. It changed from an indirect election method—an election by the National Assembly—to a direct election method—a general election by the people in the "Free Region." Other than that, the amended ROC Constitution continued to apply to the territory and the people under the control of the PRC government.[561]

In 1996 when Lee Teng-hui's term expired, he was reelected for a term of 4 years in a general election pursuant to the 1992 Amendment to the Constitution. In the spring of 1996, Lee ran for the presidency as the candidate of the KMT Party against Peng Ming-min, the candidate of the opposition party, the Democratic Progressive Party (the DPP). During the election campaign, Peng, who was once imprisoned during Jiang (Chiang) Jing-guo's term for writing a "Manifesto of the Taiwanese self-preservation," was perceived to be pro-independence. But Peng lost the

[559] The fixed numbers of deputies who represent the "Entire Country" are as follows: For the National Assembly, "80 deputies from the entire country without regard to the regions." Amendment to the Constitution, *supra* note 554, Art. 1, Item 1, Para. 4. For the Institute of Legislation, "30 deputies from the entire country without regard to the regions." Amendment to the Constitution, *Id.* Art. 2, Item 1, Para. 4. For the Institute of Control, "5 deputies from the entire country without regard to the regions." Amendment to the Constitution, *Id.* Art. 3, Item 1, Para. 4.

[560] Amendment to the Constitution of the Republic of China, 1992, adopted by the 2nd National Assembly on May 27, 1992, and promulgated by the President on May 28, 1992 (The 1992 Amendment), *available at* http://www.oop.gov.tw/roc/charter/eadded.htm. Article 12 provides "The president and the vice president shall be directly elected by the entire populace of the Free Region of the Republic of China." *Id.*

[561] After 1992, there were five more amendments to the Constitution. But none of them is relevant to the discourse of this subject.

election not because of his political stand but due to other factors. One factor was that Lee as the President had achieved some political reforms, leading some voters to perceive that Lee, a Taiwanese, was in a better position to pave a way for the eventual independence of Taiwan; another factor was that the KMT Party, which had ruled Taiwan for one half a century, had built up influence on the voters by controlling local officials of the compartmentalized municipalities, an administrative system based on the system established by the former Japanese government. The 1996 election pursuant to the amended Constitution was the first time in the history of the ROC that a general election was employed to elect the President and the Vice President. Some Taiwanese politicians claimed that the election of the President and the Vice-president by a general election turned the ROC into a new State.[562]

However, Lee disappointed many of his supporters in his 1996 inaugural speech when he called for a "peaceful reunification of China."[563] He proclaimed that "there is only one China; there is no so-called 'Taiwan independence.'"[564] The speech followed the lines of Jiang (Chiang) Kai-shek's one-China dogma. The term "reunification of China" implied that Taiwan was part of China. While Lee had been perceived by many people in Taiwan as pro-Taiwan, his proclamation in his inaugural speech confused them and created a society which was, as a New York Times reporter described it, "in a schizophrenic environment."[565] For the next 5 years, Lee maintained the same position.

Though Lee had said that the ROC was a *country* many times, to other States the ROC in Taiwan was a government of China exiled in the island. Neither of the two amendments to the Constitution made the ROC a new State, as some Taiwanese politicians claimed. To other States, it was the PRC government in Beijing, rather than the ROC government in Taipei, that represented the State of China and exercised its

[562] Speech of Annette Lu (of the DPP Party), Vice-President of the ROC from 2000 to 2008, delivered on July 11, 2010 at the Taiwanese Association Conference, Plaines Region, at St. Louis.

[563] In the inaugural speech, President Lee stated that both sides of the Taiwan Strait should seek unification of the country. When Lee advocated reunification of the state, he restated his conviction of the one-China dogma. "Mr. Lee added 'China is a country divided and under separate rule' implying that there was only one China." F.J. Khergamvala, *Taiwan's Lee To Be Sworn in Today*, HINDU, 05/20/1996, at 2.

[564] Lee's inaugural speech, *available at* http://www.taipei.org/whatsnew/speech.htm. Last visited 08/01/1998.

[565] Patrick E. Tyler, *The China and Taiwan Problem; How Politics Torpedoed Asian Calm*, N. Y. TIMES, 02/11/1996, at 1.

sovereign power. As a matter of theory, Lee's insistence on the one-China dogma that Taiwan was part of China could unintentionally lend color to the PRC's claim that "Taiwan is [China's] renegade province."

B. The "special state-to-state relationship" Statement

An event in 1999 surprised the people in Taiwan as well as foreign governments and political observers. On July 9, 1999, in an interview by a German TV reporter, President Lee said that "The Republic of China has been a sovereign country since it was founded in 1912. The 1991 Amendment to the Constitution designated the cross-Strait relationship as a special state-to-state relationship. Consequently, there is no need of declaring independence."[566]

[566] Interview of the ROC President Lee Teng-hui by Dr. Guenther Knabe, Head of Deutche Welle Asia Programs (Deutche Welle television broadcast, 07/10/1999) [hereinafter "Interview of President Lee Teng-hui"], on July 9, 1999. Deutche Welle, TV broadcasting on July 10, 1999. Interview of President Lee Teng-Hui.

The following is part of the interview broadcast on Deutche Welle (The English translation is provided by the TV station):

Knaebe: *You are considered as a renegade province by Beijing's government. That is, of course, a permanent intimidation and threat from the Mainland. How are you coping with these dangers?*

Lee: *The historical fact is, that since the establishment of Chinese Communist regime in 1949, it has never ruled the territory under the ROC (Republic of China)—Taiwan, Penghu, Kinmen, and Matsu. The 1991 Constitutional Amendment had designated cross-Strait relationship as special state-to-state relationship, rather than an internal relationship between a legitimate government and a renegade group or between a central government and local government.*

Knabe: *Declaring Taiwan as an independent state seems to be no realistic option. Beijing's "one country two systems" is not acceptable for the majority of the people in Taiwan. Is there any compromise between these two positions. And if there is one, what does it look like?*

Lee: *The Republic of China has been a sovereign country since it was founded in 1912. The 1991 amendment to the Constitution (promulgated in 1947 in Nanking, China) designated cross-Strait relation as special state-to-state relation. Consequently, there is no need to declare independence.*

Id.

After the program showing the interview, the anchorman, Brian Thomas, asked Dr. Knabe, "Based on your discussion with President Lee, did you get the impression that he was prepared to declare independence?" *Id.* Knabe replied, "I think not. He stopped short of doing that." *Id.*

See also China Threatens Envoy's Trip, GREENSBORO NEWS & RECORD, 97/17/1999, *available in* 1999 WL 6953820.

The statement of Lee stirred up political debates both in Taiwan and abroad. The statement was subsequently referred to as the "special state-to-state relationship statement." Some called it the "Two-state doctrine."

C. Reaction in Taiwan and the ROC Government's Clarification

In Taiwan, the topic was a sensitive one and the reactions to the statement were diverse. The day after the interview was broadcast in the German TV, Taiwan's newspapers printed exciting headlines, claiming that Lee Teng-hui had created two Chinas during the interview. Many Taiwanese joyfully acclaimed that Lee had declared independence. Some even started to call Lee "Father of the country."

Whether Lee intended to create confusion or his statement created an unintended consequence was a subject of debates. His officials were caught off guard. There was no advanced warning to them that he would make such a drastic statement. They were quickly engaged in damage control, lest there would be a misunderstanding inside and outside of Taiwan. The immediate action for them to take was explaining to the people in Taiwan what Lee meant by his "special state-to-state relationship" statement in the context of the one-China dogma. They did not believe that Lee had declared independence because he said that "there is no need of declaring independence." But he had said something in the interview contrary to what the KMT had thus far preached to the people after Jiang (Chiang) Kai-shek moved to the island of Taiwan.

However, the ROC officials were confused. They could not reach a consensus on the meaning of the statement. On July 12, the Commissioner of the Mainland Affairs Su Q (Chi) said that "Lee Teng-hui means 'two countries in one nation.'"[567]

On July 15, the Chief of Information Bureau Cheng Jian-ren also said that "The special state-to-state relationship means 'two countries in one nation.'"[568]

But Cheng quickly withdrew his explanation next day. He said that "'Two countries in one nation' is a wrong interpretation; I have to think it over for a better explanation."[569]

[567] *Available at* http://issue.udn.com/FOCUSNEWS/TWOSTATES/Official_Statement/T_official_statement/07_13_013.htm.

[568] *Available at* http://issue.udn.com/FOCUSNEWS/TWOSTATES/Official_Statement/T_official_statement/07_16_022.htm.

[569] *Available at* http://issue.udn.com/FOCUSNEWS/TWOSTATES/Official_Statement/T_official_statement/07_22_029.htm.

He never further publicly clarified the meaning of the statement, probably because he could not come up with a sensible explanation.

Lee himself, realizing that he had created a controversy, attempted to clarify his own statement. Less than two weeks after the interview, he took an opportunity of trying to explain his statement. At a meeting of the Taipei Chapter of International Rotary Club on July 20, 1999, when he was asked to explain the "special state-to-state relationship," he replied that "[t]he [ROC] government is not engaged in the Taiwan independence [movement]. Without equal status in a negotiation [with the PRC government], problems such as smuggling of drugs and guns or transmitting of the foot-and-mouth disease,[570] are difficult to resolve."[571] It was not much of an explanation of the controversial statement. Instead of providing the meaning of "the special state-to-state relationship," he merely explained why he made the statement.

If the ROC officials were confused, it was because the statement itself was confusing. In fact, there were outright contradictions in Lee's statements made during the interview, if the word "state" in the "special state-to-state relationship" meant an independent territorial political institution. The first aspect of contradiction regarded the time when the ROC became a "State." Lee explained in the interview that "the 1991 constitutional amendment had designated cross-Strait relationship as special state-to-state relationship, rather than an internal relationship between a legitimate government and a renegade group or between a central government and local government."[572] By 1999 when Lee was interviewed, the PRC government was already recognized by a great majority of the States as the representative government of China—a government which called Taiwan a "renegade province." Thus, Lee's statement implied that the ROC was upgraded to a State from a "local government" by the Amendment to the ROC Constitution in 1991. However, in the same interview, Lee also stated that "the ROC was a sovereign country since 1912."[573] Was it 1912 or 1991 when the ROC was established as a "State"? For sure, he did not mean that the ROC became a State limiting its territory to the island of Taiwan at the time of the interview. In fact,

[570] It is a contagious disease carried by animals from China. Deborah Kuo, *In Taiwan FMD Spreads to Chiayi, Officials Say Milk Safe*, World News Connection, 01/24/2000.

[571] *President Lee reasserts the "two countries doctrine,"* The Pacific Times (Los Angeles), 07/22/1999, p. 1.

[572] *See supra* note 566.

[573] *Id.*

as discussed earlier, when the ROC was established in 1911, it was a government of China. China was a State long before the establishment of the ROC.

The second aspect of contradiction there would be was on the statehood of the ROC, if the word "state" meant an independent territorial political institution. If the word "state" in his statement meant independent territorial political institution, Lee's statement in the interview meant both the ROC and the PRC were independent territorial political institutions. Then, the 1991 Amendment to the ROC Constitution also had the same effect of making both the ROC and the PRC States in 1991. However, in 1991 there was only one China, the ROC, under the amended ROC Constitution. To other States, though there was also only one China, the State China was represented by the PRC.

The third aspect of contradiction if the word "state" in his statement meant an independent territorial political institution was with the one-China dogma. When Lee made the statement in the 1999 interview, it would be the first time an ROC President attempted to seek an equal status between the ROC and the PRC: declaring that both were independent territorial political institutions, each with its own territory. Yet, there was no provision in the 1991 Amendment which could be interpreted to have turned the ROC into a State limiting its territory to the island of Taiwan, or have created a "special state-to-state relationship" between the ROC and the PRC. On the contrary, the ROC still attempted to exercise sovereign power over China under the 1991 amended Constitution. In amending the ROC Constitution in 1991, the ROC did not discard the KMT's one-China dogma.

If interpreting the word "state" in the "special state-to-state relationship" statement as "independent territorial political institution" makes no sense, the word "state" must be given a different meaning.

D. The Meaning of the "special state-to-state relationship" Statement

It will make more sense if the word "state" in the "special state-to-state relationship" statement is rendered as "government." The circumstances under which Lee made the statement would shed some light on the meaning of the word. In the television broadcast, during the interview while the German Deutsche Welle TV Asian expert Dr. Guenther Knabe asked questions in English, Lee replied in Mandarin Chinese with a simultaneous English translation. Lee's Chinese words that were rendered "state-to-state" in English translation were "*Guo* (country) and *Guo* (country)." Since both the Chinese terms for the Republic of China or *Zhong* (*Chung*) *Hua Min Guo* and the People's Republic of China or *Zhong* (*Chung*) *Hua Jen Min Kung He Guo* end with the word *Guo* (country), Lee's statement "*Guo* to *Guo* relationship" in fact referred to "the Republic of China" to "the People's Republic of China" relationship. As it was explained before, though both the ROC and the PRC use the word "*Guo* (country)" at the end of their Chinese names, both the ROC and the PRC are governments of the State of China. Thus, Lee's statement means that the ROC and the PRC [should be] in equal status in the relationship between the two governments.

Lee's own explanation at the Rotary Club confirmed this interpretation. He explained that "[t]he [ROC] government is not engaged in the Taiwan independence [movement]. Without equal status in a negotiation [with the PRC government], problems ... are difficult to resolve."[574] A negotiation is conducted between governments. Thus, however Lee characterized the ROC, his statement, in fact, referred to "the government to government relationship."

Maybe, Lee himself was aware that he was not talking about a normal State-to-State relationship and, thus, used the word "special" to describe the relationship between the ROC and the PRC. After more than 40 years since Jiang (Chiang) Kai-shek created the one-China dogma, much of the world politic had changed at the time when Lee was interviewed: The UN passed Resolution No. 2758 expelling the ROC from the organization; a great majority of the world community had recognized the PRC as the representative government of China. The PRC government now treated the ROC as "renegade group." It was the ROC government that struggled to seek to be an equal to the PRC government. If Lee's "government [was] not engaged in the Taiwan independence"[575] as he said, then it just sought for an equal status between the two governments for negotiation.

E. Reaction of Foreign Governments

The reaction of foreign governments was uniformly reserved. Practically, no States considered that Lee's statement had turned the ROC into a new State limiting its territory to the island of Taiwan. To foreign

[574] *See supra* note 571.
[575] *Id.*

governments and political observers, the ROC was a new government of the State of China when it was established in 1912. When the PRC was established in 1949, it was also a new government of China. Lee's "special state-to-state relationship" statement was not a declaration establishing a new State limiting its territory to the island of Taiwan.

The Deutsche Welle interviewer did not see a declaration of independence in Lee's statement either. Immediately after the German TV broadcast showing the interview, the anchorman, Brian Thomas, asked the interviewer Gruenther Knabe: "Based on your discussion with President Lee, did you get the impression that he was prepared to declare independence?" Knabe emphatically replied, "I think not. He stopped short of doing that."[576] A few days after Lee's interview, US Senator Frank H. Murkowsky (R-Alaska) dismissed a suggestion that "Taiwan has virtually declared independence by President Lee Teng-hui's statement [about the cross-Strait relationship.]"[577]

Three months after Lee made the statement, the UN Secretary General Kofi Annan also rejected any view that the ROC had become a State by Lee's statement. In September 1999, a severe earthquake struck the central part of the island. Many people died. Many more were injured, lost their houses, and traumatized. Immediately thereafter Annan announced that the United Nations had to wait for the approval of the PRC government before the UN Office for the Coordination of Humanitarian Affairs could send a disaster assessment team to what he called "the Taiwan Province of China."[578] If in Annan's view Taiwan was a "Province of China," the ROC in Taiwan could not be a State. Whether Annan was correct in characterizing the island of Taiwan as a "Province of China" is a different issue to be analyzed later, but his view was that the ROC in Taiwan was not a State because no State can be a province of another State.

576 *Id.*

577 *US Senator Sees No Change in Taiwan's China Policy*, CENTRAL NEWS AGENCY, 07/17/1999, *available in* 1999 WL 17720726.

578 *See* Antonio Chiang, *Taipei Crisis, Beijing Opportunity*, INT'L HERALD TRIBUNE, 09/27/1999; *UN Sends Coordinating Rescue Team to Taiwan*, 09/22/1999, AGENCE FRANCE-PRESSE, *available in* 1999 WL 25110592; Corky Siemaszko, *Taiwan Digging Out, Frantic Rescuers Hunt for Quake Survivors*, DAILY NEWS, 9/22/1999, at 7. *See UN Sends Coordinating Rescue Team to Taiwan*, AGENCE FR. PRESSE, 09/22/1999; Corky Siemaszko, *Taiwan Digging Out, Frantic Rescuers Hunt for Quake Survivors*, DAILY NEWS, 09/22/1999, at 7.

6. POSITION OF CHEN SHUI-BIAN ON THE POLITICAL STATUS OF THE ROC

In March 2000, a general election was held before the end of Lee Teng-hui's term. The three way race was among Chen Shui-bian of the DPP, Lian Zhan of the Chinese Nationalist Party (The KMT), and Soong Chu-yu (James Soong), who had left the KMT to form The People First Party. Chen Shui-bian (Chen) won the election. Chen, like Lee, was a native Taiwanese. It was the first time the Chinese Nationalist Party lost the executive power of the government, though the Party still retained a majority in the "congress."

Although Chen was perceived by his supporters as pro-independence, in public he wavered on his stance on the political status of the ROC throughout his presidency. During the campaign for the president of the ROC, his announced policy toward China was that of compromise and cooperation. He advocated integration of Taiwan with China. A majority of the Taiwanese cast their votes for him because the alternative was worse. In his May 20, 2000 inaugural speech, Chen angered many of his Taiwanese constituencies by announcing a blatantly negative agenda.

Chen declared that his China policy was that of "four-nos and one have-no": "as long as the Chinese Communist Party regime has no intention to use military force against Taiwan, I pledge that during my term in office I will not declare independence; I will not change the country name; I will not push forth the inclusion of the so-called 'state-to-state relationship' concept in the Constitution; I will not promote a referendum to change the status quo in regards to the question of independence or unification; I have no plan to abolish the National Reunification Council or the National Reunification Guidelines."[579]

In essence, Chen had a "no Taiwan independence" policy.

But in August 2002, Chen suddenly changed his position on the political status of the ROC. This time, he claimed that the ROC was a country separate from China. When the World Federation of Taiwanese Associations, an organization formed by the overseas Taiwanese

[579] *See* Chen Shui-bian, *Dawn of a Rising Era*, TAIPEI TIMES, 05/21/2000, *available at* http://www.taipeitimes.com/News/archives/2000/05/21/0000036938. Last visited 05/04/2010. Chen subsequently claimed that it was the US Government (the Clinton Administration) that forced him to make such policy announcement. *See infra* text accompanying note 1021.

associations, held an annual conference in Tokyo, Japan, Chen gave a speech to the group via close circuit TV on August 5. During the speech, Chen suddenly, departing from his prepared speech, proclaimed that "Taiwan and China are two countries, each on one side of the Taiwan Strait and that the (ROC) Institute of Legislation (the Legislature *Yuan*) should consider passing a referendum law [permitting the people] to protect its sovereignty."[580]

The Taiwanese were jubilant. The proclamation became known as the "two countries each on one side [of the Taiwan Strait]" statement. Chen used the word "Taiwan," even though he was the President of the ROC. He often used "Taiwan" instead of "the ROC," possibly to please the people of Taiwan. From then on, Chen claimed that Taiwan or the ROC had sovereignty.

In March 2004, Chen Shui-bian was reelected for a second term of the presidency. In the presidential campaign, the competition was between Chen, who sought a second term, and Lian Zhan of the KMT Party. Chen won again in the general election. During the campaign, Chen often proclaimed that the ROC was a "sovereign country." In February 2004, in an interview with a reporter, he said that "The ROC is a sovereignty[sic] independent country," but also said that "Taiwan is a sovereignty[sic] independent country."[581] So, after he was reelected, he announced that he would not use a referendum to create a new Constitution, just amend it.[582]

But in 2005 President Chen again angered his supporters by making an ambiguous statement on the political status of the ROC. On February 24, 2005, he and his former political rival, The People First Party Chairman James Soong, issued a joint statement. It was not clear why the President had to join with a political rival to make the statement, but the statement said that "According to the Constitution of the Republic of

[580] Sandy Huang, *Pan blue camp pans Chen's talk*, TAIPEI TIMES, Monday, 08/5/2002, P.1, *available at* http://www.taipeitimes.com/News/front/print/2002/08/05/0000159038. Last visited 03/04/2011.

[581] *Strait Talking, In an exclusive interview, Former President Chen Shui-bian rejects the mainland's 'one-China' policy.* TIME ASIA, 02/16/2004. The statement "The ROC is a sovereignty independent country" in Chinese literally means that The ROC is a country whose sovereignty is independent. The statement "Taiwan is a sovereignty independent country" in Chinese literally means that Taiwan is a country whose sovereignty is independent.

[582] Joseph Kahn and Chris Buckley, *Taiwan's President Tones Down His Pro-Independence Oratory,* N.Y. TIMES, 05/21/2004, Sec. A, p. 12, C5.

China (the ROC), our country's status and position is defined as the *de facto* and *de jure* status quo existing [with the PRC each] on the opposite side of the Strait." But then, Chen pledged in the same joint statement that "during my term as president, I will not declare independence, [and] will not promote a referendum to change the status quo on the issue of independence or unification."[583]

Although the language was ambiguous, for sure it was not a declaration establishing a new State separated from the State of China. In fact, Chen in the joint statement said clearly that he "will not declare independence." Soong, who was a pro-China politician, could not have agreed to a make a joint statement declaring independence of the ROC.

Like his predecessor Lee Teng-hui, Chen was simply confused as to the political status of the ROC thinking that it was a country. As a consequence, he constantly made statements that did not make sense in term of international law. For instance, after stating that he would not declare independence in 2005, in an interview in November of 2006 with a Financial Times reporter he claimed that "Taiwan is a sovereignty[sic] independent State."[584] With such a political leader, the people of Taiwan lived in an ever-confused environment.

A. Reactions of Other States

Notwithstanding Chen's repeated statement that "The ROC is a sovereignty [sic] independent country," or "Taiwan is a sovereignty [sic] independent country," the United Nations and its related organizations as well as the United States did not consider the ROC or Taiwan a sovereign State during his presidency.

In 2003, World Health Organization (WHO) echoed Kofi Annan's view that "Taiwan is a province of China," implying that Taiwan was not a State. For many years, the ROC applied to WHO to be an "observer," not as a member. Every time, the application was rejected. In April 2003, a disease known as "severe acute respiratory syndrome (SARS)" spread to the island of Taiwan. Not being a member of WHO, the ROC

[583] *See supra* text accompanying note 579.

[584] *Financial Times, Interview with Former President Chen*, Office of the President, Republic of China, News Release, 11/3/2006, *available at* http://www.president.gov.tw/en/news-release/print.php?id'1105499283. Last visited 11/15/2006. *Interview With Taiwanese Former President Chen Shui-bian*, THE WASHINGTON POST, Friday, 10/10/2003. www.washingtonpost.com/ac2/wp-dyn/A9815-2003Oct10.?language'printer. Last visited 11/06/2006.

government in Taiwan could not receive information provided by the organization for preventing the spread of the disease. A month earlier in March 2003, the ROC government applied, as it had done repeatedly several years in the past, to WHO to become an observer at its annual meeting, World Health Assembly (WHA). When the WHA opened its General Session in Geneva in May 2003, it again rejected the ROC's application, even though the SARS disease continued to spread in Taiwan. The WHO shared Kofi Annan's view on the political status of the ROC, and referred to Taiwan as "the Taiwan Province, China" in its website.[585] If Taiwan was a province of China, the ROC could not be a State.

Later in May 2003, Kofi Annan, as the Secretary General of the United Nations again made a statement implying that the ROC was not a State. Puzzled by the WHO's action or inaction, the UN Press Club decided to hold a press conference[586] at the UN Headquarters in New York City to discuss the WHO's decision in rejecting the ROC in its efforts to gain entry into the organization. The Press Club invited a ROC official in New York City,[587] equivalent to the rank of a consulate general, to speak at the conference. When the ROC official attempted to enter the UN building, Kofi Annan barred him from entry "because of the organization's one-China policy."[588] Kofi Annan's statement—the organization (the United Nations)'s one-China Policy—implied that Taiwan was part of China and that the ROC in Taiwan was not a State in the eyes of the United Nations.

The position of the United States was the same. It did not regard the ROC as a State. In October 2004, the US Secretary of State Colin Powell made some remarks on Taiwan's sovereignty that drew protests in Taiwan. On his way to China, Powell gave an interview to a CNN

[585] *See World Health Organization Changes Travel Recommendation for Taiwan Province, China*, June 17, 2003 (changing a previous advisory that recommended postponing all but essential travel to Taiwan, in order to contain a spread of severe acute respiratory syndrome (SARS)), *available at* http://www.who.int/mediacentre/news/. Last visited 10/01/2004; *see also* UN DAILY NEWS DIGEST, *WHO Urges Precautions in Labs After Worker in Taiwan, China, Gets SARS*, 12/17/2003 (using the expression "Taiwan, Province of China"), *available at* http://www.un.org/news/. Last visited 10/01/2004.

[586] The press conference took place on May 23, 2003. *See* Colum Lynch, *UN Bars Taiwanese Official From Briefing*, WASH. POST, 05/24/2003, at A22.

[587] Director of the Taipei Cultural and Economic Office (Previously called "Coordination Council For North American Affaires").

[588] *See UN Bars Taiwanese Official From Briefing*, *supra* note 586.

reporter on October 25, 2004. During the interview, Powell made two remarks. The first remark was, "[t]here is only one China; Taiwan is not independent. It does not enjoy sovereignty as a nation." His second remark was, "[w]e want to see both sides not take unilateral action that would prejudice an eventual outcome, a reunification that all parties are seeking."[589] While Powell's view that "[all parties] are seeking a reunification" was not correct, his first statement that "[The ROC] does not enjoy sovereignty as nation" simply reflected the position of the US Government. A senior US officer repeated the US position on the political status of the ROC in 2007. In September 2007, Dennis Wilder, Senior Director for Asian Affairs of the White House National Security Council, said that "Taiwan, or the Republic of China, is not at this point a state in the international community."[590]

7. POLITICAL STATUS OF THE ROC UNDER LEE AND CHEN IN INTERNATIONAL LAW

It was concluded in the previous Sections that regardless of the characterization of former President Lee and former President Chen on the political status of the ROC in Taiwan, other States and the United Nations did not consider the ROC a State after it moved to the island of Taiwan. This section will apply State theory and international law discussed in Chapter 2, The State and Sovereignty, to the ROC to see whether it met the requirements of a State after it moved its seat to Taiwan.

As it was observed in Chapter 2, The State and Sovereignty, a territorial political institution with the required elements of a State becomes a State by an act of declaration. It was also pointed out that after the declaration, for the political institution to establish a State effectively, it must act consistently with the fact that it is a State, i.e., asserting its statehood and acting like a State in international affairs. This section will review the

[589] *Interview With Anthony Yuen of Phoenix TV*, US Department of State, *Former Secretary of State Collin L. Powell, Speeches and Remarks*. 2004 October. During his visit to China, while in Beijing Powell gave an interview to a television reporter on October 25, *available at* http://www.state.gov/secretary/former/powell/remarks/c12960.htm. Last visited 11/7/2006.

[590] Chiehyu Lin and Y.F. Low, *UN secretary-general stops calling 'Taiwan part of China*, 09/06/2007, *available at* http://www.taiwanbasic.com/un/cna/taiwanpart.htm. Last visited 03/17/2009. *Also available at* http://www.cna.com.tw/eng/topread.php?id'200709060011. Last visited 08/19/2010.

acts of the ROC in Taiwan in the world community to see whether the ROC met the two requirements.

A. There Was No Act of Declaration Establishing a State

For the ROC to become a State, it has to declare independence from China limiting its territory to the area under its actual control—Taiwan. The ROC government under Jiang (Chiang) Kai-Shek and his son Jiang (Chiang) Jing-guo never intended to establish a new State independent of China or build a separate identity. Both the father and the son stuck to the one-China dogma.

Many people in Taiwan, in particular the Taiwanese politicians, claim that the ROC turned into a State at a certain historical event during the presidency of Lee Teng-hui or Chen Shui-bian. The most common events that have been cited were: (a) the amendment of the Constitution in 1991; (b) the election of Lee Teng-hui as the President by a general election in 1996; (c) the announcement of the "special state-to-state relationship" statement by Lee Teng-hui in 1999; and (d) the announcement of the "two countries each on one side (of the Taiwan Strait)" statement by Chen Shui-bian. This subsection will examine whether any of the events listed above amounted to an act of declaration of the ROC under Lee Teng-hui or Chen Shui-bian sufficient to establish a new State in international law.

a. The Amendment of the Constitution in 1991

When Lee Teng-hui in the 1999 TV interview said that "The 1991 Amendment to the ROC Constitution designated the cross-Strait relationship as a special state-to-state relationship,"[591] he seemed to indicate that the ROC turned into a "State" by the constitutional amendment, thus, "there is no need of declaring independence." As explained before, the amendments of the Constitution, both in 1991 and 1992, did not change the character of the Nanjing (Nanking) Constitution as a constitution for the entire country of China. A change in the method of electing the President from an indirect election to a general election in 1992 did not make the political institution a new State. Such a change in procedural rules does not effect a change in the substantive status of a political institution.

[591] *See supra* text accompanying note 566.

b. The Election of Lee Teng-Hui as the President by a General Election in 1996

Advocates of this view held that the new direct election by the people of the ROC's President and Vice President to replace the indirect election by the National Assembly created a new State. Again, this was simply a change in procedure, rather than a substantive change in the nature of the political institution. If a change in the constitution of the method of electing the President and the Vice President did not create a new State, neither would the implementation of the new method.

c. The Announcement of the "Special State-to-State Relationship" Statement by Lee Teng-Hui in 1999

Lee's "special state-to-state relationship" statement was not a declaration of independence or a declaration establishing a State. As fully discussed earlier, Lee had no intention to establish a new State limiting its territory to the island of Taiwan. In fact, Lee's statement that there was no need to declare independence in the TV interview negated any interpretation that the statement was itself a declaration of independence. A declaration for the establishment of a new State is a solemn statement and should be open and clear. The purpose of such a declaration is to make the existence of a new state open and unambiguous to the population and other States. Every State has a birthday. A new state cannot gradually evolve into existence. The modern State practice is to make such declaration by the political leader, such as the Executive head of the government, or representatives of the people, such as the legislature, in a document officially executed and announced in public to the international community. Lee's statement, made in an interview by a foreign reporter in a closed chamber, not supported by any formal document, was not a serious declaration, which would establish statehood.

d. The Announcement of the "Two Countries Each on One Side (of the Taiwan Strait)" Statement by Chen Shui-Bian

Chen's statement was not a declaration establishing a new State either. Chen made the statement to limited attendees of a conference via a closed circuit TV, not to the public in general. Such an oral statement was not qualified as an official declaration establishing a State. Similar to Lee's "special state-to-state relationship" statement, Chen's statement was not an open and unambiguous statement to the world of establishing statehood. Additionally, Chen subsequently negated any notion that

Taiwan had become a State when he said that he "[would] not declare independence."[592]

The above analyses of the events demonstrated that none of them constituted an act of declaration establishing a new State limiting its territory to the island of Taiwan. Thus, there was no point in time or event that the ROC transformed into a State during the tenure of the two ROC Presidents. A comment by the drafters of the Restatement states that "Taiwan might satisfy the elements of the definition [of a State], but its authorities have not claimed it to be a State, but rather part of the State of China."[593] Failure to formerly declare independence prevented the ROC from being a State.

B. The ROC Has Not Acted Like a State in the World Community

For a political institution to become a State effectively existing, after it declares establishment of statehood, it must assert statehood in the world community. That neither Lee Teng-hui nor Chen Shui-bian established a new State was evidenced by their subsequent government practice in participating international affairs. Both Presidents asserted that the ROC was an "independent country." If the ROC was a State, its subsequent actions did not match the words. In its attempts to participate the world organizations, the ROC did not assert statehood as illustrated by its attempts to rejoin the United Nations or its participation in the Olympic Games, APEC (Asia Pacific Economic Cooperation), and WTO (World Trade Organization).

a. The United Nations

During the presidency of Lee Teng-hui, the ROC began a campaign to join the United Nations. Since December 1971 when the UN General Assembly decided by Resolution No. 2758 that its member State, China, was to be represented by the PRC government, the ROC in Taiwan was shut out from the United Nations and its related organizations. Twenty-two years later, beginning in 1993 when Lee Teng-hui was the President, the ROC attempted to rejoin the United Nations.

Importantly, in its attempt to join the United Nations, the ROC did not apply for a new membership. Under the UN Charter, an application

[592] *See supra* text accompanying note 583.

[593] The Restatement, *supra* note 212. '201, Comment f (3d Ed., 1987).

by a State to join the United Nations as a new member is to be submitted through the Secretary General's office to the Security Council for approval. Lee Teng-hui did not apply to the Security Council for the ROC to be a new member.

Instead, Lee Teng-hui sought to regain China's seat in the United Nations, which the ROC lost in 1971. Before the UN General Assembly's session in September 1993, the ROC asked friendly countries to submit a request to the General Committee, which was in charge of arranging the General Assembly's annual meeting agenda, to include in the agenda a discussion of the return of "The Republic of China" to the United Nations. The General Committee denied the request. From 1994 to 1999, Lee Teng-hui repeated the request each year. Each time, the request was denied.

President Chen Shui-bian continued the effort to join the United Nations. Although Chen called the ROC a "sovereign independent country," he did not apply to the United Nations for a new membership either. The ROC again sought to return to China's seat, which was occupied by the PRC government. Like Lee Teng-hui, Chen also sought the assistance of friendly States to send the request for inclusion of the matter in the General Assembly's annual meeting agenda every year.[594] Each year, the General Committee rejected the request.

The reason which the ROC gave for returning to the United Nations changed many times. In Lee Teng-hui's time, at the beginning, the application challenged Resolution 2758 itself.[595] In 1998, the ROC requested the UN General Assembly to revoke the Resolution, and restore the ROC's rights at the United Nations by allowing the ROC to participate in the United Nations.[596] In 1999, the Lee administration softened the stand and requested to return to the United Nations solely to represent the people of Taiwan. In its supporting documents, the ROC requested the United Nations to allow the State of China to be represented by two governments: the PRC and the ROC. The document claimed that the twenty three-million people under the ROC were not represented in the

[594] *Request for the inclusion of a supplementary item in the agenda of the fifty-fifth session.* General Assembly. Distr.: General, 4 August 2000. In 2002, the application used the name "the Republic of China (Taiwan)," and the Explanatory memorandum claimed that "the Republic of China (Taiwan) is a sovereign state."

[595] UN G.A. Res. 2758, UN GAOR, 26th Sess., 1976th mtg. at 358 (1971).

[596] *Request for the inclusion of an item in the provisional agenda of the fifty-third session*. General Assembly. Distr.: General, 8 July 1998.

United Nations.[597] Chen Shui-bian, in the request (application) of 2002, argued that Resolution No. 2758 "has been subsequently misused to justify the exclusion of Taiwan."[598] It claimed that participation in the United Nations was the fundamental human right of the people of Taiwan.[599]

In the requests submitted to the United Nations, Chen also created a new identity for the ROC by associating the name "The Republic of China" with "Taiwan." When the Chen administration first applied to the United Nations in 2000, the document used the name "The Republic of China on Taiwan."[600] The word "Taiwan" was but a geographic name where "the Republic of China" government was located. But in 2002, the Chen administration created a new name by incorporating the word "Taiwan" into the official name when Chen used the term "The Republic of China (Taiwan)" as the applicant.[601] In 2006, the word "Taiwan" then became an alternative term for the name of "the Republic of China" when the supporting document (Explanatory memorandum) began with "the Republic of China (hereinafter referred to as 'Taiwan') is a free and peace-loving sovereign State."[602] Despite the new name used by the ROC, the General Committee rejected the requests.

Frustrated by the repeated rejections of the United Nations of the ROC's applications to become a member, President Chen in July, 2007 sent to the UN Secretary-General Ban Ki-Moon an application for a new UN membership in the name of "Taiwan."[603] Ban Ki-Moon rejected the application arbitrarily and returned it without submitting the application

[597] *Request for the inclusion of a supplementary item in the agenda of the fifty-fourth session.* General Assembly. Distr.: General, 12 August 1999.

[598] *Request for the inclusion of a supplementary item in the agenda of the fifty-seventh session.* General Assembly. Distr.: General, 20 August 2002.

[599] *Id.*

[600] The request (application) of 2000 used the name "the Republic of China on Taiwan." The 'Explanatory memorandum' stated "The Republic of China is a democratic country." *Request for the inclusion of a supplementary item in the agenda of the fifty-fifth session.* General Assembly. Distr.: General, 4 August 2000.

[601] In 2002, the application used the name "the Republic of China (Taiwan)," and the Explanatory memorandum claimed that "the Republic of China (Taiwan) is a sovereign state."

[602] In 2006, the application used the name "the Republic of China (hereinafter referred to as Taiwan)."

[603] *See* Chiehyu Lin, *UN secretary-general stops calling 'Taiwan part of China, supra* note 590.

to either the Security Council or the General Assembly for consideration. Ban cited "the UN's one-China policy based on Resolution No. 2758" as his grounds for rejection.[604]

The ROC's attempts to join the United Nations have thus far failed.[605] The failure cannot be solely attributed to obstruction by the PRC government. There was a legal aspect in the ROC's applications that was repugnant to the principle of international law. The United Nations is an organization formed by States; only political institutions with statehood may be members. Yet, the ROC government never declared establishment of a new State independent of China and never applied for a new membership as a new State. It just attempted to *return* to the UN General Assembly to share the China seat with the PRC government. As stated in Chapter 2, The State and Sovereignty, sovereignty is indivisible. Only one government can represent a State. International law does not permit dual representation of a State.

b. World Olympic Games and APEC

The ROC's athletic teams use the name "Chinese Taipei" in the World Olympic Games.[606] The ROC had used the name "the Republic of China" in the Olympic Games until 1988 when the International Olympic Committee (the IOC) refused its use of the name under pressure from the PRC.[607] In 1989, an agreement was reached between the PRC and the ROC that "in all the occasions of the IOC, Taiwan should be called 'Chinese Taipei' *(Zhonghua Taipei)*."[608] Later, when the ROC joined the APEC, it did not use the name "the Republic of China" or Taiwan but again used the name "Chinese Taipei." Thus, the ROC did not assert statehood while participating in the Olympic Games and APEC, but instead acquiesced to being referred to as a part of China.

[604] Ban returned the application on July 23, 2007.

[605] *See* Chiang, *UN Sends Coordinating Rescue Team to Taiwan*, *supra* note 578.

[606] The term "Chinese Taipei" was first used in Olympic Games. *See* CATHERINE K. LIN, NATIONALISM IN INTERNATIONAL POLITICS: THE REPUBLIC OF CHINA'S SPORTS FOREIGN POLICY-MAKING AND DIPLOMACY FROM 1972 TO 1981.)

[607] Jacques de Lisle, *The Chinese Puzzle of Taiwan's Status*, ORBIS, Jan. 1, 2000, at 35.

[608] Interview with Ma Yin-jeou, *available at* http://www.washingtonpost.com/wp-dyn/content/article/20081209-27. Last visited 12/10/2008. *See* Catherine K. Lin, *supra* note 606.

c. The GATT and WTO

In its application to join the General Agreement on Tariff and Trade (the GATT) and WTO,[609] the ROC did not assert to be a State either.[610] After World War II, in order to promote world trade, 23 States signed the GATT.[611] Initially, all signatories were States. However, some members, particularly the United Kingdom and France, had overseas territories, which, due to their special geographical and economic conditions, would suffer hardships if they were subject to the same customs duty and other import regulations as their parent States. Therefore, GATT was amended to add a new type of membership called "Customs Territories." This type of membership permitted these overseas territories, with the sponsor of their parent States, to join as members and to be treated separately from their parent States. The United Kingdom was a member of GATT and made her territory Hong Kong a Customs Territory for it to join GATT as a separate member. The United Kingdom did this before it handed Hong Kong over to China in 1987 pursuant to an international agreement of 1985.[612] In 1995, GATT transformed into the WTO.

The ROC attempted to apply for membership of GATT and later the WTO for many years before it was finally admitted in 2002. Although President Lee Teng-hui and President Chen Shui-bian claimed that the ROC was a "sovereignty[sic] independent country," when the ROC applied to join GATT and later the WTO as a member, it did not apply

[609] Agreement Establishing the Multilateral Trade Organization (World Trade Organization), Dec. 15, 1993, 33 I.L.M. 13 (1994). *Taiwan WTO Entry See To Be Delayed Until Mid-next Year*, China News, Dec. 9, 1999, *available in* 1999 WL 17736320; Jack de Lisle, *supra* note 607, at 35.

[610] Deborah Shen, *ROC Reinforces WTO Entry Bid*, Free China J., 12/13/1996, at 2.

[611] General Agreement on Tariffs and Trade, opened for signature on Oct. 30, 1947, 61 Stat. A3, 55 U.N.T.S. 187 (1950).

[612] *Joint Declaration of the Government of the United Kingdom of Great Britain and Northern Ireland and the Government of the People's Republic of China on the Question of Hong Kong*, *available at* http://www.info.gov.hk/trans/jd/jd2.htm. Last visited 10/25/2006. *See* 22 U.S.C. '5712(3) (1994) (providing that "The United States should respect Hong Kong's status as a separate customs territory"); 22 U.S.C. '5713(3) (1994) (stating that "The United States should continue to recognize Hong Kong as a territory which is fully autonomous from the United Kingdom and, after June 30, 1997, should treat Hong Kong as a territory fully autonomous from the People's Republic of China with respect to economic and trade matters"); 22 U.S.C. '5722(a) (1994) (allowing US President to suspend laws of United States with respect to Hong Kong if President "determines that Hong Kong is not sufficiently autonomous to justify treatment under a particular law of the United States.").

as a State. It could not use the name "China" because a great majority of the member States did not regard the ROC as the representative government of China. It did not apply in the name of the "ROC" because it was the name of a government and the ROC did not assert that it was a State in international affairs. Thus, the ROC applied as a Customs Territory. The ROC used the name "The Customs Territory of Taiwan, Penghu, Kinmen, and Matsu" in its application.[613]

In short, the ROC did not assert that it was a State in the international community, but instead claimed to be just a part of a State, China. In conclusion, other States did not regard the ROC in Taiwan as a State because the ROC did not act as a new State.

8. POSITION OF MA YING-JEOU ON THE POLITICAL STATUS OF THE ROC

The KMT Party regained political power in 2008. In March 2008, when Chen's term was about to expire, there was a two-way competition in a general election of the ROC President between Hsieh Chang-ting of the DPP Party and Ma Ying-jeou (Ma) of the Chinese Nationalist Party (the KMT). Ma won the election and the KMT Party regained the executive power of the ROC after eight years of the DPP rule.

After Ma, a native of Hong Kong (China), assumed the presidency of the ROC in May 2008, he announced that Taiwan was merely a region. There were two implications of the statement that "Taiwan is a region." One was that Taiwan was part of China. By referring to Taiwan as a region, Ma implied that Taiwan was China's territory. The other implication was that the ROC was not a State. He ordered his officials, in dealing with foreign countries, to refer to the island, as "Chinese Taipei," instead of "the ROC" or "Taiwan."

To the Taiwanese people, the illusion that the ROC was a State was shattered overnight. When Ma invited a PRC official Chen Yun-lin in charge of Taiwan Affairs to visit Taipei on November 6, 2008, the national flags of the ROC in the reception hall were removed before Chen's arrival; the Chinese official addressed him "Mr. Ma," not

[613] A statement accompanying the application of the Republic of China to join the General Agreement on Tariff and Trade (GATT) and the World Trade Organization (WTO) states that "[t]he Customs Territory of Taiwan, Penghu, Kinmen and Matsu (hereinafter referred to as Chinese Taipei) is preparing to accede to the General Agreement on Tariffs and Trade (GATT), which itself has been reorganized into the World Trade Organization."

"President Ma." When the people held a demonstration against him for giving up "Taiwan's sovereignty" on May 17, 2009, he rebutted that "No country in the world thinks that Taiwan was not a country." But the people knew that he made the statement simply to pacify them.

In July 2010, Ma's government and the PRC government entered into a trade agreement called "the Economic Cooperation Framework Agreement (ECFA)."[614] The ECFA, said to promote trades between Taiwan and China, was not signed by the two governments, but by governmental agencies from both sides.[615] Whether such an agreement binds the governments is an intriguing question for constitutional lawyers. Subsequently, the Agreement was sanctioned by the Institute of Legislation (The Legislature *Yuan*).

But in August 2010, Ma gave an intriguing characterization of the nature of the ECFA. The deputy news editor of Taipei Times wrote in an editorial that "Ma on Wednesday (August 4, 2010) told visiting Japanese academics that the Economic Cooperation Framework Agreement (ECFA) signed in late June was not a treaty signed between two states [because] [w]e do not recognize China as a state, so our relationship with each other is not one of state-to-state."[616] The statement implied that while the ROC was a State, the PRC was not. Ma Ying-jeou later said that "China" in the term "One China" referred to the ROC. This was the position of the KMT's one-China dogma. His characterization of the ROC was contradictory to his earlier statement that "Taiwan is a region."

Whatever characterization Ma made with respect to the ROC, he did not intend to establish a new State limiting its territory to the island of Taiwan. As London's Economist magazine observed, "Ma, unlike his predecessor, the DPP's Chen Shui-bian, has not trumpeted Taiwan's

[614] For official information on ECFA, *see* Background Information on ECFA, *available at* http://www.mac.gov.tw/public/data/042611402.pdf. Last visited 04/10/2011.

[615] The Agreement was signed by the PRC's HaiChi (The Sea Foundation) Association and the ROC's Luwei (The Mainland Affairs) Association. Ma Ying-jeu, the former President of the ROC in Taiwan, did not claim that Taiwan was a State. He referred to Taiwan as an area, which was a term that implied that Taiwan was a part of China. *Ma repeats "area-to-area" comment*, Taipei Times, by Loa Iok-sin(staff reporter), 12/22/2008, *available at* http://www.taipeitimes.com/News/taiwan/archives/2008/12/22/2003431770. Last visited 6/24/2013. Hong Kong is also part of China, now considered a special administrative region of China, abbreviated as "SAR."

[616] J. Michael Cole, *President Ma disappears the PRC*, TAIPEI TIMES, Sunday, 08/8/2010, P.8, *available at* http://www.taipeitimes.com/News/editorials/archives/2010/08/08/2003479868. Last visited 08/08/2010. Cole is the deputy news editor of Taipei Times.

separate identity."[617] The position he took was: The ROC was not a State separate from China.

9. POSITION OF TSAI ING-WEN ON THE POLITICAL STATUS OF THE ROC

In 2016, the DPP Party regained the political power in Taiwan. In a presidential election in January 2016, the contest was between the DPP's candidate Tsai Ing-wen and KMT's candidate Chu Li-lung. Tsai won a landslide victory.

In her inaugural speech, Tsai said that she wanted to maintain the established relation with the PRC government and referred to the ROC and the PRC as two "institutions representing each side across the strait."[618] She did not leave any impression that she wanted to establish a new state limiting its territory to the island of Taiwan. On May 29, when the Minister of Public Health of her administration spoke at the WHA in Geneva, he kept referring to Taiwan as "Chinese Taipei," a name which implies that the island was part of China, not a state.[619]

[617] "(Ma) [u]nlike his predecessor, the DPP's Chen Shui-bian, has not trumpeted Taiwan's separate identity." China and Taiwan, The Ties that Bind? The Economist, 07/5/2010, *available at* http://www.economist.com/node/16485487. Last visited 07/18/2010.

[618] *Tsai's inaugural speech*. Taipei Times, 2016/05/21, *at* http://www.taipeitimes.com/News/front/archives/2016/05/21/2003646753, Last visited /06/02/2016.

[619] See Alison Hsiao, Staff reporter with CNA, *Premier says use of Chinese Taipei name unsatisfactory, but acceptable*, Taipei Times, 05/27/2016, p. 3, *available at* http://www.taipeitimes.com/News/taiwan/print/2016/05/27/2003647238. Last visited 10/01/2016.

PART III

Sovereignty Over Taiwan

CHAPTER 6

China's Sovereignty Over Taiwan Before the US One-China Policy

Contents

1. A HISTORICAL OVERVIEW OF THE ISLAND OF TAIWAN

Since the Republic of China (ROC) in Taiwan is not a State, as this work concluded in Chapter 5, Political Status of the ROC in Taiwan, the ROC has no sovereignty over Taiwan. The question is then whether any State has sovereignty over Taiwan. This chapter examines China's claim of sovereignty over Taiwan.

Ever since its establishment in 1949, the People's Republic of China (PRC) government has claimed that China has sovereignty over the island of Taiwan and its inhabitants. In 1950, the PRC government claimed that the US violated its sovereignty by supporting the ROC government. In March 2005, the PRC government promulgated an "Antisecession Law," which was designed to suppress the "Taiwan independence secessionist forces to cause Taiwan's secession from China."[620] The enactment of such municipal law implied that China claimed sovereignty over the inhabitants on the island of Taiwan. The United Nations (UN)'s top official echoed the PRC's position. In 1999, Kofi Annan's refusal to send a UN Disaster Assessment team to Taiwan after a strong earthquake without

[620] *See* http://english.peopledaily.com.cn/200503/14/print20050314_176746.htm. Last visited 06/01/2005.

The One-China Policy: State, Sovereignty, and Taiwan's International Legal Status
DOI: http://dx.doi.org/10.1016/B978-0-08-102314-3.00006-9

prior approval of the PRC government implied that, in his view, China had sovereignty over the people of Taiwan.[621]

Under the theory of sovereignty and international law discussion Chapter 2, The State and Sovereignty, China has no sovereignty over the people of Taiwan unless China has title to the island of Taiwan. As observed in the first three chapters, the State, both the modern State and the neo-modern State, is predicated on territory. Consequently, title to a territory is a prerequisite of a state's sovereignty over the territory and the people inhabiting the territory. As expounded in the previous chapters, territory is an element of the State in international law; the State owns its territory. Thus, a question raised in the Introduction is whether China has title to the island of Taiwan.

Ever since the PRC government was established, it claims that China has title to the island of Taiwan. In 1950, its Premier Zhou (Chou) En-lai made a claim to the UN that "Taiwan is an integral part of China."[622] In 2000, the PRC government again claimed that Taiwan was China's territory in its White Paper.[623]

The ROC government in Taiwan also maintains the same position. The ROC government, notwithstanding its differences with its arch rival the PRC government, claims that Taiwan is a part of China. Many foreign politicians and government officials have also expressed, explicitly or implicitly, the view that the island of Taiwan is China's territory. Kofi Annan's statement "the Taiwan Province of China" also implies that the island of Taiwan is China's territory. Their view echoed China's position.[624] This chapter examines whether, based on the international law on territory discussed in Chapter 3, The Territorial State, China has acquired title to the island of Taiwan by any means asserted by the PRC government. Before discussing the title to the island of Taiwan, a historical overview of the major events relating to the

621 *See supra* text accompanying note 578. House Concurrent Resolution 98, passed in the US Congress House of Representatives on March 16, 2005, found that "(China's) Anti-secession Law [is] to create a legal framework for possible use of force against Taiwan" and "to provide a legal justification for the use of force against Taiwan, altering the status quo in the region, and thus is of grave concern to the United States." *See* the proposed Taiwan Policy Act of 2013, *infra* note 1074.

622 *Cablegram from Peiping Foreign Minister (Chou En-lai) to Secretary-General, Trygve Lie* (Aug. 24, 1950), DEP'T ST. BULL., Oct. 16,1950, at 607.[hereinafter *Chou En-Lai Cablegram*].

623 *See* the White Paper, *infra* note 664, at 53.

624 *Id.*

transitions of the major occupiers of the island will facilitate the discussions of the legal issues that follow.

Taiwan, called Formosa by the Europeans, as a geographic term is an island located on the western edge of the Pacific Ocean. To its west, 100 miles across the Taiwan Strait is China's coast. 370 miles (595 km) to its north is Okinawa island (the main island of Ryukyu Islands), and to its south 220 miles (355 km) across the Luzon Strait is the Philippines. The island has the shape of a fish or yam and is slightly larger in area than the Netherlands[625]—245 miles from north to south and 90 miles at its widest point at the southern part of the island. Penghu, called the Pescadores by the Europeans, is an archipelago consisting of many small islets located 28 miles west of the southern coast of Formosa.

The name "Formosa" is of Portuguese origin. In 1544, a Portuguese ship was sailing along China's coast to Japan when the sailors in the ship saw a pristine island with high mountains covered with green forests standing in the Pacific Ocean.[626]"*Ilha Formosa* (Beautiful Island)" shouted a sailor in Portuguese. Since then, the West has known the island as Formosa. Although these sailors in the ship did not land on the island, the island later appeared on a European map in the 1550s.[627] The Japanese called the island "Takasago" in the 16th century when a territorial magnate Toyotomi Hideyoshi (1556–98) ruled western Japan.

[625] A comparison excluding The Netherlands' created lands. Taiwan's area is 13,900 SM.

[626] The history of Taiwan in this work is primarily based on the following works: SSU MENG, TAIWANREN S BAI NIAN SHI (THE FOUR HUNDRED YEARS OF THE TAIWANESE HISTORY), Paradise Culture Associates, San Jose, Cal. (1980); Marie Lin, *Retracing the Han among the Taiwanese*, pp. 87–98, in SHYU-TU LEE AND JACK F. WILLIAMS, Ed, TAIWAN' STRUGGLE, Roman and Littlefield. (2014) Langham, Maryland; Jim Cheng, *History of the Name: Formosa, Tayouan and Taiwan.* NATPA Forum, 130705, *available at* https://mail.google.com/mail/?ticket = ST-750432-fTWS0Y5ChSfdXWzhIVYG-cas&shva = 1#inbox/13fb0c0329bd3c29. Last visited 07/07/2013. The article is based on *The Formosan Encounter* (1623–1668) from the Dutch historical documents called VOC (Dutch East Indian Company 1602–1795), *Id.;* GEORGE H. KERR, FORMOSA BETRAYED, *supra note* 399; and AN ENCYCLOPEDIA OF WORLD HISTORY, *supra* note 393, at 892.

[627] Colonel Hernando de los Rios sent a memorial from Manila to the Spanish king with a map of "Hermosa"(in 1597) suggesting the invasion of Formosa. Source: http//www.upf.es/fhuma/eeao/projectes/che/s16/rios.htm. Translation in http://64.233.179.104/translate_c?hl = en&sl = es&u = http://www.upf.es/fhuma/eeao/projecte. For a Chinese version, *see* www.taiwanus.net/history/1/20.htm. Last visited 12/4/2006. For a narrative of the gradual appearance of maps of the island of Taiwan in Western explorers, *see* JEROME KEATING, THE MAPPING OF TAIWAN; DESIRED ECONOMIES, COVETED GEOGRAPHIES, SMC Publishing, Taipei (2011).

Dutch sailors were the first Europeans to land on the island. In the early 17th century, the Dutch East India Company set up an office in Batavia (called Jakarta today), Indonesia. The Dutch government decided to colonize Indonesia and appointed a Governor to administer the area. In 1622, to establish a post for transporting merchandise, Dutch sailors landed on an island, which was part of an archipelago called "Pinghu (called 'Penghu' today)" by the natives. The Dutch traders named the archipelago "the Pescadores." They, with support of their government, built a castle on the island intending to develop trade with China and Japan from there. China's Ming officials quickly ordered the Dutch traders to leave the islands as the Ming government had regarded the Pescadores as Ming's territory. When the Dutch traders refused, the Ming officials sent the army to expel them. Upon defeating the Dutch, the Ming officials suggested to the Dutch that they moved to the nearby island Formosa in the east, as it had regarded Formosa as a land of barbarians outside of its domain; in fact, it had prohibited its subjects to go to Formosa because pirates had made the island their hiding places. Accordingly, the Dutch traders moved to the southwest corner of Formosa.

When the Dutch moved to Formosa, they came into contact with native peoples. In 1624, when the Dutch traders accompanied by soldiers moved from Pescadores to Formosa, the island was inhabited by three ethnic groups of people. One group that resided in the mountain regions was Austronesian and arrived from the south about 15,000 years ago after the last glacial period. They were subsequently called "Taiwan or Formosan Aborigines." The second group that resided in the western and northern plains was ethnic "Yueh" people of Austronesian origin from Continental Southeast Asia between 8000 and 6000 years ago. They were subsequently called "Plain Tribe Aborigines." The third group that resided in the western plains of the island moved to the island from Continental Southeast Asia coast area about 400 years ago, not long before the Dutch arrived. Men under China's rule left their economically stressed homeland to seek a new life in the unruly land by taking a perilous sea voyage over the Black River (The Taiwan Strait), unaccompanied by women. They were Minnan people and Hakka people. Until recently, Minnan and Hakka were thought to be Han Chinese. A recent analysis of their DNA discloses that these men were in fact ethnic Yueh, speaking languages different from the second group, whose ancestors living in Continental Southeast Asia coast were sinicized (culturally converted to Chinese) after the Han Dynasty extended China's rule to their homeland.

The Dutch colonized the southwest corner of Formosa. Initially when the Dutch traders moved to Formosa, they just set up a station for the Dutch East India Company to conduct trade with China and Japan. But after the Dutch traders discovered that the soil was fertile and suitable for agricultural development, they decided to settle down and colonize the area.

The Spaniards landed in northern Formosa. After the Spanish governor in Manila learnt of the Dutch activities in southern Formosa, he sent a navy ship to land at the northern corner of Formosa in 1625. The Spaniards set up a station at what is Tamsui today and called the area "San Tiego."

The Dutch developed the south where they settled down. They built a castle called "Zeelandia" in 1632 near what is Tainan City today and took up residence there. While Dutch merchants were guarded by Dutch soldiers, they, on one hand, traded with the native aborigines (mainly for deer skins) and, on the other hand, developed farmlands. Due to a lack of laborers to develop the land, the Dutch hired Minnan and Hakka men from China's Fujien and Canton Provinces, bringing them to Formosa. During the Dutch expansion of their holdings, conflict between them and the indigenous peoples often led to skirmishes.

The Dutch eventually expelled the Spaniards in the north. In 1642, when the Spanish governor in Manila decided to expand his domain in the Philippines, he recalled most soldiers stationed in Formosa back to the Philippines, leaving only a small number of soldiers to guard the station. The Dutch took the opportunity to expel the Spaniards from the island by force. In 1653, the Dutch built another and a larger castle called "Fort Provintia" near Zeelandia Castle, in the area where the native people were called "Tayouan." Thus, the native people called Fort Provintia "Tayouan Castle." The name "Tayouan" subsequently turned into "Taiwan," which eventually became the name of the island. Although before and after the arrival of the Dutch, Minnan and Hakka men in China's coastal area had migrated to the island, their number was limited.

In 1661, a large group of Chinese arrived in Formosa. In 1636, the Manchu king in Manchuria renamed his kingdom as "*Qing* (Ching)" and invaded China when it was ruled by the Ming Dynasty established by Han Chinese. In 1644, *Qing* (Ching)'s army captured Ming's capital Beijing (Peking) and began to rule China. Several of Ming's princes fled to the south and continued to resist the invaders. By 1661, *Qing* (Ching)'s army had defeated all of Ming's loyalists except General *Zheng* (Cheng) Cheng-gong or Koxinga (a name called by the Portuguese) stationed on the southern coast of China. Koxinga continued to resist *Qing* (Ching)'s army until 1661 when he with his army of 36,000 soldiers fled to southern Formosa where the Dutch had established a small colony. The Dutch residing on the island were overpowered by Koxinga's huge army and expelled from the island ending the Dutch dominance of the island for 37 years.[628]

The island came under the rule of the *Qing* (Ching) Dynasty when the Ming loyalists in Formosa surrendered. After Koxinga died in 1662, his son *Zheng* (Cheng) Jing, who had brought 6000 solders to join him earlier, succeeded him and established a regime called "Tong Ning Guo (country)." *Zheng* (Cheng) Jing established a regime, not to create a new state separate from China, but to succeed the Ming Dynasty. When *Zheng* (Cheng) Jing died in 1683, his son *Zheng* (Cheng) Ke-shuang succeeded him but surrendered to the *Qing* (Ching) government within a few months. Meanwhile, many soldiers who had retreated to Formosa with Koxinga and his son died of a contagious disease. Soon after *Zheng* (Cheng) surrendered, the *Qing* (Ching) government sent most of Ming's remaining soldiers back to China. The Minnan and Hakka laborers and Koxinga's soldiers went to Formosa unaccompanied by women. These laborers and the soldiers who stayed in the island intermarried with the local "Plain Tribe" women. Most Taiwanese today are their offspring.

Near the turn of the 20th century, Japan was involved in two wars. During the second half of the 19th century, China, Japan, and Russia, in competing to build their respective spheres of influence in the Korean Peninsula, set a collision course between themselves. The conflict led to two wars in the Far East. One was the Sino-Japanese War of 1894. The other was the Russo-Japanese War of 1904.

Japan won both wars. In the Sino-Japanese War, the *Qing* (Ching) army lost the war to Japan and the two States concluded the Treaty of Shimonoseki in 1895.[629] In the Treaty, China ceded Formosa and Pescadores (hereinafter, Formosa and Pescadores are collectively called "Formosa" or "the island of Taiwan" unless the context indicates otherwise or is in a quotation) to Japan.[630]

[628] Koxinga literally means "Lord of the Imperial(Ming) Surname." *See* Wikipedia, "Koxinga." He and his 36,000 solders occupied the island of Taiwan during the reign of Kang Xi (Hsi) Emperor. His son Zheng (Cheng) Jing brought with him another 6000 soldiers. But by the time Zheng(Cheng) Jing died, 6000 Chinese in Taiwan had died of a contagious disease.

[629] *See* the Treaty of Shimonoseki, *supra* note 453. For a brief description of the conflict between China and Japan, *see* AN ENCYCLOPEDIA OF WORLD HISTORY, *supra* note 393, at 892.

[630] For the provisions of the Treaty, *see infra* text accompanying note 671.

Although the *Qing* (Ching) government nominally reigned Formosa for 211 years, the government did not develop it for two centuries. The Chinese governments (both Ming and *Qing* (Ching) Dynasties) for a long time regarded the island of Taiwan as an unruly region, not within their territorial boundary. When the Ming loyalists surrendered in 1683, the *Qing* (Ching) government immediately promulgated an ordinance prohibiting its subjects to go to Taiwan Island. The *Qing* (Ching) government lifted the ordinance and imposed it again several times until 1885 when it lifted the ordinance for the last time and established Taiwan as a Province.

Even after Taiwan became a Province, the government never developed it. After the *Qing* (Ching) government set up Taiwan as a Province, it still did not develop the island and, according to The Times (London), "left the land virtually a wilderness."[631] When Japan demanded Formosa as part of compensation at the conclusion of the Sino-Japanese War, the *Qing* (Ching) Emperor complied without hesitation because he considered that he had given away a barren land. A London Times correspondent, in writing about Japan's ensuing colonization of Formosa, wrote that "China was willing, if not glad, to cede it, and Li-Hung-Chang (the Chinese Ambassador who signed the Shimonoseki Treaty for China) remarked sarcastically that Japan would find the island an exceedingly bad bargain."[632]

In the Russo-Japanese War of 1904, the Russian Navy fleet was annihilated in the Japan Sea by the Japanese Navy. The two States, through good offices of the US President Theodore Roosevelt, concluded the Treaty of Portsmouth in 1905.[633] In the Treaty, Russia ceded "in perpetuity and full sovereignty the southern portion of the Island of Sakhalin and all the islands adjacent thereto" to Japan.[634] Russia also acknowledged

[631] *Savage island of Formosa transformed by Japanese*, THE TIMES (London), 09/24/1904. Also published in The New York Times, 09/24/1904.

[632] *Id.*

[633] The Treaty of Portsmouth, September 5, 1905. AN ENCYCLOPEDIA OF WORLD HISTORY, *supra* note 393, at 892.

[634] Art. 9 of the Treaty provides, "The Imperial Russian Government cedes to the Imperial Government of Japan in perpetuity and full sovereignty the southern portion of the Island of Saghalin and all the islands adjacent thereto and the public works and properties thereon. The fiftieth degree of north latitude is adopted as the northern boundary of the ceded territory. The exact alignment of such territory shall be determined in accordance with the provisions of the additional article II annexed to this treaty." *Id.*

in the Treaty that "Japan possesses in Korea paramount political, military and economical interests" and agreed not to interfere.[635]

Japan developed the island of Taiwan under its rule. After the Treaty of Shimonoseki was signed, the news soon reached Taiwan. The native Taiwanese were angry and petitioned to the *Qing* (Ching) government to abrogate the Treaty. When the petition failed, the Taiwanese leaders declared the establishment of the "Taiwan Democratic State" to resist the new ruler.[636] The resistance was quashed by the Japanese army in about a year. At first, Japan distinguished Taiwan from its homeland as a colony, but later incorporated the island as its integral territory[637] and developed its agriculture and industries.

In the 1930s, Japan began its military aggression in China. In September 1931, Imperial Japan sent its troops into Manchuria.[638] By 1939, the Japanese armed forces occupied Manchuria and a vast area of the central and eastern parts of China. Japan set up a puppet State, Manchukuo, to control Manchuria. Japan's ensuing invasion into Southeast Asia alarmed the United States, which then imposed an embargo of strategic materials against Japan. The embargo prompted Japan to declare war against the United States in December 1941 and attacked Pearl Harbor the next day. The United States was forced to declare war against Japan the following day.

China issued a proclamation abrogating the Treaty of Shimonoseki. A few days after the United States declared war against Japan, the ROC government also declared war against Japan and at the same time issued a proclamation abrogating all "unequal" treaties between China and Japan, including the Treaty of Shimonoseki.

In 1943, the governments of the United States, the United Kingdom, and the Republic of China jointly issued a declaration called the Cairo

[635] Art. 2 of the Treaty provides, "The Imperial Russian Government, acknowledging that Japan possesses in Korea paramount political, military and economical interests, engages neither to obstruct nor interfere with measures for guidance, protection and control which the Imperial Government of Japan may find necessary to take in Korea." *Id.*

[636] *See* SSU MENG, THE FOUR HUNDRED YEAR OF TAIWANESE HISTORY. *supra* note 626, at 248–252.

[637] For instance, the Japanese government required all Taiwanese to adopt a Japanese surname in 1940s. *See* BRIAN LEE BRUBAKER, *Language Attitudes and Identity in Taiwan* 18 (2003) (M.A. thesis, University of Pittsburgh), *available at* http://etd.library.pitt.edu/ETD/available/etd-08192003-082704/unrestricted/Brubakerthesis.pdf. Last visited 10/02/2004. (discussing pressure placed on Taiwanese to assume Japanese surnames).

[638] *See* EDWIN O. REISCHAUER, JAPAN, PAST AND PRESENT, 3d Ed. 1964, at 170.

Declaration. While the Pacific War was in progress, the US President Franklin D. Roosevelt, British Prime Minister Winston Churchill, and China's Generalissimo Jiang (Chiang) Kai-shek met in Cairo, Egypt, from November 22 to 26, 1943 to discuss the strategy for defeating Japan.[639] In December 1943, the three governments issued a joint press release (statement), which dealt with the future of Formosa and Korea and later came to be known as the Cairo Declaration.[640]

In 1945, the three governments again issued a declaration called the Potsdam Proclamation. After Germany surrendered in May 1945, the US President Harry Truman,[641] British Prime Minister Winston Churchill,[642] and the Soviet Premier Joseph Stalin[643] convened in Potsdam, Germany, from July 17 to August 12 to discuss the postwar disposition of Europe. During the conference, on July 26 the heads of governments of the United States, the United Kingdom, and the Republic of China[644] issued a joint statement called "the Proclamation Defining Terms for Japanese Surrender," which became part of the Potsdam Proclamation announced at the end of the Conference. The Potsdam Proclamation confirmed the Cairo Declaration with respect to the future of Formosa and Korea.[645]

The US fought on two fronts during the Second World War: Europe and Asia. In Europe, the United States, the United Kingdom, France, and USSR were true military allies, fighting together against the German and the Italian armed forces. In Asia, however, after the Japanese army ran

[639] The USSR (The Soviet Union), not at war with Japan then, was not represented at the Cairo Conference. *See Cairo Declaration*, in NEW CYCLE IN ASIA 29 (Harold R. Isaacs ed., 1947). Generalissimo Jiang(Chiang) Kai-shek became the President of the Republic of China on September 13, 1943.

[640] *See* the Cairo Declaration, 9 DEP'T ST. BULL., Dec. 1943, at 393.

[641] Harry S. Truman, US President (1945–1953).

[642] Winston S. Churchill, the British Prime Minister (1940–1945; 1951–1955).

[643] Joseph V. D. Stalin, the Soviet Premier (1941–1953).

[644] The United Kingdom was originally represented by Prime Minister Winston Churchill at the Potsdam Conference. Churchill resigned after losing a parliamentary election on July 26, 1945, and was replaced by new Prime Minister Clement Attlee. *See* THE ENCYCLOPEDIA BRITANNICA, *supra* note 21, V. 29, at 92 (15th Ed. 1994). Jiang (Chiang) Kai-shek was not present at the Conference.

[645] The Potsdam Proclamation deals with the postwar disposition of Germany, Italy, Japan, Poland, *etc.* While Truman and Churchill signed the *Proclamation Defining Terms For Japanese Surrender*, President Jiang (Chiang) Kai-shek of the Republic of China, not in attendance at the conference, only concurred by despatch. *See Proclamation Defining Terms For Japanese Surrender* (July 26, 1945), DEP'T ST. BULL., July 1945, at 137 [hereinafter Potsdam Proclamation].

over Indo-China, the French and the British Armies withdrew from the battle stage in Asia. The ROC's army, with the help of America, was barely able to hold down the advance of the Japanese army in China. The USSR did not declare war against Japan until eight days before Japan surrendered, after it had learned that Japan was negotiating a surrender.[646] Thus, the United States, with a small Australian contingent in the US Army, was alone fighting the Japanese military forces.[647] It was the American Navy, the American Air Force, and the American Army that defeated the Japanese forces. General MacArthur who, as the Commander of the US South-West Pacific Forces, led the American Forces fighting the Japanese army, recalled later that "none of these powers [Russia and the United Kingdom] had been forthcoming with troops to fight the Pacific war when we needed them."[648]

When Japan surrendered, the United States became the occupying power of Japan. After the United States dropped two atomic bombs on Japan's Kyushu Island in August 1945, Japan surrendered unconditionally on August 15, 1945[649] to the United States and the United Kingdom.[650] The United States became "the occupying power" of Japan's territory, which included the island of Taiwan.[651]

After Japan lost the war, President Truman appointed General Douglas MacArthur as "the Supreme Commander for the Allied Powers in the

[646] The Soviet Union declared war against Japan on August 8, 1945. *See Soviet War Declaration of War on Japan, available at* http://metalab.unc.edu/hyperwar/PTO/Dip/sov-japan-neu.html. Last visited 10/03/2004.

[647] DOUGLAS MACARTHUR, REMINISCENCES, McGraw-Hill Co. New York, 1964, at 291. Most Australian forces were fighting in Europe.

[648] *Id.*

[649] The Emperor of Japan announced the surrender to the people of Japan on August 15, 1945. *See* MODERN JAPAN, AN ENCYCLOPEDIA OF HISTORY, CULTURE & NATIONALISM, at 290 (James L. Hoffman ed., 1998).

[650] The Japanese Emperor in the surrender announcement by radio said that "Japan surrenders to the US the UK and Chungking." *See* KERR, *supra* note 399. George Kerr explained that Chungking City was where the American military headquarters in the Far East was and the Japanese Emperor wanted to surrender to "Chungking" meaning the US forces. *See supra* note 399 and the accompanying text. According to George Kerr, the Japanese did not consider China a victorious State. *Id.* at 61 ("[Japanese Military High Command] considered that Japan had not surrendered to 'China' but to 'Chungking,' where the Chinese *and the Americans* had their military headquarters."). *Id.* (emphasis added).

[651] *See supra* note 393. Dulles, *The San Francisco Conference on Proposed Japanese Peace Treaty. Id.*

Pacific" to accept the surrender of Japan.[652] Although MacArthur assumed the official title of "the Supreme Commander for the Allied Powers in the Pacific," the term "Allied Powers" was in name only because almost all the forces under him were Americans.

The United States set up a Military Government under the command of General MacArthur to assume the administration of the four major islands of Japan-Honshu, Hokkaido, Kyushu, Shikoku- and Ryukyu Islands.[653] It also assumed the post surrender operations in South Korea, leaving the operations in North Korea to the Soviet Union, which occupied it after Japan surrendered.

Pursuant to the direction of the US Government, General MacArthur assigned the task of accepting the surrender of the Japanese commanders in Formosa to Jiang (Chiang) Kai-shek.[654]

The United States could have assumed the post surrender operation in Formosa, which was after all Japan's territory. But immediately after Japan surrendered, the US Government wanted to recall its troops home as soon as possible.[655] The war had lasted too long since the Japanese attack of Pearl Harbor. Besides, most US State Department officials believed

[652] *See* Incoming Message, WARX 49571, dated Aug. 14, 1945, from General Marshall to General MacArthur (on file with MacArthur Memorial).

[653] After Japan surrendered, the Soviet Union and the United Kingdom attempted to divide Japan into several occupied zones, as the Allies had done in Germany, but the US objected. *See* MacArthur, *supra* note 647.

[654] *See Id.* at 44. In 1955, British Foreign Sec'y Anthony Eden stated in the House of Commons that "[i]n September [of 1945], the administration of Formosa was taken over from the Japanese by Chinese forces at the direction of the Supreme Commander of the Allied Powers." 536 PARL. DEB., H.C. (5th ser.) (1955) at 159. In fact, the assignment was made at the direction of the US State Department. Before Japan surrendered, General MacArthur received from General Marshall on August 13, 1945 four proposed documents prepared by the US Government: (1) Directives to Chief Supreme Commander for the Allied Powers; (2) Proclamation by the Emperor of Japan; (3) Instrument of Surrender; and (4) General Order Number One.

Upon Japan's surrender, General Marshall notified General MacArthur on August 14, 1945 that his directive as Supreme Commander became effective. *See supra* note 652 and the accompanying text. General Order Number One was issued in the name of the Japanese Imperial General Headquarters by direction of the Emperor. It directed that "[t]he senior Japanese Commanders and all ground, Sea, air and auxiliary forces within China, excluding Manchuria, Formosa and French Indo China north of 16 degrees north latitude shall surrender to the Generalissimo Chiang Kai-shek." Incoming Message, WARX 48672, dated Aug. 12, 1945, from General Marshall to General Headquarters, US Army Forces Pacific (on file with MacArthur Memorial).

[655] *See* KERR, *supra* note 399.

that Formosa would be returned to China in a postwar settlement pursuant to the Cairo Declaration.[656] The US Navy sent ships to transport the Chinese army under Jiang (Chiang) Kai-shek from China to Formosa. On October 25, 1945, the Japanese Commander Ando Rikichi surrendered his authority in Formosa to General Chen Yi of the ROC government in Taipei, and the ROC government assumed the post surrender operation of Formosa.[657] From 1895 when Formosa was ceded by China to Japan in the Treaty of Shimonoseki until the Japanese military surrendered to Jiang (Chiang) Kai-shek's army in October of 1945, Japan governed the island for 50 years.

During the 50 years of the Japanese rule, Japan developed the island of Taiwan into a modernized society, surpassed only by Japan proper in Asia. Within a year from taking over the island in 1895, Japan placed the island under civil administration in March 1896 and introduced its own Westernized legal system based on German law. Within ten years, Japan had introduced its education system, built roads and railroads, the telecommunication system (telegraphs and telephones), banks, and post offices, and developed its agriculture and industries. By 1945, when the Japanese left the island, the island was well modernized.

In 1949, the ROC government was driven into exile to the island of Taiwan. On December 8, 1949, the ROC government, having lost the civil war to the Chinese Communists, "took," in the words of Winston Churchill, "refuge upon Formosa"[658] and has stayed there ever since. Meanwhile the Chinese Communists established a new government, called "the People's Republic of China" (the PRC) in October 1949.

Since the Korean War, the United States has protected Taiwan from Chinese Communists. When the Korean War erupted in 1950, President Truman sent the US Navy Seventh Fleet to the Taiwan Strait to deter the Chinese Communists' invasion of Taiwan. In 1954, the United States and China represented by the ROC government entered into the US–China (the ROC) Mutual Defense Treaty. Under the Treaty, the United States provided military assistance to the ROC government in Taiwan, including stationing a military advisory group in the island. But other than a brief exchange of artilleries between two sides of the Taiwan Strait in 1958 neither side has attempted to invade the other across the Strait.

656 *Id.*
657 *Id. at* 78.
658 *See Id.* at 365–66; *infra* text accompanying note 751.

The year 1971 is a decisive year for the international relations of the ROC government. In 1971, by Resolution No. 2758 the UN General Assembly expelled the ROC government from the organization. Since then the number of the States that recognize the ROC as the representative government of China decreased dramatically.

Though the United States continued to recognize the ROC as the representative government of China until 1979, the United States began to open its doors to the PRC government in 1972. In that year, President Nixon[659] made a friendly visit to Beijing to negotiate an end to the enmity between the two countries. In Shanghai, Nixon and Chinese Premier Zhou (Chou) En-lai issued a joint statement called Shanghai Communiqué. The American policy contained in the Shanghai Communiqué was later known as "the one-China Policy."

In 1979, the United States recognized the PRC and simultaneously withdrew its recognition of the ROC. When the United States withdrew its recognition of the ROC as the representative government of China, the United States also terminated the US–China (the ROC) Mutual Defense Treaty and withdrew its military advisory group from Taiwan. To protect the people of Taiwan and the security of the United States in the Western Pacific, the United States enacted the Taiwan Relations Act. Since 1979 the United States has maintained an unofficial relation with the ROC government and supplied defensive weapons to Taiwan under the Taiwan Relations Act.

2. CHINA'S CLAIM OF TITLE TO THE ISLAND OF TAIWAN

During the more than 60 years in which the ROC government and the PRC government have coexisted, the PRC government has claimed that the island of Taiwan is China's territory. Two official documents issued by the PRC government set forth the grounds of its claim. The first one was Zhou (Chou) En-lai's telegram to the UN Secretary-General in 1950. Immediately after North Korea attacked South Korea, to deter the invasion of the Chinese Communists, the US President Truman sent the US Navy Seventh Fleet to the Taiwan Strait and the US military contingents to station in the island of Taiwan.[660] On August 24, 1950, the PRC's

[659] Richard M. Nixon, US President (1969–1974).

[660] The day after the United States sent its Navy Seventh Fleet toward the Taiwan Strait, the United Nations went to war with North Korea. The UN Security Council, by a resolution, recommended that its members "furnish such assistance to the Republic of Korea as may be necessary to repel the armed attack." S. C. Res. 83, UN SCOR, 5th Sess., 474th mtg. at 5, UN Doc. S/INF/5/Rev.1 (1950).

Minister of Foreign Affairs Zhou (Chou) En-Lai sent a cablegram to the UN Secretary-General Trygve Lie, claiming that the United States had violated China's territory.[661] In the cablegram, Zhou (Chou) En-Lai accused the United States of encroaching on China's territory. The telegram stated,

> *"On 27 June this year, President Truman of the United States of America announced the decision of the United States Government to prevent with armed forces the liberation of Taiwan by the Chinese People's Liberation Army. Meanwhile, the United States Seventh Fleet move toward the Strait of Taiwan, followed by the arrival in Taiwan of contingents of the United States in an open encroachment on the territory of the People's Republic of China. This action on the part of the United States Government is a direct armed aggression on the territory of China and a total violation of the United Nations Charter."*[662]

Zhou(Chou) En-Lai based his accusation on China's claim that Taiwan was China's territory. It continued,

> *"Taiwan is an integral part of China. This is not only a fact based on history, confirmed by the situation since the surrender of Japan, but it is also stipulated in the Cairo Declaration of 1943 and the Potsdam Communiqué of 1945 as binding international agreements which the United States Government has pledged itself to respect and observe."*[663]

The second document setting forth the grounds of China's claim was the PRC's White Paper on Taiwan. On February 21, 2000 the PRC government released a position paper called the "White Paper—the One-China Principle and the Taiwan Issue" (2000) (hereafter "the PRC White Paper" or "the White Paper").[664] The PRC White Paper consolidated the grounds on which the PRC government based its argument that the island of Taiwan was China's territory. It stated,

> *"Taiwan is an inalienable part of China. All the facts and laws about Taiwan prove that Taiwan is an inalienable part of Chinese territory. In April 1895, through a war of aggression against China, Japan forced the Ching*

[661] *Taiwan is an integral part of China. Chou En-Lai Cablegram, supra* note 622.

[662] *Id.*

[663] *Id.*

[664] "White Paper-The One-China Principle and the Taiwan Issue (2000)" issued by the PRC government State Council and the Taiwanese Affairs Office on February 21, 2000, *available at* http://www.taiwandocuments.org/white.htm. (Last visited 03/1/2010), at 53. The ROC government also controls two small islands, Queymoy and Matsu, off the Chinese coast. These islands are not part of the island of Taiwan and are Chinese territories. *See supra* notes 1 & 473.

> *government to sign the unequal Treaty of Shimonoseki, and forcibly occupied Taiwan. In July 1937, Japan launched an all-out war of aggression against China. In December 1941, the Chinese government issued the Proclamation of China's Declaration of War Against Japan, announcing to the world that all treaties, agreements and contracts concerning Sino-Japanese relations, including the Treaty of Shimonoseki, had been abrogated, and that China would recover Taiwan. In December 1943, the Cairo Declaration was issued by the Chinese, United States and British governments, stipulating that Japan should return to China all the territories it had stolen from the Chinese, including Northeast China, Taiwan and the Penghu Archipelago. The Potsdam Proclamation signed by China, the United States and Britain in 1945 stipulated that 'The terms of Cairo Declaration shall be carried out.' In August of that year, Japan declared surrender and promised in its instrument of surrender that it would faithfully fulfill the obligations laid down in the Potsdam Proclamation. On October 25, 1945, the Chinese government recovered Taiwan and the Penghu Archipelago, resuming the exercise of sovereignty over Taiwan."*[665]

It continued, "after replacing the government of the Republic of China in 1949, the government of the PRC has become the sole legal government of China, enjoying and exercising sovereignty over the whole of China, including Taiwan."[666]

The PRC government still makes the same arguments today. By synthesizing the two documents mentioned above, one finds that the PRC's claim that Taiwan is China's territory is based on four grounds.[667] The first ground of the claim is based on the past ownership. The second ground is based on its own proclamations.[668] The third ground is based on the Cairo Declaration and the Potsdam Proclamation.[669] The fourth ground is based on administration of Taiwan.

All these grounds are based on the historical events that took place before the 1972 Shanghai Communiqué in which the US Government announced the "one-China Policy." Thus, the next section will examine the historical events which might have affected title to the island of Taiwan that took place prior to the Shanghai Communiqué.

[665] *Id.*
[666] *Id.* at 11.
[667] *Id.*
[668] *See* the White Paper, *supra* note 664.
[669] *See Chou En-Lai Cablegram*, *supra* note 622.

3. A LEGAL ANALYSIS OF CHINA'S CLAIM OF TITLE TO THE ISLAND OF TAIWAN

None of the PRC government's arguments is supported by international law. Each of the grounds of the PRC government's argument is analyzed below.

A. Title Based on the Past Ownership

The first of the grounds of the PRC government's argument that the island of Taiwan is China's territory is based on historical ownership. The PRC government argues that the island of Taiwan is now China's territory because it was once China's territory.

The argument based on historical ownership is not valid. There is no rule in international law that lends support to a claim of title to a territory based on past ownership. Such a rule would nullify all territorial treaties in which territories were ceded by one party to the other. Regardless of the length of time a territory was owned by a State, title to the territory may be changed by territorial treaties. The transfer of title to a territory under a territorial treaty overrides the ownership in the past. Alsace and Lorraine provide good precedents. King Louis II of the East Frankish Kingdom (later Holy Roman Empire and then Germany) acquired Alsace in 870 under the Treaty of Mersen, which divided the territories of Lothair II at his death.[670] France acquired Alsace in the Treaty of Ryswick in 1697 and Lorraine by marriage of its king in 1766 (acquisition of a territory by marriage was analogous to acquisition by a merger agreement). Germany later reacquired Alsace and Lorraine by the Peace Treaty of Versailles in 1871 which also concluded the Franco-German War. After the First World War, France again acquired Alsace and Lorraine under the 1919 Treaty of Versailles. Thus, a treaty was necessary to transfer the territory back to its original owner despite the fact that the transferee owned it in the past.

An unconditional transfer of title to a territory by a territorial treaty cuts off all the rights, including the right of reversion, of the transferor. When the *Qing* (Ching) government was defeated in the 1894 Sino-Japanese War, China and Japan entered into a treaty of peace, known as the Treaty of Shimonoseki. Article 2 of the Treaty provides,

[670] The Treaty of Mersen was between Louis the German of the East Frankish Kingdom and Charles II of France.

China cedes to Japan *in perpetuity* and full sovereignty the following territories, together with all fortifications, arsenals, and public property thereon:

(a) (Repealed)

(b) The island of Formosa, together with all islands appertaining or belonging to the said island of Formosa.

(c) The Pescadores Group, that is to say, all islands lying between the 119th and 120th degrees of longitude east of Greenwich and the 23rd and 24th degrees of north latitude.[671]

The Treaty of Shimonoseki is a territorial treaty. The word "cede" means transfer of title to a territory by a treaty.[672] As stated before, since sovereignty is based on territory, sovereignty over a territory includes title to the territory. China, by ceding sovereignty over Formosa to Japan in the Treaty, transferred whatever rights it had in or over the island of Taiwan to Japan, reserving no rights, including the right of reversion, in the island. This is the nature of territorial treaties. The words "in perpetuity" in the Treaty merely emphasize the permanent nature of a territorial treaty. Thus, regardless of the length of time during which China's governments had effective control of the island of Taiwan, China's title to the island was cut off by the Treaty.

Japan acquired title to the island of Taiwan under international law through this treaty. As mentioned in Chapter 3, The Territorial State, a peace treaty that transfers a territory to conclude a war is valid and binding.[673] The victorious State acquires good title to the territory ceded to it under the treaty. Thus, Japan acquired good title to Formosa via the treaty of Shimonoseki in 1895.

B. Title Based on Its Own Proclamations

The second of the grounds of the PRC government's argument that the island of Taiwan is China's territory is that the island was returned to China by China's own proclamations. Since China ceded the island of Taiwan to Japan in 1895, China's governments in two occasions proclaimed that the island of Taiwan was returned to China. One was made in 1941 when China declared war against Japan at the beginning of the

[671] The Treaty of Shimonoseki, *supra* note 453 (emphasis added).

[672] *See* The New Shorter Oxford English Dictionary, 3rd Ed. *supra* note 65, at 357. (providing the definition of "cede" as "grant (territory) by treaty.")

[673] *See supra* text accompanying notes 408–409.

Pacific War. When the ROC government declared war against Japan, it at the same time issued a proclamation abrogating all "unequal" treaties between China and Japan. The PRC government argued in the PRC White Paper that because the Treaty of Shimonoseki was an "unequal" treaty, it was abrogated in 1941 by the proclamation, and the island of Taiwan was immediately returned to China.[674]

As explained in Chapter 3, The Territorial State, such a proclamation to abrogate a treaty is not valid in international law.[675] The Treaty of Shimonoseki is a territorial treaty. By its nature, the Treaty cannot be abrogated. A unilateral proclamation to abrogate a treaty by a party to the treaty may be valid with respect to a treaty of executory nature, but it cannot effectively abrogate a territorial treaty.

This is true even though the defeated State regards the treaty as unequal. A treaty in which a State defeated in a war is forced to cede a territory is necessarily unequal. The defeated State is not in an equal bargaining position with the victorious State in the negotiations, or in case of an unconditional surrender, it may not even be in a position to negotiate with the victorious State. The defeated State cedes the territory to end the war and save the State from being destroyed or annexed by the victorious State.

The term "unequal treaty" is a political term rather than a legal concept recognized in international law.[676] Historically, no territorial treaty was ever effectively abrogated or revoked by the government of the defeated State that executed the treaty on the ground of inequality. A succeeding government cannot do what the government that executed the treaty cannot do. If the *Qing* (Ching) Dynasty, which signed the Treaty of Shimonoseki, could not abrogate or revoke the Treaty, no succeeding government could do so either. It follows that the 1941 proclamation of

[674] *See* the White Paper, *supra* note 664, at 53.

[675] *See* SCOTT, *infra* note 676.

[676] For a discussion of unequal treaties, *see* GARY L. SCOTT, CHINESE TREATIES: THE POST-REVOLUTIONARY RESTORATION OF INTERNATIONAL LAW AND ORDER. Oceana Publications Inc. (Dobbs Ferry, NY. 1975) 85–99. "[N]one of these writers [Grotius, Pufendorf, Vattel, and Wolf] considered that inequality in treaties was in any way a cause for abrogation or a factor invalidating treaties." *Id.* at 86. *See generally* PETER WESLEY-SMITH, UNEQUAL TREATY 1898–1997: CHINA, GREAT BRITAIN AND HONG KONG'S NEW TERRITORIES, Oxford University Press, Warwick House, Quatty Bay, Hong Kong (1998); FARIBORZ NOZARI, UNEQUAL TREATIES IN INTERNATIONAL LAW, Stockholm University (Stockholm, Sweden, 1971).

the ROC government abrogating all treaties with Japan had no effect with respect to the Treaty of Shimonoseki.

The other proclamation was made in 1945 when Japan surrendered toward the end of the Pacific War. Immediately after Japan surrendered to the United States and the United Kingdom, the ROC government seated in Chungking proclaimed that Taiwan was a "Province of China."[677] As stated before, a victorious State in a war can acquire title to a territory of the defeated State only by a territorial treaty, not by unilateral proclamation.[678] Accordingly, R. H. Turton, the Joint Under-Secretary of State For Foreign Affairs of the Churchill administration, referring to China's proclamation, said, "[u]nilateral declarations could not affect the legal political status of Formosa."[679] This statement by the United States' main ally made at the time is particularly telling of the effectiveness of China's proclamation.

Furthermore, after a territorial treaty is concluded, a subsequent aggressive act of a party to the treaty against the other does not affect the validity of the treaty.[680] Thus, Japan's subsequent aggression in China had no effect on the legal status of Taiwan. In 1955, during parliamentary debates on the sovereignty over Formosa in the British House of Commons, international law scholar Georg Schwarzenberger commented that the cession of Taiwan Island by China to Japan under the Treaty of Shimonoseki was valid and subsequent aggression by Japan should be disregarded.[681]

Thus, neither the ROC government, which made the proclamations, nor the competing PRC government can claim on behalf of China the title to the island of Taiwan based on the proclamations.

[677] The second proclamation was based on the argument that the ROC government's 1941 proclamation effected the return of Taiwan Island to China. *See* The White Paper, *supra* note 664.

[678] *See supra* text accompanying note 396.

[679] *See* 536 PARL. DEB., H.C. (5th Ser.) (1955) at 216.

[680] *See infra* text accompanying note 681.

[681] Georg Schwarzenberger, *Letter to the Editor: Formosa And China, Examination of Legal Status,* TIMES (LONDON), 02/2/1955. Schwarzenberger was a Reader in International Law at the University College of London. "China had ceded Formosa to Japan by the peace treaty of Shimonoseki of April 16, 1895. In order to judge the validity of this cession subsequent developments in international law which may, or may not, have affected the validity of cessions achieved as the result of aggressive war must be disregarded. Thus, the validity of this cession can hardly be contested." *Id.*

C. Title Based on the Cairo Declaration and the Potsdam Proclamation

The third of the grounds of the PRC government's argument that the island of Taiwan is China's territory is that the island was returned to China pursuant to the Cairo Declaration and the Potsdam Proclamation.[682] The following will examine the two declarations and their effect.

Both the Cairo Declaration and the Potsdam Proclamation were made during the Pacific War. As mentioned earlier, on December 1, 1943, the US President Franklin D. Roosevelt, British Prime Minister Winston Churchill, and China's Generalissimo Jiang (Chiang) Kai-shek issued a joint statement, known as the Cairo Declaration.[683] The Cairo Declaration stated, in part,

> *"The Three Great Allies ... covet no gain for themselves and have no thought of territorial expansion. It is their purpose that all the territories Japan has stolen from the Chinese, such as Manchuria, Formosa, and the Pescadores, shall be restored to the Republic of China. The aforesaid three great powers are determined that in due course Korea shall become free and independent."*[684]

After Germany surrendered on May 8, 1945, the US President Harry Truman, British Prime Minister Winston Churchill, and the Soviet Premier Joseph Stalin convened in Potsdam, Germany, and on July 26, 1945 issued a joint declaration called "the Proclamation Defining Terms for Japanese Surrender" (hereinafter "The Potsdam Proclamation"), when Japan had not yet surrendered.

The three leaders in the Potsdam Proclamation agreed to carry out the terms of the Cairo Declaration.[685] The Proclamation stated that "[t]he terms of the Cairo Declaration shall be carried out and Japanese sovereignty shall be limited to the islands of Honshu, Hokkaido, Kyushu, Shikoku and such minor islands as we determine."[686]

The intention of the three leaders at the time of issuing the Cairo Declaration that Formosa "shall be restored to the Republic of China" after Japan surrendered is not questioned here. However, the nature and

[682] *See Chou En-Lai Cablegram*, *supra* note 622.
[683] The Cairo Declaration, *see supra* note 640, at 393 and the text accompanying the note.
[684] *Id.*
[685] *See supra* text accompanying note 645.
[686] The Potsdam Proclamation, *supra* note 645. Sec. 8, at 137.

the legal effect of both declarations in international law are examined below.

First, the Cairo Declaration, by its nature, was not binding on the declaring governments or their succeeding governments. A joint declaration of two or more governments, like a joint communiqué, is often used to express the common foreign policy or the common intent of the issuing governments at the time of announcing the joint declaration. Such declaration of common foreign policy or of common intent is not a treaty.[687] It certainly does not have the characteristics of a contract in private law creating a binding obligation on the governments involved, let alone on the States which the governments represent.[688]

The Cairo Declaration was only a statement of common intent of the three governments at the time. Although the Cairo Declaration showed an intent to return Formosa to China at the time of the announcement, Winston Churchill, who took part in the Declaration, later emphatically said "[i]t contained *merely* a statement of common purpose."[689] With the political leader who made the Cairo Declaration clearly indicated that it was not meant to be binding, it is untenable to hold it otherwise. The Foreign Secretary Anthony Eden also said that the Declaration was "merely a statement of intention that Formosa should be retroceded to China after the war that never materialized."[690] Similarly, in May 1955 the Joint Under-Foreign Secretary R.H. Turton of the Eden Administration,

[687] On August 18, 1982, John H. Holdridge, the US Assistant Secretary for East Asian and Pacific Affairs, testified before the House Foreign Affairs on *United States—China Joint Communiqué*, said, "[referring to the Third United States—China Joint Communiqué] We should keep in mind that what we have here is not a treaty or agreement but a statement of future US policy. We intend to implement this policy in accordance with our understanding of it." Dept. of State Bulletin, October 1982, Vol. 82, No. 2067, at 21.

[688] For instance, one provision in the Potsdam Proclamation relating to the exclusion of certain Japanese officials after the war was not carried out, and no Allied powers has challenged it. The Potsdam Proclamation contains a provision (Paragraph 6) that requires the removal and exclusion of Japanese officials "who have deceived and misled the people of Japan into embarking on world conquest" in public offices. *See Id.* The exclusion was removed from the Peace Treaty of 1951. *See* MacArthur, *supra* note 647, at 298.

[689] 536 PARL. DEB., H.C. (5th ser.) (1955) at 901(emphasis added). Winston Churchill, who had been reelected Prime Minister, made the statement in response to the assertion of Rev. R. W. Sorensen, a Labor Party member, that Formosa should be handed over to the Chinese Communists under the Cairo Declaration. *See Id.*

[690] *Id.* at 159.

in responding to the questioning of a Labor Party member,[691] said that "[t]he Cairo Declaration was couched in the form of a statement of intention, and as it was merely a statement of intention, it is merely binding in so far as it states the intent at that time."[692]

The Potsdam Proclamation was also a joint statement of intention of the declaring governments. It, like the Cairo Declaration, does not bind the governments which made the declaration. In other words, it expressed an intention of carrying out the terms of the Cairo Declaration with respect to the future of Formosa and Korea. Thus, both the Cairo Declaration and the Potsdam Proclamation had no binding effect on the governments that made such declarations.

Second, the two declarations did not effect a transfer of Formosa to China. At the time when the two declarations were issued, Japan had not yet surrendered. The United States was winning the war, but had not yet defeated Japan. A general rule of law accepted by civilized nations is: one cannot give something that he does not have. Even assuming for the sake of argument that the declarations were considered contractual promises to offer Formosa to China, which they were not, they could not effect a transfer of Formosa to China. None of the three States represented by the declaring governments had title to Formosa at the time of making the declarations. Nor could they force Japan to transfer title to Formosa before Japan surrendered. Such transfer could be made at a postwar settlement in a treaty *only* after Japan surrendered and provided Japan was a party to the treaty.

That the two declarations did not effect a transfer of title to Formosa to China was also the opinion of the United States and the United Kingdom high officials. At a congressional hearing held in May 1951, General Douglas MacArthur said "[t]here were certain agreements that were entered into at Yalta, and other places, but legalistically Formosa is still a part of the Empire of Japan."[693] Thus, six years after the Cairo Declaration, General MacArthur, who assigned the task of the post surrender administration of Taiwan to Jiang (Chiang) Kai-shek, still said that Taiwan island

[691] Geoffrey Bing asserted that "the Potsdam Declaration which re-affirmed the Cairo Declaration ... was binding upon this Government." 540 Parl. Deb., H.C. (5th ser.) (1955) at 1869.

[692] *Id.*

[693] *The General Declines to Say That the US Has Lost the Initiative in Foreign Policy Matters* (Statement of General Douglas MacArthur before a congressional hearing), N.Y. Times, 05/5/1951, at A7 [hereinafter "Gen. MacArthur's Statement"].

was Japan's territory. His statement clearly implied that neither the Cairo Declaration nor the ROC government's proclamations effected a transfer of Formosa to China. The British Joint Under-Foreign Secretary R.H. Turton was of the same opinion, saying that the "Cairo Declaration cannot by itself transfer sovereignty. That document does impose certain moral obligations on those who take part in it, but it is not really germane to the present legal argument on what is or is not today the present sovereignty over Formosa."[694]

It may be true that, for a period after Japan surrendered, the US Government intended that Formosa would be returned to China in a post-war settlement. It assigned the task of the post surrender administration of Formosa to Jiang (Chiang) Kai-shek's ROC government, which still controlled a major part of China at that time.[695] The US Government even provided its Navy ship to transport the Chinese soldiers from China to Formosa. But prior to any legal disposition of the island of Taiwan, the ROC government became embroiled in a civil war with Chinese Communists. Later, Jiang (Chiang) Kai-shek was forced to take exile in Formosa. This left the United States in a difficult position. They had intended to return the island of Taiwan to China under the ROC government, their war ally at the time of announcing the Cairo Declaration, but subsequently China was ruled by the Communist PRC government. They did not wish to give the island of Taiwan to China for several reasons, but importantly, if that were done, the ROC government would have no place to go.

In describing the situation, US officials never stated that the island of Taiwan was returned to China. President Truman in the "Statement on Formosa" of January 5, 1950 stated that "[i]n keeping with the [Cairo Declaration and the Potsdam Proclamation], Formosa was surrendered to Generalissimo Jiang (Chiang) Kai-shek and for the past four years the United States and the other allied powers have accepted the exercise of *Chinese authority* over the island."[696] The US Secretary of State Dean Acheson also said: "The Chinese have administered Formosa for four years. [The] *authority* in that occupation was regarded as in accordance with the commitments."[697] While it may be inferred from the above that

[694] 540 PARL. DEB., H.C. (5th ser.) (1955) at 1870.

[695] *See supra* text accompanying note 652.

[696] *Text of Statement on Formosa*, N.Y. Times, 01/6/1950, at A3 (emphasis added).

[697] 540 PARL. DEB., H.C. (5th ser.) (1955) at 1865. Acheson made the statement on January 5, 1950. *See Id.*(emphasis added).

the US Government intended that Formosa would be returned to China in a postwar settlement, these statements did not mean that China *had acquired* title to Formosa. In the statements quoted above, the US Government used the terms "authority," "authority over the island," and "authority in that occupation," rather than the term "sovereignty" or "ownership" so as not to imply that China had title to the territory.[698] It is likely that Truman and Acheson made the statements to explain away the responsibility for a possible loss of Formosa in case the Chinese Communists overran the island.[699]

Third, the intents of the Cairo Declaration and the Potsdam Proclamation were not carried out. The Korean War changed the minds of the US and the UK Governments on the fate of Taiwan. The Cairo Declaration was based on the basic principles of nonaggression and no territorial ambitions.[700] The US and the UK Governments changed their positions because China violated the principles of the Cairo Declaration. Furthermore, the Declaration clearly stated that "The aforesaid three great powers are determined that in due course Korea shall become free and independent." The action of the PRC government, which was attributable to the State of China, in aiding North Korea's invasion of South Korea was in direct violation of the principles embodied in the Cairo Declaration. Thus, the US Government changed its position with respect to the future sovereignty over Formosa because of China's aggression in Korea. President Truman changed his position one day after

698 *See Id.*

699 A Congressional report indicates that the US government, at the time, prepared the way for the abandonment of Formosa to the Chinese Communists. The Report states,25. *The State Department directive of December 23, 1949, was a policy statement calculated to prepare the way for the abandonment of Formosa to the Chinese* Reds. On December 23, 1949, the US State Department issued hundreds of copies of a secret directive concerning the attitude to be adopted by our representatives abroad in respect to Formosa.... [T]his directive was an actual statement of policy on the part of the United States State Department in which we announced to our foreign representatives that Formosa was not of strategic importance to the United States and that its control by the Communist forces would not imperil our position in the Far East. *The Military Situation in the Far East: Hearing Before the Senate Comm. on Armed Services and Foreign Relations*, 82nd Cong. 30 (1951).

700 "The Three Great Allies ... covet no gain for themselves and have no thought of territorial expansion." The Cairo Declaration, *supra* note 640.

North Korea invaded South Korea.[701] On June 27, 1950, he issued "the Statement on Korea" in which he stated:

> *"The [Communists'] attack upon Korea makes it plain that communism has passed beyond the use of subversion to conquer independent [N]ations and will now use armed invasion and war. [T]he occupation of Formosa by Communist forces would be a direct threat to the security of the Pacific area and to [the US] forces performing their lawful and necessary functions in that area."*[702]

Although the Chinese Communists had not yet formally entered the Korean War at the time,[703] President Truman regarded North Korea's invasion of South Korea as part of a broad Communist attack scheme, and considered the Chinese Communists' invasion of Formosa imminent. He sent the US Navy Seventh Fleet toward the Taiwan Strait in order to prevent any attack on Formosa by the Chinese Communists.[704] Also voicing a change in attitude towards the PRC, Assistant Secretary for Far Eastern Affairs Dean Rusk said over the Voice of America, "[t]he Chinese Communists took part in the preparations for the treacherous North Korean assault long before it was actually launched."[705] Secretary of State Acheson also changed his earlier position. In a television interview in September 1950, he stated,

> *"The Cairo Declaration declares that Formosa should be returned to China. It also declares that Korea should be free and independent. In most of the discussions that we have about Formosa, we are reminded about the Formosan part of the Declaration, and both the Chinese and the Russians forget about the Korean part of the Declaration. Surely, the Declaration of Cairo is an important factor to be taken into consideration in the future settlement. But the future settlement is for the future."*[706]

[701] *See* The New Encyclopedia Britannica, *supra* note 7. V. 6, at 958; *see also* World Almanac 476 (William A. McGeveran Jr. et al. eds., 2004); *Foreign Policies Toward Asia, A Television Interview with Sec'y Acheson* (Sept. 10, 1950), *in* Dep't St. Bull., Sept. 1950, at 463.

[702] President Harry Truman, *Statement on Korea*, N.Y. Times, 06/28/1950, at A1.

[703] The PRC government sent a volunteer army (the "Chinese People's Volunteers") to the Korean Peninsula in October of 1950. *See* The New Encyclopedia Britannica, *supra* note 7. V. 16, at 959.

[704] *See Id.*

[705] *Our Contributions to the Peace*, Statement by Dean Rusk, Assistant Sec'y for Far Eastern Affairs (Dec. 29, 1950), Dep't St. Bull., Jan. 1951, at 64 (stating that North Korea invaded South Korea in June of 1950).

[706] *Foreign Policies Toward Asia, A Television Interview with Sec'y Acheson* (Sept. 10, 1950), *in* Dep't St. Bull., Sept. 1950, at 463.

The United Kingdom also changed its position due to China's aggression. In May 1951, British Foreign Secretary Herbert Morrison made the following policy statement in the House of Commons:

> *"The Cairo Declaration also proclaimed the intention that Korea should in due course become free and independent. It also expressed acceptance of two principles: nonaggression and no territorial ambitions. [T]he Prime Minister [Attlee] went on to remark [on December 14, 1950] that until China shows by her action that she is not obstructing fulfilment [sic] of the Cairo Declaration in respect of Korea and accepts the basic principle of that Declaration, it will be difficult to reach a satisfactory solution of this problem [of Formosa]."*[707]

British Prime Minister Winston Churchill regarded the Cairo Declaration obsolete. In February 1955, in rebutting an assertion of a Labor Party member that Formosa should be handed over to the Chinese Communists under the Cairo Declaration, Churchill, who made the Declaration more than a decade earlier, said that "since [the Cairo Declaration] was made a lot of things have happened. The problem of Formosa has become an international problem in which a number of other [N]ations are closely concerned."[708] The following day, The New York Times printed a headline *Cairo Formosa Declaration Out of Date, Says Churchill.*[709] Churchill had made it very clear that the past intentions would no longer be fulfilled. From the above analyses, it is clear that neither the ROC government nor the PRC government can claim title to the island of Taiwan for the State of China based on the Cairo Declaration or the Potsdam Proclamation.

Subsequent to the Cairo Declaration, the Allies, the United States, China, and Japan, collectively or separately, between them entered into several treaties: the Peace Treaty of San Francisco, the Treaty of Taipei (signed by the ROC and Japan), the US–China Mutual Defense Treaty (signed by the ROC), the Treaty of Peace and Friendship (signed by the PRC and Japan). As the following analyses of these treaties will show, they all negated the notion that China acquired title to the island of Taiwan under the Cairo Declaration.

[707] 478 Parl. Deb., H.C. (5th ser.) (1951) at 2301–02.

[708] 536 Parl. Deb., H.C. (5th ser.) (1955) at 901.

[709] Drew Middleton, *Cairo Formosa Declaration Out of Date, Says Churchill*, N.Y. Times, 02/2/1955, at A1.

a. The Peace Treaty of San Francisco

One treaty which is crucial to title to the island of Taiwan but which the PRC government never mentions in its claim on the island of Taiwan is the Peace Treaty of San Francisco.

In 1945, the United Nations was formed. While the allied powers were engaged in war with the Axis States both in Europe and Asia, the representatives of the United States, the United Kingdom, the Soviet Union, and the ROC met at Dumbarton Oaks, Washington, DC in August 1944 to discuss the formation of an international peace and security organization in order to prevent a third world war.[710] On April 25, 1945,[711] the allied powers convened at the UN Conference in San Francisco and formed the United Nations,[712] which officially came into existence on October 24, 1945. China, represented by the ROC government, was one of the original members and also a permanent member of its Security Council.

In August 1945, when Japan surrendered unconditionally, the United States, having defeated Japan, became the occupying power (State) of Japan.[713] As the occupying State, the United States had the power to dispose of Japan's territory. The United States assigned the ROC government to receive the surrender of the Japanese military commanders in Taiwan. Under the general principles of law accepted by civilized nations,

[710] *See* DEP'T ST. BULL., Aug. 1944, at 133. The meetings, which began on August 14, came to be known as the Dumbarton Oaks Conversations on International Peace and Security Organization'. *See* Hungdah Chiu, *The Right of The Republic of China and its 21 Million Chinese People to Participate in the United Nations*, 28 J. MARSHALL L. REV. at 247, 248 (1994). The representatives of the United Kingdom and the United States spoke with the Soviet Union's representatives first, and then with the Chinese representatives separately. *See Id. See also* the Dumbarton Conference, *available at* http://en.wikipedia.org/wiki/Dumbarton_Oaks_Conference. Last visited 10/20/2013.

[711] The date of the conference was set by US President Franklin D. Roosevelt, the UK Prime Minister Winston Churchill, and the USSR Marshall Joseph Stalin at the Crimea Conference held between February 4 and February 11, 1945.

[712] *See* UN Charter *supra* note 383; *see also* United Nations Conference on International Organization (Apr. 25, 1945), DEP'T ST. BULL., Apr. 1945, at 789. The Charter was signed on June 26, 1945 by 50 countries. The United Nations officially came into existence on October 24, 1945. *See* The United Nations, *About the United Nations, available at* http://www.un.org/aboutun/history.htm. Last visited 09/30/2004; *see also* RUTH B. RUSSELL, A HISTORY OF THE UNITED NATIONS, the ROLE OF THE UNITED STATES, 1940–1945, at 964 (Brookings Inst. 1958) (providing in-depth coverage of the formation of the UN Charter). Before the date of the Conference, President Franklin Roosevelt died (April 12, 1945), and Vice President Harry S. Truman became the 33rd US President. *See* JOSEPH N. KANE, PRESIDENTIAL FACT BOOK, at 215 (1999).

[713] *See supra* note 391.

an agency relation was implicitly created between the US Government as the principal and the ROC government as its agent with respect to the administration of Taiwan.

To prepare a postwar settlement, the allied powers began to prepare for a peace treaty. The United States and the United Kingdom assumed the task of drafting the treaty.[714] The draft was distributed to other allied powers for comments, and exchanges of notes among the allies ensued. The Peace Treaty of San Francisco, as it came to be known, was signed on September 8, 1951[715] between the Allied Powers and Japan.[716] China was neither a party nor a signatory to this treaty.[717] Consequently, neither the ROC government that administered the island of Taiwan nor the PRC government that controlled China proper was invited to sign on behalf of the State of China.

China did not acquire title to Formosa as a consequence of the Peace Treaty of San Francisco for three reasons. The first reason is that Japan did not transfer title to Formosa to China in the Treaty. Even though the ROC government had administered the affairs of Formosa for 6 years when the Peace Treaty of San Francisco was concluded, the Allied Powers did not intend to confer title to Formosa to China in the Peace Treaty. While the ROC government had allied with the US Government in fighting against Japan, it was no longer in control of China's territory. As discussed previously, since the United States did not wish to benefit the new Communist government of China, it did not allow China to be a signatory in the Treaty.

[714] The United Kingdom and the United States each produced a text of its own before they jointly drafted a reconciled text. Sec'y John Foster Dulles, *Statements at the Second Plenary Session (Sept. 5, 1951)*, *in* DEP'T ST. BULL., Sept. 1951, at 452–54.

[715] *See* the Peace Treaty of San Francisco, *supra* note 403.

[716] The following countries signed the Peace Treaty with Japan as Allied Powers: Argentina, Australia, Belgium, Bolivia, Brazil, Cambodia, Canada, Ceylon, Chile, Columbia, Costa Rica, Cuba, Dominican Republic, Ecuador, Egypt, El Salvador, Ethiopia, France, Greece, Guatemala, Haiti, Honduras, Indonesia, Iran, Iraq, Laos, Lebanon, Liberia, Luxembourg, Mexico, Netherlands, New Zealand, Nicaragua, Norway, Pakistan, Panama, Paraguay, Peru, The Philippines, Saudi Arabia, South Africa, Syria, Turkey, United Kingdom, United States, Uruguay, Venezuela, Vietnam. *See Id.*

[717] John Foster Dulles said, "[T]he Sino-Japanese War cannot be formally terminated at this occasion [the signing of the Peace Treaty of San Francisco]." Sec'y John Foster Dulles, *Statements at the Second Plenary Session*, *supra* note 714, at 458. Subsequently, the ROC government and Japan signed the Treaty of Peace on April 28, 1952. ROC–Japan, 163 UNTS 38 [hereinafter the 'Treaty of Taipei']. It entered into force on Aug. 5, 1952. For a discussion of the Treaty of Taipei, *see infra* text accompanying note 752.

The Peace Treaty of San Francisco is a territorial treaty. The only provision that deals with the territory of Formosa is Article 2(b), which provides that "Japan renounces all right, title and claim to Formosa and the Pescadores."[718] There is no mention of China at all, much less a provision for the return of Formosa to China.

China did not receive title to Formosa by any interpretation of the Treaty. There are two approaches in interpreting a treaty: the objective approach and the subjective approach.[719] Article 31 of the Vienna Convention adopts the ordinary meaning (the "objective" approach), as well as the meaning derived from the words supplemented by other methods, such as the intention of the parties (the "subjective" approach).[720] Under the objective approach, i.e., by the plain and ordinary meaning of the treaty, China did not receive title to Formosa under the language of the Peace Treaty of San Francisco. The Treaty does not use the word "cede," which is in general usage the word used in a treaty to transfer a territory between the parties to the treaty. Instead, it uses the word "renounce." The plain and ordinary meaning of the word "renounce" is "to give up,"[721] "to abandon."[722] It has the same meaning as the word "relinquish" employed in the Treaty of Paris between Spain and the United States.[723] A territorial treaty is like a deed in municipal law. In municipal law, the deed must designate a transferee in order for title to a piece of land to pass to the transferee. The Peace Treaty of San

718 The Peace Treaty of San Francisco, *supra* note 403, Art. 2(b).

719 *See* WALLACE, *supra* note 36, at 239–40.

720 *See* Vienna Convention on the Law of Treaties, *supra note* 365. Art. 31 (providing interpretive methodologies for all treaties); WALLACE, *supra* note 36, at 204 (Sweet & Maxwell, 1986).

721 *See* MERRIAM-WEBSTER'S COLLEGE DICTIONARY 991 (10th Ed. 1996) (providing the definition of "renounce" as "to give up"); *see also* OXFORD ADVANCED LEARNER'S DICTIONARY, *supra* note 4, at 991(providing definition of "renounce" as "to abandon"). In the Peace Treaty of Sevres concluded after the World War I between Ottoman Empire (Turkey) and the Allied Powers, Turkey "renounced all claims to non-Turkish territories." ENCYCLOPEDIA OF WORLD HISTORY, *supra* note 393, at 954.

722 *See* OXFORD ADVANCED LEARNER'S DICTIONARY. *Id.* at 1.

723 *See* The Treaty of Paris, Dec. 10, 1898, United States–Spain, 30 Stat. 1754, Art. 1., *see infra* note 1010. In January 1955, Sec'y of State John Dulles, said, "[Formosa and the Pescadores] became part of the Japanese Empire in 1895. They continued as such for half a century, until they were *relinquished* by Japan as a result of her defeat in war." Sec'y John Foster Dulles, *Our Foreign Policies in Asia, Address before the Foreign Policy Association* (Feb. 16, 1955), *in* DEP'T ST. BULL., Feb. 1955, at 329 (emphasis added).

Francisco does not mention any transferee. For that reason, no State could receive any right or title to Formosa under the Treaty according to its terms, not even China.

Under the subjective approach of interpretation, i.e., the intention of the parties to the Peace Treaty of San Francisco, it is clear that the Allied Powers did not intend for China to receive the title to Formosa. The United States and the United Kingdom had changed their positions with respect to the intent announced in the Cairo Declaration, and instead, decided to leave the future of Formosa undetermined. Accordingly, they wanted Japan to abandon title to Formosa, but *did not* want China to receive it. Using the word "renounce" for disposing of the title to Formosa was not without careful deliberation of the drafters of the Peace Treaty of San Francisco.[724] The Soviet Union was aware of the disposition of the island of Formosa in the draft Treaty. In fact, the government of the Soviet Union, in its memorandum to the US Ambassador, objected to the proposed disposition.[725] The Soviet Union's memorandum stated,

> *"In the meantime the [US] draft treaty and the memorandum of the United States of America of May 19 testify to the fact that the Government of the United States is going on with direct violation of the national rights of China with respect to its territory in refusing to fulfilling the Cairo agreement regarding the return of Taiwan island and the Pescadores Islands to China as well as with exclusion of China from preparation of a peace treaty with Japan."*[726]

Likewise, the government of India was fully aware that Formosa was not to be returned to China under the draft Peace Treaty of San Francisco.[727] In its memorandum to the US Department of State,[728] the Indian government expressed its intent not to participate in the Peace Treaty of San Francisco on the ground, among others, that,

> *"[T]he Government of India attach[es] the greatest importance to the Treaty providing that the Island of Formosa should be returned to China. The time and manner of such return might be the subject of separate negotiations but*

[724] *See* DULLES, *The San Francisco Conference on Proposed Japanese Peace Treaty*, *supra* note 391.

[725] *See Memorandum of the USSR* (June 10, 1951), USSR–US, DEP'T ST. BULL., June 1951, at 138.

[726] *Id.* at 142.

[727] *See India Refuses To Be Party to Treaty, Memorandum of India*, Aug. 23, 1951, India–US, DEP'T ST. BULL., Sept. 1951, at 386.

[728] *Id.*

> to leave the future of the Island undetermined, *in spite of past international agreements, in a document which attempts to regulate the relations of Japan with all Governments that were engaged in the last war against her does not appear to the Government of India to be either just or expedient.*"[729]

Both the Soviet Union and India characterized the nature of the Cairo Declaration as an "agreement," implying that the Declaration created a legal obligation on the parties to implement the agreement. If the Cairo Declaration was an agreement, it could not bind Japan which owned Formosa at the time of the Declaration because Japan was not a party to the agreement. Besides, neither the Soviet Union nor India were parties to the Cairo Declaration. They were not in a position to interpret the nature of the joint statement of other governments. The United States and the United Kingdom simply disregarded their comments.

At the Conference in San Francisco for signing the Peace Treaty, John Dulles, who drafted the Treaty, referring to the disposition of Formosa, remarked,

> *"[A]rticle 2 ... merely delimit[s] Japanese sovereignty. [S]pecify[ing] precisely the ultimate disposition of each of the ex-Japanese territories [w]ould have been neater. But the Allies quarrel about what shall be done with what Japan is required to give up. The wise course was leaving the future to resolve doubts by invoking international solvents other than this Treaty."*[730]

President Truman at the conference explained the disposition of Formosa by reminding the conference delegates of the Communists' aggression.[731] The US Secretary of State Dean Acheson, who presided at the Conference, added at the closing of the Conference that "[w]e signed this great treaty this morning, but we must live this treaty from this day on," well aware that the fate of Formosa was not decided by the treaty.[732] Thus, there was no doubt to all the parties involved that the Allied Powers did not intend China to acquire title to Formosa under the Peace Treaty of San Francisco.

The attitude of the United States and the United Kingdom toward the Taiwan problem changed over the years. As it was pointed out in

729 *Id.* at 386 (emphasis added).

730 John Foster Dulles, *Statements at the Second Plenary Session*, *supra* note 712, at 454.

731 Truman said: "Unfortunately, today, the world is faced with new threat of aggression. Many of the countries represented here are now engaged in a hard fight to uphold the United Nations against international lawbreaking." *Opening Address by President Truman (Sept. 4, 1951)*, *in* DEP'T ST. BULL., Sept. 1951, at 447.

732 *Id.* at 460.

Chapter 3, The Territorial State, under international law a victorious State has the power to dispose at will the territory of a defeated State that surrendered unconditionally in a war. Although at the Cairo Conference of 1943, the US President Franklin Roosevelt and British Prime Minister Winston Churchill intended to return Formosa to China after the war with Japan ended, subsequent to Japan's surrender, however, the two leading victorious powers, i.e., the United States and the United Kingdom, changed their positions due to the aggression of China in Korea, and instead simply required Japan to renounce her title to Formosa in the Peace Treaty.

The second reason that China did not acquire title to Formosa as a consequence of the Peace Treaty of San Francisco is that China is not a party to the Treaty. Under the general rule of international law mentioned in Chapter 3, The Territorial State, only a party to a territorial treaty can transfer or receive title to a territory in the treaty. The Peace Treaty of San Francisco is more specific. According to Article 23, China is not a party to the Peace Treaty of San Francisco. Article 23 provides,

> *"The present Treaty shall be ratified by the States which sign it, including Japan, and will come into force to all the States which have then ratified it, when instruments of ratification have been deposited by Japan and by the majority, including the United States of America as the principal occupying Power, of the following States, [here appear the names of such of the following States as signatories to the present Treaty] namely Australia, Canada, Ceylon, France, Indonesia, the Netherlands, New Zealand, Pakistan, the Philippines, the United Kingdom of Great Britain and Northern Ireland, and the United States of America."*[733]

China is not listed in Article 23.

Under Art. 25, only an Allied Power can receive any rights, titles, or benefits conferred by the Treaty. Article 25 provides that "Subject to the provisions of Article 21, the present Treaty shall not confer any rights, titles or benefits on any State which is not an Allied Power as herein defined; *nor shall any right, title or interest of Japan be deemed to be diminished or prejudiced by any provision of the Treaty in favor of a State which is not an Allied Power as so defined*."[734]

China is not an Allied Power as defined in the first paragraph of Article 25, which provides that, "[f]or the purposes of the present Treaty the Allied Powers shall be the States at war with Japan, or any State which

[733] The Peace Treaty of San Francisco, *supra* note 403, Art. 23.
[734] *Id*. Art. 25,at 74 (emphasis added).

previously formed a part of the territory of a State named in Article 23, *provided in each case the State concerned has signed and ratified the Treaty*."[735]

China cannot receive title to Formosa under an exception to Article 25 either. The exception is in Article 21, which provides that "[n]otwithstanding the provisions of Article 25 of the present Treaty, China shall be entitled to the benefits of Articles 10 and 14(a)2."[736] Neither Art. 10 nor Art. 14(a)2 deals with territory of Japan. Article 10 deals with the rights and interests of Japan *in* China, not with Japan's territories. Article 10 provides,

> *"Japan renounces all special rights and interests in China, including all benefits and privileges resulting from the provisions of the final Protocol signed at Peking on September 7, 1901, and all annexes, notes and documents supplementary thereto, and agrees to the abrogation in respect to Japan of the said protocol, annexes, notes and document."*[737]

Article 10 specifically provides for the renunciation of rights and interests acquired by Japan on September 7, 1901. The Article does not include the territory or any rights acquired by Japan in the 1895 Treaty of Shimonoseki. As mentioned in Chapter 3, The Territorial State, a general principle of law is: Where a document enumerates specific items, it is construed to exclude any items not enumerated.

Article 14 of the Treaty deals with reparations and acceptance of surrender,[738] not with territory. Thus, because China is not a party to the Treaty and not an "Allied Power" under the Treaty, China cannot receive title to a territory owned by Japan under the Treaty.

[735] *Id.* Art. 25 (emphasis added).

[736] *Id.* Art. 21.

[737] *Id.* Art. 10.

[738] *See Id.* Art. 14. Art. 14(a)2 of the Peace Treaty of San Francisco does not confer to the ROC government any right to govern the island of Taiwan. Art. 14(a)2 provides:

[E]ach of the Allied Powers shall have the right to seize, retain, liquidate or otherwise dispose of all property, rights and interests of

a. Japan and Japanese nationals,
b. person acting for or on behalf Japan or Japanese nationals, and
c. entities owned or controlled by Japan or Japanese nationals, which on the first coming into force of the present Treaty were subject to its jurisdiction.

The Peace Treaty of San Francisco, *supra* note 403, Art. 14(a)(2), 136 UNTS at 59. Thus, though China, not being an Allied Power as defined, was conferred no right, titles, or benefits by the Peace Treaty of San Francisco (Article 25), Article 21 provides an exception so that China had the benefits specified under Article 14(a)2.

The third reason why China did not acquire title to Formosa as a consequence of the Peace Treaty of San Francisco is that title to Formosa did not revert to China as a result of the Treaty.[739] Title to Formosa did not revert to China for two reasons. First, the Allied Powers did not intend that the title to Formosa reverted to China as a consequence of the Peace Treaty of San Francisco. If the Allied Powers had intended that the title to Formosa reverted to China, the Treaty would have simply required Japan to cede the island to China. But the treaty did not do so.

Second, no provisions in the Peace Treaty of San Francisco can be interpreted to result in a reversion of title to Formosa to China. Legalistically, such reversion of title to China can occur only if the Treaty of Shimonoseki, which conveyed the island by China to Japan, is revoked or terminated. However, the Peace Treaty of San Francisco does not revoke or terminate the Treaty of Shimonoseki. The Treaty of Shimonoseki is a territorial treaty, which as stated in Chapter 2, The State and Sovereignty, cannot be revoked or terminated.[740] Besides, the Peace Treaty of San Francisco does not even mention the Treaty of Shimonoseki.

Article 2(b) of the Peace Treaty of San Francisco does not result in a reversion of title to Formosa to China.[741] The Peace Treaty of San Francisco does not require Japan to renounce her rights, title, and claim to Formosa that it acquired in the Treaty of Shimonoseki. In Article 2(b), Japan simply renounces the title and claim to Formosa without reference to the Treaty of Shimonoseki. The language in Article 2(b) of this Treaty is similar to that in Article 2(f), in which "Japan renounces all right, title and claim to the Spratly Islands and the Paracel Islands."[742] In these two provisions, Japan renounced her claim to the territories without qualification and without any attempt to transfer their title, but leaving it unresolved.

In summary, the Peace Treaty of San Francisco leaves the Treaty of Shimonoseki intact. It does not affect the validity of the Treaty of Shimonoseki, in which China transferred title to Formosa to Japan. In fact, that the Peace Treaty of San Francisco requires Japan to renounce

[739] *See* the Peace Treaty of San Francisco, *supra* note 403.
[740] *See supra* text accompanying note 406.
[741] *See* the Peace Treaty of San Francisco, *supra* note 403, Art. 2(b).
[742] The Peace Treaty of San Francisco, *Id.*, Art. 2(f), at 48.

the title to Formosa indicates that the Peace Treaty recognizes Japan's title to Formosa acquired under the Treaty of Shimonoseki.[743]

For the three reasons discussed above, China undoubtedly did not acquire the title to Formosa as a consequence of the Peace Treaty of San Francisco. The Peace Treaty of San Francisco has one very important implication: it specifically and deliberately does not carry out the war time intention of the three governments announced in the Cairo Declaration and the Potsdam Proclamation. The Peace Treaty rejects the Formosan part of the two declarations. The Allied Powers, which signed the Peace Treaty of San Francisco, formally rejected the two declarations regarding the return of Formosa to China. As Britain's Foreign Secretary Anthony Eden stated in the House of Commons,

> *"In the Cairo Declaration of November, 1943, the Allies stated that it was their purpose 'that all the territories which Japan has stolen from the Chinese such as Formosa and the Pescadores, shall be restored to the Republic of China.' This Declaration was a statement of intention that Formosa should be retroceded to China after the war. This retrocession has, in fact, never taken place."*[744]

Thus, the island of Taiwan was not returned to China pursuant to the Peace Treaty of San Francisco.

b. The Post-Peace Treaty Interpretations of the United States and the United Kingdom

After the Peace Treaty of San Francisco was concluded, the United States and the United Kingdom, the two leading Allied Powers, had occasions to interpret the Peace Treaty with respect to sovereignty over Formosa.[745] Both the United States and the United Kingdom held that no State had acquired sovereignty over Formosa under the Peace Treaty of San Francisco.

Their views were expressed three years after the conclusion of the Treaty. The Eisenhower Administration considered that China had not acquired title to the island of Taiwan under its proclamations, the Cairo Declaration, the Potsdam Proclamation, or the Peace Treaty of San Francisco, and regarded the sovereignty over Formosa as an issue that was not settled by the Peace Treaty. In February 1955, when the United

[743] *See* the Treaty of Shimonoseki, *supra* note 453.

[744] 536 Parl. Deb., H.C. (5th ser.) (1955) at 159.

[745] The United Kingdom and the United States are the "cosponsors of the text." Sec'y Dean Acheson, *Opening Statement Before the San Francisco Conference* (Sept. 5, 1951), *in* Dep't St. Bull., Sept. 1951, at 450.

States signed a mutual defense treaty with the ROC government, the US Secretary of State, John Foster Dulles, in urging the US Senate to approve the Treaty, remarked that "[t]echnical sovereignty over Formosa and the Pescadores has never been settled. That is because the Japanese peace treaty merely involves a renunciation by Japan of its right and title to these islands. But the future title is not determined by the Japanese peace treaty, nor is it determined by the peace treaty which was concluded between the Republic of China and Japan."[746] Thus, the Peace Treaty of San Francisco left the sovereignty over Formosa undetermined.

The UK's position was the same—that China did not acquire Formosa under the Peace Treaty of San Francisco. British Prime Minister Churchill did not consider Formosa part of China when he said in 1954 that "Chiang Kai-shek who was driven *out of his country* by a Communist revolution took refuge upon Formosa, where he still remains."[747] Likewise, in 1955, in response to a Laborite's suggestion in the British House of Commons that Formosa should be handed over to Communist China pursuant to the Cairo Declaration, British Foreign Secretary Anthony Eden said:

> *"[Formosa and the Pescadores] have been in Chinese Nationalist hands ever since the Japanese surrender in 1945. [Formosa and the offshore islands Quemoy and Matsu] have always been treated as separate issues ... Formosa has never in this century been a part of China and the status of Formosa ... was dealt with by the Treaty of San Francisco, signed by the [Attlee] Government. The offshore islands [Quemoy and Matsu] have always been regarded, and are now regarded, by us as part of China. [The] distinction which the House should carefully maintain."*[748]

A week later, British Prime Minister Winston Churchill, who participated in the issuance of the Cairo Declaration, said that the future of the island was now an international problem and the question of its future sovereignty was left undetermined by the Japanese peace treaty.[749] The

[746] Sec'y John Foster Dulles, *Remarks at News Conference on the Purpose of Treaty with ROC* (Dec. 1, 1954), *in* DEP'T ST. BULL., Dec. 1954, at 896. *See also* Dulles, *Our Foreign Policies in Asia, Address before the Foreign Policy Association* (Feb. 16, 1955), *supra* note 723.

[747] 530 PARL. DEB., H.C. (5th ser.) (1954) at 494 (emphasis added).

[748] 536 PARL. DEB., H.C. (5th ser.) (Jan. 26, 1955) at 160. The Treaty was signed on Sept. 8, 1951 and went into force on Apr. 28, 1952.

[749] *See* Drew Middleton, *Cairo Formosa Declaration Out of Date, Says Churchill*, N.Y. TIMES, 02/2/1955, at 1.

British Foreign Secretary Anthony Eden confirmed Churchill's statement in the British House of Commons. Eden stated,

> *"[U]nder the Peace Treaty of April, 1952, Japan formally renounced all right, title and claim to Formosa and the Pescadores; but again this did not operate as a transfer to Chinese sovereignty, whether to the People's Republic of China or to the Chinese Nationalist authorities. Formosa and the Pescadores are therefore, in the view of Her Majesty's Government, territory the* de jure *sovereignty over which is uncertain or undetermined."*[750]

British Joint Under-Foreign Secretary R. H. Turton reiterated the United Kingdom position in the House of Commons in May of 1955.[751] Thus, the two leading Allied Powers were in consensus regarding the meaning of the terms of the Peace Treaty of San Francisco disposing the title to Formosa—that the Treaty did not give China the title to Formosa.

c. The Treaty of Taipei Signed by the ROC and Japan

China was not a party to the Peace Treaty of San Francisco. Thus, neither the ROC government nor the PRC government was invited to sign the Treaty. After the conclusion of the Treaty of San Francisco, Japan concluded two separate peace treaties with China. One was "the Treaty of Peace" between Japan and China represented by the ROC government, sometimes called "The Treaty of Taipei."[752] The other was "the Treaty of Peace and Friendship," also between Japan and China but represented by the PRC government. The two treaties are examined below.

The Treaty of Taipei of 1952 is not a territorial treaty because it does not dispose of a territory. Although the Treaty of Taipei ended the war between China and Japan, it did not address the title to Formosa, but simply confirmed Japan's disposition in the Peace Treaty of San Francisco. Article II of the Treaty of Taipei provides that "It is recognized that under Article 2 of the Treaty of Peace with Japan signed at the city of San Francisco in the United States of America on September 8, 1951, Japan has renounced all right, titles and claim to Taiwan (Formosa) and Penghu (The Pescadores) as well as the Spratly Islands and Paracel Islands."[753] The Treaty of Taipei that merely recognized the disposition of territory in

[750] 536 Parl. Deb., H.C. (5th ser.) (1955) at 159.

[751] *See* 540 Parl. Deb., H.C. (5th ser.) (1955) at 1871.

[752] *See* the Treaty of Taipei of 1952, *supra* note 717. The ROC government, in signing the treaty, represented the State of China.

[753] *See* the Treaty of Taipei of 1952, *Id.* Art. II.

another treaty is not a territorial treaty. By recognizing that Japan had abandoned Formosa in the Treaty of San Francisco, China officially accepted Japan's action in the Peace Treaty of San Francisco as valid. China not only did not acquire the title to Formosa under the Treaty of Taipei, but also formally accepted the disposition of Formosa by the Peace Treaty of San Francisco.

Under the general principles of law, China could not acquire title to the island of Taiwan under the Treaty of Taipei. Japan, having renounced her title and claim to the island of Taiwan in the Peace Treaty of San Francisco in 1951, no longer had any title or right to the island of Taiwan to give away at the time of concluding the Treaty of Taipei in 1952. As mentioned before, this result was confirmed by the US Secretary of State John Foster Dulles, who said that "[T]he future title [to the island of Taiwan] is not determined by the Japanese peace treaty [the Treaty of San Francisco], nor is it determined by *the peace treaty which was concluded between the Republic of China and Japan* [referring to the Treaty of Taipei]."[754] In 1978, when Japan and the PRC government signed the Treaty of Peace and Friendship, Japan terminated the Treaty of Taipei. That the Treaty of Taipei could be terminated by one party also indicates that the Treaty of Taipei was not a territorial treaty.

d. The US–China (the ROC) Mutual Defense Treaty

In 1954, the United States and China represented by the ROC government entered into a mutual defense treaty. After the Korean War ended, in order to defend Taiwan against the possible invasion by the Chinese Communists, the Eisenhower Administration signed a mutual defense treaty with the ROC government in Taiwan in 1954.[755] In February 1955, in urging the US Senate to approve the Treaty, Secretary of State John Foster Dulles rejected a suggestion that signing a mutual defense agreement with the ROC President Jiang (Chiang) Kai-shek would change the legal status of Formosa and would give the Nationalists (the ROC government) sovereignty over them. Dulles said that the Eisenhower Administration "does not regard the sovereignty of Formosa and the Pescadores as settled and the [Mutual Defense T]reaty would not

[754] *See supra* text accompanying note 746 (emphasis added).

[755] *See* the Mutual Defense Treaty, Dec. 2, 1954, United States–China (the ROC government), 6 U.S.T. 433. Although the treaty was signed by the ROC government, technically the treaty was between China and the United States because a treaty is between two States.

give General Chiang sovereignty over these islands."[756] The US Senate Foreign Relations Committee Chairman, Senator Walter F. George, commented that the committee's "understanding" of the treaty was that "Senate approval of the Treaty would neither strengthen nor weaken the Chiang [the ROC] Government's claim to sovereignty over Formosa, the international status of which is yet to be decided."[757] It is clear from this comment that the United States had no intention to change its position on the legal status of Formosa through this treaty.

The British government interpreted the US–China Mutual Defense Treaty in the same way. To a House member's argument that the United States would accord formal recognition of Formosa as a territory of the ROC by signing the Mutual Defense Treaty, British Joint Under-Foreign Secretary Turton in the Eden Administration rebutted that "It is clear from what Mr. Dulles said at the time of signing of the Treaty that he was in no conflict with us on the legal interpretation of the position."[758]

Thus, the position of the United States and the United Kingdom immediately prior to the Shanghai Communiqué was that the US–China Mutual Defense Treaty of 1954 did not effect a transfer of the island of Taiwan to China. When the US switched recognition from the ROC government to the PRC government in 1979, the United States terminated the US–China Mutual Defense Treaty because the Treaty was no longer consistent with the political situation. That the United States could unilaterally terminate the Mutual Defense Treaty indicates that the Treaty was not a territorial treaty that could change title to a territory.

e. *The Treaty of Peace and Friendship Signed by the PRC and Japan*

The second peace treaty between Japan and China—the Treaty of Peace and Friendship—was signed by the PRC government and the government of Japan in 1978.[759] Back in 1972, the two governments issued a Joint Communiqué in which they stated a mutual desire to normalize the relations between the two countries. The Joint Communiqué with respect to Taiwan stated,

[756] James Reston, *New Formosa Bid*, N.Y. Times, 02/7/1955, at A1.

[757] William S. White, *Senate Approves Formosa Treaty*, N.Y. Times, 02/10/1955, at A1.

[758] 540 Parl. Deb., H.C. (5th ser.) (1955) at 1865, 1870–71.

[759] The Treaty of Peace and Friendship between Japan and the People's Republic of China, Aug. 12, 1978, Japan–PRC, 1981 U.N.T.S. 269 [hereinafter the "Treaty of Peace and Friendship"]. Technically, the treaty is between Japan and China. The PRC government, in signing the treaty, represented the State of China.

"The Government of the People's Republic of China reiterates that Taiwan is an inalienable part of the territory of the People's Republic of China. The Government of Japan fully understands and respects this stand of the Government of the People's Republic of China, and it firmly maintains its stand under Article 8 of the Potsdam Proclamation."[760]

This Joint Communiqué, like other joint communiqué, is not a territorial treaty. It could not and did not effect a transfer of a territory. Besides, in the Joint Communiqué, Japan only stated that it understood and respected the PRC government's position. An acknowledgment of China's position was not consent or acquiescence to China's position.

The Treaty of Peace and Friendship provides for development of "lasting relations of peace and friendship between the two countries on the basis of mutual respect for the principles of sovereignty and territorial integrity, mutual nonaggression, nonintervention in each other's internal affairs, mutual benefit, and peaceful coexistence." The only part of the Treaty indirectly concerning Taiwan is the reference to the 1972 Joint Communiqué in the preamble. It provides,

"Having recalled with satisfaction that, since the issuance of the joint statement by the Government of Japan and the Government of the People's Republic of China on 29 September 1972 at Beijing, friendly relations between the Governments and the peoples of the two countries have developed extensively on a new basis, affirming that the aforementioned joint statement constitutes the basis for relations of peace and friendship between the two countries and that the principles set out in that statement should be strictly observed."

The Treaty of Peace and Friendship does not confer Formosa's title to China. The Treaty, which acknowledges a previous communiqué, is not a territorial treaty either. It does not even mention the Peace Treaty of San Francisco or Taiwan. In addition, the Treaty can be terminated by either party pursuant to its provision. Article 5 of the Treaty provides,

1. This Treaty is subject to ratification and shall enter into force on the day of the exchange of the instruments of ratification at Tokyo. This Treaty shall remain in force for 10 years and thereafter until the statement of termination provided for in paragraph 2 of this article is made.
2. Upon the expiration of the initial 10-year period or at any time thereafter, either Contracting Party may terminate this Treaty by informing

[760] Joint Communiqué of the Government of Japan and the Government of the PRC (Sept. 29, 1972), *available at* http://www.taiwandocuments.org/japan01.htm. Last visited 10/12/2004.

the other Contracting Party in writing one year beforehand of its intention to do so.

That the Treaty can be terminated also indicates that it is not a territorial treaty because a territorial treaty, as mentioned in Chapter 3, The Territorial State, cannot be terminated.

More recently, Japan clarified its stance on the legal status of Taiwan, particularly with respect to the 1972 Joint Communiqué. In 2010, the Japanese Ambassador to China said that Japan never recognized that Taiwan was part of China. At a press conference in Tokyo on July 26, 2010, the newly appointed Japanese Ambassador Uichiro Niwa said that "In the 1972 Joint Communiqué of Japan and China, with respect to China's claim on the territorial sovereignty over Taiwan, Japan's position was, it simply 'understood and respected China's stand on Taiwan,' but never recognized its claim. Japan will maintain the same position in the future."[761] No official in the Japanese Ministry of Foreign Affairs disclaimed or criticized Niwa's statement. It is inconceivable that Ambassador Niwa would express such an important policy position without prior clearance with Japan's Ministry of Foreign Affairs.

This section, by analyzing the Cairo Declaration and the treaties between the Allies, Japan, and China, demonstrates that China's argument that the island of Taiwan was returned to China pursuant to the Cairo Declaration and the Potsdam Proclamation is not supported by international law.

D. Title Based on the Administration of Taiwan

The fourth ground of the PRC government's argument that the island of Taiwan is China's territory is that China acquired title to the island by the ROC's administration of Taiwan. The PRC government argues that "[o]n October 25, 1945, the Chinese government recovered Taiwan and the Penghu Archipelago."[762] The date October 25, 1945 was the day when the ROC government received the surrender of the Japanese army in Taiwan and began the administration of the island. So, "the Chinese government" that the PRC government refers to is the ROC government, not the PRC government itself. Thus, the PRC's argument implies that

[761] *Japanese Ambassador: Japan never recognizes that Taiwan is part of China.* The Liberty Times, 07/27/2010, 1, *available at* http://www.libertytimes.com.tw/2010/new/jul/27/today-t2.htm. Last visited 07/29/2010.

[762] *See supra* text accompanying note 665.

China has acquired title to the island of Taiwan by the ROC government's administration of Taiwan. Some world-class publications also echo China's position. The Encyclopedia Britannica in its entry for "Taiwan" states, "Following World War II Taiwan was ceded to China."[763] Academic American Encyclopedia is more specific. In its entry for "Taiwan," it states that "Taiwan, also known as Formosa, is the main island of the Republic of China (Nationalist China). It was a colony of Japan after 1895 and returned to Chinese sovereignty in 1945."[764] The statement implies that Taiwan was "returned to Chinese sovereignty in 1945" when the ROC government began the administration of the island.[765] None of these descriptions is correct.

China has not acquired title to the island of Taiwan due to the fact that the ROC government administered Taiwan for two reasons. First, the United States, as the occupying power, has not acquired title to the island of Taiwan by occupation. On September 2, 1945 when the Japanese government officials signed the Instrument of Surrender,[766] the United States became the occupying power (State) of Japan's territory, including the island of Taiwan. It is common for a victorious army in a war to occupy the territory of the defeated State. However, as discussed in Chapter 3, The Territorial State, it is a customary international law that the occupation of an enemy's territory after the enemy surrenders and before a peace settlement does not give the occupying State title to the territory that it occupies.[767] The Hague Convention Respecting the Laws and Customs of War on Land codifies the international customary law rule.[768] As stated in Chapter 3, The Territorial State, it has become a rule of customary international law that if title to a territory of the

[763] THE NEW ENCYCLOPEDIA BRITANNICA, *supra* note 7, V. 11, at 511, 512 (the entry of "Taiwan").

[764] ACADEMIC AMERICAN ENCYCLOPEDIA, *supra* note 12. V. 19, at 12 (the entry of "Taiwan").

[765] *See also* Wikipedia "Government in exile." "The Republic of China (ROC) is currently the state which governs Taiwan and some of its surrounding islands," *citing* HENCKAERTS, JEAN-MARIE (1996), THE INTERNATIONAL STATUS OF TAIWAN IN THE NEW WORLD ORDER: LEGAL AND POLITICAL CONSIDERATIONS, Kluwer Law International, at 337, *available at* http://en.wikipedia.org/wiki/Government_in_Exile. Last visited 01/09/2010.

[766] The Instrument of surrender, like an armistice, ended the hostility, but not the war.

[767] *See supra* text accompanying note 398.

[768] *See supra* note 400.

defeated State is to be changed after a war, then it must be achieved by a territorial treaty.[769]

The United States has long recognized this international customary rule.[770] The 1956 US Department of the Army Field Manual for The Law of Land Warfare also recognizes the rule. It provides that "Being an incident of war, military occupation does not transfer the sovereignty to the occupant."[771] Thus, the United States, as the occupying power, has not acquired the title to Formosa. This conclusion may be inferred from the statements of the US high officials. On June 26, 1950, immediately after North Korea invaded South Korea, the US President Truman proclaimed that "[t]he determination of the future status of Formosa must await the restoration of security in the Pacific, a peace settlement with Japan, or consideration by the United Nations."[772] General MacArthur also shared the same view. In 1951, six years after MacArthur, pursuant to the instruction of the US Government, assigned the ROC government to administer Formosa, he said that Formosa was a still part of Japan. On May 4, 1951, in answering a question posed by Senator Russell, asking whether "the status of Formosa [had] ever been finally determined by any formal treaty," MacArthur answered that "[I]t has not. Legalistically [Formosa] is still a part of defeated Japan. The disposition of the various segments of the Empire of Japan has not yet been formally determined."[773]

The United Kingdom also recognized this customary rule. In November 1949, while Formosa was under the administration of the ROC government, British Foreign Secretary Mayhew, in answering a question in the House of Commons with respect to the eventual settlement of the Formosa issue, said that "[a]ny change in the legal status of Formosa *can only be formally effected in a treaty of peace* with Japan. But what the eventual settlement will be is a matter which His Majesty's

769 *Id.*

770 *See Am. Ins. Co.* v. *Cantor, supra* note 397. ("The usage of the world is, if a nation be not entirely subdued, to consider the holding of conquered territory as a mere military occupation, until its fate shall be determined at the treaty of peace.")

771 *See* Hague Convention Respecting The Laws and Customs of War on Land, *supra* note 400, Par. 358.

772 *Statement on Korea, supra* note 702 at A1.

773 *Gen. MacArthur's Statement*, *supra* note 693. The war between Japan and the Allied Powers formally ended on April 28, 1952 when the Treaty of Peace with Japan (the "Peace Treaty of San Francisco") entered into force. *See* the Peace Treaty of San Francisco, *supra* note 403. *Gen. MacArthur's Statement*, *Id.*

Government cannot decide alone."[774] In July 1950, the succeeding British Foreign Secretary Younger stated that "because of the provisional nature of the present administration of Formosa [by the ROC government], it is the hope of His Majesty's Government that the disposal of Formosa will be decided, as has always been contemplated, in connection with the peace settlement, with Japan."[775]

These statements made by the high officials of the United States and the United Kingdom not only attest to the existence of a rule in international law that if title to a territory of the defeated State is to be changed after a war, then it must be achieved by a territorial treaty,[776] but also demonstrated that the United States did not acquire title to the island of Taiwan by occupation through administration of the ROC government. Under the same reasoning, even if the ROC was the occupying power, which it was not, it could not acquire title to the island of Taiwan by occupation.

The United States as the occupying State acquired, in the legal term, "possession" of Japan's territory, including the island of Taiwan, in September 1945 when Japan formally delivered the Instrument of Surrender to the United States. This is the view of the Truman Administration.[777] In August 1950, after Truman sent the US Navy Seventh Fleet toward the Taiwan Strait and provided military assistance to the ROC's Nationalists in Taiwan, the Soviet Union circulated a paper to the members of the UN Security Council charging the United States with aggression against Taiwan. Truman instructed Ambassador Warren Austin to deliver a letter to the UN Secretary-General, in which it stated,

> *"The actual status of the island is that it is territory* taken from Japan *by the victory of the Allied Forces in the Pacific. Like other such territories, its legal*

[774] 469 Parl. Deb., H.C. (5th ser.) (1949) at 1679 (emphasis added).

[775] 478 Parl. Deb., H.C. (5th ser.) (1950) at 60.

[776] *See supra* text accompanying note 399.

[777] *See Statement on Korea*, *supra* note 702, at A1. *Also see* William Lowther, *CIA Report Shows Taiwan Concern*, Taipei Times, 06/9/2013, p. 1. "Declassified CIA report in March 1949 states 'Pending a Japanese peace treaty, the island remains occupied territory in which the US has proprietary interests'." *Id.*, *available at* http://www.taipeitimes.com/News/front/archives/2013/06/09/2003564336. Last visited 06/10/2013. This proprietary interest is right of possession, not title.

> *status cannot be fixed until there is international action to determine its future. The Chinese Government was asked by the Allies to take the surrender of the Japanese forces on the island. That is the reason the Chinese are there now."*[778]

Truman's letter did not specifically say by whom the island was "taken from Japan." Since the United States was the occupying State of the Japanese territory after Japan surrendered, Truman's statement implied that it was the United States that "took" *possession* of the island from Japan.

The right of occupation (possession) of a territory and the right to its title are two distinct rights. For instance, in the 1898 Treaty of Paris concluded to end the Spanish-American War, Spain "relinquished" the title to the island of Cuba and the United States was given the right of occupation (possession) without the title to the island pending final resolution.[779]

The United States acquired possession of, but never received the title to, the island of Cuba.

Second, if the United States did not acquire title to the island of Taiwan by possession, the ROC government did not acquire the same by administration of Taiwan. As stated before, when the United States, as the occupying power, assigned the ROC government to administer Taiwan on its behalf, an agency relationship was implicitly created between the United States as the principal and the ROC government as its agent. The authority of an agent is limited by its mandate given by the principal. While the United States had possession of the island of Taiwan, it only gave *custody* of Taiwan to the ROC government for administration. The purpose of the administration of Taiwan by the ROC government was for a post surrender operation, and for that purpose only. If the United States, as the principal, did not acquire the title to the island, the ROC, as its agent, could not either. Thus, it is beyond dispute that the ROC did not acquire the title to Formosa by occupation before the Peace Treaty of San Francisco. This was the view of the US General

[778] *Letter from the US to Sec'y-Gen. Lie*, Aug. 25, 1950, DEP'T ST. BULL., Sept. 1950, at 412 (emphasis added).

[779] The Treaty of Paris, *supra* note 723. Article I provides:

> Spain relinquishes all claim of sovereignty over and title to Cuba. And as the island is, upon its evacuation by Spain, to be occupied by the United States, the United States will, so long as such occupation shall last, assume and discharge the obligations that may under international law result from the fact of its occupation, for the protection of life and property. Id.

MacArthur. On May 4, 1951, in answering a question raised by the Chairman of the US Senate Foreign Relations Committee, Senator Richard Russell, MacArthur responded that "[t]he Allies turned over the administration and the *trusteeship* of Formosa to China[the ROC], just as Japan was turned over to us, and it is still in that status."[780]

The British echoed that same view. The British governments, both of the Labor Party and of the Conservative Party, held the view that the ROC government did not acquire the title to the island of Taiwan by administering the island. In 1949, British Foreign Secretary Mayhew of the Attlee (Labor Party) Administration said in the House that "the Chinese Nationalist authorities are in control of the island [of Formosa]. However, [any] change in the legal status of Formosa can only be formally effected in a treaty of peace with Japan."[781] In 1950, British Foreign Secretary Younger of the Attlee Administration stated that "Formosa is still *de jure* Japanese territory. Following on the surrender of Japan, the Chinese Government of the day assumed, with the consent of the remaining Allies, the provisional administration of the territory pending the final determination of its status at a peace settlement."[782]

The agency relationship between the United States and the ROC government has not been terminated after the Peace Treaty of San Francisco entered into force. The ROC government continues to administer Taiwan after the Peace Treaty was concluded. If the title to the island of Taiwan were transferred to the State of China in the Treaty, then the agency relationship between the United States and the ROC government would have to be terminated and the ROC government would be administering the island as the reigning government or on behalf of the reigning government of China. But the Peace Treaty did not transfer the title to the island of Taiwan to China or any other State. The United States, as the occupying power, allowed the ROC government to continue to administer the island.

Since the Peace Treaty of San Francisco entered into force, no factual or legal event took place that would have changed the relationship between the United States and the ROC government with respect to the occupation of Taiwan. No official statement or act of the ROC government or the United States that terminated, or attempted to terminate, the

[780] *Gen. MacArthur's Statement*, *supra* note 693 (emphasis added).
[781] 469 Parl. Deb., H.C. (5th ser.) (1949) at 1679.
[782] 478 Parl. Deb., H.C. (5th ser.) (1950) at 60.

agency relationship.[783] In fact, after the Peace Treaty of San Francisco was concluded, a US policy maker confirmed that the agency status of the ROC government was not terminated by, at, or after the signing of the Peace Treaty of San Francisco. In 1955, three years after the Treaty was concluded, the US Secretary of State John Foster Dulles in the Eisenhower[784] Administration said that "[i]n 1945, [t]he Republic of China was *entrusted* with authority over (Formosa and the Pescadores),"[785] and "General Chiang [Kai-shek] *was merely asked to administer them* (Formosa and the Pescadores) *for the Allied and associated powers* pending a final decision as to their ownership."[786]

The British government expressed the same view. In 1955, the British Foreign Secretary Anthony Eden (Conservative Party), in describing the right of the ROC government, said in the House that

> "*[i]n September, 1945, the administration of Formosa was taken over from the Japanese by Chinese forces* at the direction of *the Supreme Commander of the Allied Powers. [B]ut this was not a cession, nor did it in itself involve any change of sovereignty. The arrangements made with Chiang Kai-shek put him there on a basis of military occupation pending further arrangements, and did not of themselves constitute the territory Chinese.*"[787]

The comment of British Joint Under-Foreign Secretary R.H. Turton in 1955 was more direct. He said at the House that "Formosa['s] sovereignty was Japanese until 1952. The Japanese Treaty entered into force, and at that time Formosa was being administered by the Chinese Nationalists, to whom *it was entrusted* in 1945, as a military occupation. This military occupancy could not give [the Chinese Nationalists] legal sovereignty."[788] In 1955, the British Foreign Secretary Anthony Eden in the House stated that "[i]n September (of 1945), the administration of Formosa was taken over from the Japanese by Chinese forces at the direction of the Supreme Commander of the Allied Powers. The arrangements made with Jiang (Chiang) Kai-shek put him there on a basis of military

[783] The agency relationship may be terminated by mutual consent or by either party. In any event, at the termination of an agency relationship, the agent cannot retain the possession of the territory. *See generally Gov't Guarantee Fund of the Republic of Finland* v. *Hyatt Corp.*, 95 F.3d 291 (3d Cir. 1996).

[784] Dwight Eisenhower, US President (1953–1961).

[785] *See* Sec'y John Foster Dulles, *Our Foreign Policies in Asia*, *supra* note 723 at 329 (emphasis added).

[786] Reston, *supra* note 756, at A1 (emphasis added).

[787] 536 Parl. Deb., H.C. (5th ser.) (1955) at 159 (emphasis added).

[788] 540 Parl. Deb., H.C. (5th ser.) (1955) at 1871 (emphasis added).

occupation pending further arrangements."[789] The statement of British Prime Minister Winston Churchill that "Chiang Kai-shek took refuge upon Formosa, where he still remains"[790] made in 1954 also implies that China had not acquired title to the island of Taiwan even though the ROC government was administering the island.

Thus, both the United States and the United Kingdom leaders concurred that China did not acquire the title to the island of Taiwan by the ROC government's administration of Taiwan. In short, the administration of Taiwan by the ROC government could not and did not give the State of China title to the island of Taiwan.

Thus, there are no legal grounds under which the State of China can claim title to the island of Taiwan based on the fact that the ROC government has administered the island. In administering Taiwan, the ROC government acted as an agent of the United States, not of the PRC government or of China. In addition, by administering Taiwan the ROC government did not acquire title to the island of Taiwan for itself or for anyone else.

Thus far, this work has analyzed the four grounds of the PRC government's argument that China has acquired title to the island of Taiwan: title based on the past ownership; title based on its own proclamations; title based on the Cairo Declaration and the Potsdam Proclamation; and title based on administration of Taiwan. As the above analyses show, none of the arguments of the PRC government is supported by international law.

This was the position of the Truman Administration that signed the Peace Treaty of San Francisco. It was also the positions of the three successive US Administrations prior to the issuance of the Shanghai Communiqué—Eisenhower, Kennedy, and Johnson. A brief review of the positions of these Administrations follows.

The position of the Eisenhower Administration that the island of Taiwan was not China's territory was explicit.[791] Most Americans still had fresh memories of the Korean War, in which the US soldiers had fought the Chinese army. The US Secretary of State was John Foster Dulles, who drafted the Peace Treaty of San Francisco in which China

[789] 536 PARL. DEB., H.C. (5th ser.) (1955) at 159.

[790] 530 PARL. DEB., H.C. (5th ser.) (1954) at 494. Churchill said, "Chiang Kai-shek was driven out of his country by a Communist revolution and took refuge upon Formosa, where he still remains [in 1954]." *Id.*

[791] *See supra* text accompanying note 785.

was not given Formosa or the Pescadores and in 1951 testified in Congress that "[i]n 1945, [t]he Republic of China was *entrusted* with authority over (Formosa and the Pescadores)."[792] The position of the Eisenhower Administration was manifested in the State Department Bulletin and quoted by a US court in *Cheng Fu Sheng* v. *Rogers*[793] in its decision. The Federal Court said,

> *A Department of State Bulletin, Vol. XXXIX, No. 1017, dated December 22, 1958, which constitutes an official expression of the foreign policy of the United States, contains the following discussion of the problem: "On September 2, 1945, the Japanese Government, in the instrument of surrender, accepted the provisions of the declaration. The Supreme Allied Commander for the Allied Powers then issued Directive No. 1 under which the Japanese Imperial Headquarters issued General Order No. 1 requiring Japanese commanders in Formosa to surrender to Generalissimo Chiang Kai-shek of the Republic of China.*
>
> *"Since September 1945 the United States and the other Allied Powers have accepted the exercise of Chinese authority over the island. In article 2 of the Japanese Peace Treaty, which entered into force April 28, 1952, Japan renounced all 'right, title and claim' to Formosa. Neither this agreement nor any other agreement thereafter has purported to transfer the sovereignty of Formosa to China."*
>
> *From the foregoing official pronouncements of the Department of State, it appears that* the United States recognizes *the Government of the Republic of China as the legal government of China; that the provisional capital of the Republic of China has been at Taipei, Taiwan (Formosa) since December 1949; that the Government of the Republic of China exercises authority over the island; that the sovereignty of Formosa has not been transferred to China; and* that Formosa is not a part of China as a country. *Formosa may be said to be a territory or an area occupied and administered by the Government of the Republic of China, but is not officially recognized as being a part of the Republic of China. Expressions of the State Department are drawn with care and circumspection to refrain from such recognition.* Formosa is not regarded by the Department of State as part of China.[794]

Thus, seven years after the Peace Treaty of San Francisco went into force, both the Eisenhower Administration and a US court held that the island of Taiwan was not China's territory.

Neither President John F. Kennedy,[795] who engaged the Soviet Union, an ally of China, in a cold war, nor President Lyndon B.

[792] *Id.* (emphasis added).
[793] *Cheng Fu Sheng v. Rogers*, *supra* note 510.
[794] *Id.* (emphasis added).
[795] John F. Kennedy, US President (1961–1963).

Johnson,[796] who sent American soldiers to fight the Vietcong in Viet Nam, had any reason to change the US' position on the title to the island of Taiwan. Both Administrations refused to recognize the PRC as the representative government of China and blocked the attempts by the Soviet bloc to replace the ROC government with the PRC government in the United Nations by persuading the majority of the UN members to designate the representation question as an *important question* under the UN Charter. Although both Administrations continued to recognize the ROC government seated in Taiwan as the representative government of China, they never proclaimed the island of Taiwan to be China's territory.

4. CHINA'S SOVEREIGNTY OVER TAIWAN BEFORE THE ONE-CHINA POLICY

In 1972, President Nixon and China's Premier Zhou (Chou) En-Lai jointly announced the Shanghai Communiqué, in which the US Government formulated its "one-China policy." The above analysis of China's claim over Taiwan indicates that immediately prior to the announcement of the Shanghai Communiqué, the US' and UK's position confirmed the conclusion that China did not acquire title to the island of Taiwan after the Second World War. The conclusion had three implications in international law immediately before the Shanghai Communiqué was issued. The first is that China had no sovereignty over Taiwan. The sovereignty of the modern State and the neo-modern State over a territory is based on the ownership and control of the territory. This concept, known as "territorial sovereignty," was discussed in Chapter 3, The Territorial State. Thus, any sovereignty of China over Taiwan had to be based on the title to the island of Taiwan. China had no sovereignty over Taiwan because it had no title to the island of Taiwan.

The second implication is that under international law the legal status of Taiwan was not a domestic issue of China. If China had no title to the island of Taiwan, the United States did not encroach upon China's sovereignty by providing military assistance to the governing authorities in Taiwan.

The third implication is that the Taiwan Strait was a part of the High Seas, and not China's internal waters. Thus, every State had the right to

[796] Lyndon B. Johnson, US President (1963—1968).

navigate its ships through the Strait without interference under international law. The next chapter will analyze the US' one-China policy to see whether the United States has conceded to China's claim over Taiwan as a result of the US policy announced in the Shanghai Communiqué.

CHAPTER 7

Sovereignty Over Taiwan Under US' One-China Policy

Contents

1. US' ONE-CHINA POLICY AND ITS POSITION ON THE LEGAL STATUS OF TAIWAN

A. The Background of a New US Policy

As the previous chapters have shown, when Nixon became the President in 1969, the position of the US Government, as well as that of the contemporaneous British government, was that China had not acquired title to the island of Taiwan in or after the Peace Treaty of San Francisco. While the islands of Kinmen (Quemoy) and Matsu were China's territories, the island of Taiwan (Formosa and the Pescadores) was not.[797]

The Peace Treaty of San Francisco binds the United States as a controlling law under the US Constitution.[798] After the Peace Treaty of San Francisco entered into force in 1952, the Treaty was self-executing in the United States and became supreme law of the land under the

[797] *See supra* text accompanying note 747.
[798] *See* De Lima v. Bidwell, 182 US 1, at 195 (1901).

The One-China Policy: State, Sovereignty, and Taiwan's International Legal Status
DOI: http://dx.doi.org/10.1016/B978-0-08-102314-3.00007-0

US Constitution.[799] Thus, the disposition of the island of Taiwan by the Treaty cannot be changed by a foreign policy of a US Administration, the Congress, or a court.

Even though the US Government cannot change the title to the island of Taiwan, its statements expressing its foreign policy can create distorted perceptions on its position in international relations and geopolitics. In 1972, President Nixon and China's Premier Zhou (Chou) En-lai jointly announced a communiqué in which the United States announced a new policy toward China. This chapter examines the circumstances leading to the formulation of the new US policy toward China and analyzes the US Government's position during and after the Nixon Administration on the legal status of Taiwan under its new policy.

a. US Attitude Toward the PRC Immediately After the Korean War

After the Chinese Communists established the (People's Republic of China) PRC government in 1949, the US Government refused to recognize it as the representative government of China. The Truman Administration refused to recognize the PRC government even after the regime had the effective control of China proper because Truman considered the PRC a satellite regime of the Soviet Union. The Korean War of the early 1950s in which the US soldiers fought the 180,000 Chinese "volunteer" soldiers and sustained heavy casualties further convinced the succeeding three Presidents—Eisenhower, Kennedy, and Johnson—that the PRC was an aggressive regime. The three Administrations continued to maintain diplomatic ties with the (Republic of China) ROC government in Taiwan and supported the ROC government in the United Nations.

b. Nixon's Attitude Toward the PRC Prior to the UN Resolution 2758

Nixon was a staunch anti-Communist statesman when he succeeded Johnson as the President. He was a Republican US Senator when the United States was fighting the Chinese army in the Korean War, which

[799] *See* US CONST. Art. VI, cl. 2. The Constitution states that:

> *This Constitution, and the Laws of the United States which shall be made in Pursuance thereof; and all treaties made, or which shall be made, under the Authority of the United States, shall be the supreme law of the land; and the judges in every state shall be bound thereby, anything in the Constitution or laws of any state to the contrary notwithstanding.*

Id.
Also see text accompanying note 406.

deepened the anti-China sentiment in the United States. When Nixon took office in 1969, he had not forgotten the Korean War and the general American sentiment.

After Nixon took office, his policy toward the PRC was rejection and containment. There had been no official contact between the United States and China for 20 years when Nixon took the office. Nixon was a Senator when the US Senate approved the Peace Treaty of San Francisco, in which China did not acquire the title to the island of Taiwan. Nixon as the President of the United States refused to recognize the PRC government and continued to recognize the ROC in Taiwan as the representative government of China. He had no reason to concede to the PRC's claim over Taiwan.

Nixon also continued to support the ROC government in the United Nations until 1971 when the UN General Assembly adopted Resolution 2758. Ever since Nixon took the office in 1969, he blocked the PRC government's repeated attempts to replace the ROC government in the United Nations. In 1969, to prevent a simple majority vote in the United Nations on the question of China's representation, the Nixon Administration again persuaded Western States to vote on the question as an "important question," which required a two-thirds majority vote in the General Assembly, as the previous Administrations had done so repeatedly since 1961. In 1971, the pressure in the United Nations to replace the ROC government with the PRC government mounted. A majority of the UN members already recognized the PRC as the representative government of China. In October 1971, attempting to save the ROC' s seat in the General Assembly, Nixon proposed dual representation for China in the United Nations and, when the proposal failed, directed the US representative to vote against Albania's proposal for replacing the ROC with the PRC.[800] The UN General Assembly voted to adopt Albania's proposal by Resolution No. 2758, which decided that the State of China from then on was to be represented by the PRC government, and expelled the representatives of the ROC government.

The adoption of Resolution 2758 in the United Nations did not change the US' position on the title to the island of Taiwan. At a press conference on the morning after the adoption of the Resolution, to a reporter's question "[I]sn't the vote an implicit acknowledgment that

[800] *See supra* text accompanying note 548.

Taiwan is a province of China, and if so, what would we do if Peking now asked us to remove our troops from there?,"[801] Secretary of State William Rogers replied, "Well, I don't want to speculate [about the PRC government asking us to remove our troops from Taiwan]. We have made our position clear. Our policy is unaffected by this vote."[802]

B. The Shanghai Communiqué

After the UN General Assembly adopted Resolution No. 2758, the United States was in an odd and awkward situation in its foreign relations. While the United States together with other members of the UN recognized the PRC as the government representing the State of China in the United Nations and related organizations, it still recognized the ROC as the representative government of China outside of international organizations.

Nixon was the first US President who changed the US policy toward the PRC government. By July 1971, the PRC government had been established for more than 20 years and it was clear that the ROC government had lost the chance and ability to "recover the mainland" as Jiang (Chiang) Kai-shek had repeatedly claimed ever since he lost China. Internationally, the ROC government also lost the support of a majority of the world community. Realizing this, the Nixon Administration began to change the policy toward the PRC government even before the UN Resolution No. 2758. He changed from a policy favoring containment of the PRC to a rapprochement with the regime.[803]

Nixon broke the ice between the US Government and the PRC government in 1972, and softened his attitude toward China. His policy toward China was reflected in the Shanghai Communiqué of 1972 (known simply as the "Shanghai Communiqué").[804] A brief review of

[801] *Sec'y of State William Rogers, Statements at Press Conference Discussing United Nations' Decision on Chinese Representation*, *in* DEP'T ST. BULL., Dec. 1971, at 541.

[802] *Id.*

[803] The geopolitical reasons for Nixon to establish some kind of informal relationship with China included a cease fire in Vietnam and an alliance with China against Soviet Union. For the reason in the background for the US Government and the PRC government to make contact, *see* HENRY KISSINGER, OBSERVATIONS: SELECTED SPEECHES AND ESSAYS, Little, Brown and Company, Boston, 1982, at 141.

[804] Shanghai Communiqué (Feb. 27. 1972), *in* DEP'T ST. BULL., 1972, at 437 (emphasis added).

the background and circumstances under which the Shanghai Communiqué was drafted will shed some light on the meaning of the policy statements made by the US Government in the Communiqué.

The rapprochement between the US Government and the PRC government began with a dialogue between the two governments. At the time, Nixon and the PRC's leader each had his own geopolitical and strategic reasons to be, or at least to look, friendly with the other.[805] So, in July 1971 Nixon began a high-level dialogue with the PRC government by sending Henry Kissinger, the Assistant to the President for National Security Affairs, as an envoy to meet with the PRC leaders in Beijing and to negotiate and arrange a meeting of the two top government leaders in China. The negotiation of Kissinger and the PRC's officials included drafting a joint declaration to be announced during Nixon's visit in the following year. In February of 1972, President Nixon met China's Premier Zhou (Chou) En-lai in Beijing. The two leaders afterward went to Shanghai and there announced a joint communiqué, subsequently known as the "Shanghai Communiqué."

The Shanghai Communiqué was a unique joint declaration in world politics and created a problematic US foreign policy. It was unique because its nature was different from traditional joint declarations or joint communiqués. A joint declaration or communiqué by two or more governments, such as the Cairo Declaration, traditionally expresses a common foreign policy or common intention of the declaring governments on a particular foreign affair.[806] In the Shanghai Communiqué, however, each government declared its own view on the same issues. It was problematic for the United States because the statements of the PRC government contained a false claim on the legal status of the island of Taiwan and the statements of the US Government allowed the PRC government an opportunity subsequently to make another false claim regarding the US position.

The PRC government tried to use the occasion to recover whatever face it had lost in the prolonged stalemate with the United States. After 20 years of stalemate between the two governments, the PRC wanted to show the world that it was the United States that gave in to end the stalemate; that Nixon, the President of the most powerful Nation on

[805] *See Id.* at 141.

[806] *See* the Cairo Declaration, *supra* note 640; *see also* the Potsdam Proclamation, *supra* note 645.

earth, would agree to go to China's capital was like the king of a tributary personally visiting the Chinese emperor and paying homage to him in the pre-modern China. As for the tribute, nothing could be better than the US acceptance of the PRC's position on the Taiwan issue, which was, after all, the root of the stalemate. In the official text of the Shanghai Communiqué, a general introduction was followed by the PRC government's statements on its positions on Korea, Taiwan, and Vietnam. On the Taiwan issue, the PRC government stated,

> *The Chinese side reaffirmed its position: the Taiwan question is the crucial question obstructing the normalization of relations between China and the United States; the Government of the People's Republic of China is the sole legal government of China; Taiwan is a province of China which has long been returned to the motherland; the liberation of Taiwan is China's internal affair in which no other country has the right to interfere; and all US forces and military installations must be withdrawn from Taiwan. The Chinese Government firmly opposes any activities which aim at the creation of "one China, one Taiwan," "one China, two governments," "two Chinas," an "independent Taiwan" or advocate that the "status of Taiwan remains to be determined."*[807]

There were three basic propositions in the PRC's claim. The first one was that there was only one State called "China" in the world; accordingly, the ROC was not a State and there was no other State also called China. The second proposition was that the government of the PRC was the sole legitimate government of China; accordingly, the ROC was not the legitimate government of the State of China. The PRC's third proposition was that the island of Taiwan was China's territory; and that the US encroached upon China's sovereignty. Since the term "province" referred to a territorial and administrative division of China, when the PRC government claimed that "Taiwan is a province of China," it meant that the island of Taiwan was China's territory. It was not clear what the statement "Taiwan ... has long been returned to the motherland" meant from the PRC's statement. Later, the PRC government in its 2000 White Paper explained that Taiwan was returned to China in 1945.[808] The PRC White Paper stated, "[O]n October 25, 1945, the Chinese government recovered Taiwan and the Penghu Archipelago."[809]

The PRC's statements were followed by the US Government's statements, which were made as a response to the PRC's claims. Nixon could

[807] The Shanghai Communiqué, *supra* note 804, at 437.
[808] *See* the White Paper, *supra* note 664, at 53.
[809] *Id.*

not accept most of the PRC government's propositions. However, if he expected to be greeted by a former enemy with open arms, he could not reject all the propositions claimed by his host.

Of the three propositions claimed by the PRC government, Nixon could accept only its first one "[T]here is only one state called China" because it reflected a fact. In 1971 when the Shanghai Communiqué was being drafted, the two governments, the PRC and the ROC, coexisted and both claimed that there was only one China, even though each one claimed that it, not the other, represented China. The PRC's proposition in the text presented no problem to Nixon because the ROC government in Taiwan did not intend to create a second China[810] and the US government could not do anything about it.

On the PRC's second proposition "the Government of the People's Republic of China is the sole legal government of China," Nixon had difficulty responding to it. Although the UN Resolution No. 2758 decided that the PRC government had replaced the ROC government as the representative government of China in the United Nations, the US Government at the time of Nixon's visit still recognized the ROC as the representative government of China. The Nixon Administration could not formally accept the PRC government's proposition. Nixon avoided designating which was the legitimate government—the ROC or the PRC—by cleverly referring to the two governments as "all Chinese on either side of the Taiwan Strait."[811]

Nixon could not accept the PRC's third proposition that Taiwan was China's territory either, for two reasons. The first reason is that politically Nixon could not accept China's claim. When Nixon went to China in 1972, the Vietnam conflict was ongoing. If Nixon was not ready to recognize the PRC regime that provided military aid to the North Vietnamese in combating the US armed forces as the legitimate government of China, he was even less willing to accept the regime's claim on the island of Taiwan.

The second and more fundamental reason was a legal one: the PRC's proposition was based on a false claim. As discussed earlier, China never reacquired the title to the island of Taiwan after it ceded the island to

[810] *See* Warren I. Cohen, *On an Island, with Dreams of the Mainland*, L.A. TIMES, 03/28/2004, at R13 (reviewing JONATHAN FENBY CARROLL, CHIANG KAI-SHEK: CHINA'S GENERALISSIMO AND THE NATION HE LOST (2004)). Jiang (Chiang) Kai-shek swore "to recover the Mainland" until his death in 1975.

[811] *See infra* text accompanying note 812.

Japan in 1895. When the US Senate approved the Peace Treaty of San Francisco for President Truman to ratify it, Nixon was a Senator. He was undoubtedly aware of the disposition of the title to the island of Taiwan under the Peace Treaty of San Francisco.

But Nixon could not flatly reject the PRC's third proposition without undermining his willingness to compromise. He had to say something about the legal status of Taiwan. The closest word that Nixon finessed was "acknowledge." The final text in the Communiqué turned out to be "[t]he US declared: The United States *acknowledges* that all Chinese on either side of the Taiwan Strait maintain there is but one China and that Taiwan is a part of China. The US Government does not challenge that position."[812]

Thus, Nixon's response was simply acknowledging China's claim. The Nixon Administration only took notice of what the Chinese governments on both sides of the Taiwan Strait claimed.[813] It was the extent to which Nixon was willing to meet with the PRC's demand. The US statements in the Shanghai Communiqué indicated that Nixon, in drafting the statement, chose the words carefully, so as not to imply that the United States accepted or recognized the PRC government's position that Taiwan was part of China.[814]

The statement of the US "[t]he United States Government does not challenge that position"[815] simply meant that the US Government did not deny the fact that Chinese took the position that Taiwan was part of

[812] The Shanghai Communiqué, *supra* note 804, at 437(emphasis added).
Item 12 of the Shanghai Communiqué states,

> *The US side declared: The United States acknowledges that all Chinese on either side of the Taiwan Strait maintain there is but one China and that Taiwan is a part of China. The United States Government does not challenge that position. It reaffirms its interest in a peaceful settlement of the Taiwan question by the Chinese themselves. With this prospect in mind, it affirms the ultimate objective of the withdrawal of all US forces and military installations from Taiwan. In the meantime, it will progressively reduce its forces and military installations on Taiwan as the tension in the area diminishes. The two sides agreed that it is desirable to broaden the understanding between the two peoples. To this end, they discussed specific areas in such fields as science, technology, culture, sports and journalism, in which people-to-people contacts and exchanges would be mutually beneficial. Each side undertakes to facilitate the further development of such contacts and exchanges.*

[813] This point is confirmed by Harvey Feldman. *See infra* text accompanying note 832.
[814] *See* the Shanghai Communiqué, *supra* note 804, at 437 (emphasis added).
[815] *Id.* at 438.

China.[816] It did not mean that the US Government agreed to or conceded to the position taken by the PRC government. Although such interpretation was not apparent by the statement itself in the Shanghai Communiqué, it was confirmed later in the Second Communiqué announced by President Carter to be discussed later.[817]

Since the United States did not necessarily agree with the PRC's position on the legal status of Taiwan, the United States response tactfully disposed of the PRC's demand that "the liberation of Taiwan is China's internal affair in which no other country has the right to interfere, and all US forces and military installations must be withdrawn from Taiwan" because the demand was based on the grounds not conceded by the United States, and thus required no response.[818]

The Shanghai Communiqué formulated a new fundamental US policy toward China, which has lasted to date.[819] In these policy statements, the Nixon Administration did not accept China's claim on the island of Taiwan. However, the language finessed by Nixon in the Shanghai Communiqué was such that it created an opportunity for the PRC government, despite Nixon's reservation, to distort the US position and repeatedly claimed that the US Government in the Shanghai Communiqué accepted its claim that Taiwan was part of China.

Gerald Ford[820] took over the presidency after Nixon resigned in 1974. Ford did not change the China policy established by Nixon because during his tenure as the President there was no occasion that required him to express or clarify the US position on the legal status of Taiwan.

The Carter Administration was the first US Administration that accorded recognition to the PRC.[821] On December 15, 1978, the Carter Administration withdrew recognition of the ROC and recognized the PRC as the representative government of China by establishing diplomatic relations with it. After that, many States which had recognized the

[816] *Id.* at 437–38.

[817] *See* the Second Communiqué, *infra* note 823.

[818] *See* the Shanghai Communiqué, *supra* note 804, at 437.

[819] *See* Barbara Franklin, *China: Friend or Enemy?*, Lecture Before the Heritage Foundation (June 20, 1996), *available at* http://www.heritage.org/research/asiaandthe-pacific/hl566.cfm.

[820] Gerald R. Ford, US President (1974–1976).

[821] James E. Carter, Jr., US President (1977–1981).

ROC until then followed the US lead and switched the recognition to the PRC. As of March 2017, only 21 States still recognized the ROC.[822] The recognition of the ROC was government recognition, not a State recognition. In international law, these States still recognize the ROC as the representative government of China.

But in recognizing the PRC government, the Carter Administration did not recognize China's claim on the legal status of Taiwan. The US position was clear in the policy statements made in the Joint Communiqué on Establishment of Diplomatic Relations Between the United States of America and the People's Republic of China announced on January 1, 1979.[823] The Communiqué was later called "the Second Communiqué." The Carter Administration again, like Nixon's, only *acknowledged* China's claim over Taiwan. The Second Communiqué states, "The United States of America and the People's Republic of China reaffirm the principles agreed on by the two sides in the Shanghai Communiqué, and emphasize once again that: The government of the United States of America *acknowledges* the Chinese position that there is but one China and Taiwan is part of China."[824]

In the Second Communiqué, the Carter Administration did not accept or concede to the *position* taken by the PRC government. By saying that the two governments "reaffirm the principles agreed on by the two sides in the Shanghai Communiqué," the Carter Administration

[822] By December 20, 2010 the following 23 States recognized the ROC government as the representative government of China and maintain diplomatic relations with that government:

Belize, Burkina Faso, Dominican Republic, El Salvador, The Gambia, Guatemala, Haiti, Holy See, Honduras, Kiribati, Marshall Islands, Nauru, Nicaragua, Palau, Panama, Paraguay, Saint Christopher and Nevis, Saint Lucia, Saint Vincent and the Grenadines, São Tomé and Princípe, Solomon Islands, Swaziland, Tuvalu, *available at* http://www.gio.gov.tw/taiwan-website/5-gp/yearbook/ch06.html. Last visited 11/20/2010.

As of March 1, 2017, two more countries (the Gambia and São Tomé and Princípe) have switched sides after the ROC government refused their horrendous financial demands.

On June 12, 2017, Panama terminated the diplomatic relation with the R.O.C. government and establishes a diplomatic relation with the P.R.C. government.

[823] The Joint Communiqué on Establishment of Diplomatic Relations Between the United States of America and the People's Republic of China, (Jan. 1, 1979) [hereinafter "the Second Communiqué"], *available at* http://www.china.org.cn/english/china-us/26243.htm. Last visited 10/01/2004.

[824] *Id.* (emphasis added).

continued to maintain the US position in the Shanghai Communiqué, i.e., the United States acknowledged that the PRC's position was that Taiwan was a part of China.

Thus, the Second Communiqué confirmed the earlier interpretation in this work of the ambiguous statement "The United States Government does not challenge that position" in the Shanghai Communiqué that the statement simply meant that the US Government did not *challenge* the fact that Chinese took the position that Taiwan was part of China.[825] The Second Communiqué dropped the ambiguous sentence that appeared in the Shanghai Communiqué because the PRC had distorted its meaning.

Immediately after withdrawing recognition of the ROC government, the United States enacted Taiwan Relations Act (TRA). When the United States withdrew recognition of the ROC as the representative government of China in 1979, the diplomatic tie between the US Government and the ROC government in Taiwan was dissolved. Consequently, the United States also terminated the US–China (the ROC) Mutual Defense Treaty. The withdrawal of the recognition of the ROC and termination of the mutual defense treaty also terminated the international mechanism to protect the people of Taiwan. For the protection of the people of Taiwan and the security of the United States in the Western Pacific, some form of unofficial relation between the two governments had to be established. The US utilized an unprecedented measure in international relations: employing a domestic law to implement a foreign policy. The Carter Administration prepared a bill entitled "Taiwan Relations Act" for maintaining the informal relation with Taiwan, but the Congress considered Carter's bill too weak to protect the people of Taiwan and passed its own version of TRA for Carter to sign. The TRA, which prescribes that "in furtherance of the policy of this Act, the United States will make available to Taiwan such defense articles and defense services in such quantity as may be necessary to enable Taiwan to maintain a sufficient self-defense capabilities"[826] became law on January 1, 1979.

The purpose of TRA is the maintenance of the peace and security of the Western Pacific and protection of the people of Taiwan, implicitly

[825] The Shanghai Communiqué, *supra* note 804, at 437–38.

[826] Sec. 3 of Taiwan Relations Act, *supra* note 503. The Act was approved by the Congress on April 10, 1979, but was effective retroactively on January 1, 1979.

against the invasion of the PRC army. The Act establishes the American Institute in Taiwan (AIT) as the US unofficial representative for maintaining relations with Taiwan. Section 2(b) of TRA[827] sets forth the main objects of the Act. It states,

> *"(3) to make clear that the United States decision to establish diplomatic relations with the People's Republic of China rests upon the expectation that the future of Taiwan will be determined by peaceful means; (4) to consider any effort to determine the future of Taiwan by other than peaceful means, including by boycotts or embargoes, a threat to the peace and security of the Western Pacific and are of grave concern to the United States; (5) to provide Taiwan with arms of a defensive character; and (6) to maintain the capacity of the United States to resist any resort to force or other forms of coercion that would jeopardize the security, or the social or economic system, of the people on Taiwan."*[828]

The statement in item (3) "[T]he future of Taiwan will be determined by peaceful means" has two implications. One is, the Act creates a US policy that "China shall not take Taiwan by force." Among others, the Act reenforces a proposition of the one-China policy that "both sides of the Taiwan Strait should peacefully settle their dispute." Under this proposition, the ROC government in Taiwan is not allowed to attack China; the Act does not authorize the US Government to provide Taiwan with weapons of offensive nature. On the other hand, China shall not use force, direct or indirect, to take Taiwan. The US one-China policy and TRA together have become the guiding US policy on Taiwan since 1979.

The other implication of the statement is, TRA confirms a proposition in the one-China policy that the United States does not recognize the island of Taiwan as China's territory. The provisions in Section 2(b) indicate that the United States does not treat Taiwan as a part of China. The statement "the future of Taiwan will be determined by peaceful means" implies that "the future of Taiwan" is not settled. If the island of Taiwan were China's territory, the PRC government would be within China's sovereign power to take the island by any means, including the

[827] *See* Taiwan Relations Act, *supra* note 503.
[828] *Id.*

use of force.[829] In fact, the Act positively indicates that Taiwan is not China's territory. Item (4) of Section 2(b) provides that "[the United States] consider[s] any effort to determine the future of Taiwan by other than peaceful means, including by boycotts or embargoes, a threat to the peace and security of the Western Pacific."[830] The statement "any effort to determine the future of Taiwan" necessarily includes acquiring the title to the island of Taiwan. Other provisions in the Section are also inconsistent with any notion that China has the title to the island of Taiwan or sovereignty over it. From the language, it can be concluded that TRA treats the island of Taiwan as a territory not owned by any State. This point was later confirmed by Harvey Feldman, who was involved in drafting the Act.[831] Feldman recalled,

> *Because President Carter switched diplomatic recognition from Taipei to Beijing to gain an ally against the Soviet Union, successive administrations have said the US follows a "one-China policy." But our "policy" is not at all like Beijing's "[one-China] principle." Washington's "one-China policy" says we have diplomatic relations only with Beijing, though we maintain all other relations with Taipei, and we "acknowledge" China's claim to the island, but* we make no statement about Taiwan's status.[832]

[829] The traditional view of sovereignty is that the State has absolute power to rule its people. *See* Louis Henkin, *That "S" Word: Sovereignty, and Globalization, and Human Rights, Et Cetera, Address as part of the Robert L. Levine Distinguished Lecture Series*, 68 FORDHAM L. REV. 1, 4–6 (1999). In the 20th century, under the doctrine of human rights, the sovereign power is not absolute. *See* Father Robert Araujo, *Sovereignty, Human Rights, and Self-Determination: The Meaning of International Law*, 24 FORDHAM INT'L L.J. 1477, 1486–89, 1497 (2001). Under this doctrine, States have the right to protect the people of another State which abuses human rights of its own people. But State practice has not uniformly accepted such doctrine. For instance, when the government soldiers of Yugoslavia (Serbia) killed the ethnic people in Kosova, a region within its own territory, the North Atlantic Treaty Organization (NATO) intervened based on the doctrine of human rights of the ethnic people. On the other hand, when the Russian army killed Chechens in Chechnya, a region within its own territory, no other State intervened. *See generally* Fred Weir, *Summit Delegates in Istanbul Debate Russia's Chechen Attacks*, CHRISTIAN SCIENCE MONITOR (Nov. 18, 1999).

[830] *See* Taiwan Relations Act, *supra* note 503.

[831] Harvey Feldman was a retired ambassador and a senior fellow at the Heritage Foundation. He participated in the drafting of Taiwan Relations Act.

[832] Harvey Feldman, *Commentary: United States is Caught Between Two Governments Glaring Across a One-China Policy*, L.A. TIMES, 12/8/2003, at B11.

That the US adopted the Act indicates that the United States was still an occupying power of Taiwan at the time of its enactment. As will be discussed later, the Act being a US municipal law, the US Government implements the purposes of the law as the occupying power of Taiwan.[833]

Ronald Reagan, who succeeded Carter as the President,[834] was a conservative Republican. By the time Reagan took office, the TRA had been enacted for 2 years. He must have been aware of the position of the United States on the legal status of the island of Taiwan under the Act.

But Reagan's attempt to work together with the PRC government "in order to limit the Soviet Union's opportunities for exploiting its military power" in Asia[835] worried the ROC officials in Taiwan. In May 1981 the US Secretary of State Alexander Haig, who had already made a plan to go to China, delivered a speech in St. Louis indicating that the Reagan Administration sought to improve its relations with the PRC.[836] On June 16, 1981 when Haig was in Beijing, at a news conference after meeting with the Chinese leaders, he said that "[I]t is apparent that the strategic realities which prompted reconciliation between the United States and China more than a decade ago are more pressing than ever. Our common resolve to coordinate our independent policies in order to limit the Soviet Union's opportunities for exploring its military power has, likewise, grown stronger."[837]

Later, two more occasions made the ROC officials in Taiwan even more nervous. One was in July 1981 when US Assistant Secretary for East Asia and Pacific Affairs John H. Holdridge testified before the US House Foreign Affairs Committee on the possible sale of military weapons to China. He said that "[T]he US–China relationship is a major component in our global and regional security policies. We concluded that we should revise the regulations on international traffic in arms to permit the licensing of commercial sales to China on a case-by-case basis."[838] The other occasion was in October 1981 when China's Foreign Minister Huang Hua met with President Reagan and the US Secretary of

[833] *See infra* text accompanying note at 1046.

[834] Ronald Reagan, US President (1981–1989).

[835] Sec'y Alexander Haig, *Remarks at News Conference*, Beijing (June 16, 1981), *in* DEP'T ST. BULL., Aug. 1981, at 34–35.

[836] *See* Sec'y Alexander Haig, *Speech at St. Louis Town Hall Forum* (May 29, 1981), *in* DEP'T ST. BULL., July 1981, at 13.

[837] Alexander Haig, *Remarks at News Conference*, *supra* note 835, at 35.

[838] John H. Holdridge, *Assessment of US Relations With China*, Address before the House Foreign Affairs Committee (July 16, 1981), *in* DEP'T ST. BULL., Oct. 1981, at 38.

State Alexander Haig in Washington, DC. It was widely reported that the two sides discussed the US' reduction of arms sales to Taiwan and possible sale of arms to China.

The fear of the ROC officials was not ameliorated by a few comforting comments by the United States officials that the United States would continue its unofficial relationship with the people of Taiwan.[839] At the news conference in June, 1981 in Beijing, Haig also said that "[r]egarding Taiwan, I explained [to the PRC officials] that the unofficial relationship which has characterized the contacts between the people of the United States and the people of Taiwan since normalization of relations with the People's Republic of China will be continued, and this was understood."[840] At the August 18, 1981 Congressional hearing, Holdridge also said that "[t]he Chinese insisted that we agree to the ultimate termination of arms sales [to Taiwan]. We refused because the level of our arms sales must be determined by the needs of Taiwan, and we could not agree to a termination date, as the Chinese demanded, which might impair our ability to meet those needs."[841]

During or immediately after Huang Hua's visit in October 1981, the Reagan Administration agreed with the PRC government to issue another joint declaration.[842] While the negotiation between the Reagan Administration and the PRC government for a joint declaration was going on, the ROC officials in Taiwan presented the Reagan Administration with a few points that they wished the United States would use as guidelines in conducting the US–China relations.[843]

To alleviate the fear of the ROC officials in Taiwan, President Reagan sent to President Jiang (Chiang) Jing-guo of the ROC a private letter which contained a policy statement on July 14, 1982. The letter, which listed six points that the US Government "would not accede to in any agreement with mainland China,"[844] came to be

[839] *See Id.* (referencing Secretary Haig's visit to Beijing, June 14–17, 1981).

[840] Sec'y Alexander Haig, *Remarks at News Conference*, *supra* note 835, at 35.

[841] Holdridge, *supra* note 687, at 19.

[842] *See* John H. Holdridge, *Assessment of US Relations With China*, Address Before the National Council on United States–China Relations, New York (Dec. 13, 1982), *in* DEP'T ST. BULL., Feb. 1983, at 8 ("I need not review in detail the 10-month long negotiating or period leading up to the issuance of our August 17 joint Communiqué."). *See Id.* This indicates that the negotiation for drafting the communiqué began in October 1981, the month the Chinese Premier visited Reagan.

[843] *See infra* note 845.

[844] Steve Lohr, *Taiwan Expresses Regret Over Communiqué*, N.Y. TIMES, 08/18/1982, at A13.

known as the Six Assurances. The Six Assurances offered by the US Government to the ROC government are that, in dealing with the PRC government, the United States will not (1) set a date for termination of arms sales to Taiwan; (2) consult with China on arms sales to Taiwan; (3) play a mediation role between PRC and Taiwan; (4) revise Taiwan Relations Act; (5) alter its position regarding sovereignty over Taiwan; or (6) exert pressure on Taipei to enter into negotiations with Beijing.[845]

[845] *See* Jay Chen & Deborah Kuo, *US Congress Congratulates Taiwanese People on Successful Election*, World Rep., Mar. 29. 2000, *available at* 2000 WL 2360456. Rep. Benjamin Gilman (R-NY) praises Taiwan's courageous democracy. *See Id.*; *see also* Larry M. Wortzel, *Why the Administration Should Reaffirm the "Six Assurances" to Taiwan*, Backgrounder #1352. The Heritage Foundation, March 16, 2000, *available at* www.heritage.org/library/backgrounder/bg1352.html. Last visited 09/14/2004.It was James Lilley, Director of AIT, who delivered the private letter to President Jiang Jin-guo in person. As the letter was never published, various versions of the Six Assurances exist. The difference among these versions is in the tense used. Wortzel describes the Six Assurances as follows:

> *The United States: [1]* Had not agreed *to set a date for ending arms sales to the Republic of China on Taiwan; [2]* Had not agreed *to hold prior consultations with the Chinese government on arms sales to the Republic of China on Taiwan; [3]* Would not play *any mediation role between Taiwan and China; [4]* Had not agreed *to revise the 1979 Taiwan Relations Act; [5]* Had not altered *its position regarding sovereignty over Taiwan; and [6]* Would not exert *pressure on the Republic of China on Taiwan to enter negotiations with the People's Republic of China. Wortzel, supra. The US House of Representatives Foreign Affairs Committee in the Taiwan Policy Act of 2013, used present perfect tense.* See infra *note 1076.*

The Taiwan Documents Project describes the Six Assurances, similar to the version in the text, uses future tense as follows:

1. The United States will not set a date for termination of arms sales to Taiwan;
2. The United States will not alter the terms of Taiwan Relations Act;
3. The United States will not consult with China in advance before making decisions about US arms sales to Taiwan;
4. The United States will not mediate between Taiwan and China;
5. The United States will not alter its position about the sovereignty of Taiwan which was, that the question was one to be decided peacefully by the Chinese themselves, and would not pressure Taiwan to enter into negotiations with China;
6. The United States will not formally recognize Chinese sovereignty over Taiwan.

Taiwan Documents Project, *The "Six Assurances" to Taiwan* (July 1982), *at* www.taiwandocuments.org/assurances.htm. Last visited 09/15/2004.

The assurance that "[t]he United States will not alter its position regarding sovereignty over Taiwan"[846] is the most crucial one in the discourse of the legal status of Taiwan. This assurance means that Reagan, consistent with the US' position in the TRA, will not change the long-held position of the United States on the legal status of the island of Taiwan—that the United States does not recognize Taiwan as China's territory.

On August 17, 1982, in an attempt to stipulate on the arm sales to Taiwan, the Reagan Administration and the PRC government issued a third joint communiqué called the Third US–China Joint Communiqué on Arms Sales to Taiwan (known as "the Third Communiqué"). Notwithstanding a TRA's provision that the United States "will make available to Taiwan such defense articles and defense services in such quantity as may be necessary to enable Taiwan to maintain a sufficient self-defense capabilities," the Third Joint Communiqué announced that "arms sale to Taiwan will not exceed, either in quantitative or qualitative terms, the level of those supplied in recent years."

With respect to the legal status of Taiwan, the Third Communiqué confirmed what the Shanghai Communiqué and the Second Communiqué did: the United States simply took notice of what the PRC government claimed. The Third Communiqué stated that "the United States of America *acknowledges the Chinese position that there is but one China and Taiwan is part of China*."[847]

But the Third Communiqué did not stop at simply acknowledging the PRC's claim on Taiwan. It positively indicated that the island of Taiwan was not China's territory. The Communiqué stated that a principle guiding US–China relations since the Shanghai Communiqué was respecting each other's sovereignty. It stated that the United States and China's "[r]espect for each other's sovereignty and territorial integrity and noninterference [in] each other's internal affairs constitute the fundamental principles guiding [US]–China relations. These principles were confirmed in the Shanghai Communiqué of 1972 and reaffirmed in the

[846] *The "Six Assurances" to Taiwan, Id. See Implementation of the Taiwan Relations Act: Hearing and Markup Before the House Comm. on Foreign Affairs and its Subcomm. on Human Rights and Int'l Orgs. and on Asian and Pacific Affairs of the H.R.*, 99th Cong. 127–31 (1986) (statement of Martin Lasater, Dir. of Asian Studies, the Heritage Found.); *see also* Don Oberdorfer, *China Sees Diplomatic Victory in Pact; Gradual Cut for Taiwan Pledged*, WASH. POST, 08/18/1982, at A1.

[847] The Second Communiqué, *supra* note 823 (emphasis added).

[Second] Joint Communiqué [of] 1973."[848] The United States then declared in the same Communiqué that it "ha[d] no intention of infringing on Chinese sovereignty and territorial integrity, or interfering in China's internal affairs."[849] Yet, in the ensuing statement, the US Government also stated that it would continue "its arms sales to Taiwan."[850] Thus, in the eyes of the Reagan Administration, arms sales to Taiwan did not "infring[e] on China's sovereignty and territorial integrity."[851] Such a statement implies that the island of Taiwan is not China's territory.

After the Third Communiqué was issued, the PRC government changed the course of its foreign policy. It began to adopt a foreign policy which stressed its identification with the Third World and even resumed a dialogue with Moscow.[852] The new development made the Reagan Administration uncomfortable. So, Reagan planned to send the Secretary of State George Shultz, who succeeded Alexander Haig, to China "for what we hope will be serious, constructive, and wide-ranging talks with the Chinese leadership."[853] Former Secretary of State Henry Kissinger, in commenting on the forthcoming mission of Shultz to Beijing, stated that Schultz could not change the legal frame work of Taiwan,[854] which undoubtedly included the question of sovereignty over the island of Taiwan.

[848] *Id.*

[849] *Id.*

[850] *Id.*

[851] *Id.*

[852] *See* Holdridge, *Assessment of US Relations With China*, *supra* note 838, at 8.

[853] *Id.*

[854] *See* Henry Kissinger, Mr. Shultz Goes to China: What Should Come Out of This Trip, Wash. Post, 01/30/1983, reprinted in Henry Kissinger, Observations at 145 (1985). "In the Shanghai Communiqué of 1972, [and] the accord on normalization of 1979, ... the United States has committed itself to the proposition that there is only one China and that it would not support any variety of a two-China solution. Moreover, the United States has already recognized Peking as the government of all of China. . . . [F]ormal diplomacy has exhausted the subject; the legal framework cannot be stretched further." Id. (The second emphasis added).

C. US One-China Policy

Subsequently, the US officials called the US policy toward China formulated in the Shanghai Communiqué "one-China policy." By 2017, the United States had maintained the "one-China policy" for more than four decades. Although government officials and political commentators often describe the US policy toward China since 1972 as "the one-China policy,"[855] the policy is toward Taiwan as much as China.

The US officials use the term "one-China policy" without defining it.[856] As mentioned earlier, the term "one-China" appeared in late 1970 when the UN General Assembly debated whether the PRC government should replace the ROC government to take China's seat in the United Nations. At the time, the PRC government, which had attempted to replace the ROC government in the United Nations, charged the US Government and the Japanese government with plotting to create two Chinas.[857] On November 22, 1970, after the General Assembly voted on the question of China's representation, the Japanese Ambassador to the UN Min Aichi announced that "Japan will continue to espouse the "onc-China" policy despite the closeness of the vote."[858] It was the first time in the world politics that the term "one-China" appeared on record. The term "one-China" was used by Aichi in connection with the

[855] *See, e.g., Television Interview with Sec'y of Defense William Cohen* (CNN television broadcast, Mar. 10, 2000).

[856] *See* Robert Kaiser, *What We Said, What They Said, What's Unsaid*, WASH. POST, 04/15/2001, at B1.

[857] *See* N.Y. TIMES ABSTRACTS, 02/24/1970, at 6.Communist China charges US and Japan promote independence movement in Taiwan to foster policy of 2 Chinas; says they smuggled Peng Ming-min out of country to enable him to continue his activities for Taiwan independence; charges USSR plays "extremely despicable role" in furthering movement; cites recent visit to Moscow by Newsweek (pub) correspondent and '69 visit to Taiwan by Soviet correspondent for London Evening News as further evidence of Soviet "plotting." *Id. See also* N.Y. TIMES ABSTRACTS, 04/19/1970, at 8.

> *Canadian Minister Sharp reports Canada and China, in 14-month-old talks on establishing diplomatic relations, are "moving closer on main question of Taiwan"; at issue has been China's initial requirement that Canada back Peking's claim to Taiwan; Canada reportedly has convinced Peking that it has no secret desire for two-Chinas policy; Canadian position and possible courses of action reviewed; Canada seen more anxious than China to establish ties; further issues that remain to be resolved outlined. Id.*

[858] *See supra* statement of Min Aichi and text accompanying note 498.

conjectured recognition of the PRC. It simply indicated Japan's policy of not recognizing the PRC. His term "one-China" had nothing to do with title to the island of Taiwan.

The US officials and commentators often used the term "one-China policy" with different connotations. At times, it was said that the "one-China Policy" was the policy announced in the Shanghai Communiqué. At other times, it was said that the policy of the United States on Taiwan was "based on one-China policy and Taiwan Relations Act," or "based on the Three Joint Communiqués and Taiwan Relations Act,"[859] implying that the one-China policy was a combined policy announced in the three Joint Communiqués. More recently, the United States high officials frequently said that the US' policy on Taiwan was "a one-China policy," without mentioning the "Taiwan Relations Act," but in the ensuing explanation of the policy, mentioned the Act as if the Act was a part of the "one-China policy."[860]

For the purpose of discussions in this work, the term "one-China policy" refers to the combined policy of the three Communiqués. The term "one-China policy" as used in this work does not include TRA because the Act is a US statute and while an administration may change its policy, it not only cannot change but is rather obligated to implement a Federal statute.

The one-China policy derived from the three Communiqués consists of the following five major propositions. The first proposition is that there is only one State called China. This is the basic proposition of the Shanghai Communiqué, which is the primary among the three Communiqués. The second proposition is that the PRC government is the legitimate government of the State called China. This is the principal proposition of the Second Communiqué. The Carter Administration had just switched the recognition of China's representative government from the ROC to the PRC when it announced the Second Communiqué. The third proposition is that the ROC is not a State separate from China. This is also a proposition in the Shanghai Communiqué. The ROC was not a State, but was recognized as the representative government of the State called China by the United States until 1979. The fourth proposition is that the United States does not recognize the island of Taiwan as China's territory. This is a proposition of all three Communiqués. While

[859] *See infra* "nonpaper" and text accompanying note 908.
[860] *Id.*

the Second Communiqué only confirmed the US position in the Shanghai Communiqué that the US Government took notice of China's claim over Taiwan and made no statement about Taiwan's legal status,[861] the Third Communiqué by its language, together with the principles of the TRA and Reagan's Six Assurances, positively implied that the Reagan Administration did not consider the island of Taiwan as China's territory. The fifth proposition is that both sides of the Taiwan Strait should peacefully settle their dispute. This proposition is derived from the Shanghai Communiqué.

D. The Legal Status of Taiwan Under the One-China Policy

The following examines US Government's position on the legal status of the island of Taiwan under the one-China policy subsequent to the Reagan Administration.

President George H. W. Bush[862] succeeded Reagan in 1989. Bush was in office less than a year when the Tiananmen Square Incident occurred. On June 4, 1989, the PRC government sent the Chinese army and tanks into the Square in its capital Beijing to suppress a civilian demonstration and killed numerous students who had gathered in the city days before.[863] Bush harshly criticized the PRC government. He said that "It is clear that the Chinese Government has chosen to use force against Chinese citizens who were making a peaceful statement in favor of democracy. I deeply deplore the decision to use force against peaceful demonstrators and the consequent loss of life."[864] The relationship between the US Government and the PRC government was at a low point. But the Bush Administration did not announce any specific changes to its policy toward China. So, officially the Administration did not change the existing US position on the legal status of the island of Taiwan.

President William J. Clinton,[865] who succeeded George H.W. Bush in 1993, did not appear to be friendly toward the PRC government before

[861] *See supra* note 832 and the accompanying text.

[862] George H.W. Bush, US President (1989–1993).

[863] *See* Nicholas D. Kristof, *China Tightens Grip with a Ban on Groups Calling for Democracy*, N.Y. TIMES, 06/13/1989, at A10.

[864] George H.W. Bush, *President's Statement* (June 3, 1989), *in* DEP'T ST. BULL., Aug. 1989, at 75.

[865] William J. Clinton, US President (1993–2001).

he became the President. When he campaigned for the presidency, Clinton accused President Bush of "coddling dictators," referring to Bush's China policy.[866]

When Clinton became the President, the five propositions discussed earlier constituted his policy to maintain the "status quo of Taiwan." In 1995, the Clinton Administration issued a visa to the ROC's President Lee Teng-hui for a private visit to his alma mater Cornell University. The PRC government protested accusing the United States of violating its own one-China policy. The Clinton Administration's response to the PRC's protest was simply warning Lee of not to engage in any political activities which might provoke China.

In 1996, President Clinton still stood up to the threat of the PRC government against Taiwan. The ROC government in Taiwan scheduled a presidential election in March of 1996. The contest was between incumbent President Lee Teng-hui, who as the candidate of the ruling Chinese Nationalist Party (The KMT) was opposed to Taiwan independence on his campaign platform, and Peng Ming-Min, who as the candidate of the Democratic Progressive Party (the DPP) was pro-independence. To intimidate the voters in Taiwan and discourage them from voting for Peng, the PRC government conducted a missile drill by shooting seven or eight missiles toward the island of Taiwan. As a show of force against the PRC's threat, Clinton sent two aircraft carrier battle-groups to the region and as a result the PRC stopped firing missiles.

Subsequently, Clinton changed his attitude toward the PRC government, largely due to the pressure of the US business and trade groups. He changed his China policy from Nixon's rapprochement to cooperation. In 1997, Clinton announced that the PRC government was a "strategic partner" of the United States.[867] He eventually became perceived as more pro-China than any previous President in postwar US history.[868]

[866] *Clinton Easing Up on China*, Com. Appeal, Aug. 24, 1994, at 2 A.

[867] E.J. Dionne, Jr., *China Policy Full of Contradictions*, Denv. Post, 04/10/2001, *available at* http://www.brookings.edu/printme.wbs?page=/pagedefs/c7c1d214d3c2ff3a7ff-f2e680a141465.html. *See* Patrick E. Tyler, *The United States—China Slide: A Relationship Strained by Trade Tension Could Worsen Further Over Taiwan*, N.Y. Times, 05/23/1995, at A10.

[868] Scott Wheeler, *Hu sizes up the White House*, The Daily Caller, the National Republican Trust, 01/26/2011, *available at* http://www.goptrust.com/Hu_Sizes_Up_White_House.html. Last visited 01/28/2011.

Clinton shocked the conservatives in the US and the ROC officials by making a policy announcement in 1998. In June 1998, Clinton made an official trip to China. While in Shanghai, Clinton made a policy statement, subsequently called the "Three-nos statement,"[869] before a group of Chinese college students.

The "Three-nos statement" was "no [US] support for an independent Taiwan, no recognition for a separate Taiwan Government, and no support for Taiwan's entry into international organizations."[870] Clinton created new policy by the statement "no US support for an independent Taiwan" as it is not a proposition of the original one-China policy. It may be considered a special and the sixth proposition of Clinton's one-China policy on Taiwan.[871]

Clinton denied that he changed the US policy on Taiwan. As soon as Clinton made the "Three-nos statement," he was criticized by conservative groups in the United States as selling out Taiwan to the PRC. The Clinton Administration quickly assured the leaders of the ROC government that there was no policy change.[872] However, Clinton's friendly

[869] *See* Philip Shenon, *No Policy Turn, US Assures Taiwan Again*, N.Y. TIMES, 07/7/1998, at A9; *see also* Herman Pan, *Washington Post Editorial Finds "Noes" Fault with Clinton*, CENT. NEWS AGENCY (Taiwan), 07/2/1998.

[870] John J. Tkacik, *Stating America's Case to China's Hu Jintao: A Primer on United States–China-Taiwan Policy*, Backgrounder #1541, THE HERITAGE FOUNDATION, April 26, 2002. at 10. There is no agreement among the US officials and the commentators on the exact wording of Clinton at the meeting. According to Tkacik, President Clinton subsequently sent a letter to China's President Jiang Zemin to clarify his position in the "three-nos" statement. *Id.* "State Department spokesman Jamie Rubin explained, 'We certainly made clear that we have a one China policy, that we don't support a one China or one Taiwan policy, we don't support a two Chinas policy. We don't support Taiwan independence, and we don't support Taiwanese membership in organizations that require you to be a member state. We certainly made that very clear to the Chinese.' *See* US Department of State, *Noon Briefing*, October31, 1997." *Id.* note 45 at 18.

[871] Sec'y of Defense, William Cohen, called it a one-China policy. *See* Jonathan S. Landay, *Cohen Reiterates US "One-China" Policy, Urges Beijing, Taipei to Calm Down*, KNIGHT RIDDER WASH. BUREAU, 03/17/2000.

[872] *See* Shenon, *supra* note 869, at A9. During a meeting in Shanghai last week, Mr. Clinton appeared to make a concession to his Chinese hosts by making a public declaration of a policy known as the "three-nos"—no [US] support for an independent Taiwan, no recognition for a separate Taiwan Government and no support for Taiwan's entry into international organizations. "Nothing that the President said in China changes our relationship with Taiwan," said P.J. Crowley, a White House spokesman. *Id.*

"[T]he escalation of the threat of military action against Taiwan is a direct consequence of Administration efforts to appease Beijing. The President's unexpected statement in Shanghai in June 1998, known as the "three-no's," laid out the three principles behind the Administration's policy toward Taiwan." Wortzel, *supra* note 843.

attitude toward the PRC government[873] made the US position on the legal status of Taiwan murkier. Clinton's special policy implied that the Taiwan authority should not assert sovereignty as to provoke the PRC government. The statement was "cited by the PRC government as further justification of its claims of sovereignty [over Taiwan.]"[874]

However, a careful analysis of the language in the "Three-nos statement" does not lead to a conclusion that the Clinton Administration recognized or conceded to China's claim on Taiwan. In fact, the "Three-nos statement" did not involve a US position on title to the island of Taiwan. The first "no" statement, "No support for an independent Taiwan," simply meant that the United States would not actively support the creation of the State of Taiwan. It did not mean that the island of Taiwan was China's territory.

The second "no" statement, "No recognition for a separate Taiwan government," did not involve title to the island either. It meant that the US Government would not recognize two Chinese governments at the same time. In international law, a State has one representative government, and only one. Since 1979 when the Carter Administration shifted recognition of China's government from the ROC to the PRC, the US Government no longer recognized the ROC as China's representative government.[875] Therefore, it was legally impossible for the United States or other States that had recognized the PRC government also to recognize the ROC government. The second "no" statement does not contain any notion that the island of Taiwan is China's territory.

The third "no" statement, "No support for Taiwan's entry into international organizations," certainly had nothing to do with territory. It was the corollary of the first and the second "no" statements. The first two "no" statements indicated that Taiwan was not a State. Since membership of international organizations was limited to States, Taiwan could not be

[873] See Jane Moore, Relation with China a Top US Concern, State's, Zoellick Says: Domestic concerns, global stakes bind the countries, deputy secretary says. Robert Zoellick, Congressional Hearing before House International Relations Committee (Chair: Henry Hyde), May 10, 2006. Topic "A resurgent China: responsible stakeholder or robust rival," available at http://www.america.gov/st/washfile-english/2006/May/20060510172111ajesrom0.
8644068.html. Last visited 08/17/2010.

[874] Wortzel, *supra* note 845.

[875] *See* Taiwan Relations Act, *supra* note 505.

a member of any international organization. Thus, though the "Three-nos statement" was criticized as a policy that appeased the PRC government, it did not change US' position on title to the island of Taiwan.

Notwithstanding that the Clinton Administration adopted the policy of "constructive engagement" with the PRC government,[876] it was still determined to protect Taiwan. On March 17, 2000 in order to assuage the PRC government, the US Secretary of Defense William Cohen stressed that "We have a one-China policy that we continue to support." But when Cohen was asked by a reporter if the United States would defend Taiwan militarily if the PRC government were to attack the island, he replied, "We also are committed under TRA to provide defensive equipment and support [to Taiwan]."[877] This last comment indicated that the Clinton Administration continued to maintain US' position on the territorial status of Taiwan because, as discussed before, TRA did not recognize the PRC's position that the island of Taiwan was China's territory.[878]

In March 2000, Chen Shui-bian of the DPP Party was elected President of the ROC. Before Chen's inauguration, Clinton privately wielded his power over the Chen Administration. According to Chen's own account later, he announced the "four-nos and one have-no" policy, which included the statement "no [declaration of] independence" and "no referendum to change the status quo [of Taiwan]," in the May 2000 inauguration[879] under the pressure of the Clinton Administration.[880]

2. THE PRC'S ONE-CHINA PRINCIPLE

A. The PRC White Paper

The PRC government claims that China has sovereignty over Taiwan. When the ROC government in Taiwan scheduled to hold a presidential election in March 2000, the PRC government released a White Paper one month before the election to intimidate the voters in Taiwan and discourage them from voting for the pro-independence candidate.[881] In the White Paper, the PRC government threatened to use force against

876 See Otto Kreisher, Defense Chief Urges "Constructive Engagement" with China Continue, San Diego Union-Trib., 03/25/2000, at A16.

877 *Id. See* Landay, *supra* note 871.

878 *See supra* text accompanying note 832.

879 *See supra* text accompanying note 579.

880 *See infra* text accompanying note 1021.

881 *See generally* the White Paper, *supra* note 664, at 53.

Taiwan if the "total unification of the country [is] postponed indefinitely."[882] According to a commentator, Clinton's "three-nos statement" lent China color to its claim over Taiwan in the White Paper. Larry M. Wortzel wrote that "The [White] paper cites the [Three-nos] statement made by President Clinton as further justification of its claims of sovereignty. [C]learly the White Paper demonstrates that the escalation of the threat of military action against Taiwan is a direct consequence of [Clinton] Administration efforts to appease Beijing. The President's unexpected statement in Shanghai in June 1998, known as the "three-nos statement," laid out the principles behind the Administration's policy."[883]

In the 2000 White Paper, the PRC government accused the US Government of violating China's sovereignty: First, when the US Government sold weapons to the ROC government in Taiwan[884]; and second, when it issued a visa to the ROC's President Lee Teng-hui for a private visit to the United States in 1995.[885]

But what is more important is, China created a new term "the one-China principle" for its claims in the White Paper. Initially, since US officials and many political commentators referred to US' one-China policy without defining it,[886] the PRC government attempted to interpret US' one-China policy to serve its own purposes.[887] The PRC government claimed that the US Government in the Shanghai Communiqué conceded to its claim over Taiwan, thus, US' one-China policy also contained a proposition that Taiwan was China's territory, making China sovereign over Taiwan. But when the PRC government subsequently realized that the United States did not recognize Taiwan as China's territory in US' one-China policy, it had to create a different slogan to serve its claims. The term which it created was the "one-China principle." The

[882] *Id.* at 10, 17. *See* Landay, *supra* note 871.

[883] Larry M. Wortzel, *supra* note 845.

[884] *See* the White Paper, *supra* note 664 at 15. "While the Chinese were willing to state their peaceful policy [toward Taiwan] in strong terms, they at first resisted any relationship between that policy and our arms sales to Taiwan. The Chinese resisted this relationship because of their view that *the sale of arms to Taiwan constitutes an interference in China's internal affairs.*" John H. Holdridge, *supra* note 687, at 19 (emphasis added).

[885] *See* the White Paper, *Id.* at 9. Lee Teng-hui visited the United States in 1995. *See* Barbara Franklin, *China: Friend or Enemy? See supra* note 819.

[886] *See* Robert Kaiser, *supra* note 856.

[887] See Anniversary of Shanghai Communiqué: Sino-US "Alliance" Has Increased Tension, (BBC television broadcast, Mar. 3, 1982).

"one-China principle" claims the following three propositions: (a) There is but one China; (b) the PRC government is the legitimate government of China; and (c) Taiwan is China's territory. The one-China principle's major difference with the US' one-China policy is the last proposition.

The claim that Taiwan is China's territory in the PRC White Paper is not valid in international law. The White Paper is no more than a unilateral proclamation. Such a proclamation, as discussed before, cannot effect a change of title to a territory. Under international law, territory can only be acquired in a limited number of ways, and a unilateral proclamation is not one of them unless it is on a newly discovered land. China did not point to any specific basis which supported it's claim to Taiwan. When China issued its White Paper, the position of the US Administrations from President Nixon to President Clinton under the one-China policy was that Taiwan was not China's territory.

B. China's Position on Sovereignty Over Taiwan Under its One-China Principle

A question raised in the Introduction is whether China has sovereignty over the island of Taiwan and its inhabitants. China claims that it has had sovereignty over Taiwan since 1945. The PRC White Paper stated that "on October 25, 1945, the Chinese government recovered Taiwan and the Penghu Archipelago, resuming the exercise of sovereignty over Taiwan. The government of the PRC naturally should fully enjoy and exercise China's sovereignty, including its sovereignty over Taiwan."[888]

The PRC government claims sovereignty not only over the island of Taiwan, but also over the people of Taiwan under its one-China principle. On March 14, 2005, the Chinese National People's Congress adopted the Anti-secession Law.[889] The law prohibits the Taiwanese people to "secede" from China. Article 2 of the Anti-secession Law provides

[888] The One-China Principle and the Taiwan Issue (2000). *See* the White Paper, *supra* note 662, at 53.

[889] *See* The Anti-secession Law, adopted at the Third Session of the Tenth National People's Congress and promulgated on March 14, 2005, *available at* http://www.chinadaily.com.cn/english/2005-03/14/content_424643.htm. Last visited 05/01/2005. Article 2 provides "There is only one China in the world. Both the mainland and Taiwan belong to one China. China's sovereignty and territorial integrity brook no division. Safeguarding China's sovereignty and territorial integrity is the common obligation of all Chinese people, the Taiwan compatriots included. Taiwan is part of China. The state shall never allow the 'Taiwan independence' secessionist forces to make Taiwan secede from China under any name or by any means." *Id.*

that "Taiwan is part of China. The state shall never allow the 'Taiwan independence' secessionist forces to make Taiwan secede from China under any name or by any means."[890]

The Anti-secession Law threatens the people of Taiwan that the PRC government will resort to nonpeaceful means, including use of force, to suppress Taiwan independence. Article 8 provides,

> *"In the event that the 'Taiwan independence' secessionist forces should act under any name or by any means to cause the fact of Taiwan's secession from China, or that major incidents entailing Taiwan's secession from China should occur, or that possibilities for a peaceful reunification should be completely exhausted, the state shall employ nonpeaceful means and other necessary measures to protect China's sovereignty and territorial integrity."*[891]

Under international law, the Anti-secession law has no validity against the people of Taiwan. The Chinese domestic law which authorizes the PRC government to employ "nonpeaceful means and other necessary measures" is intended to apply to the people of Taiwan. But, under the theory of sovereignty discussed in Chapter 2, The State and Sovereignty, and international law, China's sovereignty over the people of Taiwan is contingent upon having the title to the island of Taiwan. As China never reacquired the title to the island of Taiwan by any recognized means in international law after the Treaty of Shimonoseki, the State of China has no sovereignty over the island of Taiwan and its inhabitants.

C. US Response to the One-China Principle

When President George W. Bush[892] took office in January 2001, his policy was not friendly toward the PRC government. He called the PRC government a "strategic competitor" to replace Clinton's "strategic partner."[893] In April 2001, three months after Bush took office, he pledged in a televised interview to do "whatever it took to help Taiwan defend herself,"[894] notwithstanding China's claim under its one-China Principle in the 2000 White Paper.

[890] *Id.* Art. 2.

[891] *Id.*

[892] George W. Bush, US President (2001–2008), is a son of George H.W. Bush, US President (1989–1993).

[893] *See* Dionne, *supra* note 867; *See also Issues 2000: Every Presidential Candidates' View on Every Issue. More Headlines: George W. Bush on China, available at* http://www.issues2000.org/Celeb/More_George_W_Bush_China.htm; Kreisher, *supra* note 874, at A16.

[894] Kelly Wallace, *Bush Pledges Whatever it Takes to Defend Taiwan, available at* http://www.cnn.com/2000/ALLPOLITICS/04/24/bush.taiwan.abc/. Last visited 09/09/ 2004.

However, Bush changed his attitude toward the PRC government after the "September 11" event. On September 11, 2001, when Al Qaeda groups attacked the United States with three commercial airplanes, Bush's attitude toward the PRC changed. He approached the PRC government for assistance.

In 2003, Bush for the first time expressed his opposition to Taiwan independence in public. In December of 2003, President Chen Shui-bian proposed that the ROC government, coinciding with the presidential election in March 2004, conduct a referendum in Taiwan pursuant to the ROC's Referendum Law. The Bush Administration condemned the proposal charging that it was a move toward independence.[895] Later, when Chinese Premier Wen Jiabao met with President Bush in Washington on December 9, 2003, Bush, standing next to Wen, rebuked Chen for proposing to hold a referendum. After the meeting, Bush said, "[W]e oppose any unilateral decision by either China or Taiwan to change the status quo. And the comments and actions made by the leader of Taiwan indicate that he may be willing to make decisions unilaterally that change the status quo, which we oppose."[896]

The Bush Administration opposed President Chen Shui-bian's application to join the United Nations in the name of "Taiwan." In July 2007, when Chen sent to the UN Secretary-General Ban Ki-Moon an application for a UN membership in the name of "Taiwan" instead of the names such as "the Republic of China" or "the Republic of China (Taiwan)" used in the past, the US State Department immediately condemned Chen for making the proposal.[897]

The Bush Administration also condemned Chen's proposal for a referendum in Taiwan to join the United Nations. In August 2007, when President Chen was frustrated by the repeated rejections of the UN General Committee on the ROC's applications to rejoin the United Nations, he proposed a referendum by the people of Taiwan to apply to join the United Nations as a member in the name of "Taiwan." The Bush Administration warned him not to alter the "status quo" unilaterally. Deputy Secretary of State John Negroponte, in criticizing Chen's

[895] David Sanger, *On Eve of Chinese Premier's Visit, White House Warns Taiwan,* N.Y. Times, 12/8/2003.

[896] Lin Chieh-yu & Charles Snyder, *Chen Still Defiant After Bush Rebuke*, TAIPEI TIMES, 12/11/2003, at 1, *available at* http://www.taipeitimes.com/News/front/archives/2003/12/11/2003079111. Last visited 11/08/2004.

[897] *See supra* text accompanying note 605.

proposal a few days later, told a Hong Kong-based Phoenix TV reporter that Taiwan's efforts to hold a democratic plebiscite would constitute a move "towards a declaration of independence of Taiwan."[898]

The Bush Administration considered Chen's proposal repugnant to its China policy. In January 2009, when Negroponte was asked of the US position on Taiwan's status at the American Chamber of Commerce in China, he replied that "We of course maintain our position of a One-China Policy. The issue of cross-Strait relations must be resolved by peaceful means."[899]

Bush's opposition to Taiwan independence is stronger than Clinton's "no [support for] Taiwan independence." Bush's policy outright suppressed Taiwan independence. He even opposed a referendum for the people of Taiwan to determine their political future. Thus, the Bush Administration added a new, and the seventh, proposition to the one-China policy—no referendum for the people of Taiwan. For the Bush Administration, a referendum in Taiwan for the people to decide their political future was somehow not a peaceful means to settle the dispute between two sides of the Taiwan Strait.

Despite Bush's change of attitude toward the PRC government,[900] his Administration maintained the past US position on the legal status of Taiwan. At one point an alarm sounded in Taiwan as if the Bush Administration had changed its position on the legal status of Taiwan. In May 2002, the US Deputy Secretary of Defense Paul Wolfowitz delivered a speech at Brookings Institute on the US policy toward China. During the speech, he said that the Bush Administration "has no intention, no desire to separate Taiwan from the mainland."[901] The statement "seemingly mean[t] that the US Government recognizes Taiwan is part of

[898] John Negroponte, *US Presses Taiwan to drop Referendum Plan*. August 24, 2007, *available at* http://www.globalsecurity.org/wmd/library/news/taiwan/2007/taiwan-070828-voa01.htm. Last visited 04/15//2011.

[899] *US Relations With the People's Republic of China (2009)*. Press Release, US Department of State. Remarks of John D. Negroponte, Deputy Secretary of State at the American Chamber of Commerce in China, Chaoyang Westin Hotel, Beijing, China, January 8, 2009.

[900] See Jane Moore, Relation with China a Top US Concern, State's Zoellick Says: Domestic concerns, global stakes bind the countries, deputy secretary says. Robert Zoellick, Congressional Hearing before House International Relations Committee (Chair: Henry Hyde) May 10, 2006. Topic: A resurgent China: responsible stakeholder or robust rival?

http://www.america.gov/st/washfile-english/2006/May/20060510172111ajesrom0.8644068.html. Last visited 08/17/2010.

[901] *United States Against Taiwan Independence, Defense Official Wolfowitz Says*, BRIT. BROADCASTING CORP., 5/31/2002.

China."[902] Wolfowitz's statement surprised political observers and reporters because the statement from the usually hawkish part of the US Government, the Department of Defense, if true, meant an abrupt change to the past position of the US Government on the legal status of Taiwan.

The alarm turned out to be a false one. Wolfowitz quickly took an opportunity to clarify his statement a few days later. During a flight to Singapore on May 30, 2002 for a Southeast Asia Regional Security Meeting, when a reporter asked Wolfowitz whether his speech at Brookings Institute indicated that the Bush Administration had changed the position toward Taiwan, he flatly denied it. Wolfowitz said,

> *"That's very good caution against any improvisation. I mean the President (George W. Bush) has been very clear. And we have a very clear statement. I appreciate actually the opportunity to say it emphatically. The president said from the beginning we have a one-China policy. It basically rests on two propositions. One is that we do not support Taiwan independence, but just as strongly and, I believe, central to the whole notion, we oppose the use of force."*[903]

A US senior administrator recalled that during the visit of the Chinese Premier Wen Jiabao in December 2003, Bush told the Chinese Premiere "in no uncertain terms" that the United States "would have to get involved if China tried to use coercion or force to unilaterally change the legal status of Taiwan."[904] The statement that the US opposes the use of force by the PRC government to take Taiwan implied that Taiwan was not China's territory because if Taiwan were China's territory, China with its sovereign power could use any means, including force, to take Taiwan under international law.

Thus, even though Bush tried to please the PRC leader, he was firm on the US position on the legal status of Taiwan. A statement jointly issued by the US Government and the Japanese government in 2005 also implied that the Bush Administration did not regard the island of Taiwan as China's territory. In February of 2005, the Japanese Foreign Minister Nobutaka Machimura and the Defense Agency Director General Yoshinori Ono met with Secretary of State Condoleezza Rice and Secretary of Defense Donald H. Rumsfeld in Washington to consult the issues of regional and global peace and stability in the United States–Japan Alliance and to strengthen the United States–Japan security and defense cooperation. At the conclusion of the meeting, the United States–Japan Security Consultative Committee

[902] *Id.*
[903] *Id.*
[904] Lin Chieh-yu & Charles Snyder, *supra* note 896.

issued a Joint Statement on February 19, 2005. In the Joint Statement the two countries agreed to "[enhance] regional and global peace and stability and the formation of "common strategic objectives" to "develop a cooperative relationship with China, [and] encourage the peaceful resolution of issues concerning the Taiwan Strait through dialogue."[905] The Joint Statement indicates that the United States–Japan alliance under the United States–Japan Mutual Defense Treaty included maintaining the peace of the Taiwan Strait. That statement indicated that the Taiwan Strait was not China's internal water, implying that Taiwan was not China's territory. In June 2007, in a response to an inquiry on the legal status of the island of Taiwan, the US State Department, by a letter to the inquirer, stated that "[a]lthough the United States recognizes the PRC Government as the sole legal government of China, we have not formally recognized Chinese sovereignty over Taiwan. In fact, we have not made any determination as to Taiwan's political status."[906]

The Bush Administration took the same stand in a message to the UN Secretariat. When President Chen Shui-bian of the ROC sent to the UN Secretariat an application to join the United Nations in the name of "Taiwan" in July 2007, the Secretary-General Ban Ki-Moon rejected the application on the ground that "Taiwan is part of China."[907] Although the

[905] *Joint Statement of United States–Japan Security Consultative Committee*, Washington, D.C., Feb. 19, 2005. Also Joel Brinkley, *Japan Said to Support US on Security of Taiwan*. N.Y. Times, 2/19/2005.

[906] Letter of Sue Bremner, Deputy Director, Taiwan Coordination Office. (2008/07).

Dear (the name of the addressee omitted):Thank you for your letter of June 4 to Secretary Rice. You asked whether the United States has been "holding" Taiwan's sovereignty since 1945 and whether Taiwan, like Puerto Rico, is part of the United States.

The United States has never claimed to have acquired title to Taiwan by law, treaty or conquest. Our relations with Taiwan are governed by the three Joint Communiqués and Taiwan Relation Act. The 1972 Shanghai Communiqué "acknowledges that all Chinese on either side of the Taiwan Strait maintains there is but one China and that Taiwan is a part of China." Although the United States recognizes the PRC Government as the sole legal government of China, we have not formally recognized Chinese sovereignty over Taiwan. In fact, we have not made any determination as to Taiwan's political status. Our consistent position remains that sovereignty of Taiwan is a question to be decided peacefully by the Chinese people on both sides of the Taiwan Strait. I hope this information is useful to you. Sincerely, Sue Bremner, Deputy Director, Taiwan Coordination Office.

(A copy of the letter is in this writer's file.)

[907] *See supra* text accompanying note 605.

Bush Administration was against the application of the ROC, it rebuked the UN Secretariat for repeatedly describing Taiwan as a "Province of China" by a message in the form of "nonpaper" verbally delivered to the UN Under Secretary General for Political Affairs.[908] In the message, the United States informs the Under Secretary General that the "The United States reiterates

[908] In July of 2007, the US Secretary of State Condoleezza Rice instructed the US Representative at the United Nations to meet with the UN Under Secretary General for Political Affairs Lynn Pascoe to convey the points listed below in the form of Demarche on China/Taiwan nomenclature at the U.N.*2. (U) USUN should seek the following objectives in its meeting with U/SYG* Pascoe:

– Reiterate the United States' "one China" policy based on our three Joint Communiqués with the PRC and the Taiwan Relations Act. Consistent with this policy, we "acknowledge" the Chinese view "that Taiwan is a part of China," but we take no position on the status of Taiwan. We neither accept nor reject the claim that Taiwan is a part of the PRC.
– Explain that the United States has long urged that Taiwan's status be resolved peacefully, to the satisfaction of people on both sides of the Taiwan Strait. Beyond this, we do not define Taiwan in political terms.
– Express concern that, as the PRC has become more active in international organizations, it has called on Secretariats and member States to accept its claim of sovereignty over Taiwan. In some cases, as a condition for the PRC's own participation in international organizations, Beijing has insisted that organizations or member States use nomenclature for Taiwan, e.g., 'Taiwan, China," that suggests endorsement of Chinese sovereignty over the island. Express concern also that some UN organizations have recently asserted that UN precedent requires that Taiwan be treated as a part of the PRC and be referred to by names in keeping with such a status.
– Note that we have become aware that the UN has promulgated documents asserting that 'the United Nations considers Taiwan for all purposes to be an integral part of the People's Republic of China' (e.g., in a March 28 communiqué from the SYG to the Republic of Nauru). While this position is consistent with Chinese policy, it is not universally held by UN member States, including the United States.
– Note that the UN documents asserting that the organization views Taiwan as an integral part of the PRC indicate that UNGA resolution 2758, adopted on October 25, 1971, is the basis for accepting the PRC's sovereignty claim on Taiwan. Explain that, in fact, the resolution does not establish that Taiwan is a province of the PRC. The resolution merely recognizes the representatives of the Government of the PRC as the only lawful representatives of China to the United Nations, recognizes the PRC as one of the five permanent members of the Security Council, and expels the representatives of Chiang Kai-shek from the seat that they occupied at the United Nations and all UN-related organizations. There is no mention in resolution 2758 of Chinese claims of sovereignty over Taiwan.
– Explain that while we do not support Taiwan's membership in organizations such as the United Nations for which statehood is a prerequisite, we do support meaningful participation by Taiwan's expels, as appropriate, in such organizations. We support Taiwan's membership, as appropriate, in organizations for which statehood is not required.

its One China policy which is based on the three United States–China Communiqués and TRA, to the effect that the United States *acknowledges* China's view that Taiwan is a part of China. We take no position on the status of Taiwan. We neither accept nor reject the claim that Taiwan is a part of China. If the UN Secretariat insists on describing Taiwan as a part of the PRC, or on using nomenclature for Taiwan that implies such status, the United States will be obliged to dissociate itself on a national basis from such position."[909] Thus, under the US one-China policy, the status quo of Taiwan includes a proposition that the United States does not recognize Taiwan as China's territory. Although the note contained a typical diplomatic ambiguity, the Bush Administration expressly stated that it did not hold the position that Taiwan was a part of China.

Although the Bush Administration did not recognize that Taiwan is part of China, it did not consider either the ROC or Taiwan as a State. In October 2004, the US Secretary of State Colin Powell made some remarks on Taiwan's sovereignty that drew protests in Taiwan. On his way to China, Powell gave an interview to a CNN reporter on October 25, 2004. During the interview, Powell made two remarks: The first remark was "There is only one China; Taiwan is not independent. It does not enjoy sovereignty as nation"; the second remark was "We want to see both sides not take unilateral action that would prejudice an eventual outcome, a reunification that all parties are seeking."[910]

- Urge the UN Secretariat to review its policies on the status of Taiwan and to avoid taking sides in a sensitive matter on which UN members have essentially agreed to disagree for over 35 years.
- Caution that if the UN Secretariat insists on describing Taiwan as a part of the PRC or on using nomenclature for Taiwan that implies such a status, the United States will be obliged to disassociate itself on a national basis from such positions. Source: The Office of Information Programs and Services, SA-2, Department of State, Washington, DC. KODAKB.021005.

The nonpaper drafted by the US Representative to the United Nations includes additional background not reproduced herein. The nonpaper was to be delivered verbally and included an instruction that "USUN should not leave behind any written points or nonpaper."

For the nonpaper, *also see* John Tkacik *Taiwan's "Unsettled" International Status: Preserving US Options in the Pacific*. The Heritage Foundation. Backgrounder #2146. June 19, 2008, *available at* www.heritage.org/Researc/AsiaandPacific/bg2146.cfm. According to John Tkacik, Jr, a retired US career diplomat and former Senior Fellow at The Heritage Foundation, a nonpaper is so called because it does not address a particular proposal in the United Nations. *Id.*

[909] *Id.* (emphasis added).

[910] *See supra* text accompanying note 589.

Although many politicians in Taiwan criticized Powell for making the remarks, Powell was correct in saying that Taiwan was not a State. But he was misguided when he remarked that "a reunification [of Taiwan and China] that all parties are seeking." In 2004, when Powell made the remarks, not only were a majority of the people of Taiwan not seeking "a unification with China," but President Chen Shui-bian, who in August 2002 claimed that the ROC was a country separate from China in his "two countries each on one side [of the Taiwan Strait]" speech,[911] never expressed any desire for the unification of Taiwan and China at the time. This remark would be correct in the earlier era when the KMT Party was in control of the government in Taiwan and "both sides" referred to the government of the PRC and the government of the ROC, but not correct when Chen Shui-bian was the ROC's President. Clearly Powell's second remark was not supported by facts.

Thus, against China's newly created "one-China principle" the Bush Administration confirmed that its policy toward China was the one-China policy: Taiwan was not China's territory. Bush added to his one-China policy two special propositions. One is, the US opposes the use of force by the PRC government to take Taiwan. The other is, the US opposes Taiwan independence: no referendum for the people of Taiwan.

When Barak Obama became the President, he initially played down the conflict between China and the United States.[912] In February 2009 when Obama was sworn in as the President, the country was in an unprecedented economic crisis. While the country carried an enormous national deficit and debt, an economic depression of the 1929 magnitude was looming. The US Government needed foreign money to support its stimulus programs. China was the largest holder of the US Treasury bonds (sovereign debts). The US Government was in the weakest bargaining position in history in dealing with the PRC government. Needing China's support, Obama sent Treasury Secretary Timothy Geithner to Beijing on a special mission in June 2009.[913] Geithner's mission was to convince the Chinese officials that China's continual investment in the

[911] Sandy Huang, *supra* note 580.

[912] President Barak Obama (2009–2017) said "[S]ome in China think that America will try to contain China's ambitions; some in America think that there is something to fear in a rising China. I take a different view." Mark Lander, *Obama Lists Wide Agenda As Talks With China Open*, N.Y. Times. 07/28/2009, Sec. A, C. 1, p. 9.

[913] David Barboza, *Geithner Says China Has Faith in US* N.Y. Times, 06/3/09, *available at* http://www.nytimes.com. Last visited 09/03/2009.

US bonds was beneficial to both countries' economy.[914] Obama also needed China's cooperation to suppress the nuclear projects of North Korea and Iran. Thus, Obama, a Nobel Peace Prize winner, was not heard criticizing or commenting on the human rights issues in China until January 2011 when China's President Hu Jing-tau visited him.

But an event in August of 2009 provided an opportunity to test the courage of the Obama Administration against China. On August 8, 2009 typhoon Maraket struck southern Taiwan and caused a historical flooding and landslides. The storm, which caused 500 deaths and thousands of homeless people, paralyzed President Ma Ying-jeou's ROC government. On August 17, 2009, the US military authority stationed in Okinawa Air Base, seeing that Ma Ying-jeou's government was helpless, quickly dispatched four helicopters and two Marine C-130s based on Okinawa Island to southern Taiwan and delivered four pallets of plastic sheeting and a half-ton of water-purifying chlorine tablets.[915]

In this episode, the Obama Administration showed some political strength against the PRC government. The US military authority in Okinawa would not have done so without authorization of the Department of Defense. The US authority took the action without permission from the PRC government. According to a newspaper account, the US military authority acted without giving an advance notice to the PRC government,[916] although there was a conflicting report on the giving of notice to the PRC.[917] But what was not in dispute was that the US Government did not seek the PRC's permission to land the US Navy helicopters in Taiwan. The incident was in sharp contrast to the reaction of the UN Secretary-General Kofi Annan during the 1999 earthquake in Taiwan when he announced that the United Nations had to wait for the approval of the PRC government before the UN Office For the Coordination of Humanitarian Affairs could send a disaster assessment

[914] David Barboza, *Id.*

[915] Wendell Minnick, *US Forces on Taiwan for Typhoon Relief Mission*, Defense News, 08/19/2009, *available at* www.defensenews.com. Last visited, 09/01/2009. *See* also Gordon Lubold, *Helping after Taiwan typhoon, US avoids confronting China*, The Christian Science Monitor, 08/18/2009.

[916] "State Department spokesman Philip Crowley said, 'I don't believe that we felt it was necessary to inform China in advance. Obviously, this is serious humanitarian situation that Taiwan is facing.'" Gordon Lubold, *Id.*

[917] "Walter Lohman, director of the Asian Studies Center at The Heritage Foundation in Washington said, 'There had to be some kind of signal sent, it would only be prudent.'" Gordon Lubold, *Id.*

team to Taiwan.[918] The strength which the Obama Administration showed was even more significant considering that it needed the cooperation and assistance of the PRC government in other aspects.

The action which the US Government took in southern Taiwan in the aftermath of typhoon Moraket was more than a humanitarian mission. The Obama Administration used the occasion to demonstrate that the United States did not consider the island of Taiwan as China's territory. In international law, if China had sovereignty over the island of Taiwan and its inhabitants, no other States could intrude into China's territory without a request or permission from its government. China has had numerous disasters, both natural and manmade, killing hundreds of people in the past. No other States have sent in a rescue team or aid, let alone military aircrafts, to China without its request. The action which the US Government took in this incident was more powerful than angry rhetoric. It was quite a surprise to political observers that no complaint was lodged by the PRC government against the action of the US military force in Taiwan.

What the Obama Administration expressed in its action in Taiwan was significant in geopolitics in the Western Pacific. The landing of military helicopters in Taiwan without China's permission was a message to the Asia Pacific region that the United States would defend its allies against any military action endangering the security of the region. On November 17, 2009, while visiting China, President Obama told reporters in Beijing that "I have been clear in the past that my administration fully supports a one-China policy. We don't want to change that policy and that approach."[919]

[918] *See supra* note 578.

[919] *People's Daily Online,* 11/17/2009, *available at* http://english.people.com.cn/90001/90776/90883/6815654.html. Last visited 10/01/2010. According to UPI, Nov. 16, 2010, quoting Xinhua's report, Obama repeated the statements in Shanghai, *available at* http://www.upi.com/Top_News/US/2009/11/16/Obama-supports-one-China-policy/UPI-90501258374573. Last visited 10/01/2010. By stating "I have been clear in the past," Obama might be referring to his statement to Hu Jintao, President of the PRC, when the two leaders met during the "Group of 20 countries" summit held in London in April of 2009. "Obama reiterated Washington's 'one-China policy' based on the three US–PRC Communiqués that have governed the US policy toward China for three decades and also pointedly mentioned the Taiwan Relations Act of 1979." Editorial, *What Obama-Hu met means for Taiwan*, TAIWAN NEWS, 04/07/2009, p. 6, *available at* http://www.etaiwannews.com/etn/news_content.php?id=913194.

In 2013, the Obama Administration confirmed its policy again. In August 2013, US Secretary of Defense Chuck Hagel met with Chinese Minister of Defense General Guan Youfei in Washington. Afterwards, US Representative Michael McCaul asked Hagel in a letter whether the United States had consulted with China about sales of weapons to Taiwan. In a reply released on November 1, US Undersecretary of Defense James Miller said the US government's approach to Taiwan was founded on the three joint United States—China Communiqués and the TRA. Miller continued in the letter,

> *"This approach has been a constant for eight US administrations and will not change. As a matter of policy, and consistent with previous assurances we have given to Taiwan, the United States does not consult with China prior to a decision to sell arms to Taiwan, and did not agree to do so when General Chang met with Secretary Hagel. [T]he administration of US President Barack Obama would continue to make defense articles and services available to Taiwan in such quantity as may be necessary for Taiwan to maintain a sufficient self-defense capability. The Department of Defense views support to Taiwan as consistent with both the TRA and with US security interests to ensure peace and stability in Northeast Asia."*[920]

Thus, the PRC's one-China principle has not changed the position of the United States on the legal status of Taiwan. Although the language used by Bush, either to please the PRC's leader or to rebuke the leader in Taiwan, sounded unfriendly to the ROC government or to Taiwan, his statements did not lend color to China's claim over Taiwan, notwithstanding its 2000 White Paper. The Bush Administration explicitly stated that its policy toward Taiwan was based on the three official Communiqués and TRA. Obama also announced that "his administration supports a one-China policy," implying that Taiwan was not part of China.

Based on the above analyses of the US policy toward China, the one-China policy of the United States is significantly different from the one-China principle advocated by the PRC government. The United States does not recognize or concede to the PRC's claim that the island of Taiwan is China's territory in its one-China principle. The PRC government distorts the meaning of US' one-China policy when it equates US' one-China policy with its own one-China principle.

[920] William Lowther (Staff reporter), *PRC not consulted over arms: US*, Taipei Times, 11/03/2013, *available at* http://www.taipeitimes.com/News/taiwan/archives/2013/11/03/2003576040.

Occasionally, political commentators express a distorted view. For instance, Richard Allen, a senior fellow at Stanford University's Hoover Institution, who was chief foreign policy adviser to Richard Nixon in 1968 and to Ronald Reagan in 1980, said that the US one-China policy conceded to the PRC's claim that Taiwan was part of China. In 2009, Allen wrote in Wall Street Journal that,[921]

> *"In recent years – until the 2008 election of President Ma Ying-jeou – Taiwan had become problematic in terms of US policy and goals by toying with the notion of 'independence' from the PRC. Such a move would run directly counter to the US policy of the past 40 years, begun by Nixon, that there is but one China, and* Taiwan is part of China*; and that the US remains legally committed to the preservation of Taiwan's freedom from forcible absorption by the PRC."*[922]

A statement like this from a past policy advisor to US Presidents is surprising. However, as the analyses and discussions above indicate, if he had advised Nixon to give up the strategic island and conceded to China's claim to Taiwan, he did not succeed. Even if Nixon had conceded to China's claim of Taiwan, China could not acquire the island of Taiwan by a concession under international law. Nixon would be in violation of the Peace Treaty of San Francisco which the US drafted and became its supreme law under its Constitution. A subsequent concession to a claim of a territory by a single party to the Treaty cannot override the Treaty disposition. Allen further said that "US commitments under TRA could be met by proceeding with the pending arms sale and initiating free-trade discussions with Taiwan."[923] If "Taiwan is part of China" as Allen claims, his suggestion that the US Government makes sales of weapons to Taiwan amounts to persuading the US Government to violate international law. In fact, Allen's views were contrary to the US' proclamations in the Second and the Third Communiqués.

[921] Richard Allen, *The Next Step in the Taiwan-China Dance,* WALL STREET JOURNAL, 08/17/2009.

[922] *Id.* (emphasis added). Such advocacy may encourage China to repeat its assertion. In October 2012, The PRC government began to issue its new passports with a map of China showing that its territory included the island of Taiwan, South China Sea, and part of the territory in dispute with India. The US Assistant Secretary of State Kurt Campbell formally asked China to "rethink its new passports." William Lowther, *US' Campbell asks China to rethink new passports*, TAIPEI TIMES, 12/1/2012, p. 3.

[923] *Id.*

A few days after Allen's article appeared, John Tkacik, Jr., a former senior diplomat to China and Taiwan, criticized Allen's view in the same newspaper. Tkacik, in a letter to WALL STREET JOURNAL, rebutted as follows,

> *"It may be ancient history, but Richard V. Allen's memory of Nixon's Taiwan policy is garbled (*The Next Step in the Taiwan-China Dance*, Aug. 17). As a US foreign service officer I worked on China and Taiwan affairs for 20 years, and I can attest that the US has never subscribed to China's territorial claims on Taiwan. Nor did President Richard Nixon ever publicly articulate such a policy."*[924]

The one-China principle advocated by the PRC government is correct in its claims that there is only one China and the PRC is its representative government, but it is not correct in its claim that Taiwan is a part of China.

In summary, China has never reacquired the title to the island of Taiwan since the Treaty of Shimonoseki by any recognized means in international law: it has not acquired the island of Taiwan under the Cairo Declaration; it has not acquired it by the Peace Treaty of San Francisco or any other treaty. Furthermore, China has not acquired the island through occupation.

[924] John Tkacik, Jr., *The US Doesn't Recognize China's Claims to Taiwan*. WALL STREET JOURNAL, 09/1/2009.

CHAPTER 8

The UN's Position on the Sovereignty Over Taiwan

Contents

1. KOFI ANNAN'S POLICY STATEMENTS

Discussions now turn to Kofi Annan's two policy statements relating to the legal status of Taiwan mentioned earlier. The first policy statement made by him is "the Taiwan Province of China" when he refused to send a UN disaster assessment team to the island after a powerful earthquake in 1999.[925] The second policy statement is "the organization's one-China policy" made by him as the grounds to deny a Republic of China (ROC) official access to the UN Headquarters to attend a press conference in 2003.[926] By the statement "the Taiwan Province of China," he clearly means that Taiwan is China's territory. His statement "[UN]'s one-China Policy" also implies that Taiwan is part of China.[927]

925 *See supra* text accompanying note 578.

926 *See supra* text accompanying note 588. *See also UN Bars Taiwanese Official From Briefing*, *supra* note 586. The press conference took place on May 23, 2003. *See UN Bars Taiwanese Official From Briefing*, *Id.*

927 That Koffi Annan denied the Taiwan's official access to the UN Headquarter on the ground of UN's "one-China policy" can only mean that Taiwan is part of China.

The One-China Policy: State, Sovereignty, and Taiwan's International Legal Status
DOI: http://dx.doi.org/10.1016/B978-0-08-102314-3.00008-2

There is no question that Annan's statements were influenced by China. China's role in the United Nations is undoubtedly important, being a founding member of the United Nations and a permanent member of its Security Council.[928] Since October 25, 1971 when the People's Republic of China (PRC) government replaced the ROC government as the representative government of China in the United Nations, the PRC government has exerted a strong influence in the United Nations.

Since its establishment, the PRC government has claimed that Taiwan is China's territory.[929] Kofi Annan was the chief executive of the United Nations. At first glance, it would appear that Annan's statements reflected the position of the organization on the legal status of Taiwan. That may not necessarily be so.

An examination of the position of the Security Council and the General Assembly that follows will show that Annan's statements did not truly reflect UN's policy.

2. THE UN SECURITY COUNCIL'S POSITION ON THE LEGAL STATUS OF TAIWAN

This section reviews the position of the Security Council with respect to China's claim of title to the island of Taiwan. The only occasion since the formation of the United Nations in which the Security Council had an opportunity to deal with the question of the title to the island of Taiwan occurred in 1950. On that occasion the Security Council did not take a position that the island of Taiwan was China's territory. A review of the events leading to this conclusion follows.

In June of 1950, the Korean War erupted. On the morning of Sunday, June 25, 1950, North Korean armed forces crossed the 38th parallel line into South Korea. On the same day, the UN Security Council received from the Representatives of the United States a complaint of "Aggression upon the Republic of Korea." The Security Council thereupon called an emergency meeting. In the meeting, the Security Council adopted a resolution, which called upon the authorities of North Korea to cease hostilities and to withdraw their armed forces. It also called upon "all

[928] *See* THE UN CHARTER *supra* note 383, Art. 7, Sec. 1.

[929] *See Chou En-Lai Cablegram*, *supra* text accompanying note 622.

Members to render every assistance to the United Nations in the execution of this resolution and to refrain from giving assistance to the North Korean authorities."[930]

On June 27, 1950 President Truman issued "the Statement on Korea" and sent the US Navy Seventh Fleet to the Taiwan Strait in order to prevent any attack on Formosa by the Chinese Communists. On August 24, 1950, the PRC's Minister of Foreign Affairs Zhou (Chou) En-Lai sent a cablegram to the UN Secretary-General Trygve Lie, claiming that the United States had violated China's territory.[931] At the same time, the Soviet Union also circulated a memorandum to the members of the UN Security Council accusing the United States of violating China's territory by its aggression against Formosa.[932]

The US Government in a strong statement denied that it violated China's territory because the island of Taiwan was not China's territory. On August 25, 1950, the US Ambassador to the UN Warren Austin delivered a letter to the UN Secretary-General stating that "[t]he United States has not encroached on the territory of China."[933] The letter continued, "The actual status of the island is that it is territory taken from Japan by the victory of the Allied Forces in the Pacific. Like other such territories, its legal status cannot be fixed until there is international action to determine its future."[934]

In September 1950, while the Security Council continued to deal with the Complaint of aggression upon the Republic of Korea, it received a "Complaint of armed invasion of Taiwan (Formosa)" from the representatives of the USSR filed on behalf of the People's Republic of China.[935] On November 27, 1950, when a Security Council meeting was convened at the request of the USSR, the Security Council, over the objection of the USSR, joined the

[930] UN S.C. Resolution 82 (1950); S/1501.

[931] *See supra* note 622.

[932] *See* Warren R. Austin, *Position on the Formosan Question, Letter to UN Sec'y-Gen., Trygve Lie* (Aug. 25, 1950), *in* DEP'T ST. BULL., Sept. 1950, at 411.

[933] *Id.* at 412.

[934] *Id.*

[935] Upon receipt of the complaint, the Security Council passed a resolution to postpone the decision until the regular meeting. The resolution first "noted the declaration of the People's Republic of China regarding the armed invasion of Formosa" and then decided "to defer consideration of [the] question until the first meeting of the Council." S.C. Res. 87, UN SCOR, 506th mtg. at 87–88, UN Doc. S/1836 (1950).

Complaint (a) of armed invasion of Taiwan (Formosa) with the Complaint (b) of aggression upon the Republic of Korea in the same agenda for discussion.[936] Since Complaint (b) dealt with the Korean War, only Complaint (a) will be discussed here.

At the morning meeting of the Security Council on November 28, 1950, the US Representative Warren Austin reiterated the US position as stated in his letter of August 25 to the UN Secretary-General.[937] When the meeting resumed in the afternoon, Representative Wu Hsiu-chuan of the Central People's Government of the PRC argued that since June 27, 1950 the Seventh Fleet of the United States had been invading the territorial waters of China around Taiwan so as to prevent the Central People's Government of the People's Republic of China from exercising sovereignty on Taiwan. He stated,

> *"People with any common sense know that Taiwan is an inseparable part of the territory of China. Long before Christopher Columbus the Chinese people were already in Taiwan. Long before the United States achieved its own independence, Taiwan had already become an inseparable part of the territory of China, civilized nations of the whole world have never conceded that the occupation of Taiwan by imperialist Japan during the fifty-year period from 1895 to 1945 was justifiable."*
>
> *"Precisely because Taiwan is an inseparable part of China, the Cairo Declaration jointly signed on 1 December 1943 by the Government of China, the United States of America and the United Kingdom explicitly stipulated that 'it is their'—the three great Powers- 'purpose ... that all territories Japan has stolen from the Chinese, such as Manchuria, Formosa and the Pescadores, shall be restored to the Republic of China.'"*
>
> *"[T]he Cairo Declaration is a solemn international commitment which the United States Government has pledged itself to observe. As one of the principal provisions concerning the unconditional surrender of Japan, this solemn international commitment was again laid down in the Potsdam Declaration which was signed jointly on 26 July 1945 by China, the United States and United Kingdom, and was subsequently adhered to by the Soviet Union."*
>
> *"On 2 September 1945, Japan signed the Instrument of Surrender, the first article of which explicitly provided that Japan 'accept'—I am quoting from the original wording—'the provisions set forth in the Declaration*

936 UN SCOR, 525th Mtg. Nov. 27, 1950, S/PV .525.
937 UN SCOR, 526th Mtg. Nov. 28, 1950; S/PV.526.

> *issued by the heads of the Governments of the United States, China and Great Britain on July 26, 1945, at Potsdam, and subsequently adhered to by the Union of Soviet Socialist Republics.' When the Chinese Government accepted the surrender of the Japanese armed forces in Taiwan and exercised sovereignty over the island, Taiwan became, not only* de jure, *but also* de facto, *an inalienable part of Chinese territory, and this has been the situation as regards Taiwan since 1945. For this reason, during the five post-war years from 1945 to 27 June 1950, no one has ever questioned the fact that Taiwan is an inalienable part of Chinese territory,* de jure *and* de facto.*"*[938]

At the end of the discussion, two proposed Resolutions were put to separate votes. One was prepared by the government of the USSR. The other was prepared by the PRC government. The proposed Resolution for Complaint[939] prepared by the USSR was put to a vote first. The pro-

[938] UN SCOR, 527th mtg, Nov. 30, 1950; S/PV.527, 19. *See* http://www.un.org/en/ga/search/view_doc.asp?symbol=S/PV.527 (Last visited 06/19/2014).

[939] The proposed Resolution submitted by the Soviet Union follows: "*The Security Council*, "*Considering* the appeal of the Central People's Government of the People's Republic of China regarding the act of aggression committed by the Government of the United States of America in the form of the invasion by armed forces of the United States of America of the Island of Taiwan, which is an inalienable part of the territory of China, as is admitted in the Cairo Agreement between the three Powers, *viz*. the United States of America, Great Britain and China, of 1 December 1943, and of the intervention thereby on the part of the Government of the United States of America in the internal affairs of China. "*Considering* also the declaration of the representative of the United States of America to the United Nations, Mr. Austin, concerning the appeal of the Central People's Government of the People's Republic of China to the Security Council on the question of Taiwan, "Condemning the said acts of the Government of the United States of America as an act of aggression and as an intervention in the internal affairs of China," *And resolves*, with the object of putting an end to such illegal acts, which violate the State sovereignty of the Chinese Republic, to propose to the Government of the United States of America that it immediately withdraw all its air, sea and land forces from the island of Taiwan and form other territories belonging to China."

UN SCOR, 530th mtg. S/PV .530, 22; S/1757.

posal was rejected.[940] Then the proposed Resolution prepared by the PRC[941] was put to a vote. The proposal was also rejected.[942]

Since the proposals were rejected, no Resolution was adopted. Thus, the Security Council did not make or adopt any position with respect to the title to the island of Taiwan and certainly did not make any statement, express or implied, indicating that Taiwan was China's territory.

Legalistically, in August 1950 when the PRC claimed title to the island of Taiwan in the United Nations, the island of Taiwan was still Japan's territory. After Japan surrendered unconditionally in August 1945, the United States became the occupying power of Japan under international law. As the occupying power, the United States had right to send in its armed forces to the occupied territory to protect the territory and its inhabitants.

[940] The votes were: one in favor (the USSR), nine against (China, Cuba, Ecuador, Egypt, France, Norway, United Kingdom, United States of America, Yugoslavia), and one did not participate in voting (India). *Id.*

[941] The proposed Resolution submitted by the People's Republic of China and sponsored by the Soviet Union follows:

"The Security Council,"

"Recognizing that the invasion and occupation of Taiwan by armed forces of the Government of the United States of America constitute open and direct aggression against Chinese territory,"

"Condemns the Government of the United States of America for its criminal acts of armed aggression against the Chinese territory of Taiwan, and armed intervention in Korea";

> 'Resolves *to demand the complete withdrawal by the Government of the United States of America of its forces of armed aggression from Taiwan, in order that peace and security in the Pacific and in Asia may be ensured; and further"*
>
> 'Resolves *to demand the withdrawal from Korea of the armed forces of the United States of America and all other countries and to leave the people of North and South Korea to settle the domestic affairs of Korea themselves, so that a peaceful solution of the Korean question may be achieved."*

UN SCOR, 530th mtg. S/PV .530, 22; S/1757.

[942] The votes were: one in favor (the USSR), nine against (China, Cuba, Ecuador, Egypt, France, Norway, United Kingdom, United States of America, Yugoslavia), and one did not participate in voting (India). *Id.*

3. THE UN GENERAL ASSEMBLY'S POSITION ON THE LEGAL STATUS OF TAIWAN

When the Peace Treaty of San Francisco entered into force in 1952, the United Nations was bound by the Peace Treaty on its disposition of the island of Taiwan. Five years after the United Nations was formed, the Peace Treaty of San Francisco was signed. All signatories of the Treaty except Japan were members of the United Nations at the time. Although the United Nations itself is not a signatory to the Treaty, it is also bound by the territorial disposition of the Treaty for three reasons. The first reason is that the United Nations has no capability to take a position on the title to a territory. The United Nations is loosely formed by sovereign States and has no legal personality. It, unlike a corporation in municipal law, has no will of its own and makes decisions only by collective actions. A UN resolution or its position on a matter simply reflects the collective will or position of its majority members.

Fundamentally the United Nations has no capability to take a position on the title to a territory. The United Nations is an organization formed by sovereign States to maintain international peace and security. It is not empowered by the UN Charter or other authorities to decide the territory of States. In addition, the only way for the United Nations to express its position on the legal status of a territory is by members voting either in the General Assembly or in the Security Council. In international law, the title to a territory cannot be decided by unrelated States or an international organization in any way. There are only a few recognized ways to acquire a territory in international law. Voting by unrelated States in the United Nations is not one of them.

The second reason that the United Nations is bound by the Peace Treaty of San Francisco is the nature of the Treaty. As stated in Chapter 3, The Territorial State, all States, including States that are not parties to a territorial treaty, are bound by the provisions of a treaty that disposes of territory. By a corollary, the United Nations, an international organization made up of States, is also bound by the territorial arrangement of territorial treaties, including the Peace Treaty of San Francisco.[943]

The third reason that the United Nations is bound by the Peace Treaty of San Francisco is that the United Nations cannot now take a position against the will of its majority members expressed in the Treaty.

[943] *See* Vienna Convention, *supra* note 365, Art. 38; *see also* WALLACE, *supra* note 36, at 206.

All 49 Allies that signed the Peace Treaty of San Francisco were the UN members in 1951. At the time, the total members of the UN numbered only 60. That means that when the Treaty was signed, more than four-fifths of the UN members were parties to the Treaty and were, thus, bound by it. Thus, the Treaty was signed by a majority of UN's members at the time and the United Nations had an obligation toward its members to abide the territorial disposition of the Peace Treaty of San Francisco. Any collective decision of the United Nations now on a position on the title to the island of Taiwan different from the territorial disposition of the Treaty would necessarily contravene the collective will of its majority members in 1951. On the part of the UN members that signed the Treaty, they are aware that Japan did not cede the island of Taiwan to China under the Treaty and cannot vote in the General Assembly or the Security Council for a position that the island of Taiwan is China's territory without contravening what they had agreed to in the Treaty.

4. UN'S "ONE-CHINA POLICY"

A. Secretary-General's Statement on Taiwan's Legal Status

In 2003, Secretary-General Kofi Annan created a term: "The (UN's) one-China policy." When an ROC official (The General Director of Taipei Economic and Cultural Office) from Taiwan attempted to enter the UN Headquarters to attend a press conference in May 2003, Kofi Annan barred him from entry "because of the organization (the UN)'s one-China policy."[944] This is the first time that a chief executive of the United Nations referred to such a policy. As mentioned earlier, Annan at the time used the statement "the organization's one-China policy" to infer that Taiwan was part of China.

B. Origin of UN's One-China Policy

By the nature of the organization, the United Nations cannot have a policy without a resolution of its Security Council or General Assembly. As pointed out earlier, when the Japanese Ambassador to the UN Min Aichi in 1970 used the term "one-China" to express Japan's policy, it addressed the conjectured recognition of a new State and not with title to the island of Taiwan.[945] If the United Nations had a policy on Taiwan, it could be

[944] *See UN Bars Taiwanese Official From Briefing*, *supra* note 586.
[945] *See supra* text accompanying note 858.

created only from Resolution No. 2758 of 1971 because it was the only resolution adopted in the United Nations concerning the ROC government or Taiwan.

The Secretariat of the United Nations from time to time has stated that its policy is that Taiwan is a province of China. The policy is in fact derived from Resolution 2758. In 1997, the Committee for Admission of Taiwan to the United Nations (the CATUN), a private organization in the United States and sympathetic to Taiwan's cause, sent to the UN Secretary-General Kofi Annan a large box containing thousands of checks, each in the amount of $4.40 payable to the United Nations, collected from US citizens, together with letters of support of Taiwan's membership in the United Nations.[946] Denis Halliday, Officer-in-Charge of Department of Administration and Management, replied in a UN official letterhead, in part,

> *"Please note that under the United Nations Financial Regulations and Rules, voluntary contributions to the Organization may be accepted by the Secretary-General provided that, inter alia, the purposes for which the contributions are made are consistent with the policies, aims and activities of the Organization.*
>
> *"In this connection, I wish to draw your attention to General Assembly resolution 2758 (XXVI) of 25 October 1971, which recognized the Government of the People's Republic of China as the only lawful representative of China to the United Nations. Pursuant to this resolution, the official position of the Secretariat of the United Nations is that* Taiwan is one of the provinces of China.
>
> *"In light of the foregoing, you will understand that the Secretary-General is not in a position to accept the cheques which were collected by the CATUN. I am, therefore, returning herewith the cheques, together with the letters of support."*[947]

The statement in Secretariat's letter that "Pursuant to [Resolution 2758], the official position of the Secretariat of the United Nations is that Taiwan is one of the province of China" was reiteration of a position taken by Kofi Annan.

Annan used the term "the Taiwan province of China" as the reason to reject the ROC's applications to rejoin or join the United Nations or its

946 At the time, the US Government withheld some payments due the United Nations. The $4.40 is the amount of money which represented each US citizen's share of the payments withheld.

947 Letter by Denis Halliday, Officer-in-Charge of Department of Administration and Management of the United Nations dated 3 January 1997(emphasis added). A copy of the letter is in the file of this writer.

related organizations which required statehood for membership, such as the WHO. The term "the Taiwan province of China" logically means that Taiwan is China's territory. It appears that Halliday simply followed Annan's instruction. The following pages will examine whether Resolution 2758 states or indicates that Taiwan is a part of China.

C. The Resolution No. 2758

Resolution No. 2758 of 1971 was one of the major events in the history of the United Nations and changed the fate of the ROC government. For 22 years the ROC government represented the State of China and the 700 million people inhabiting China, whom it did not govern, from October 1949 to October 1971, Thus, the issue before the General Assembly in the October 1971 debates was which government, the ROC government or the PRC government, should represent the State of China and the people inhabiting China in the United Nations. The issue was not who should govern Taiwan and represent the people of Taiwan. Resolution 2758 was a victory for the PRC government. It has three propositions: One, there is only one member State called "China" in the United Nations; Two, the PRC government is the legitimate government of the State of China; Three, in the United Nations, the people in China will be represented by the PRC government thereafter.

The United Nations has no official policy that maintains that China has the title to the island of Taiwan or China has sovereignty over the inhabitants of Taiwan. If the Resolution has created a UN policy, the policy, whether it is now called "one-China" policy or not, does not include a proposition that Taiwan is part of China. The UN General Assembly never discussed an issue concerning title to the island of Taiwan, let alone decided that Taiwan was part of China.

Thus, when Kofi Annan used the statement "the UN's one-China Policy" to infer that the UN's position was that Taiwan was China's territory, he misrepresented the UN's policy. It appears that though neither the UN Security Council nor the General Assembly ever decided or expressed the view that the island of Taiwan was China's territory, the Secretariat of the United Nations adopted a position not authorized by either the Security Council or the General Assembly. Kofi Annan's "the UN's one-China Policy" merely echoed China's one-China principle, rather than any position officially adopted by the United Nations.

The UN Secretariat has simply given in to China's demands. For many years, the PRC government has pressured the United Nations to accept its position that Taiwan is part of China; that the United Nations or other international organizations which require statehood for membership should not admit the ROC or Taiwan as a member; that the associated organizations which do not require statehood for membership should permit the ROC to participate only it uses a name implying that Taiwan is part of China, such as "Chinese Taipei."

Annan's reference to "the Taiwan province of China" was not supported by the Resolution 2758 as he claimed. Annan, as the chief executive of the United Nations, was obliged not to make any statement that misrepresented UN's position. This is especially true when such a statement is not supported by international law, under which the institution was formed and operated. Although his label of "the Taiwan province of China" could not legitimize China's claim to the island of Taiwan, he has misled others in international politics.

The successor to Kofi Annan, Ban Ki-Moon, also expressed the view that Resolution 2758 had produced UN's "one-China policy." On July 19, 2007 when President Chen Shui-bian of the ROC sent to the UN Secretariat an application for it to join the United Nations in the name of "Taiwan," Ban Ki-Moon rejected the application on the ground of the UN's one-China policy based on Resolution 2758.[948] On July 27, when Ban Ki-Moon was asked about the ROC's application, Ban replied that membership of the United Nations was only granted to "sovereign countries" and that "the position of the United Nations is that Taiwan is part of China."[949]

Almost immediately after that time, the UN Secretariat received a verbal message called "nonpaper" from the Bush Administration.[950] The message of the nonpaper was that the UN Secretariat's policy statement that "Taiwan is a part of China" is a "mistake".[951] It urged the UN Secretariat to review its policy on the status of Taiwan and to avoid taking

[948] *See UN secretary-general stops calling 'Taiwan part of China, supra* note 590.

[949] *Id.* "The United Nations has promulgated documents asserting that 'the United Nations considers Taiwan for all purposes to be an integral part of the People's Republic of China' (e.g., in a March 28[2007] commucation from the SYG to the Republic of Nauru)." Nonpaper, *supra* note 908.

[950] *See supra* text accompanying note 908.

[951] *Id.*

sides in a sensitive matter.[952] On July 31, 2007, when Chen sent a second letter to Ban urging him to reconsider his decision on the application, the letter was returned by Ban without any comment.[953] A news article reported that "the UN Secretary-general stops calling Taiwan part of China."[954]

The issue of the title to the island of Taiwan has never been brought before the General Assembly since the creation of the United Nations. This work has discussed in detail the debates on the question of China's representation in the United Nations from 1950 to 1971 to demonstrate that not once did the discussions in the United Nations involve the title to the island of Taiwan before or during the debates leading to Resolution 2758. When the General Assembly adopted Resolution 2758, members of the General Assembly voted on only one issue: which government's representatives should sit in China's seat.

D. The Resulting Effect of UN's One-China Policy

The United Nations was organized to maintain the peace of the world and promote the welfare of the peoples through the enforcement of international law. On the one hand, it should uphold justice and respect right rather than might. On the other hand, it should not allow itself to create a situation in which international conflict persists.

Two recent Secretaries-General of the United Nations created the erroneous perception that Taiwan was a part of China under the so-called UN's "one-China policy."[955] Kofi Annan and his successor Ban Ki-Moon repeatedly said that under the UN's one-China policy, Taiwan was "a province of China."

The two Secretaries-General have misrepresented the policy of the United Nations. If the United Nations has a "one-China policy" under Resolution 2758, the policy has three propositions mentioned in Chapter 5, Political Status of the ROC in Taiwan. None of them touches

952 *Id.*

953 President Chen Shui-bian's letter to UN Secretary-General Ban Ki-moon on July 31. [2007], *available at* http://www.taiwanunme.tw/ct.asp?xItem=258&CtNode = 2&Prev=313&next=326. Last visited 10/2/2007. *Also see* Chiehyu Lin. *supra* note 590.

954 *Id.*

955 "[I]n 2007, the United Nations issued a quiet declaration that it considers Taiwan for all purposes to be an integral part of the People's Republic of China."(John Tkacik, Jr. "*Taiwan's 'Unsettled' International Status: Preserving US Options in the Pacific,*" *supra* note 904.

upon the issue of territory. Thus, UN's policy, if there is any, does not include a notion that "Taiwan is part of China."

As mentioned earlier, in 2007 the US Department of State, realizing that the UN Secretariat had often made erroneous statements, notified the Secretary General Ban Ki-Moon that he should stop referring to Taiwan as a province of China. The United Nations and its officials, including its Secretaries-General, have an obligation to refrain from making erroneous statements, such as "Taiwan is part of China" or making reference to "The Taiwan province of China." Other international organizations should do the same.

CHAPTER 9

The Legal Status and the Political Status of Taiwan in International Law

Contents

This chapter examines the legal status of Taiwan and then analyzes the political status of Taiwan in international law. In analyzing Taiwan's political status, it first examines what Taiwan is *not* before it attempts to characterize what Taiwan is in international law.

1. THE LEGAL STATUS OF TAIWAN IN INTERNATIONAL LAW

Since a territorial political institution subject to sovereignty of a State cannot be a State, before examining the political status of Taiwan (whether Taiwan is a State), it must be determined first that Taiwan is not subject to any sovereignty. That Taiwan is not subject to sovereignty of China is extensively discussed in Chapters 6, China's Sovereignty Over Taiwan Before the US One-China Policy, and 7, Sovereignty Over Taiwan Under US' One-China Policy. This section will examine whether any other State has sovereignty over Taiwan.

For some time, a few commentators in Taiwan have argued that the island of Taiwan is a US territory.[956] More recently, some people have claimed that Taiwan is under the sovereignty of the United States. Some in Taiwan even brought a suit in US courts to force a declaratory

[956] John Hsieh, *Who has sovereignty?* Taipei Times, 06/25/2006, p. 8. Roger Lin, *Letter to Editor: Taiwan is US territory*, Taipei Times, 12/31/2006, p. 8.

The One-China Policy: State, Sovereignty, and Taiwan's International Legal Status
DOI: http://dx.doi.org/10.1016/B978-0-08-102314-3.00009-4

decision on the matter. In *Roger C.S. Lin, et al.* v. *the USA*,[957] the plaintiffs, who were residents of Taiwan and members of the Taiwan Nation Party, alleged that they had "attempted multiple times to submit applications for US passports to the American Institute in Taiwan (AIT) [in Taipei][958] for processing; the AIT refused to accept the applications." They then brought an action against the United States in the US District Court of the District of Columbia. The Plaintiffs sought in the action "essentially two declarations: (1) The AIT's refusal to process the individual plaintiffs' passport applications wrongfully deprived them of their status as US nationals and attendant rights; and (2) Plaintiffs are US nationals entitled to all associated rights, particularly those flowing from the First, Fifth, Eighth, and Fourteenth Amendments [of the US Constitution]."[959]

The Plaintiffs claimed that they were entitled to US passports because, they argued, "they have rights and privileges as United States nationals." They alleged that "the US [is] the principal occupying Power [after Japan surrendered at the end of the Second World War], holding sovereignty over Taiwan and title to its territory in trust for the benefit of the Taiwanese people." The District Court dismissed the case on the ground of lack of subject matter jurisdiction under the political question doctrine. The court reasoned that "*the sovereignty of Taiwan* was an undecided question"[960] and "[t]he determination of who is sovereign over specific territory is non-justiciable,"[961] meaning that it was not a matter that a court could decide.

On appeal by the plaintiffs, the US Court of Appeals for the District of Columbia reviewed the case[962] and affirmed the decision of the district court. The Court of Appeals stated that "[i]dentifying *Taiwan's sovereign* is an antecedent question to [Plaintiffs'] claim,"[963] meaning that the sovereign of Taiwan must be determined in order to decide whether the

[957] *Roger C. S. Lin, et al.* v. *the U.S.A.*, 539 F. Supp.2d 173 (US District Ct for the District of Columbia, 2008); 561 F.3d 502; US Ct. of App. D.C. 191.(2009); 130 S. Ct. 202, (2009).(US Supreme Court, certiorari denied.).

[958] American Institute in Taiwan was created under Taiwan Relations Act. *See supra* note 503, Sec. 6.

[959] As summarized by the Court of Appeals from Amended Complaint 18–19 in 561 F.3d 502.

[960] *Id.* 508 (emphasis added).

[961] *Id.* 506.

[962] *Id.* In reviewing the decision below, the Court of Appeals retried the case. ("review the district court's [decision] de novo.")

[963] *Id.* 506 (emphasis added).

residents of Taiwan were the US nationals. The Court then said that "[u]nder the political question doctrine, a court must decline jurisdiction if there exists "a textually demonstrable constitutional commitment of the issue to a coordinate political department,"[964] citing a US Supreme Court case, *Baker v. Carr,* as authority.[965] This meant that the court would not decide an issue that should clearly be the function of another branch of the government. The Court concluded that "[b]ecause deciding *sovereignty of Taiwan* is a political task, [Plaintiffs'] case is nonjusticiable."[966] It concluded that "[a]ddressing [Plaintiffs'] claims would require *identification of Taiwan's sovereign*; The Executive Branch has deliberately remained silent on this issue and we cannot intrude on its decision. Therefore, as the district court correctly concluded, consideration of [Plaintiffs'] claims is barred by the political question doctrine."[967]

Both the US District Court and the US Court of Appeals dismissed plaintiffs' case on the ground that the plaintiffs' nationality could not be decided without deciding who had sovereignty of Taiwan, which was a political question.

The US Constitution, in setting up three branches (the executive; the legislative; and the judiciary) of the government for exercising the State power, does not use or define the term "political question." In *Baker* v. *Carr*[968] cited by the District Court, the US Supreme Court enumerated six factors that may render a case nonjusticiable under the Political Question doctrine: (1) textually demonstrable constitutional commitment of the issue to a coordinate political department; (2) a lack of judicially discoverable and manageable standards for resolving it; (3) the impossibility of deciding without an initial policy determination of a kind clearly for nonjudicial discretion; (4) the impossibility of a court's undertaking independent resolution without expressing lack of respect due coordinate branches of government; (5) an unusual need for unquestioning adherence to a political decision already made; or (6) the potentiality of embarrassment of multifarious pronouncements by various departments on one question.[969] The US District Court in *Schneider*[970] said that "[t]o find a

[964] *Id.*
[965] Baker v. Carr, 369 US 186, 82 S. Ct. 691, 7 L. Ed. 2d 663 (1962).
[966] 561 F.3d 502, 505 (emphasis added).
[967] *Id.* 508 (emphasis added).
[968] *Baker* v. *Carr. See supra* note 965.
[969] *Id*, at 217.
[970] *Schneider* v. The US, 412 F.3d.190 (US District Court, District of D.C.).

political question, [the Court] need only conclude that one factor is present, not all."[971]

Political questions are the tasks of the Executive and the Legislative branches to decide. Some questions, such as the question of recognition of a new State and recognition of a new government, are clearly political questions for the Executive to decide. The question of which State has sovereignty over a particular territory is also a political question, and the judicial branch follows the decisions of the Executive and the Legislative.[972] The US Supreme Court Justice Gray in *Jones* v. *United States*[973] wrote as follows: "Who is the sovereign, de jure or de facto, of a territory, is not a judicial, but a political question, the determination of which by *the legislative* and *executive departments* of any government conclusively binds the judges, as well as all other officers, citizens, and subjects of that government."[974]

In *Roger C. S. Lin,* both the District Court and the Court of Appeals posed the determining question as "Who has sovereignty of Taiwan?" The Court of Appeals said that "addressing the Plaintiffs' claim requires identification of Taiwan's sovereign." It then stated that "'sovereignty of Taiwan' was a political question," but "[the] Executive Branch has deliberately remained silent on this issue[975] [and] [d]espite the executive renunciation of ties with the (Republic of China) ROC, Congress pledged to maintain relations with the people on Taiwan, and to supply the government with weapons. Thus began decades of *strategic ambiguity* with respect to sovereignty over Taiwan."[976]

However, the issue in *Roger C.S. Lin* was narrower than what the Courts posed. The plaintiffs argued that the United States had sovereignty over the residents of Taiwan because "the United States was the true occupying power of Taiwan" under the Peace Treaty of San Francisco,[977] and thus had sovereignty of Taiwan.

US' sovereignty over the US citizens and nationals is based on its sovereignty over its territory. Thus, the US Congress defines a noncitizen

971 *Id.* at 194.

972 *See supra* text accompanying note 511. The US Court of Appeal for the District of Columbia. *Roger C. S. Lin, et al.* v. *the U.S.A.*, *supra* note 957.

973 *Jones* v. *United States*, 137 US 202, at 212, 11 S. Ct. 80, at 83, 34 L. Ed. 691.

974 *Id.* (emphasis added).

975 561 F.3d 502, at 508.

976 *Id.* 505 (emphasis added).

977 *See Roger C. S. Lin, et al.* v. *the U.S.A.*, *supra* note 957.

national as a person "born in an outlying possession of the United States on or after the date of formal acquisition of such possession."[978] The issue in the present case was actually: Whether the United States had sovereignty of Taiwan, not "Who had sovereignty of Taiwan" as broadly phrased by the Court.[979]

Deciding whether the United States has sovereignty of Taiwan is a much easier task than deciding who had sovereignty of Taiwan. Whether the United States has sovereignty of Taiwan depends on whether the United States has the title to the island of Taiwan. As it was pointed out in Chapter 3, The Territorial State, sovereignty of the neo-modern State is based on territory. Whether the United States had sovereignty of Taiwan when the plaintiffs applied for the US passports depended on whether the United States had the title to the island of Taiwan at the time. This question could be decided on the opinions (actions) or the policy already expressed by the Executive and Legislative branches.

The United States did not acquire the title to the island of Taiwan by conquest, treaty, or occupation. An examination of each of these scenarios follows. The United States has not acquired the island of Taiwan by conquest. As discussed earlier, when two States engage in a war, the victorious State may annex the defeated State that has unconditionally surrendered by conquest. John Foster Dulles said that "the United States, [as] the occupying power [of Japan], could practically do [as] much as it wanted."[980] Although there was a voice for annexing Japan after it surrendered, the United States chose not to do so. Had the US annexed Japan when she surrendered, it would have the title to the island to Taiwan today.

The United States did not acquire the title to the island of Taiwan by any treaty. The United States acquired all its Territories by treaties or agreements: Guam and Puerto Rico from Spain in the 1898 Treaty of Paris; American Samoa by a 1900 treaty with Germany; Virgin Islands from Denmark by a purchase agreement in 1917; the Northern Mariana Islands, which were included in the US Trust Territory of the Pacific after WWII, by a mutual agreement in 1978 with the approval of the United Nations. The United States did not receive the title to the island of

[978] 8 U.S.C. ' 1408.

[979] A person born outside of the US territory may acquire the US citizenship. But the plaintiffs in this case claim that they are "the US nationals" because the United States has sovereignty over Taiwan.

[980] DEP'T ST. BULL., Aug. 1951, at 347 (emphasis added).

Taiwan under the Peace Treaty of San Francisco. The same reasons that China did not acquire title to the island of Taiwan under the Peace Treaty applied to the United States. The Peace Treaty of San Francisco leaves the island of Taiwan free of any State's sovereignty. Under the terms of the Treaty, Japan simply abandoned Taiwan. Nor did the United States receive the title to the island of Taiwan under any other treaty.

Finally, the United States did not acquire the title to the island of Taiwan by occupation. As explained in Chapter 6, China's Sovereignty Over Taiwan Before the US One-China Policy, the United States, as the occupying power, has possession of the island of Taiwan,[981] even though it did not maintain actual possession by establishing governmental offices and services, such as post offices, or a military government, but asked the ROC government to administer Taiwan on its behalf. However, the United States did not acquire the title to the island of Taiwan by occupation.[982] In summary, the United States has not acquired the title to the island of Taiwan by any recognizable means in international law.

More important is that the United States has never claimed that Taiwan is a US territory. No territory can be part of a State unless the State claims it. More specifically, no people in a territory can claim that they are the nationals of the United States unless the US claims title to the territory. The US Executive branch never claimed title to the island of Taiwan. The US Government did not require Japan to cede the island of Taiwan to the United States in the Peace Treaty of San Francisco. As pointed out earlier, the Deputy Director of the Taiwan Coordination Office in the State Department in the Bush Administration, said in her 2007 letter to a US citizen that "The United States has never claimed to have acquired title to the island of Taiwan by law, treaty or conquest."[983] An official document issued by the US Government specifically provides that "the US territory includes the 50 states, the District of Columbia, Puerto Rico, the Virgin Islands, Guam, the Northern Mariana Islands, American Samoa, and the territorial waters adjoining the land areas of the United States."[984] The list does not include Taiwan.

[981] *See supra* text accompanying note 777.

[982] *American Insurance Co.* v. *Cantor. See supra* note 397. The 1907 Hague Convention Respecting the Laws and Customs of War on Land, *supra* note 400, Art. 55.

[983] *See* Letter of Sue Bremner, *supra* note 906.

[984] The US Code, Title 48, Chap. 10, Sec. 1469a lists US territories and insular possessions. Taiwan is not one of them.

The US Congress has never adopted any statute or resolution that provides or implies that the island of Taiwan is a US territory. In defining the US territory, the US Code on "Foreign Relations" defines the "United States" as "the continental United States, Alaska, Hawaii, Puerto Rico, Guam, the Virgin Islands of the United States, and all other United States territories and possessions."[985] The term "the [US] possessions" in the definition of "noncitizen national of the United States"[986] and in the definition of "outlying possessions of the United States"[987] does not include Taiwan. In fact, the Court of Appeals in *Roger R.S. Lin* applied these statutes in rejecting the Plaintiffs' claim that they were US nationals.[988]

Specifically with respect to the title to the island of Taiwan, the US Senate, which approved the Peace Treaty of San Francisco in 1952, was aware that the United States did not acquire the title to the island of Taiwan under the Treaty. The enactment of the Taiwan Relations Act in 1979 by the US Congress is positive proof that the US Congress does not regard the island of Taiwan a US territory. Section 3 of the Act provides that "the United States will make available to Taiwan such defense articles and defense services in such quantity as may be necessary to enable Taiwan to maintain a sufficient self-defense capability." The provision in the Act implies that the United States did not regard Taiwan a US territory. As early legal writers and political philosophers have said, the purpose of establishing a State is to create a hard shell to protect its territory and its people. The government, which exercises the State power, is entrusted by the people of the responsibility to protect its people and

[985] Title 22: Foreign Relations, Sec. 51.1(j).

[986] 8 U.S.C. ' 1408. "Noncitizen national of the United States" mean "a person who, though not a citizen of the United States, is born in an outlying possession of the United States on or after the date of formal acquisition of such possession."

[987] *Id.* ' 1101(a)(29). "Outlying possessions of the United States" means "American Samoa and Swains Island."

[988] *Roger C. S. Lin, et al.* v. *the U.S.A.*, *supra* note 957. On 2/27/2015, Roger C.S. Lin, Julian T. A. Lin, and Taiwan Civil Government filed a new complaint against United States of America and the Republic of China in the US District Court for the District of Columbia, pleading the court, among others, for a Declaratory judgment declaring that the ROC's 1946 Nationality Decrees stripping the entire population of Taiwan of their Japanese nationality were promulgated without authority. *Roger Lin Roger C.S. Lin, Julian T. A. Lin, and Taiwan Civil Government* v. *United States of America and the Republic of China,*177 F. Supp. 3d 242(2016). The case was dismissed for lack of subject matter jurisdiction. An appeal filed by the plaintiffs is still pending as of March 2017.

territory from foreign invasions. Such responsibility is so fundamental and obvious that it does not need any Executive order or legislation to spell out. No country in the world will leave the national defense of a part of its territory to that territory itself. The Taiwan Relations Act proclaims that the US Government is committed to protect Taiwan from outside invaders. If the US Government had considered the island of Taiwan a US territory, as a matter of law, it would not have needed to enact the Taiwan Relations Act.

Without the title to the island of Taiwan, the United States has no sovereignty over Taiwan and its inhabitants. The "strategic ambiguity" was created by the US Administrations by their expressions regarding China's claim on Taiwan. The ambiguity is on China's claim to the island of Taiwan, not the US' title to the island. Thus, the United States has no sovereignty over Taiwan; the plaintiffs were not nationals of the United States. The Court could have decided the case more narrowly by following the policy already made or expressed by the Executive and Legislative branches, instead of avoiding the question.

Finally, Taiwan was not placed under the UN's trusteeship after the Second World War because no mandate was issued by the United Nations for Taiwan. In summary, none of the major players in the Far East—Japan, China, and the United States—has the title to the island of Taiwan. Since no other State claims the title to the island, Taiwan is not subject to the sovereignty of any State.

2. THE POLITICAL STATUS OF TAIWAN IN INTERNATIONAL LAW

Although Taiwan is not subject to the sovereignty of any State, it is not a State. As discussed in Chapter 2, The State and Sovereignty, a territorial political institution must claim statehood in order to be a State. An official comment to Section 201 of the Restatement states that "an entity is not a state if it does not claim to be a state."[989] The present President of the ROC in Taiwan Tsai Ing-wen does not claim that Taiwan is a State. She refers to the two sides of the [Taiwan] Strait as two institutions.[990]

Even though former President Chen Shui-bian claimed that Taiwan was a "sovereign independent country," Taiwan was not a State under his

[989] The Restatement, *supra* note 212, ' 201, Comment f (3d Ed., 1987).
[990] Tsai Ing-wen's inaugural speech. *See supra* note 619.

administration. The following will analyze and comment on several views expressed by political leaders and the commentators in Taiwan who characterized Taiwan as a State.

Former President Chen Shui-bian of the ROC expressed his view that Taiwan was a country on several occasions. He often did not distinguish "the Republic of China" and "Taiwan" and used the two terms interchangeably. After he declared that "the Republic of China is a sovereign independent country," he further confused the people by also making the statement "Taiwan is a sovereign independent country."[991] There was no clear indication on why he made the two statements interchangeable. The ROC and Taiwan have completely different meanings and connotations. "The ROC" refers to what was once the government of China, and "Taiwan" refers to the island or a political institution across the Taiwan Strait from China. One possibility was that he wanted to appease some people in Taiwan by showing them that when he mentioned "the Republic of China," he meant "Taiwan."

It is important to recognize that the question of whether Taiwan is a State is different from the question of whether the ROC is a State. The two questions involve different issues. That the ROC is a government, not a State, was explained in details in Chapter 5, Political Status of the ROC in Taiwan. Taiwan is also not a state, but for different reasons.

Taiwan was not a State under President Chen Shui-bian for three reasons. The first reason is that fundamentally the territory had no government of its own essential for establishing a State. In the State theory discussed in Chapter 2, The State and Sovereignty, one of the essential elements of the neo-modern State is government. The government means a governing authority set up by the people of the territory to manage the State.[992] Although there was a governing authority in Taiwan—the ROC government—it was a government of China in exile. Its official position was that it was the legitimate government of China.[993]

The ROC is not the government of Taiwan. The ROC was organized in China under the ROC Constitution. A constitution is adopted by the

[991] *See supra* text accompanying note 581.

[992] *See supra* text accompanying note 209.

[993] While Ma Ying-jeou was the president of the ROC, he said that "China" in the term "One China" refers to the Republic of China. Staff Reporter, *Ma's "one ROC, two areas" declaration peeves Chinese scholars*. WANT CHINA TIMES, 05/22/2012, *available at* http://www.wantchinatimes.com/news-subclass-cnt.aspx?id=20120522000086&cid=1101. Last visited 07/08/2012.

ruler of a kingdom or the people of a republican State to lay down the fundamental political structure of the State, including a government. A government essential for establishing a State in a territory cannot be one organized under the constitution of the peoples outside of its territory. The ROC Constitution was China's constitution adopted in 1946 in Nanjing (Nanking) by the people of China for the State of China at the time when the island of Taiwan was not part of China. In 1950, while the ROC government administered Taiwan under the assignment of the US Government, British Foreign Secretary Younger in the Attlee administration stated, "[T]here is no Government of Formosa as such."[994] The statement implied that the ROC was not the government of Formosa (Taiwan).

The people of Taiwan did not adopt the ROC Constitution as their own. At no time in the past did the people of Taiwan adopt the ROC Constitution as their constitution. Election of the ROC officials, including elections of the Presidents by the people of Taiwan, and amendments of the ROC Constitution made by the ROC's National Assembly did not make the ROC Constitution a constitution of the people of Taiwan. Thus, the ROC government could not legally be the government of the people of Taiwan. From the beginning, the ROC government was a foreign government to the people of Taiwan. It still is today. A territorial entity without its own government cannot be a State.

The second reason that Taiwan was not a State under President Chen Shui-bian was that Taiwan, as a political institution, never declared establishment of a State. As discussed in Chapter 2, The State and Sovereignty, a territorial political institution with all the required elements of State that has not declared establishment of a State cannot become a State. Thus, even if the ROC under Chen Shui-bian was considered the government of Taiwan, Taiwan was not a State because it never declared the establishment of a new State. A good example is Palestine. Palestine, a political institution with a people residing in a territory with a governing authority, is not a State until it declares establishment of a State. Conversely, once Kosovo declared independence from Serbia and establishment of a new State, Kosovo acquired statehood. The International Court of Justice in an advisory opinion

[994] 478 Parl. Deb., H.C. (5th ser.) (1950) at 60.

declared that the people of Kosovo effectively established a State by such a declaration.[995]

No executive head in Taiwan, including President Lee Teng-hui and President Chen Shui-bian, or representatives of the people have ever declared establishment of a new State of Taiwan, limiting its territory to the island of Taiwan. When Lee Teng-hui made the "special state-to-state" statement, the statement was not a declaration of establishment of a State, as discussed in Chapter 5, Political Status of the ROC in Taiwan.[996] Even if the statement were considered a declaration establishing a State, it would be for the ROC, not for Taiwan.

When Chen Shui-bian of the ROC said that "Taiwan is a sovereign independent country," the statement was not a declaration of establishing a State. That was a statement describing what he believed Taiwan to be, rather than an open and unambiguous declaration of statehood. When a political institution becomes a State by declaration, the new State needs a new political structure and new political order. It has to organize a government under a new political structure to replace the old one. Chen did not abandon the ROC Constitution, but instead continued to operate the government established under the ROC Constitution. He called his government "the Republic of China" and himself the 11th President of the Republic of China,[997] the first President being Jiang (Chiang) Kai-shek.

Unless a political institution meets the requirements of establishing a State discussed in Chapter 2, The State and Sovereignty, no self-proclaimed description of any kind can turn the political institution into a State. During the Chen administration, the DPP (Democratic Progressive Party) politicians in Taiwan, in claiming Taiwan a state, came up with a few variations of its name. Some, including the then Vice-President Annette Lu of the ROC, introduced a description "Taiwan is a country; its name is the Republic of China." Likewise, the ruling DPP Party created a formula equating the ROC with Taiwan (the ROC Taiwan) in an attempt to legitimize the ROC's.

[995] *See* International Court of Justice advisory opinion on Kosovo's declaration of independence, *available at* http://en.wikipedia.org/wiki/International_Court_of_Justice_advisory_opinion_on_Kosovo's_declaration_of_independence. Last visited 04/11/2011.

[996] *See supra* text accompanying note 575.

[997] Chen Shui-bian was the 10th ROC President during his first term.

rule of Taiwan. Without a declaration of establishing a new State, hoping to make Taiwan a State by replacing the name "the ROC" with "Taiwan" or equating the two is illusory because eventually, like an adopted algebraic symbol, "Taiwan" will be replaced by the true name, the "ROC," which is not a State. Joining the two terms "the Republic of China" and "Taiwan" together in any way will not make either the Republic of China or Taiwan a State no matter how they are mixed or twisted.

Still, some people claim that Taiwan is a "*de facto* State." But "de facto State" does not exist in State theory. It is not a legal term in international law. While the term "*de facto* government" is a recognized term,[998] the concept of "*de facto* State" is unknown in international law. A political institution is either a State or not a State. There is nothing inbetween. The Palestinian Authority has said several times in the past that it would declare the establishment of the State of Palestine at a future date. It did not do so because Israel threatened to annex the Palestinian land under its control if Palestine declared statehood without a peace accord with Israel. The Palestinian Authority does not call Palestine a "*de facto* State."

The third reason that Taiwan was not a State under President Chen is that it did not act like a State. A political institution that has become a State must act like one after it is established. The Chen administration never asserted or presented itself in the world community that it was the government of a new State, Taiwan. Notwithstanding Chen's desire to join the United Nations, its administration did not apply to the UN Security Council for "the State of Taiwan" to join as a new member as the UN Charter prescribed. The Chen administration applied to "rejoin" the United Nations every year. At the beginning it used the name "the Republic of China on Taiwan,"[999] but later

[998] After the USSR was established in 1917, the US Government refused to recognize the new government until 1936. But the new government was treated as a "de facto" government of Russia by the US Courts. *See Wulfsohn v. Russian Socialist Federated Soviet Republic, supra* note 379.

[999] *Request for the inclusion of a supplementary item in the agenda of the fifty-fifth session (2000)*, Appendix 1 Explanatory memorandum.

switched to "the Republic of China (Taiwan)."[1000] "The Republic of China" and "Taiwan" are not synonyms. While the Republic of China is a government, Taiwan is not. Even if "Taiwan" is synonymous with the ROC, Taiwan cannot be a State because "The Republic of China" itself is not a State.

After repeated failures of the ROC to "return" to the United Nations in the name of "the Republic of China," in July 2007 President Chen of the ROC sent to the United Nations an application for a membership in the name of "Taiwan."[1001] The Secretary-General Ban Ki-Moon (Ban) returned the application next day on the ground of the UN's one-China policy. Chen did not explain that he was seeking to join as a new state, unrelated to China. In joining WTO, the Chen administration did not apply as a State. He applied to join the organization in the name of "The Customs Territory of Taiwan, Penghu, Kinmen and Matsu, also called Chinese Taipei."[1002] Although some government officials argued that this was done to avoid opposition from China, they should have known that at the time China was not even a member of WTO. Additionally, taking on the name "Chinese Taipei" implied that Taiwan was part of another country, rather than an independent sovereign state.

Taiwan as a political institution has no sovereignty because it is not a State. As discussed before, in the neo-modern State, sovereignty is inseparable from the State. Each State is a sovereign; only a State has sovereignty. Thus, the statement "Taiwan is a sovereign independent country" has no support in State theory and international law.

[1000] *Request for the inclusion of a supplementary item in the agenda of the fifty-eighth session (2002)*, Appendix 1 Explanatory memorandum. By appending the word *Taiwan* to the term *the Republic of China* in parentheses, the term "the Republic of China (Taiwan)" equates "the Republic of China" with "Taiwan." The application to rejoin the UN in 2005 stated that "The Republic of China (Taiwan) is a free and peace-loving sovereign State." But Paragraph 7 of the document states, "Taiwan's participation in the United Nations will help maintain peace, prosperity and stability in Asia and the Pacific." It treats "Taiwan" a synonym of "the Republic of China."

[1001] *See supra* text accompanying note 603.

[1002] The statement accompanying the application of the Republic of China to join the General Agreement on Tariff and Trade (GATT) and the World Trade Organization (WTO) stated that "[t]he Customs Territory of Taiwan, Penghu, Kinmen and Matsu (hereinafter referred to as "Chinese Taipei") is preparing to accede to the General Agreement on Tariffs and Trade (GATT), which itself has been reorganized into the World Trade Organization."

Still, some people in Taiwan hold that "Taiwan's sovereignty resides with the 23 million people." This cannot be true even if Taiwan is a State. The notion of "sovereignty in the people," as discussed in Chapter 2, The State and Sovereignty, means that the people in a democratic State have the ultimate political power; the sovereignty is still in the State. So, in Taiwan which is not a State, the notion of "sovereignty in the people" has no support in the theory of sovereignty. The US Secretary of State Colin Powell's remark "Taiwan is not independent: It does not enjoy sovereignty as a nation" is, unfortunately for the people of Taiwan, true.

At the present, only a few people in Taiwan realize that Taiwan is not a State. The people of Taiwan cannot agree on the political status of Taiwan. And those who claim that Taiwan is a State cannot agree on the name of their country. Colin Powell might have made a remark which displeased many people in Taiwan, but if his remark reflected the view of the world community, the remark should provide the people of Taiwan with an opportunity to reexamine the situation in which they found themselves.

Taiwan is an unusual civil society. After the conclusion of the Peace Treaty of San Francisco, Taiwan has developed into an unusual civil society which is neither an entity subject to any sovereign power nor a State. The Peace Treaty of San Francisco created the unusual situation. A territorial treaty, by its nature, provides final settlement of title to a territory. When the Allied Powers forced Japan to renounce title to the island of Taiwan without making any reservations in the Peace Treaty of San Francisco, both Japan and the Allied Powers lost the power and legal right to dispose of the island. John Dulles, at the Conference in San Francisco for signing the Peace Treaty, said that "[A]rticle 2 merely delimit[s] Japanese sovereignty. The wise course was leaving the future to resolve doubts [on sovereignty over the island of Taiwan] by invoking international solvents other than this Treaty."[1003] Therefore, the island is no longer owned by any State and has not been subject to any sovereignty since then.

This is true even though the United States, as the occupying power, assigned the R.O.C. government to administer Taiwan. In *Roger C.S. Lin,* the US Court of Appeals declined to decide Taiwan's sovereign

[1003] Sec'y John Foster Dulles, *Statements at the Second Plenary Session*, *supra* note 714, at 454.

because it was a political question and "the Executive Branch has deliberately remained silent of this issue."[1004] Thus, as to the United States, the people of Taiwan are not under any sovereignty: they are stateless people. The Court stated that "[T]he people on Taiwan have lived without any uniformly recognized government. In practical terms, this means they have uncertain status in the world community".[1005] Since the island of Taiwan is not subject to sovereignty of any State, a question is: What is the political status of Taiwan in international law?

It is important to recognize that not all civil societies are States. A society in a territory may be a political institution, yet is neither an entity subject to any sovereignty nor a State. Taiwan is such an entity. The US Court of Appeals in *Rogers* v. *Cheng Fu Sheng*[1006] stated that "Formosa is a well-defined geographical, social and political entity."[1007] This work will refer to such society as an *independent territorial entity.*

Although an independent territorial entity is not owned by any State, it is the *people's property,* a concept derived from the Roman law concept of *res humani iuris* or "things subject to human dominion."[1008] *People's property* is property owned by a society or, more specifically, the people of the society as a whole.

Taiwan is not unique in the status of "independent territorial entity" in international law. In the past, Cuba was also at one time such a territorial entity. In the 1898 Treaty of Paris between the United States and Spain, signed to conclude the Spanish–American War, Spain relinquished her title to the island of Cuba without ceding it to any State.[1009] When Cuba was thereafter briefly occupied by the United States until Cuba established statehood, the territory and the society in it were not under

[1004] *Roger C. S. Lin, et al.* v. *the U.S.A.,* 561 F.3d 502; US App. D.C. 191.(2009), *supra* note 957.

[1005] *Id.* at 1.

[1006] *Cheng Fu Sheng* v. *Rogers, supra* note 510.

[1007] *Id.* 3.

[1008] Gaius in Book II, Section 2 states, "The first division of things is into two classes: things subject to divine dominion, and things subject to human dominion." Section 10 states, "Things subject to human dominion *res humani iuris* are either public or private." GAIUS, ELEMENTS OF ROMAN LAW 157, 158 (Edward Poste trans., 2nd Ed. 1994).

[1009] The Treaty of Paris of 1898 between the United States and Spain after the end of the Spanish-American War, *supra* note 723.

any sovereignty.[1010] During that period, Cuba, under the US occupation, was an independent territorial entity. East Timor, for a short period after its independence and before the establishment of a State, was also in a similar status.[1011] Palestine is the same.[1012]

[1010] See Article I of the Treaty of Paris, *supra* note 779.

[1011] After the Indonesian Parliament ratified the inhabitants' votes for independence in the August 1999 referendum, East Timor was not under any sovereignty. Pending a preparation for establishing statehood under the UN administration, the territory was an independent territorial entity. The territory belonged to the people and was owned by the people of East Timor collectively. *See* Daniel Fitzpatrick, *Land Issues in a Newly Independent East Timor*, DEP'T OF THE PARL. LIBRARY (Austl.), Research Paper 21 (2001).

[1012] *See supra* note 325.

PART IV

US Control Over Taiwan

CHAPTER 10

US Policy on Taiwan

Contents

Part IV examines US control over Taiwan. It first analyzes US policy on Taiwan and then examines Taiwan under US control. Finally, it suggests a solution for the Taiwan problem. This chapter discusses the present policy of the United States on Taiwan and the implementation of its policy.

1. US PRESENT POLICY ON TAIWAN

The present US policy on Taiwan is based on the "one-China policy" and the Taiwan Relations Act (TRA).[1013] In 2015, President Obama reiterated his commitment to the Three Joint Communiqués and the TRA when China's President Xi Jinping visited the White House.[1014] The US

[1013] *See* "nonpaper," *supra* note 906. "Our relations with Taiwan are governed by the three Joint Communiqués and the Taiwan Relation Act." *See* Letter of Sue Bremner, *supra* note 906. In 2009, President Obama stated that his administration fully support a one-China policy. *See supra* note 917.

[1014] On September 25, 2015, when China's President Xi Jinping visited President Obama at the White House, President Obama at a press conference said "I reiterated [to Mr. Xi] my strong commitment to the Three Joint Communiqués and the Taiwan Relations Act." William Lowther/Staff reporter, *Obama 'support' Taiwan in Xi talks.* TAIPEI TIMES, Sun, 09/27/2015 p1. http://www.taipeitimes.com/News/front/archives/2015/09/27/2003628680.

The One-China Policy: State, Sovereignty, and Taiwan's International Legal Status
DOI: http://dx.doi.org/10.1016/B978-0-08-102314-3.00010-0

present policy which has been discussed in detail is summarized as follows:

A. The One-China Policy

As pointed out in Chapter 7, Sovereignty Over Taiwan Under US' One-China Policy, the term "one-China policy" in this work refers to the policy formulated in the three Joint Communiqués: The 1972 Shanghai Communiqué of President Richard Nixon; the 1979 Second Communiqué of President Jimmy Carter; and the 1982 Third Communiqué of President Ronald Reagan.

The three Communiqués together set forth five principal propositions:

1. There is only one State called China;
2. The People's Republic of China (PRC) government is the legitimate government of China;
3. The Republic of China (ROC) is not a State;
4. The United States does not recognize the island of Taiwan as China's territory;
5. Both sides of the Taiwan Strait should peacefully settle their dispute.[1015]

B. Taiwan Relations Act

The TRA[1016] enacted in 1979 also created a guiding policy toward Taiwan.[1017] While the Act, on one hand, establishes the American Institute in Taiwan (AIT) to maintain relations with the people of Taiwan and provides its governing authority with defense weapons, on the other hand, it indirectly warns China that "[it] shall not take Taiwan by force."[1018]

The Clinton Administration added a proposition to form the present US policy toward Taiwan. When Clinton became the President, the five propositions of the one-China policy mentioned above constituted his policy to maintain the "status quo of Taiwan." In 1998, President Clinton made the "three-nos statement,"[1019] which included the statement "no US support for an independent Taiwan."[1020]

Since 2000, the US Government has further discouraged the ROC President from advocating Taiwan independence. According to an

[1015] *See supra* text accompanying notes 860.
[1016] *See* Taiwan Relations Act, *supra* note 503.
[1017] *See supra* text accompanying note 826.
[1018] *Id.*
[1019] *See supra* text accompanying note 869.
[1020] *Id.*

account of Chen Shui-bian, the Clinton Administration forced him to pledge in his presidential inauguration in 2000 the policy of "four-nos and one have-no." This policy includes "no Taiwan independence" as long as China will not attack Taiwan.[1021]

If Chen's account is reliable, the Clinton Administration's new policy in 2000 prohibited Chen to advocate Taiwan independence. If language is important in foreign affairs, as it usually is, a change of the tone from a statement of "no support for an independent Taiwan" in the "three-nos statement" to the prohibition of advocating "Taiwan independence" imposed on Chen Shui-bian was a significant change of policy. The policy that the United States "would not support an independent Taiwan" left open a possibility that the United States would allow the people of Taiwan to establish a new State without US assistance.[1022] Clinton's instruction to Chen was, however, a mandate prohibiting him to advocate Taiwan independence. The policy may be considered as the sixth proposition of Clinton's one-China policy on Taiwan.[1023]

President Bush also opposed Taiwan independence. He added a special proposition "no referendum for the people of Taiwan" to his one-China policy. He openly condemned President Chen Shui-bian for proposing a referendum for Taiwan. Thus, the Bush Administration added a new, the seventh, proposition to his one-China policy—no referendum for the people of Taiwan.

When President Obama announced that his administration fully supported the one-China policy without qualification, he acceded to a policy composing the abovementioned propositions.

In January 2017, Donald Trump became the President of the United States. Before the inauguration, Trump answered a telephone call from President Tsai Ing-wen of the ROC in Taiwan to congratulate him. It was the first time, a US President had spoken directly to a president of the ROC in Taiwan since the US officially recognized the PRC government in 1979. The PRC government was furious, charging Trump for violating the one-China policy. On February 9, 2017 President Trump called President Xi Jinping of China. It was said that during the

[1021] *See supra* text accompanying note 579.

[1022] Larry M. Wortzel, criticizing the "three-nos" statement, stated that "Even the January 1, 1979, Communiqué transferring US diplomatic recognition from Taipei to Beijing did not deny the possibility that the democratic Republic of China on Taiwan was a state." *See* Wortzel, *supra* note 845.

[1023] *See supra* text accompanying note 871.

conversation, President Trump agreed to honor "the one-China policy." It is too early to predict how Trump will define and apply the one-China policy in the future.

2. THE IMPLEMENTATION OF THE US POLICY

A. US Protection and Control of Taiwan After Japan Surrendered

The peace and security of the Western Pacific region are vital to the geopolitical strategy of the United States. After the Pacific War and the Korean War, the United States realized that the security of the Western Pacific is as important as the security of Western Europe to the United States.

The major players in the Western Pacific region are China, Japan, and the United States. Taiwan's location and industrial capacity were of particular value to the United States. During the Korean War and the Vietnam Conflict, the United States considered that South Korea, Japan, Taiwan, and the Philippines formed a defensive chain of friendly territories which could be used to stage military forces in a conflict with Communist nations. In 2007, Kerry Dumbaugh, a specialist in Asian affairs, in her report to the US Congress reminded the Congressional Committee members that "The status of Taiwan is a key issue for US foreign policy and a critical point of contention in US relations with China."[1024] Recent surge of China's naval power and its territorial assertion in East China Sea and South China Sea has reinforced her conclusion in the report.

The legal status of Taiwan in international law is particularly important in the geopolitics of the United States and Japan. Since Japan surrendered at the end of World War II, a thorny point of the United States–China relations has been the Taiwan problem. The PRC has always claimed that Taiwan is China's territory. But the United States has not recognized or conceded to its claim. When the PRC Congress was discussing the enactment of the Anti-secession Act in February 2005, whether by coincidence or not, the United States and Japan jointly announced that their "common strategic objectives" included peaceful

[1024] *Underlying Strains in Taiwan-US Political Relations* CRS Report for Congress, by Kerry Dumbaugh, Specialist in Asian Affairs, Foreign Affairs, Defense, and Trade Division. Summary. Congressional Research Service, The Library of Congress. Order Code RL33684, Updated April 20, 2007, *available at* http://www.fas.org/sgp/crs/row/RL33684.pdf. Last visited 04//15/2011.

resolution of issues concerning the Taiwan Strait through dialogue.[1025] The statement implied that China had no sovereignty over Taiwan. Judging from the timing of the joint statement, it is clear that both the United States and Japan wished to remind the PRC of their position regarding Taiwan.

The United States has protected Taiwan for the last 65 years. Ever since President Truman sent the US Navy Seventh Fleet to protect Taiwan from the invasion of Chinese Communistsin 1950, the ROC government and the PRC government have coexisted till now. The ROC government in Taiwan could not have survived for so long without the military support of the US Government.

At the same time, the United States has also controlled the life of the people of Taiwan. It controlled the life of the people of Taiwan indirectly by controlling the political leaders in Taiwan. All US Presidents refused to help Jiang (Chiang) Kai-shek in Taiwan recover China proper after he had lost it. At the beginning of President Chen Shui-bian's term, the Clinton Administration gave him specific instructions on how to conduct the foreign affairs in order to implement US policy. Chen's "four-nos and one have-no" policy severely limited his executive power. It is hard to imagine that a government leader would make such detailed commitments restricting his own political agenda at the beginning of his presidency unless he was forced to do so by someone wielding formidable power.

The Bush Administration also warned President Chen not to take any action or make any statement which might disturb the "status quo" of Taiwan. In 2003 when Chen proposed that his government conduct a referendum in Taiwan, President Bush rebuked Chen for making the proposal.[1026] Later, Deputy Secretary of State Negroponte explained that "President Chen has made commitments to the American President, to the international community, and to the people of Taiwan not to take any kind of steps that would represent a unilateral alteration of the status quo, such as a change in the official name of Taiwan."[1027]

Chen's "commitments" in Negroponte's statement referred to none other than the "commitment" in the "four-nos and one have-no" policy,[1028] which Chen announced in his 2000 presidential inauguration

[1025] Joint Statement, *supra* note 905.
[1026] Lin Chieh-yu & Charles Snyder, *see supra* note 896.
[1027] *See supra* text accompanying note 898.
[1028] *See supra* text accompanying note 579.

because it was the only occasion when Chen had a chance to make such kind of "commitment" to "the American President [and] to the international community." Chen's inaugural speech angered many Taiwanese voters because he did not campaign for the presidency on such a platform.

Chen subsequently claimed that the US Government forced him to make the policy statement. In September 2009, while in a jail waiting on an appeal from a life sentence rendered by a District Court in Taiwan for alleged embezzlement of government funds,[1029] Chen filed a petition with the US Court of Appeals for the Armed Forces in Washington, DC against the United States.[1030] The petition requested an "intervention by the US Court to free him"[1031] because, according to the petition, the indictment against him by the KMT's administration and the conviction by the Taipei court were a scheme of political persecution.

Chen petitioned the US Court of Appeals For the Armed Forces for relief because, he claimed, that during 8 years as the ROC President, he acted for "the US Military Government" as an agent. Chen stated in his affidavit that "[D]uring my term of office, I accepted the instructions of the Chairmen of the AIT on many occasions, even when their instructions interfered with my Presidential decision-making."[1032] Although the petition was dismissed by the court on the grounds of lack of jurisdiction, his complaint under an oath that he acted as an agent of the US Government cannot be swept away lightly.

Chen's Petition claims that he was convicted by the court controlled by pro-China KMT not because he had committed the alleged crimes

[1029] Chen was convicted for embezzlement and money laundering, and sentenced by Taipei District Court to life sentence. On appeal, the sentence was reduced to 18 and a half years of imprisonment.

[1030] In *Chen Shui-bian* v. *United States*, a petition filed with the US Court of Appeals for the Armed Forces, Misc. No.10-8003, on Sep. 21, 2009, the Petition was dismissed for lack of jurisdiction. US Ct of Appeals for the Armed Forces, Daily Journal. No. 10-024, Tuesday, Oct. 6, 2009, *available at* http://www.armfor.uscourts.gov/newcaaf/journal/2009/2009Oct.htm. Last visited 08/30/2012. *See also Taiwan Ex-President Appeals In US Court For Release*, NYTimes.com. 09/24/2009. (Reporting by Jeremy Pelofsky; Editing by Xavier Briand), *available at* http://www.nytimes.com/reuters/2009/09/24/world/international-uk-taiwan-usa-expresident.html?_r=1. Last visited 09/29/2009.

[1031] The Petition prays for a writ of mandamus ordering the "United States Military Government for Taiwan" to intervene and for immediate release of Chen Shui-bian from captivity, confinement and restoration of his civil and human rights in a Taiwan jail.

[1032] *In re Chen Shui-bian*, *supra* note 1030. Chen's Affidavit, par. 8.

but because during his tenure as the President of the ROC he had "promoted the eventual independence of Taiwan from China" and "these [listed] acts alone earned [him] the everlasting enmity of the Kuomintang [KMT] political organization."[1033] If Chen was engaged in "the eventual independence of Taiwan," his announced "no Taiwan independence" policy was not in his political agenda, but in fact the policy of Clinton and Bush.

B. US Government's Source of Power to Implement its Policies Toward Taiwan

A government often sets a foreign policy to conduct its foreign affairs. While the government may express its foreign policy by making a policy announcement or voting in an international organization, it needs some power to implement its foreign policy beyond its borders. This subsection discusses the power in international law that the US Government has utilized to implement its policy toward Taiwan since 1945.

The State utilizes the external sovereign power to implement its foreign policy beyond its border. As discussed in Chapter 4, The State and Governments of China, the State has external power to engage with other States. The external power includes the power to wage war and the power (competence) to conclude treaties with other States.[1034]

The power that the US Government has employed to implement its policy toward Taiwan since 1945 came from three sources: the power as the occupying State; the power under the United States–China (the ROC government) Mutual Defense Treaty; and the power pursuant to the TRA. A brief analysis follows.

a. The Power of the Occupying State

One source of US power recognized by international law to implement its policy is from the war with Japan. By defeating Japan, the United States became the victorious State in the Pacific War. In the documents relating to the War with Japan and the Peace Treaty of San Francisco, the term "Allied Powers" referred to the victorious States that defeated Japan. In fact, the State that defeated Japan was the United States. As mentioned earlier, it was the United States that fought with much sacrifice to

[1033] *Id*, at 10.

[1034] The war power is, however, subject to international law, both customary and conventions.

defeat Japan.[1035] It was the military forces under the command of General MacArthur, as the Commander of the US South West Pacific Forces, that defeated Japan. It was the United States that drafted Orders for the Japanese Emperor to announce the surrender arrangement. It was to the United States that Japan surrendered.[1036] When President Truman appointed General Douglas MacArthur as "the Supreme Commander for the Allied Powers in the Pacific," the fighting was already over. MacArthur was appointed, not to fight Japan, but to occupy Japan. All the soldiers under his command were American. His title "the Supreme Commander *for the Allied Powers* in the Pacific" was in name only.

The United States became the occupying power of Taiwan. Upon unconditional surrender of Japan on August 14, 1945,[1037] the United States became what Secretary of State John Foster Dulles called "the occupying power"[1038] of Japan. As Japan's territory included the island of Taiwan at the time, the United States also became the occupying power of Taiwan.[1039]

While in a political term the United States became the occupying power of Taiwan in 1945, legalistically the United States acquired legal possession of the island of Taiwan. When Japan surrendered unconditionally, the United States had the right to occupy Japan by taking possession of Japan's territory, which included Formosa (the island of Taiwan).[1040] Thus, when the United States took possession of Japan's territory, the United States also took possession of Taiwan. The United States in its letter to the USSR, stated that "(The island of Taiwan) was territory taken from Japan [by the US] by the victory of the Allied Forces."[1041]

[1035] *See* MacArthur, *supra* note 647, at 291 and the accompanying text.

[1036] *See supra* note 650 for Japanese Emperor's surrender announcement.

[1037] *See Incoming Message*, WARX 49571, dated Aug. 14, 1945, from General Marshall to General MacArthur (on file with MacArthur Memorial).

[1038] At the Conference on Proposed Japanese Peace Treaty in San Francisco. *See* DULLES, *The San Francisco Conference on Proposed Japanese Peace Treaty*, *supra* note 391 in Chapter 3. Art. 23 of the Peace Treaty of San Francisco also refers to the United States as the "occupying power." *See supra* text accompanying note 731.

[1039] *See supra* text accompanying note 649.

[1040] "The actual status of the island is that it is territory *taken from Japan* by the victory of the Allied Forces in the Pacific." *See supra* note 778 for the US' letter to the Secretary General of the United Nations in 1950.

[1041] *See supra* text accompanying note 778.

In international law, an occupying State has the power to administer the occupied territory and thereby implement its policy in the territory.[1042] The United States, as the victorious State, won the right to dispose of Japan's territory as it wished.[1043] The US Government set up a Military Government to administer the four main islands of Japan and Ryukyu Islands, but assigned Jiang (Chiang) Kai-shek to accept the surrender of the Japanese Army on the island of Taiwan.[1044] Thus, the US Government, while retaining legal possession of Taiwan, gave custody of Taiwan to Jiang (Chiang) Kai-Shek's ROC government, thereby creating an agency relationship between the US Government and the ROC government.

The United States has continued to be the occupying power of Taiwan after the peace treaty with Japan. After the Peace Treaty of San Francisco entered into force in 1952, the United States terminated the occupation of the four Japanese main islands; it terminated its Military Government in Japan and returned the governing authorities to the Japanese government. But the US Government kept the occupation of Ryukyu Islands and the island of Taiwan, which was still under the administration of the ROC government.

The Peace Treaty of San Francisco, in which Japan renounced the title to the island of Taiwan, was silent on the post treaty administration of Taiwan. Thus, the United States has continued to be the occupying State of Taiwan after it returned Ryukyu Islands to Japan in 1972. The agency relationship between the US government and the ROC government continued. Although the United States never openly claimed the power of the occupying State, it retains the inherent power and continues to exert the power to implement its policies on Taiwan to date.

b. The Power Under the United States—China (the ROC Government) Mutual Defense Treaty

The second source of power was from the United States—China (the ROC) Mutual Defense Treaty (the "Defense Treaty"). After 1954, for 25 years the United States had an additional power to implement its

[1042] *See* Department of the Army Field Manual (for) The Law of land warfare, *supra* note 400, par. 363, 365.

[1043] *See* Dulles, *The San Francisco Conference on Proposed Japanese Peace Treaty, supra* note 391.

[1044] *See Incoming Message*, WARX 48672, *supra* note 652.

policy on Taiwan by way of a treaty. In 1954, the United States and China (represented by the ROC government) concluded the United States–China (the ROC government) Mutual Defense Treaty to deter the Chinese Communists from taking Taiwan by force.

This Defense Treaty was an unusual mutual defense treaty in two aspects. Firstly, it was not a mutual defense treaty against a third State. Usually, in a mutual defense treaty, the parties of the treaty are mutually committed to each other under the treaty to provide military assistance to the other party in case the other party is attacked by a third State. This Defense Treaty between the United States and China was for the defense not against a third State, but against an insurgency within the other party.

Secondly, usually one party to a mutual defense treaty makes a commitment to defend the other party and the other party's territory. The island of Taiwan, which the United States committed to defend under the Treaty, was not the ROC's or China's territory. Secretary of State John Foster Dulles of the Eisenhower Administration expressly stated at the US Senate hearing for approving the Treaty that "the [United States–China (the ROC)] Mutual Defense Treaty would not give General Chiang sovereignty over Formosa and Pescadores."[1045] Thus, under the Defense Treaty, the United States agreed to protect a territory, not of the other party—the ROC or China—but legally in the possession of the United States as the occupying State.

Under the Defense Treaty, the United States was under a treaty obligation to prevent the PRC government from taking Taiwan by nonpeaceful means. A proposition of the US one-China policy formulated in the Shanghai Communiqué is "Both sides of the Taiwan Strait peacefully settle their dispute." In other words, neither side should use force against the other. This proposition was backed by the Defense Treaty under which the United States had legal obligation to defend Taiwan.

The Defense Treaty provides the United States with a treaty right and power in international law. It empowered the United States to send the military affairs advisory group and members of the US Air Force to be stationed in Taiwan.

[1045] *See supra*, text accompanying note 756.

c. The Power Pursuant to Taiwan Relations Act

The third source of power to implement US policy toward Taiwan was the TRA.[1046] When the United States terminated the United States–China (the ROC) Mutual Defense Treaty in 1979, US' obligation and power under the Defense Treaty also terminated. Consequently, the United States withdrew the military affairs advisory group and the US Air Force from the island. It then enacted the TRA as a substitute for the Treaty.

The TRA is an unusual statute. Under the US Constitution, the Congress, pursuant to its constitutional power, enacts domestic (Federal) laws to govern the country, while the Executive has the power to take the initiative to make foreign policy and conduct foreign affairs. TRA is a domestic statute in which the Congress laid down a foreign policy guideline for the Executive (the US Government) to implement.

But the TRA cannot apply to a foreign government and territory outside of the United States. The Act, unlike a mutual defense treaty, is a domestic law. Though the US Government is obliged by the Act to implement the purposes of the Act, the Act cannot empower the US Government to implement its policy in a foreign country. For instance, the Act authorizes the US Government to sell weapons to the governing authorities in Taiwan, but it does not, and cannot, impose an obligation on Taiwan's governing authorities to buy or receive weapons from the United States. Likewise, Taiwan's governing authorities have no right to demand the United States to sell weapons to them. It is true that the US Government has the power to influence Taiwan's governing authorities by controlling the sale of weapons to it but such power is the power of might, not of right.

However, it is submitted that the US Government has a power in international law to implement its policy in Taiwan. The power is the inherent power of the occupying State. As long as the sovereignty over Taiwan is not settled, no event since Japan surrendered has interrupted the authority of the United States as the occupying State. Thus, the United States has retained a power in international law over Taiwan.

In fact, the US Government has acted like the government of an occupying State. Although the United States never claimed openly that it, as the principal, assigned the ROC government as its agent to administer Taiwan, the US Government has acted like it, wielding a subtle power

[1046] *See supra* note 503.

over Taiwan and its governing authorities. When Jiang (Chiang) Kai-shek was the ROC President, the US Government used the power to restrain him from attacking the PRC. When Lee Teng-hui and Chen Shui-bian were the Presidents, the US Government prohibited them from making any statements or moves that the United States considered advocating independence of Taiwan. No power other than that of an occupying State allowed the US Government to control the governing authorities and the people in Taiwan so much.

CHAPTER 11

Taiwan Under US Protection and Control

Contents

This chapter discusses Taiwan under US past and present policy.

1. TAIWAN UNDER US POLICY

A. The Policies of the US and the UK on Taiwan Immediately After World War II

Since 1952 when the Peace Treaty of San Francisco entered into force, the people of Taiwan have lived in an unsettled environment: Taiwan is not a State; it is not subject to any sovereignty, yet it has come under the administration of a foreign government in exile.

After Japan surrendered, the United States intended to solve the Taiwan problem with various policies. Before the Peace Treaty of San Francisco was concluded, at one time the United States proposed that the Taiwan problem be solved by the United Nations. In June 1950, President Truman in his "Statement on Korea" stated that "[t]he determination of the future status of Formosa must await the restoration of security in the Pacific, a peace settlement with Japan, or consideration by the United Nations."[1047] In August 1950, he instructed the US Ambassador to the UN Warren Austin to deliver a letter to the UN Secretary-General recommending the United Nations to consider the problem of Formosa.

[1047] TRUMAN, *Statement on Korea*, *supra* note 702.

The One-China Policy: State, Sovereignty, and Taiwan's International Legal Status
DOI: http://dx.doi.org/10.1016/B978-0-08-102314-3.00011-2

The letter stated that "The United States would welcome UN consideration of the case of Formosa. We would approve full UN investigation here or on the spot. We believe that UN consideration would contribute to a peaceful, rather than a forceable solution of that problem."[1048] Again, on September 21, 1950 Secretary of State Acheson, in requesting the "question of Formosa" to be included on the UN General Assembly agenda for consideration, stated that "The United States believes that the future of Formosa and of the nearly eight million people inhabited there should be settled by peaceful means in accordance with the Charter of the United Nations."[1049] Later, in May 1951, Truman, facing the possible invasion of Formosa by the Chinese Communists army, took the position of shielding Formosa with the US Navy Seventh Fleet "until its status could be settled through consideration by the United Nations."[1050]

The United Kingdom also intended to solve the Taiwan problem through the United Nations. Before the Peace Treaty of San Francisco was concluded, the Labor Party wanted to refer the Taiwan problem to the United Nations for a solution. In November of 1950, British Foreign Secretary Ernest Davies of the Attlee administration stated in the House of Commons that "The main aim of His Majesty's Government is to help in securing a generally acceptable and peaceful solution of the Formosan problem. Naturally we shall take advantage of any opportunity which may arise within the United Nations to bring about a solution."[1051] In May of 1951, the Attlee administration again expressed the desire to refer the Taiwan problem to the United Nations. During the Korean War, British Foreign Secretary Herbert Morrison said in the British House of Commons that "In the view of His Majesty's Government, [the problem of Formosa] is a question which could usefully be considered by the United Nations at the appropriate time."[1052] Similarly, the Conservative

[1048] Austin, *supra* note 778.

[1049] Discussion of the item was, at the proposal of the United Kingdom, adjourned *sine die. See Memorandum from the Office of Legal Advisor, Dep't of State, to the Director of the Office of Republic of China Affairs* (July 13, 1971), *available at* http://www.heritage.org/Press/Events/loader.cfm?url=/commonspot/security/getfile.cfm&PageID=56573; *See also* J.P. Jain, *The Legal Status of Formosa: A Study of British, Chinese and Indian Views*, 57 AM. J. INT'L L. 25, 30 n.19 (1963).

[1050] *See Gen. MacArthur's Statement*, *supra* note 693.

[1051] 478 PARL. DEB., H.C. (5th ser.) (1950) at 174.

[1052] 487 PARL. DEB., H.C. (5th ser.) (1951) at 2302. In May 1951, British Foreign Secretary Herbert Morrison said that "the problem of Formosa has now become an international problem." 487 PARL. DEB. H.C., (5th ser.) (1951) at 2302.

Party, which succeeded the Labor Party in control of Parliament, expressed the same view in 1952. The House members agreed with British Foreign Secretary Major Beamish of the Churchill administration that "the future of Formosa should be settled by the United Nations and not by force of arms."[1053]

After the Peace Treaty of San Francisco entered into force, the United Kingdom still proposed to put Taiwan under UN's control. In 1954, Winston Churchill, after being reappointed as British Prime Minister for the second time, said in the House of Commons that "Nor do I see any reason why at some subsequent date Formosa should not be placed in the custody of the United Nations."[1054]

At one point, both the United States and the United Kingdom suggested creation of the State of Taiwan. When Allied Powers forced Japan to renounce title to the island of Taiwan in the Peace Treaty of San Francisco, they had decided that the island of Taiwan would not become China's territory. The United Kingdom and the United States intended to create the State of Taiwan. The UK government in 1955 suggested creation of the State of Formosa to solve the Taiwan problem.[1055] It further suggested that both China and the new State of Formosa be included in the United Nations.[1056] The New York Times reported that "It is said on good authority that the [British] Government would not be doing this without some sign from President Eisenhower and Secretary of State Dulles that they, too, consider that this is the only long-term solution now apparent."[1057]

B. The Policy of "No Taiwan Independence"

The US policy of "no Taiwan independence" creates erroneous perception that Taiwan is China's territory; independence of Taiwan will encroach on China's sovereignty. As discussed earlier, independence and secession are closely related concepts. A successful secession by a region in a State leads to its independence from its ruling State. Thus, Bush's

[1053] 496 Parl. Deb., H.C. (5th ser.) (1952) at 1027.

[1054] 530 Parl. Deb., H.C. (5th ser.) (1954) at 494.

[1055] In January 1955, British Foreign Secretary Anthony Eden suggested the establishment of the State of Formosa. *See* Drew Middleton, *Britain's Formosa Solution Is Two Chinas, Both in UN*, N.Y. Times, 01/29/1955, at A1.

[1056] *See Id.*

[1057] *Id.* at 2.

policy of "no Taiwan independence" amounts to saying "no secession from China," and creates an erroneous perception that Taiwan is part of China.

This work, by analyzing the Peace Treaty of San Francisco and opinions of the earlier US and the UK Government leaders in details, concludes that the island of Taiwan has not been China's territory after the Treaty of Shimonoseki. In fact, one of the propositions in US' one-China policy is that the United States does not recognize Taiwan as China's territory. Taiwan Relations Act re-enforces that position.

Taiwan does not need secession from China to establish a State. Since Taiwan is not China's territory, if the people of Taiwan have a common will to establish a State, there is no secession problem. Establishment of a State of Taiwan does not encroach upon the sovereignty of any State because Taiwan is not under any sovereignty.

The one-China policy formulated in the three Communiqués does not recognize the island of Taiwan as China's territory. That is the understanding of the Congress in enacting Taiwan Relations Act. In 2004, Congressman Steve Chabot said that "so long as 'one China' is not understood to mean that Taiwan is part of China, then I have no problem with [the one-China policy] at all."[1058]

When President Clinton announced the "three-nos statement," the people of Taiwan were indignant and worried. The first proposition in the "three-nos statement," "no US support for an independent Taiwan," made them feel abandoned by their friend. The policy of the statement meant that the United States would not support Taiwan independence if they decided to establish their own State.

The tone of Bush's policy was even stronger. His "no Taiwan independence" policy meant, not only will the Bush Administration not support "Taiwan independence," but it prohibits the people of Taiwan to establish their own State. The "no Taiwan independence" policy reversed the proposals and intention of earlier political leaders of the United States and the United Kingdom to leave the Taiwan problem for the United Nations or to allow the people of Taiwan to establish their own State.

[1058] The Honorable Robert E. Andrews & The Honorable Steve Chabot, *Two Congressmen Look at "One China,"* Address given at the Heritage Foundation (Sept. 16, 2003), *available at* www.heritage.org/asiaandthepacific/hl821.cfm. Last visited 10/28/2004.

The "no Taiwan independence" policy[1059] deviated from the US policy laid down in the three Joint Communiqués. The US one-China policy formulated in the three Joint Communiqués did not embody any notion that Taiwan should not become a State. The dispute referred to in the Shanghai Communiqué was between the PRC government and the ROC government. At the time of drafting the Shanghai Communiqué, the ROC and the PRC were two rival governments, neither of which had or exercised sovereignty over Taiwan. Each one claimed that it was the legitimate government to represent the State of China. The people of Taiwan were not a party to the dispute. Their right to decide their political future was also not an issue in the dispute. The Taiwan Relations Act, which was enacted by the US Congress to protect the interest of the people of Taiwan, certainly does not include a policy statement or intent of "no Taiwan independence."[1060] There was no legitimate reason to explain why Clinton announced such a policy in his three-nos statement while he was in China except that he wanted to appease his Chinese host.

C. The Policy of "No Referendum for Taiwan"

The Bush Administration, by condemning Taiwan's political leader for advocating Taiwan independence, denied the people of Taiwan a right to determine their future. In 2002, when President Chen Shui-bian in his "two countries each on one side [of the Taiwan Strait]" speech proposed that "[T]he (ROC) Institution of Legislation (the Legislature *Yuan*) should consider passing a referendum law [permitting the people] to protect its sovereignty,"[1061] the Deputy Secretary of State John Negroponte of the Bush Administration criticized Chen's proposal. However, the policy of "no referendum by the people of Taiwan to determine their future

[1059] *See* Darryl N. Johnson, *US—Taiwan Relations: Building on Success, Address Before the American Institute in Taiwan*, Twenty-Second Annual Joint Business Conference (Nov. 10, 1998), *available at* http://ait.org.tw/en/news/officialtext/viewer.asp?ID=1998111701&GROUP=BG; *see also* Charles Snyder, *US' Taiwan Policy in Doubt: Academic*, Taipei Times, 12/4/2003, *available at* http://www.taipeitimes.com/News/front/archives/2003/12/04/2003078256.

[1060] A government policy cannot change the mandate of a Congressional statute. *See infra* text accompanying note 1075. A recent Congressional resolution "Reaffirming the Taiwan Relations Act and the Six Assurances" re-enforces this point. *See infra* note 1078.

[1061] Sandy Huang, *supra* note 580.

('no referendum for Taiwan')" was not found in the three Joint Communiqués or in the Taiwan Relations Act. It was a new policy created by the Bush Administration.

D. The People of Taiwan Under US Present Policy

Since 1998, the US Government has expanded the content of the "one-China policy" announced in the three Joint Communiqués and Taiwan Relations Act beyond their original context, and in a manner that suppressed the will of the people of Taiwan.

The US policy in the three Joint Communiqués did not accept or concede to China's claim to the title to the island of Taiwan. When the three Joint Communiqués were issued, the island of Taiwan was administered by the ROC government, the rival of the PRC government in a civil war. When the United States in the Shanghai Communiqué stated that "The United States reaffirms its interest in a peaceful settlement of the Taiwan question by the Chinese themselves," Nixon did not refer to settling the title to the island of Taiwan. The phrase "Chinese themselves" referred to the two rival Chinese governments. The dispute was a political one. What the ROC government and the PRC government could settle "peacefully" was the dispute between the two governments on the right to represent the State of China, not the title to the island of Taiwan.

From the beginning, when Nixon announced in the Shanghai Communiqué that both parties should settle the "dispute peacefully," the policy did not deprive the right of the people of Taiwan to determine their political future. Thus, when Negroponte, in criticizing Chen Shui-bian's proposal to conduct a referendum for Taiwan, said that "We of course maintain our position of a One-China Policy. The issue of cross-Strait relations must be resolved by peaceful means,"[1062] he distorted the one-China policy and ignored the right of the people of Taiwan to determine their future. It is inconceivable that Negroponte would have the ROC, a Chinese government exiled in Taiwan, and the PRC government, another Chinese government, neither of which exercised sovereignty over the people of Taiwan, to decide the future of the people of Taiwan.

[1062] *US Relations With the People's Republic of China (2009)*, Press Release, US Department of State. Remarks of John D. Negroponte, Deputy Secretary of State at the American Chamber of Commerce in China, Chaoyang Westin Hotel, Beijing, China, January 8, 2009.

As the US Court in *Roger C. S. Lin* pointed out, "for many years the [US] Executive has gone out of its way to avoid making determination [of Taiwan's sovereign], creating an information deficit for determining the status of the people on Taiwan."[1063] The policy of "no Taiwan independence" and the policy of "no referendum for Taiwan" have created ambiguity which may create a wrong impression that the US Government has conceded to China's claim to Taiwan.[1064]

The present US policy is inconsistent with American values, the idea of modern democracy, and the fundamental principle of the UN Charter. A brief explanation follows.

a. Inconsistency With American Values

First, the policy of "no Taiwan independence" is inconsistent with American values. One of the American values since the establishment of the State is people's freedom of choice. American political thought is that the people have the natural right to decide their own affairs, including their political future. America's founding fathers themselves established the State in the name of such a tenet.

A long-standing general policy of the United States is to support the peoples in other parts of the world of their right of self-determination. It is inconceivable that the US Government will prohibit the people of Taiwan, who are not under its sovereignty, to determine their own political future. Whether the people of Taiwan have the common will to establish a State is a question for them. The present US policy of "no Taiwan independence," intentionally or inadvertently, deprives them of their freedom of choice.

b. Inconsistency With the Idea of Modern Democracy

Second, the policy of "no referendum by the people of Taiwan" is inconsistent with the basic idea of modern democracy. This US policy discredits the modern political philosophy of democracy. Elections and referenda are two peaceful methods for the people to make decisions by the majority: An election is for selecting government officials and their representatives; a referendum is for making decisions on grave matters

[1063] *Roger C. Lin, supra* note 957, at 9.

[1064] *See China Says It Will Not Use Nuclear Weapons Against Taiwan*, N.Y. TIMES, 09/3/1999, (The threats have been met by concern from the United States, which recognizes Beijing's claim to the island but is bound by [U.S.] law to aid Taiwan's defense.), *Id.* at A3.

concerning the livelihood of the people. Plebiscites or referenda has been in use as a democratic method for making important decisions by the people in the West for centuries. The United States has supported peaceful attempts in other regions of the world to gain independence. The policy of "no referendum by the people of Taiwan" is repugnant to the fundamental idea of modern democracy, which the United States so proudly espouses.

c. Inconsistency With the UN Charter

Third, the policy of "no Taiwan independence" and the policy of "no referendum for Taiwan" are inconsistent with a founding principle of the UN Charter. When the US Secretary of State Acheson requested the United Nations to include the "question of Formosa" on the UN General Assembly agenda for consideration in 1950, he stated that "The future of Formosa and of the nearly eight million people inhabited there be settled by peaceful means in accordance with the Charter of the United Nations."[1065] The Charter of the UN embodies the principle of self-determination.[1066]

After the Second World War ended, many new States were established by self-determination of the people. The most peaceful means for self-determination is by a referendum. In a referendum, the people decide their future by a majority vote. The United States itself conducted such a referendum for the people of Ryukyu Islands when it terminated its occupation of the islands. The United Nations has supported such referenda in East Timor, Kosovo, South Sudan, and other regions of the world. Thus, the US policy of "no Taiwan independence" and the policy of "no referendum for Taiwan" are contrary to the position that the United States has taken in supporting self-determination by the people who have determined to establish their own States and deprive the people of Taiwan the rights that are recognized in the UN Charter.[1067]

In summary, the US policy of "no Taiwan independence" and the policy of "no referendum for Taiwan" are detrimental to the fundamental rights and interest of the people of Taiwan and discredit American values,

[1065] *See supra* note 1049.

[1066] *See supra* text accompanying note 431.

[1067] *Id.* The most recent example is South Sudan. Pursuant to a peace accord between Sudan and South Sudan of 2005, a referendum was held in South Sudan in January of 2011. On July 9, 2011, South Sudan declared establishment of the State of South Sudan.

the idea of democracy, and the principles of the UN Charter. Circuit Judge Brown in *Roger C. S. Lin* sympathetically commented that "America and China's tumultuous relationship over the past 60 years has trapped the inhabitants of Taiwan in political purgatory. During this time the people on Taiwan have lived without any uniformly recognized government. In practical terms, this means they have uncertain status in the world community which infects the population's day-to-day lives."[1068]

The predicament in which the people of Taiwan are in today is partly attributable to the US Taiwan policy. The United States has wielded its power over Taiwan for 70 years. It, on one hand, does not recognize China's claim to the island of Taiwan but, on the other hand, does not allow the people of Taiwan to determine their own future. The ambiguity in its policy toward Taiwan has created uncertainty and inconsistency. The uncertainty has left the Taiwan problem unsettled. The inconsistency in its policy has created confusion for the society of Taiwan, in which the people have lost their direction.

The US bears some responsibilities to assist the people of Taiwan under international law.

First, the US bears certain responsibilities to the people of Taiwan as an occupying State. An occupying State bears certain obligations in international law. The Hague Convention Respecting the Laws and Customs of War on Land recognizes these responsibilities. Art. 55 of the said Convention provides that "The occupying State [of a territory of the hostile State] shall be regarded only as administrator and usufructuary of public buildings, real estate, forests, and agricultural estates belonging to the hostile State, and situated in the occupied country. It must safeguard the capital of these properties, and administer them in accordance with the rules of usufruct."[1069] The US Government also recognizes such responsibilities. The US Department of the Army Field Manual for The Law of Land Warfare imposes similar responsibility.[1070] Paragraph 365 of the Field Manual provides that "Protected persons who are in occupied territory shall not be deprived, in any case or in any manner whatsoever,

[1068] *See supra* note 957.

[1069] Hague Convention Respecting The Laws and Customs of War on Land, *supra* note 15 in Chapter 3, Annex to the Convention, Regulations Respecting the Laws and Customs of War on Land, Section III Military Authority Over the Territory of the Hostile State, Art. 55.

[1070] *See* DEPARTMENT OF THE ARMY FIELD MANUAL (FOR) THE LAW of LAND WARFARE. *See supra* note 400.

of the benefits of the present (Geneva) Convention by any change introduced, as the result of the occupation of a territory, into the institutions or government of the said territory, nor by any agreement concluded between the authorities of the occupied territories and the Occupying Power, nor by any annexation by the latter of the whole or part of the occupied territory (Geneva Convention Art. 47.)"[1071] The United States recognized a responsibility to protect the people of Taiwan not long after it assigned Jiang (Chiang) Kai-shek to administer Taiwan. In 1949, when Jiang (Chiang) Kai-shek's army was retreating to Taiwan, the US Government recognized a responsibility for preventing the island of Taiwan from falling under the control of Chinese Communists.[1072]

Second, the US bears certain responsibilities as a party to the Peace Treaty of San Francisco. As pointed out earlier, the Peace Treaty of San Francisco, as a treaty, is the supreme law of the United States, second only to the Constitution. Legally and politically, the US Government is obliged to act according to the territorial disposition of the United States in the Treaty. The territorial disposition of the Treaty of the island of Taiwan cannot be changed by a governmental policy. After the Peace Treaty of San Francisco was concluded, successive US Administrations unambiguously held a position that Taiwan was not China's territory. The treaty did not provide for Taiwan to be ceded to China. Neither the three Joint Communiqués nor the Taiwan Relation Act recognized China's claim on Taiwan. However, the recent US policy on Taiwan for more than a decade has created ambiguity. In 1998, when President Clinton made the "three-nos statement," the policy of "no Taiwan independence" has created a perception that the United States had conceded to China's claim over Taiwan. If the ambiguity was strategically created by the US Government in dealing with the PRC government, the ambiguity has permitted China to twist the arms of other States and international organizations to concede to its claim over Taiwan. The WHO and other international organizations frequently list Taiwan as "a province of China."

The United States can hardly shake off such responsibilities on the grounds that it has assigned another government, the ROC, to administer the territory. The responsibilities of the occupying State are the same

[1071] *Id. See* Article I of the Treaty of Paris, *supra* note 779.

[1072] *See* US Department of State/Foreign relations of the U.S. 1949. *The Far East: China*. Vol. IX (1949) *Policy of the U.S. toward Formosa (Taiwan): concern of the U.S. regarding possible conquest by Chinese Communist*, p. 261–47 (74.8 MB) [Washington] July 6, 1949.

when it delegates its power to another governing authority. The Field Manual Paragraph 368 provides that "It is immaterial whether the government over an enemy's territory consists in a military or civil or mixed administration. Its character is the same and the source of its authority the same. It is a government imposed by force, and the legality of its acts is determined by the law of war."[1073] The United States forced Japan to abandon the island of Taiwan in the Peace Treaty of San Francisco, but allowed the ROC government to continue its administration of the island. The United States, through the ROC government, exercises its power constantly, putting the people of Taiwan under its remote control. The US control of Taiwan through its agent, the ROC government, is not so much over the tangible property, but on the life and general welfare of the people. The occupying State is responsible for the protection of the life and general welfare of the people of the occupied territory as much as of their tangible property.

In solving the Taiwan problem, the US Government has to follow the rules of international law. The present US policy on Taiwan does not offer any means to solve the Taiwan problem. The one-China policy that recognizes the PRC as the only government of China has solved China's representation problem, but does not solve the Taiwan problem. Even though the US Government has no direct control on the governing authorities in Taiwan, it can exert pressure on them to respect the rights of the people of Taiwan.

2. TAIWAN POLICY ACT

In August of 2013, the Foreign Affairs Committee of the US Congress House of Representative unanimously adopted a bill entitled "Taiwan Policy Act."[1074] Although the bill was not enacted into law, the fact that it passed the Committee by unanimous votes reflected the sentiment of the Committee members.

[1073] *See* DEPARTMENT OF THE ARMY FIELD MANUAL (FOR) THE LAW OF LAND WARFARE, *supra* note 400. par. 368.

[1074] H.R. 419: Taiwan Policy Act of 2013, Sec. 2. Findings (10), 113th Congress, 2013–2015. The bill, as amended (offered by Ms. Ros-Lehtinen of Florida), was passed in the House Foreign Affairs Committee on August 1, 2013. Text as of Jan 25, 2013 (Introduced), *available at* http://www.govtrack.us/congress/bills/113/hr419/text. Last visited 06/25/2013.The amended Act is *available at* http://docs.house.gov/meetings/FA/FA00/20130801/101239/HMKP-113-FA00-20130801-SD767.pdf. Last visited 08/01/2013.

Since the enactment of the Taiwan Relations Act of 1979, many US Administrations adopted some special policies toward Taiwan, which might or might not be friendly to the people of Taiwan, including Reagan's Third Communiqué of 1982, Clinton's policy of "no Taiwan independence," and Bush's policy of "no referendum for Taiwan."

There were two reasons for the Congressional Committee to show its concern by adopting such a bill. One reason for its concern was that the US Administrations for the last decades had not followed the mandate of the Taiwan Relations Act. For instance, notwithstanding that the Taiwan Relations Act prescribes that "the United States will make available to Taiwan such defense articles and defense services in such quantity as may be necessary to enable Taiwan to maintain a sufficient self-defense capabilities," the Third Joint Communiqué issued by the Reagan Administration reduced the level of US commitment under the Taiwan Relations Act by providing that "arms sale to Taiwan will not exceed, either in quantitative or qualitative terms, the level of those supplied in recent years." The proposed Taiwan Policy Act points out that "The language contained in the [Third] Joint Communiqué shall not, to any degree, diminish the responsibility of the United States, as legislatively mandated in Taiwan Relations Act." Likewise, neither Clinton's policy of "no Taiwan independence" nor Bush's policy of "no referendum for Taiwan" finds support in the three Joint Communiqués or Taiwan Relations Act.

The other reason for the Committee's concern was that when Ma Ying-jeu became the President of the ROC, his policy was coddling, if not kowtowing, to China. Its Economic Cooperation Framework Agreement with the PRC government pushed Taiwan closer to China. What made the situation worse was the indifference or the silence of the Taiwanese people in the face of the silent invasion—the flooding in of Chinese visitors and money—in Taiwan. The Committee probably sensed that the indifference or silence of the people of Taiwan was due to the loss of confidence of the Taiwanese people in the US commitment to protect them. Thus, the draft Taiwan Policy Act on one hand wants to remind the US Executive the mandate of the Taiwan Relations Act (Nothing in this Act will be construed to amend or supersede the Taiwan Relations Act.)[1075]; on the other hand it wants to show the people of Taiwan the level of the US commitment to protect them.

[1075] Sec. 3 of Taiwan Policy Act, *Id.*

Although the proposed Taiwan Policy Act has not become law, the purpose and content of the draft Act will be examined below for the purpose of reference. The draft Act is comprehensive. It deals with political relations, security relations, economic and trade relations with Taiwan as a territorial political institution. In political relations with Taiwan, the draft Act provides that "Notwithstanding any Communiqués entered into between the United States and the People's Republic of China, the United States continues to assent to the six assurances provided to Taiwan in July 1982, including that the United States (1) has not agreed to set a date for ending arms sales to Taiwan; (2) has not agreed to hold prior consultations with the PRC on arms sale to Taiwan; (3) will not play any mediation role between Taipei and Beijing; (4) has not agreed to revise the Taiwan Relations Act; (5) has not altered its position regarding sovereignty over Taiwan; and (6) will not exert pressure on Taiwan to negotiate with the People's Republic of China."[1076]

In security relations with Taiwan, the draft Act announces that "any determination of the nature and quantity of defense articles and defense services to be made available to Taiwan that is made on any basis other than the defense needs of Taiwan, whether pursuant to the August 17, 1982, [the Third Joint] Communiqués signed with the People's Republic of China, or any similar executive agreement, order, or policy would violate the intent of Congress specified in Section 3(b) of the Taiwan Relations Act."[1077]

In economic and trade relations, the draft Act mandates that at the appropriate time the United States should seek the negotiation of a free trade agreement with Taiwan.

On one hand, the United States does not recognize Taiwan as a State; on the other hand, the policy guidelines prescribed in the draft Act do not contain a policy of "no Taiwan independence" or "no referendum for Taiwan" as seen in the policies of Clinton and Bush. The draft Act is friendlier to the people of Taiwan than the policies of previous US Administrations.

The draft Act provides that "The US Government shall respect the right of the Taipei Economic and Cultural Representative to display its flag on the premises." In addition, it also "support[s] a decision by Taiwan to change the name of the Taipei Economic and Cultural Representative

[1076] Sec. 106, *Id.*
[1077] Sec. 201(a), *Id.*

Office." The crucial words are [a decision] "by Taiwan," not by the ROC government. Sec. 101 of the draft Act provides that "[t]he policies of the United States shall be (1) supporting Taiwan, Taiwan's democracy, and the human rights of its people." By its implication, the United States will respect a name of the representative's office and a flag which the people of Taiwan may choose. What the draft Act does not spell out but implies is that the Congress does not oppose if Taiwan wants to establish a new State limiting its territory to the island of Taiwan provided that is the common will of the people of Taiwan.

In July 2016 the US Congress passed a bill "Reaffirming the Taiwan Relations Act and the Six Assurances." It "[a]ffirms that the Taiwan Relations Act and the Six Assurances are both cornerstones of United States—Taiwan relations; urges the President and Department of State to publicly, proactively and consistently affirm the Six Assurances as a cornerstone of United States—Taiwan relations."[1078]

[1078] H. Con. Res. 88. – 114th Congress (2015–2016). It passed the House on 5/16/2016. On 07/06/2016 the Senate passed the bill without amendment and with a preamble by Unanimous Consent. (Consideration: CR S4837).

CHAPTER 12
Solution

The (People's Republic of China) PRC government in the Anti-secession Law threatens to take Taiwan by force if the people of Taiwan do not agree to the "unification" with China. As the previous chapters have pointed out, China has no sovereignty over the island of Taiwan and the its inhabitants. The use of force by the PRC to take Taiwan would be unlawful and be considered an act of aggression in international law.

After the Second World War, both the United States and the United Kingdom wanted the United Nations to solve the Taiwan problem based on the interests of the people of Taiwan.[1079] The British Foreign Secretary Major Beamish of the Churchill administration, in reminding members of the House not to overlook the will of the Formosans themselves, said that "Article 73 of the United Nations Charter lays it down clearly that territories detached from enemy States come under the trusteeship section, where the principle is laid down that the interests of the inhabitants of these territories are paramount."[1080] Notwithstanding such opinion, Taiwan was never placed under the UN's trusteeship. Had the United Nations at the time accepted the task of solving the Taiwan problem, the United Nations would most likely have given the people of Taiwan an opportunity to decide their future, as it had done so in other territories under its Trusteeship. It has been more than half a century since the conclusion of the Peace Treaty of San Francisco. It is now too late for the United Nations to decide the future of Taiwan.

The time has come for the people of Taiwan to decide their own political future. As it was pointed out in previous chapters, after the Peace Treaty of San Francisco entered into force the island became an independent territorial entity and a *people's property.* Since the property is owned by the people as a whole, the common will of the people should be respected.

The idea that the future of Taiwan should be determined by its people has support in the past. In 1951, British Foreign Secretary Morrison of

[1079] *See supra* text accompanying notes 1047 & 1051.
[1080] 496 Parl. Deb., H.C. (5th ser.) (1952) at 1027.

The One-China Policy: State, Sovereignty, and Taiwan's International Legal Status
DOI: http://dx.doi.org/10.1016/B978-0-08-102314-3.00012-4

the Attlee administration said that "It is clearly desirable that the wishes of the inhabitants of Formosa should be taken into account [in determining its future]."[1081] The position of the United States was once the same, albeit not an explicit one. In answering the question of the Soviet government on the Peace Treaty with Japan, the US Government stated,

> *"[T]he Cairo Declaration of 1943 stated the purpose to restore "Manchuria, Formosa and the Pescadores to the Republic of China." That Declaration, like other wartime declarations such as those of Yalta and Potsdam, was subject to any final peace settlement where all relevant factors should be considered. The United States cannot accept the view, apparently put forward by the Soviet Government, that the views of other Allies not represented at Cairo must be wholly ignored. Also, the United States believes that* declarations such as that issued at Cairo must necessarily be considered in the light of the United Nations Charter, *the obligation of which prevail over any other international agreement."*[1082]

As pointed out before, the UN Charter supports the principle of self-determination.[1083]

The 20th century doctrine of self-determination—the right of the people in a region of the State to secede from their ruling State and establish a new State—is a controversial one. The doctrine is not accepted universally because, as discussed in Chapter 3, The Territorial State, successful secession from the ruling state encroaches on the sovereignty of the State.

But in the case of Taiwan, the people may determine their political future without resorting to the traditional doctrine of self-determination. They do not face the legal hurdle that other groups of people seeking self-determination do—challenging the sovereignty of the ruling State in breaking free from it. The people of Taiwan, in deciding to establish a State, would not be challenging the sovereign power of any State, including China. The US policy of "no referendum for Taiwan," which restricts the right of the people of Taiwan to decide their political future, should be discarded.

A referendum by the people of Taiwan on a single issue—whether the people of Taiwan wish to establish a State—is the best solution for the

[1081] 487 Parl. Deb., H.C. (5th ser.) (1951) at 2302.

[1082] *Answer to Soviet Questions on Principles for Japanese Treaty,* Aide-Mémoire Delivered to J.A. Malik, Soviet Rep. to the UN (Dec. 27, 1950) *in* Dep't St. Bull., Jan. 1951, at 65–66 (emphasis added).

[1083] *See supra* note 431.

Taiwan problem. Most referenda conducted in the past in the process of self-determination were on one single issue—whether the people wish to establish a new State. Although Taiwan has held general elections many times in the past, a general election, including the election of the President and the Vice-President, does not reflect the common will of the people regarding their political future, i.e., whether they wish to establish statehood, because in a general election, voters choose a candidate or candidates based on various factors, including their personality and policies. Thus, in the referendum for Taiwan, the only question is whether the people of Taiwan wish to establish a new State under a new name, limiting its territory to the island of Taiwan and adjacent islands (but not including Kinmen and Matsu islands, which are China's territories).

However, the people of Taiwan may not be able to express their will freely in a referendum conducted by the present governing authorities in Taiwan in the present political environment. Since the PRC government was established in 1949, it has threatened the use of force to "reunite" Taiwan with China. In 1996, the PRC government threatened the people of Taiwan by firing missiles into the Taiwan Strait to intimidate the voters in Taiwan during the presidential election. In 2000, the PRC government, in its White Paper, again threatened to use force against Taiwan if Taiwan further delayed the "reunification" talks. In 2005, the PRC government promulgated the "Anti-secession Law" to intimidate the Taiwan independence movement.[1084] Under these military threats, the people of Taiwan cannot express their will freely in a referendum without fear of a military invasion.

The United States may play an important role in the process of the referendum. It can call for a referendum in Taiwan. The United States, as the occupying State, has moral, if not legal, responsibility to support a referendum in Taiwan for the people, as it has supported elections in Iraq and Afghanistan. This measure has support in the US Congress.[1085] In order to

[1084] Taiwan Policy Act of 2013, *supra* note 1074. Sec. 2. Findings (7).

[1085] On Oct. 16, 2009, the US Rep. Robert Andrews submitted a proposed Resolution of the US Congress to the House (111th Congress, 1st Session H. Con. Res. 200, Expressing the sense of Congress regarding the freedom, security, and stability of Taiwan.). It calls the US Congress to declare that "it is the sense of the Congress [that]: (3) the future of Taiwan should be determined free from coercion by the People's Republic of China, peacefully, and with the express consent of the people of Taiwan." *Id.*

assure that the people of Taiwan may express their will freely in a referendum without fear of military threats by the PRC government, the United States should announce to the people of Taiwan that it guarantees the implementation of the outcome of the referendum. Meanwhile, its officials should stop making public statements that the US Government does not support Taiwan independence, or that the US Government opposes a referendum in Taiwan. The policies behind such statements are not consistent with the US position on the title to the island of Taiwan, nor with the US position regarding other territories seeking statehood. These statements worsen the Taiwan problem instead of solving it.

The United Nations may also play a crucial role in the process. The present predicament in which the people of Taiwan are in is partly attributable to UN Secretaries-General's misrepresentation of UN's policy. While it is too late for the United Nations to decide the fate of Taiwan now, it can play an important role in solving the Taiwan problem by administering a referendum in Taiwan,[1086] using the universal rule in practice based on the majority votes, instead of the Referendum Law of the Republic of China (ROC) which set unusually high hurdles for passing (two third of the votes cast).

Referenda have been the ultimate solution of the territories under the UN's custody or in UN Trusteeship. Many of the UN member States were established by way of referenda. East Timor, Montenegro, and South Sudan are recent examples.[1087] Before a referendum is conducted, the Secretary-General should stop calling Taiwan "Province of China" because such an expression lends color to China's unfounded claim on the island of Taiwan.

This is a peaceful means to solve the Taiwan problem and consistent with the intention of the earlier US Administrations immediately after the Second World War, as well as the UN Charter and International Covenant on Civil and Political Rights.[1088]

In settling the disputes on international conflicts, claims and defenses should be analyzed in light of recognized international law, whether one considers international law is law in the positive sense or not. The solution suggested here is based on the conclusions reached by applying

[1086] *See* Charles Hill, *Why East Timor Matters*, Hoover Digest (2000), *available at* http://www.hooverdigest.org/001/hill2.html. Last visited 11/18/2004.

[1087] *See* Fitzpatrick, *supra* note 1011, at 3–4.

[1088] *See supra* note 353.

settled rules of international law to the situation of Taiwan, and is the most viable long-term solution to the Taiwan problem. Former Secretary of State Hillary Clinton stated that the international law is the key to resolving international problems. Former Japanese Prime Minister Mr. Noda also emphasized that the international law is vital in the international community.

If the States that helped create international law for maintaining the world order set their policies contrary to international law, they will eventually destroy the world order that the international law helped build. Michael P. Scharf, a prominent international law scholar, observed that "[W]hen a State elects to ignore or reinterpret an existing international rule according to its own short-term interests, it runs the risk of being unable to invoke the rule in the future, to its ultimate detriment."[1089]

[1089] Michael P. Scharf, *International Law in Crisis: A Qualitative Empirical Contribution to the Compliance Debate*, CARDOZO LAW REV, Vo. 31, No. 1, Sept. 2009. at 63.

CONCLUSION

In the first part of this work on the state and its characteristics, it is observed that the modern State has two characteristics: one is that the modern Sate is a territorial State; the other is that it is a sovereign State. The territorial State means that the State is predicated on territory. In the modern State, the ruler governs his people within his territory directly.

Sovereignty of the modern State resides in the ruler. For a republican State, which has no ruler, sovereignty is in the State. This work employs "the neo-modern State" as a term for a State where sovereignty resides in the State. Since in the neo-modern State, sovereignty resides in the State, sovereignty is inseparable from the State. Hence, the common notion of *sovereignty in the people* is a misnomer and merely means that the people of the State have ultimate political power.

In State theory and international law, a proposition commonly accepted is that a political institution is a State once it has the four requirements prescribed in the Montevideo Convention: permanent population; defined territory; government; and the capacity to enter into relations with other States. By examining the State practice on the creation of States and the nature of the neo-modern State, this work concludes that a territorial political institution with all those requirements does not become a State unless and until it declares the establishment of statehood or of similar import, such as a declaration of independence. Thus, a political institution does not evolve gradually into a State; it must openly and unambiguously declare itself into existence.

In the modern State and the neo-modern State, territory is an element of the State. Sovereignty of the State is based on its title to the territory. In other words, unless a State has the title to a territory, it has no sovereignty over the territory and its inhabitants.

In the transfer of a piece of territory between two States, an international customary law is that if the title to a piece (part) of the territory of the defeated State is to be changed after a war, then it must be achieved by a treaty. Thus, a victorious State does not acquire the title to a piece of the territory of the defeated State by occupation in the absence of a territorial treaty.

The second part of this work examines the political status of the Republic of China (R.O.C.) and Taiwan as well as the United States (U.S.)

policy toward Taiwan. By applying the principles and the rules in international law drawn in the first part, this work concludes that neither the R. O.C. nor Taiwan is a State.

The People's Republic of China (P.R.C.) claims that Taiwan is part of China. Its claim is based on historical ownership, self-proclamations, the Cairo Declaration, the Potsdam Proclamation, and the peace treaties between China and Japan, as well as the administration of Taiwan. But when the rules of international law on the acquisition and transfer of territory are applied to the grounds of China's claim, it is clear that China did not acquire the title to the island of Taiwan under any of them. Thus, after the Treaty of Shimonoseki in which China ceded Taiwan and Pescadores to Japan, China has not reacquired the title to the island of Tiawan.

China's claim of Taiwan in its one-China principle has no support in international law. China has no sovereignty over Taiwan and its inhabitants because China has no title to the island of Taiwan. Consequently, the P.R.C.'s Anti-secession Law cannot apply to the people of Taiwan. Furthermore, the U.S. one-China policy and Taiwan Relations Act do not recognize or concede to China's claim of Taiwan.

The present U.S. policy on Taiwan is based on the one-China policy and the Taiwan Relations Act. For the last 40 years, the U.S. Government has implemented its policies toward Taiwan as the occupying power. However, although the U.S. Government has provided protection to the people of Taiwan, its policy has also restricted the people of Taiwan from expressing their will and deprived their right to decide their political future. The policy of "no Taiwan independence" and the policy of "no referendum for Taiwan" have created ambiguity regarding the title to the island of Taiwan and put its people in an unsettled environment.

Secretaries-General of the U.N. have also created confusion in international politics. Both Kofi Annan and his successor Ban Ki-Moon referred to Taiwan as a "Province of China" under the "U.N.'s one-China policy." By analyzing the resolutions of the Security Council and the General Assembly, this work concludes that none of the U.N. resolutions ever decided that Taiwan was China's territory. The two Secretaries-General clearly misrepresented the U.N.'s policy.

Taiwan is not a State, yet it is not subject to the sovereignty of any State. The political status of Taiwan in international law is called an "independent territorial entity" in this work.The entangled claims of statehood and sovereignty, further complicated by the ambiguous U.S. position on the legal status of Taiwan, have left the people of Taiwan in a schizophrenic environment, or a state of "political purgatory" as Circuit Judge Brown describes it.

The predicament in which the people of Taiwan are today is attributable to the policies of the U.S. and the U.N. Both the U.S. and the U.N. may provide the people of Taiwan relief from the present situation by providing them with a peaceful solution to the Taiwan problem. This work suggests a solution for the Taiwan problem—a referendum by the people of Taiwan administered by the U.N. with a guarantee of the U.S. Government to implement the outcome of the referendum. Before that takes place, the U.S. and other States should reformulate their foreign policy toward China and Taiwan in accordance with the findings of this work.

BIBLIOGRAPHY

(1) Treatises and international agreements

Agreement Establishing the Multilateral Trade Organization (World Trade Organization), 1993, 33 I.L.M. 13.

American Charter on Human and Peoples Rights (Banjul Charter), 1981, 21 I.L.M. 59.

American Convention on Human Rights, 1969, 9 I.L.M. 673 (1970).

Convention Against Torture and Other Cruel, Inhuman, or Punishment, 1984, 23 I.L.M. 1027, as modified, 24 I.L.M. 535.

Convention on the Elimination of All Forms of Discrimination Against Women, 1979, 19 I.L.M. 33.

Convention Respecting The Laws and Customs of War on Land, 1907, 36 Stat. 2277; TS 539; TIAS 3365.

Convention on the Rights of the Child, 1980, 28 I.L.M. 1448.

Convention on Rights and Duties of States (The Montevideo Convention), 1933, 49 Stat. 3097, 3100; 165 L.N.T.S. 21, 25.

Convention for the Unification of Certain Rules Relating to International Carriage by Air, 1929, 49 Stat. 3000, T.S. No. 876, 137 L.N.T.S.11.

European Convention for the Protection of Human Rights and Fundamental Freedoms, 1950, 312 U.N.T.S. 221, E.T.S. 5.

General Agreement on Tariffs and Trade, 1947, 61 Stat. A3, 55 U.N.T.S. 187.

International Covenant on Civil and Political Rights, 1966, 999 U.N.T.S. 171.

International Covenant on Economic, Social and Cultural Rights, 1966, 993 U.N.T.S. 3.

International Convention on the Elimination of All Forms of Racial Discrimination, 1966, 5 I.L.M. 352.

Joint Declaration of the Government of the United Kingdom of Great Britain and Northern Ireland and the Government of the Peoples Republic of China on the Question of Hong Kong, 1984, 1399 UNTS 33.

Oslo Accords, 1993, 9 I.L.M. 673.

Peace of Westphalia (*Die Westfaelischen Friedensvertaege vom 24. Oktober 1648. Texte under Uebersetzungen* (*Acta Pacis Westphalicae. Supplementa electronica*, 1), *available at* http://www.pax-westphalica.de/ 06/01/2007).

The Treaty of Paris, U.S.-Spain, 1898, 30 Stat. 1754.

Treaty of Peace between China and Japan (Treaty of Shimonoseki), May 8, 1895, 181 Consol. T.S. 217.

Treaty of Peace with Japan (Peace Treaty of San Francisco), Sept. 8, 1951, 136 U.N. T.S. 46 (entered into force Apr. 28, 1952).

The Treaty of Peace, the R.O.C. – Japan (the Treaty of Taipei), April 28, 1952, 163 U.N.T.S. 38 (entered into force on Aug. 5, 1952).

The Treaty of Peace and Friendship Between Japan and the People's Republic of China, P.R.C.-Japan, Aug. 12, 1978, 1225 U.N.T.S. 269.

U.N. Convention on the Law of the Sea, 1982, 1833 U.N.T.S. 3, at 397.

The Universal Declaration of Human Rights, Dec. 10, 1948, U.N. G.A. Res. 217.

Vienna Convention on the Law of Treaties, 1969, U.N. Doc. A/CONF. 39/27, 1155 U.N.T.S. 331.

(2) Statutes and laws

(a) People's Republic of China

The Anti-Secession Act.

(b) Republic of China

The Constitution of the Republic of China.

Amendments to the Constitution.

(c) France

The Declaration of the Rights of Man and Citizen (1789).

The Constitution of the First French Republic (1791).

The Constitution of the (Fourth) Republic of France (1946).

The Constitution of the Fifth French Republic (1958).

(d) Germany

Act of the German Confederation (1815).

Constitution of the German Empire (1871).

German Civil Code.

The Reich Constitution (Weimar Constitution) (1919).

(e) U.S.

The Article of Confederation (1777).

The U.S. Constitution (1789).

Taiwan Relations Act (1994).

(f) U.N.

U.N. Charter (1945).

Statute of the International Court of Justice (1945).

(3) Cases

(a) The International Court of Justice

The Advisory Opinion of June 21, 1971. I.C.J. Rep. 1971.

(b) U.S. SUPREME COURT

American Insurance Company vs. Canter, 26 U.S. 1, Pet. 511 (U.S) (1828).

Baker vs. Carr, 369 U.S. 186 (1962).

Burnet vs. Chicago Portrait Co., 285 U.S. 1 (1932).

Cherokee Nation vs. Georgia, 30 U.S. 1 (1831).

DeLima vs. Bidwell, 182 U.S. 1 (1901).

Jones vs. United States, 526 U.S. 227 (1999).

Mateo Carino vs. Insular Government of The Philippine Islands, 212 U.S. 449 (1909).

United States vs. Jones, 565 U.S. 400 (2012).

United States vs. Pink, 315 U.S. 203 (1942).

(c) OTHER U.S. COURTS

Atlantic Mut. Ins. vs. Northwest Airlines, 24 F.3d 958 (7th Cir. 2004).

Chen Shui-Bian vs. United States, 68 M.J. 223 (C.A.A.F. 2009).

Cheng Fu Sheng vs. Rogers, 177 F. Supp. 281 (U.S.D.C. for the D.C. 1959).

Government Guarantee Fund of the Republic of Finland vs. Hyatt Corp., 95 F.3d 291 (3d Cir. 1996).

Jackson vs. The People's Republic of China, 794 F.2d 1490 (8th Cir. 1986).

John Lee and Margaret Lee vs. China Airlines Ltd., 669 F. Supp. 979 (C.D. Cal. 1987).

Mingtai Fire & Marine Insurance Co., Ltd. vs. United Parcel Service, 177 F.3d 1142, 1144-46 (9th Cir. 1999).

New York Chinese TV Programs, Inc. vs. U.E. Enterprises, Inc. et al., 954 F.2d 847, 853 (2d. Cir. 1992).

Rogers vs. Cheng Fu Sheng, 280 F.2d 663 (U.S. Ct of App. D.C. Cir. 1960).

Schneider vs. Kissinger, 412 F.3d 190 (U.S. Ct of App, D.C. Cir. 2005).

Roger C. S. Lin, et al. vs. the U.S.A., 539 F. Supp. 2d 173 (U.S.D.C. for D.C. 2008); 561 F.3d 502; U.S. Ct. of App. D.C. Cir. 191 (2009); 130 S. Ct. 202 (2009) (Certiorari denied).

Lin and Taiwan Civil Government vs. United States of America and the Republic of China, 177 F. Supp. 3d 242 (2016), affirmed U.S. Ct of App. D.C. Cir. (Mar. 30, 2017).

Wulfsohn vs. Russian Socialist Federated Soviet Republic, 234 N.Y. 372 (1923).

(4) Official documents

(a) U.N.

(Security Council)

U.N. S.C. Res. 82, U.N. SCOR, 5th Sess., 474th mtg. S/1501 (1950).

U.N. S.C. Res. 83, U.N. SCOR, 5th Sess., 474th mtg. S/1511 (1950).

U.N. S.C. Res. 84, U.N. SCOR, 476th mtg. (1950).

U.N. S.C. Res. 87, U.N. SCOR, 506th mtg. (1950).

(General Assembly)

G.A. Res. 396, U.N. GAOR, 5th Sess., 325th plen. mtg. (1950).

G.A. Res. 490, U.N. GAOR, 5th Sess., 277th plen. mtg. (1950).

G.A. Res. 800, U.N. GAOR, 8th Sess., 432d plen. mtg. (1953).

G.A. Res. 903, U.N. GAOR, 9th Sess., 473d plen. mtg. (1953).

G.A. Res. 990, U.N. GAOR, 10th Sess., 516th plen. mtg. (1954).

G.A. Res. 1239, U.N. GAOR, 13th Sess., 755th plen. mtg. (1957)

G.A. Res. 1351, U.N. GAOR, 14th Sess., 803rd plen. mtg. (1958).

G.A. Res. 1493, U.N. GAOR, 15th Sess., 895th plen. mtg. (1959).

G.A. Res. 1668, U.N. GAOR, 16th Sess., 1080th plen. mtg. (1961).

G.A. Res. 2271, U.N. GAOR, 22d Sess., 1610th plen. mtg. (1967).

G.A. Res. 2389, U.N. GAOR, 23d Sess., 1724th plen. mtg. (1968).

G.A. Res. 2500, U.N. GAOR, 24th Sess., 1808th plen. mtg. (1969).

G.A. Res. 2642, U.N. GAOR, 25th Sess., 1913th plen. mtg. (1970).

G.A. Res. 2758, U.N. GAOR, 26th Sess., 1976th plen. mtg. (1971) [Res. 2758].

(b) U.S.

The Declaration of Independence (1776).

The Cairo Declaration, 9 Dept St. Bull., Dec. 1943, at 393.

Proclamation Defining Terms For Japanese Surrender, July 26, 1945, Dept St. Bull., July 1945, at 137 (Potsdam Proclamation).

Incoming Message, WARX 48672, dated Aug. 12, 1945, from General Marshall to General Headquarters, U.S. Army Forces Pacific (on file with MacArthur Memorial).

Incoming Message, WARX 49571, dated Aug. 14, 1945, from General Marshall to General MacArthur (on file with MacArthur Memorial).

Cablegram from Peiping Foreign Minister (Chou En-lai) to Secretary-General, Trygve Lie (Aug. 24, 1950), Dept St. Bull., Oct. 16, 1950, at 607 (Chou En-Lai Cablegram).

Warren R. Austin, Position on the Formosan Question, Letter to U.N. Secy-Gen., Trygve Lie (Aug. 25, 1950), Dept St. Bull., Sept. 1950, at 411.

Foreign Policies Toward Asia, A Television Interview with Secy Acheson (Sept. 10, 1950), Dept St. Bull., Sept. 1950, at 463.

Memorandum of the U.S.S.R. (June 10, 1951), U.S.S.R.-U.S., Dept St. Bull., June 1951, at 138.

Opening Address by President Truman (Sept. 4, 1951), Dept St. Bull., Sept. 1951, at 447.

Secy John Foster Dulles, Statements at the Second Plenary Session, The San Francisco Conference (Sept. 5, 1951), Dept St. Bull., Sept. 1951, at 450.
Department of the Army Field Manual (for) The Law of land warfare, FM 27-10, Department of the Army, July 1956, amended July 15, 1976.
Adlai E. Stevenson, United Nations Rules Out Change in Representation of China, Plen. Statement Before the General Assembly (Dec. 1 and Dec. 14, 1961), Dept St. Bull., Jan. 1962, at 117.
Christopher H. Phillips, Twenty-fifth General Assembly Rejects Move to Change Representation of China in the U.N., Plen. Statement Before the General Assembly (Nov. 12, 1970), Dept St. Bull., Dec. 1970, at 734.
William Rogers, Secy Rogers Announces U.S. Policy on Chinese Representation in the U.N., Statement to News Correspondents (Aug. 2, 1971), Dept St. Bull., Aug. 1971, at 193.
George H.W. Bush, U.N. Votes to Seat Peoples Republic of China and Expel Representatives of Republic of China, Plen. Statement Before the General Assembly (Oct. 18, 1971), Dept St. Bull., Nov. 1971, at 549.
Secy of State William Rogers, Statements at Press Conference Discussing United Nations Decision on Chinese Representation, Dept St. Bull., Dec. 1971, at 541.
Shanghai Communiqué (Feb. 27. 1972), Dept St. Bull., 1972, at 437.
The Joint Communiqué on Establishment of Diplomatic Relations Between the United States of America and the People's Republic of China, (Jan. 1, 1979) (The Second Communiqué), 79 Dept St. Bull., 25–26, Jan. 1979.
John H. Holdridge, Assessment of U.S. Relations With China, Address before the House Foreign Affairs Committee, July 16, 1981, Dept St. Bull., Oct. 1981, at 38.
U.S.-China Joint Communiqué on Arms Sales to Taiwan, Aug. 17, 1982 (The Third Communiqué), 82 Dept St. Bull. 20, Oct. 1982.
George H.W. Bush, President's Statement, June 3, 1989, Dept St. Bull., Aug. 1989, at 75.
Underlying Strains in Taiwan-U.S. Political Relations, CRS Report for Congress, by Kerry Dumbaugh, Specialist in Asian Affairs, Foreign Affairs, Defense, and Trade Division. Summary. Congressional Research Service, The Library of Congress. Order Code RL33684, Updated Apr. 20, 2007, *available at* http://www.fas.org/sgp/crs/row/RL33684.pdf.

(c) U.K.
(Parliamentary Debates, House of Commons. 1943–1956)
469 Parl. Deb., H.C. (5th ser.) (1949) (HC Deb 31 October 1949 vol 469 c).
478 Parl. Deb., H.C. (5th ser.) (1950, 1951) (HC Deb 24 July 1950 vol 478 c).
487 Parl. Deb., H.C. (5th ser.) (1951) (HC Deb 23 April 1951 vol 487 c).
496 Parl. Deb., H.C. (5th ser.) (1952) (HC Deb 19 February 1952 vol 496 c).
530 Parl. Deb., H.C. (5th ser.) (1954) (HC Deb 12 July 1954 vol 530 c).
536 Parl. Deb., H.C. (5th ser.) (1955) (HC Deb 25 January 1955 vol 536 c).
540 Parl. Deb., H.C. (5th ser.) (1955) (HC Deb 19 April 1955 vol 540 c).

(d) The People's Republic of China
White Paper-The One-China Principle and the Taiwan Issue (2000).

(e) Others
Declaration of the Establishment of the State of Israel (1948).

(5) Books (By order of author's last name)
Academic American Encyclopedia, Arete Publishing Co., Princeton, NJ (1980).
D. Bigongiari (Ed.), The Political Ideas of St. Thomas Aquinas, Free Press, New York (1953).

J. Bodin, On Sovereignty (*Six livres de la republique*) (trans. J. Franklin), Cambridge University Press, Cambridge, UK (1992).

B.E. Carter & P.R. Trimbal, International Law, 2nd ed, Little Brown & Co., Boston, MA (1995).

B.E. Carter & P.R. Trimbal, International Law: Selected Documents (Supplement), 1999–2000 ed, Aspen Law & Business, New York (1999).

A. Cassese, Self-Determination of Peoples: A Legal Reappraisal, Cambridge University Press, Cambridge, UK (1995).

L.-C. Chen & H.D. Laswell, Taiwan, China and the United Nations, St. Martin's Press, New York (1967).

R. Churchill & V. Lowe, The Law of the Sea, 3rd ed., Manchester University Press, Manchester, UK (1999).

A Compilation of the Laws of the Republic of China, Kang Chi-Chao, Taipei, Taiwan (1967).

Continental's Concise English-Chinese Dictionary, rev. ed., Ta Lu Book Co., Taipei, Taiwan (1978).

J. Crawford, The Creation of States in International Law, 2nd ed., Oxford University Press, London (2006).

I. DeLupis, International Law and the Independent State, Crane, Russak & Co., New York (1974).

W.Y. Elliott & N.A. McDonald, Western Political Heritage, Prentice-Hall, New York (1950).

The Encyclopedia Britannica, 15th ed., Encyclopaedia Britannica, Inc., Chicago, IL (1994).

J.K. Fairbank, The United States and China, 4th ed, Harvard University Press, Cambridge, MA (1979).

J.K. Fairbank & E.O. Reischauer, China, Tradition and Transformation, rev. ed., Houghton Mifflin, Boston, MA (1989).

M.R. Fowler & J.M. Bunck, Law, Power, and the Sovereign State: The Evolution and Application of the Concept of Sovereignty, Pennsylvania State University Press, Philadelphia, PA (1995).

Gaius, Elements of Roman Law (trans. E. Poste), Gaunt, Holmes Beach, FL (1994).

German Civil Code, *Buergelichesgesetzbuch* (trans. C.H. Wang), Stevens and Sons, Ltd., London (1907), reprinted by Gaunt Inc., Holmes Beach, FL (2000).

H.A. Giles, A Chinese-English Dictionary, Shanghai, China (1892), 2nd ed., Shanghai and London (1912), reprinted by Che'eng-Wen Publishing Co., Taipei, Taiwan (1967).

H. Grotius, Rights of War and Peace (*De jure belli ac pacis*) (trans. W. Whewell) (1625), Cambridge University Press, Cambridge, UK (1853).

H. Grotius, Commentary on the Law of Prize and Booty (*De jure Praedae Commentarius*), Vol. I (trans. G.L. Williams) (1604), G.L. Williams & W.H. Zeydel (Eds.), Clarendon Press, Oxford (1950).

G.H. Hackworth, Digest of International Law, U.S. Government Printing Office, Washington, DC (1940).

H. Hannum, Autonomy, Sovereignty, and Self-Determination: The Accommodation of Conflicting Rights, University of Pennsylvania Press, Philadelphia, PA (1990).

H.V. Harrison (Ed.), The Role of Theory in International Relations, Van Nostrand, New York (1964).

H. Hart, The Concept of Law, 2nd ed, Oxford University Press, New York (1994).

J.-M. Henckaerts, The International Status of Taiwan in the New World Order: Legal and Political Considerations, Kluwer Law International, London (1996).

Henry Steele Commanger (Ed.), Documents of American History, 3rd ed., F.S. Croft & Co., New York (1943).
T. Hobbes, Leviathan, C.B. Macpherson (Ed.), Penguin Books, Ltd., Harmondsworth, UK (1651), republished by Pelican Books, Ltd., Harmondsworth, UK (1968).
L. Holborn, G. Carter & J. Herz, German Constitutional Documents Since 1871: Selected Texts and Commentary, Praeger, Westport, CT (1970).
S. Hopkins, Introduction. In: P. Campbell (Ed.), The Rights of Colonies Examined (1764); reprinted by The Rhode Island Bicentennial Foundation, Providence, Rhode Island (1974).
C. Hsuüeh, China's Foreign Relations, Praeger, New York (1982).
A. Jackson & B. Schlink, Introduction, Constitutional Crisis, the German and the American Experience, In: Weimar: A Jurisprudence of Crisis, 1st ed., University of California Press, Berkeley, CA (2000).
M.W. Janis, An Introduction to International Law, 2nd ed., Little Brown & Co Law & Business, Frederick, MD (1993).
G.H. Kerr, Formosa Betrayed, Houghton Mifflin, Boston, MA (1965).
A. Khan, The Extinction of Nation States: A World Without Borders, Kluwer Law International, Boston, MA (1996).
H. Kissinger, Observations: Selected Speeches and Essays, 1st ed., Little Brown and Co, Boston, MA (1982).
Lassa Oppenheim, International Law: Vol. I., Longmans, Green, & Co., London and New York (1905); H. Lauterpacht (Ed.), 8th ed., David McKay Co., Inc., New York (1955).
D.T. Lee, The Making of the Taiwan Relations Act, Oxford University Press (China Ltd), New York (2000).
S.-T. Lee, J.F. Williams (Eds.), Taiwan's Struggle, Roman and Littlefield, Langham, MD (2014).
J. Locke, In: T.P. Pearson (Ed.), The Second Treatise of Government (1690), Bobbs-Merrill Co. Inc., New York (1952).
H. Lubasz (Ed.), The Development of the Modern State, MacMillan Co, New York (1964).
D. MacArthur, Reminiscences, McGraw-Hill Co., New York (1964).
Mei Kai Koku Go Ji Ten (Mei Kai Dictionary of National [Japanese] Language), rev. ed., Sansei Do Co., Tokyo (1966).
A Memorial for Professor Chen Wen-Chen—A Taiwanese, Chen Wen-Chen Memorial Foundation, Inc., Ann Arbor, MI (1982).
S. Meng, *Taiwanren S Bai Nian Shi* (The Four Hundred Years of the Taiwanese History), Paradise Culture Associates, San Jose, CA (1980).
Merriam Webster Collegiate Dictionary, 10th ed., Merriam-Webster, Inc., Springfield, MA (1993).
P.W. Montague-Smith, Late Editor, Debrett's Peerage, The Royal Line of Succession, Pitkin Guides Ltd., Andover, UK (1986).
Moore, International Law Digest, U.S. Government Printing Office, Washington, DC (1906).
The New Encyclopedia Britannica, 15th ed., Encyclopaedia Britannica, Inc., Chicago, IL (2002).
The New Shorter Oxford English Dictionary, 3rd ed., Oxford University Press (1993).
The New Wildhagen German Dictionary, Follett Publishing Co., Chicago, IL (1965).

Oxford Advanced Learner's Dictionary, 5th ed., Oxford University Press (1995); 6th ed., Oxford University Press (2000).

Oxford English Dictionary, 2nd ed., Oxford University Press (1989).

M.J. Peterson, Recognition of Governments: Legal Doctrine and State Practice, 1815-1995, St. Martin's Press, Inc., New York (1997).

C. Purtschet, *Histoire des institutions Xe -XVIIIe siecle*, Masson et Ci.e., Paris (1972).

K. Rabl, C. Stoll, & M. Vasold, From the U.S. Constitution to the Basic Law of the Federal Republic of Germany [*Von der amerikanischen Verfassung zum Grundgesetz der Bundesrepublik Deutschland.*] (in both English and German), Verlag Moos & Partner, Munich, Germany (1988).

M.M. Rebecca, Wallace, International Law, Sweet & Maxwell, London (1986).

E. Reischauer, Japan, Past and Present, 3rd ed., rev., Alfred A. Knopf, New York (1964).

The Restatement of the Foreign Relations Law of the United States, 3rd ed. (1987).

R. Russell, A History of the United Nations Charter, the Role of the United States, 1940-1945, Brookings Institution, Washington, DC (1958).

Shin eiwa chu ji ten (New College English-Japanese Dictionary), 7th ed., Kenkyusha Co., Tokyo (2003).

Shin Sen Koku Go Ji Ten (Shin Sen Dictionary of National [Japanese] Language), rev. ed., Shou Gaku Kan Co., Tokyo (1965).

W.R. Sorley, A History of British Philosophy to 1900, Cambridge University Press (1965).

P. Stein, Legal Evolution, The Story of an Idea, Cambridge University Press, Cambridge, UK (1980).

M. Stolleis & T. Dunlap, A History of Public Law in Germany 1914-1945, 1st ed., Oxford University Press, Oxford (2004).

J. Tkacick Jr., Reshaping the Taiwan Strait, The Heritage Foundation, Washington, DC (2007).

O. von Gierke, The Development of Political Theories, as No. VII of the *Untersuchungen zur Deutchen Staats- und Rechtsgeschiste* (trans. B. Freyd), W.W. Norton & Company, Inc. (1880), Howard Fertig, Inc., New York (1966).

M. Weinstein & R. Kimbrough, Summary of American Law, 1st ed, Lawyers Co-operative Pub. Co, Rochester, NY (1988).

A. West, Y. Desdevices, A. Fenet, D. Gaurrier & M.-C. Heussaff, The French Legal System, An Introduction, Fourmat Publishing, London (1992).

Zheng Zhong Xing Ying Yi Zong He Da Zi Dian (Cheng Chong's Character, Phonetics, and Semantics Comprehensive Dictionary), Cheng Chong Book Co., Taipei, Taiwan (1971).

(6) Journal articles

C. Attix, Between the Devil and the Deep Blue Sea: Are Taiwan's Trading Partners Implying Recognition of Taiwanese Statehood? 25 Cal. West. Int. Law J. 357 (Spring 1995).

L. Backer, Reifying Law—Government, Law and the Rule of Law in Governance Systems, 26(3) Penn. State Int. Law Rev. 521 (Winter 2008).

F. Boyle, The Creation of the State of Palestine, 1(1) Eur. J. Int. Law 301 (1990) *available at* <http://www.ejil.org/pdfs/1/1/1136.pdf>.

C.J. Carolan, The "Republic Of Taiwan": A Legal-Historical Justification for a Taiwanese Declaration of Independence, 75 N.Y. Univ. Law Rev. 429 (May 2000).

A.G. Chen, Taiwan's International Personality: Crossing the River by Feeling the Stones, 20 Loy. L.A. Int. Comp. Law J. 223 (January 1998).

L.-C. Chen, Taiwan's Current International Legal Status, 32 New Eng. Law Rev. 675 (Spring 1998).
H. Chiu, Compilation of Treaties of the People's Republic of China, 61(4) Am. J. Int. Law 1095 (1967).
H. Chiu, The Right of the Republic of China and Its 21 Million Chinese People to Participate in the United Nations, 28 John Marshall Law Rev. (Chicago) 247 (1994).
J. Crawford, The Creation of the State of Palestine: Too Much Too Soon? 1(1) Eur. J. Int. Law 307 (1990).
J. de Lisle, The Chinese Puzzle of Taiwan's Status, 44(1) Orbis 35 (January 2000).
H. Dowdall, The Word 'State', 39 Law Q. Rev. 98 (1923).
G.E. Edwards, Applicability of the "One Country, Two Systems" Hong Kong Model to Taiwan: Will Hong Kong's Post-Reversion Autonomy, Accountability, and Human Rights Record Discourage Taiwan's Reunification with the People's Republic of China?, 32 New Eng. Law Rev. 751 (Spring 1998).
H.L.A. Hart, Positivism and the Separation of Law and Morals, 71 Harv. Law Rev. 593 (1958).
L. Henkin, That S Word: Sovereignty, and Globalization, and Human Rights, Et Cetera, 68 Fordham Law Rev. 1 (1999).
J.H. Herz, The Rise and Demise of the Territorial State. 9(4) World Politics 473–474 (1957), Cambridge University Press, New York.
C. Hill, Why East Timor Matters, Hoover Digest (2000), *available at* http://www.hooverdigest.org/001/hill2.html.
O. Hintze, The Emergence of the Democratic Nation-State *[Das Durchbruch des demokratischen Nationalstaates in der amerikanischen und franzoesischen Revolution] Staat und Verfassung* (2nd ed. Guettingen, Vandenhoeck & Ruprecht) (trans. Lubasz). In: H. Lubasz (Ed.), The Development of the Modern State, MacMillan Co., New York (1964).
E.T.-L. Huang, Taiwan's Status in A Changing World: United Nations Representation and Membership for Taiwan. 9 Ann. Surv. Int. Comp. Law 55 (Spring 2003), Golden Gate University School of Law.
J.P. Jain, The Legal Status of Formosa: A Study of British, Chinese and Indian Views, 57(1) Am. J. Int. Law 25 (1963).
C.-F. Lee, China's Perception of the Taiwan Issue, 32 New Eng. Law Rev. 695 (Spring 1998).
H.J. Morgenthau, The Intellectual and Political Functions of a Theory of International Relations. In: H.V. Harrison (Ed.), The Role of Theory in International Relations, Van Nostrand, Princeton, NJ (1964).
J.P. Nettl, The State as a Conceptual Variable, 20(04) World Politics 559 (1968).
G. Ritter, Origins of the Modern State (*Die Neugestaltung Europas im 16. Jahrhundert*, Verlag des Druckhauses Tempelhof, Berlin 1950) (trans. H. Lubasz). In: H. Lubasz (Ed.), The Development of the Modern State, MacMillan Co, New York (1964).
M. Scharf, International Law in Crisis: A Qualitative Empirical Contribution to the Compliance Debate, 31(1) Cardozo Law Rev. 63 (2009).
M. Scharf, Seizing the Grotian Moment: Accelerated Formation of Customary International Law in Times of Fundamental Change, 43(3) Cornell Int. Law J. 442 (Fall 2010).
J. Shen, Critical Essay: Sovereignty, Statehood, Self-Determination, and the Issue of Taiwan, 15 Am. Univ. Int. Law Rev. 1101 (2000).
D. Tarnapol, The Role of the Judiciary in Settling Claims Against the P.R.C, 25 Harv. Int. Law J. 355 (1984).

J. Tkacik, Jr., Taiwan's "Unsettled" International Status: Preserving U.S. Options in the Pacific (2008), *available at* <http://www.heritage.org/Researc/AsiaandPacific/bg2146.cfm>.

P. Tozzi, Constitutional Reform On Taiwan: Fulfilling a Chinese Notion of Democratic Sovereignty? 64 Fordham Law Rev. 1193 (December 1995).

S. Wei, Some Reflections on the One-China Principle, 23(4) Fordham Int. Law J. 1169 (April 2000).

A.M. Weisburd, The Executive Branch and International Law, 41 Vand. Law Rev. 1205 (1998).

D. Wippman, Treaty-Based Intervention: Who Can Say No? 62(2) Univ. Chin. Law. Rev. 607–634 (1995).

(7) News articles

B.L. Brubaker, Language Attitudes and Identity in Taiwan (2003) (M.A. thesis, University of Pittsburgh), *available at* http://etd.library.pitt.edu/ETD/available/etd-08192003-082704/unrestricted/Brubakerthesis.pdf (unpublished).

J. Cheng, History of the Name: Formosa, Tayouan and Taiwan, *NATPA Forum*, 130705, *available at* https://mail.google.com/mail/?ticket = ST-750432-fTWS0Y5ChSfdXWzhlVYG-cas&shava = 1#inbox/13fb0c0329bd3c29.

W.R. Cumming, Self-Determination and National Security Concerns, *available at* http://faculty.lls.edu/~manheimk/ns/cumming.htm.

B. DeLong, Review of Akira Iriyes, The Origins of the Second World War in Asia and in the Pacific (2004), *available at* http://www.j-bradford-delong.net.

E.J. Dionne, Jr., China Policy Full of Contradictions, *Denver Post*, 04/10/2001, *available at* http://www.brookings.edu/printme.wbs?page = /pagedefs/c7c1d214d3c2ff3a7ff-f2e680a141465.html.

C.-Y. Lin, U.N. Secretary-General Stops Calling Taiwan Part of China, 09/06/2007, *available at* http://www.taiwanbasic.com/un/cna/taiwanpart.htm.

C.-Y. Lin & C. Snyder, Chen Still Defiant After Bush Rebuke, *Taipei Times*, 12/11/2003, at 1, *available at* http://www.taipeitimes.com/News/front/archives/2003/12/11/2003079111.

D. Middleton, Cairo Formosa Declaration Out of Date, Says Churchill, *New York Times*, 02/02/1955, at 1.

R. Reeves, United Nations: A Tale of Two Speeches, *Tulsa World*, 09/24/1999.

J. Reston, New Formosa Bid, *New York Times*, 02/7/1955, at A1.

INDEX

D

S

T

U

V

W

Z

FSC
www.fsc.org
MIX
Papier | Fördert gute Waldnutzung
FSC® C083411

Kolibri 360 GmbH
Ferdinand-Jühlke-Straße 7
99095 Erfurt, Deutschland
produktsicherheit@kolibri360.de